Donald McQuarie attended undergraduate school at the University of Texas, and was awarded his Ph.D. from that university in 1975. Since 1973 he has been teaching at the Department of Sociology at Bowling Green State University, Ohio, where he is now Assistant Professor. He is the author of several articles on Karl Marx's work and Marxist sociology.

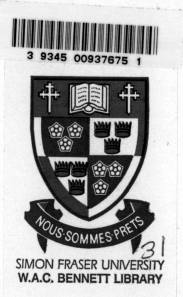

# MARX:
# SOCIOLOGY/SOCIAL CHANGE/
# CAPITALISM

Ϙ _____

Edited by DONALD McQUARIE

QUARTET BOOKS
LONDON MELBOURNE NEW YORK

First published by Quartet Books Limited 1978
A member of the Namara Group
27 Goodge Street, London W1P 1FD

Introductions copyright © 1978 by Donald McQuarie

ISBN Hardcover 0 7043 2147 5
        Paperback 0 7043 3177 2

Distribution in the U.S.A. by
Horizon Press, 156 Fifth Avenue
New York, NY 10010

Photoset, printed and bound
in Great Britain by
REDWOOD BURN LIMITED
Trowbridge & Esher

# CONTENTS

v

# INTRODUCTION*

While Karl Marx's work has exercised a great and lasting influence upon the development of social science theory, this influence has been rather disjointed and haphazard as a result of the distinctive manner of appropriation of Marx's ideas by successive social theorists. The very theoretical complexity of Marx's sociological system, as well as its fragmented state of presentation throughout many volumes of both published books and unpublished manuscripts (many of which have only been published within the last thirty years – see Avineri, 1968:1), has made the piecemeal appropriation of various elements of the system of scholars practically inevitable. Thus, the Marxian impact has been strongest in certain particular areas of sociological inquiry, such as the study of ideology (in the work of Mannheim and Merton), social class (in the work of Weber, Pareto, and later students of stratification), and industrial sociology (the entire body of literature on alienation).

Yet, valuable as all this work has been, and as fruitful as each of these individual elements of Marxian thought has proven to be, together they fail to deal adequately with the contribution of Marx's thought to general social theory. Thus, among social scientists there has been no adequate discussion of such central aspects of Marx's sociology as his methodology of theory construction, his solution of the crucial problem of historical periodization, and the central organizing tool of his social theory: the abstract model of the social formation – the mode of production. The absence of any sub-disciplines within Western social science corresponding to central problematics within Marx's thought has led to the virtual neglect by sociologists of significant portions of Marxist theory. The larger consequence of this failure has been the distortion of other elements of the theory, and a more general misunderstanding of Marxist theory. Thus, Marx's work has been viewed as an idealistic religion of revolution (Tucker, 1961, 1969; Hunt, 1950), a mystical Hegelian dialectic (Wilson, 1940), a philosophical and ethical 'humanism' (Fromm, 1961; Petrovic, 1967; Avineri, 1971), an appeal to the basest instincts of men (Ryan, 1967), a technological determinism (Bober, 1962), or an economic determinism (Seligman, 1902; Seé, 1929).

* I would like to thank the editors and publishers of *Sociological Analysis and Theory* for their permission to republish in this essay elements of my article 'Central Problems in Karl Marx's Sociology' which appeared in the October 1976 issue of that journal (vol. 6, no. 3).

1

On the other hand, these distortions and misunderstandings have not been corrected to any extent by the theoretical doctrines of Marxist-Leninism, or other such 'orthodox' Marxisms, in which theoretical issues are all too often tied to the political needs of a party or state. The socialist scholar Isaac Deutscher accurately summed up the general intellectual quality of the sectarian debate between the various official Marxisms with the phrase 'pidgin Marxism' (Deutscher, 1966:211).

Yet Marx's work has fared little better at the hands of more 'dispassionate' academic scholars. For the most part, and especially in Western Europe and the United States, Marx's work has been treated as a philosophy rather a sociology, that is, as a question of *dialectics*.

## SOCIOLOGY AND THE DIALECTIC

This reduction of Marxism to a dialectical ontology and method may be broken into three broad categories of interpretation within the literature. Differences between these general categories involve the perceived relationship of the Marxian to the Hegelian dialectic.

For one group of scholars, generally distinguished by a common philosophical background and interest in French existentialism, the question of method has resolved itself into the proposition that the Marxian method, and therefore Marx's work, involves merely an extension of the Hegelian dialectic (see Lefebvre, 1968a, 1968b; Korsch, 1970; Sartre, 1963; Gramsci, 1957; Lukács, 1966, 1971; Meszaros, 1970; Hyppolite, 1969; Marcuse, 1960 – for a different statement of this same thesis, see Popper, 1950).

Marx's work is here interpreted as profoundly philosophical in nature – he is 'the philosopher of praxis' (see Korsch, 1970; Lukács, 1971; Petrovic, 1967) – and the general approach of this school reveals an intense hostility toward the consideration of Marx's work as an empirical sociology. Henri Lefebvre flatly states: 'Marx is not a sociologist' (Lefebvre, 1968b:22).

The position of this school on the question of method is adequately summarized by Karl Korsch:

> From the outset, Marx and Engels had to clarify their position . . . with regard to the Hegelian method. They never doubted that they had issued from it. Their only problem was how to change the Hegelian dialectic from a method proper to a superficially idealist, but secretly materialist conception of the world, into the guiding principle of an explicitly materialist view of history and society. [Korsch, 1970:90]

Marx is interpreted here as the true successor of Hegel – the one a

2

philosopher whose idealist method secretly harbored a materialist conception of the world, the other a philosophical materialist who secretly adopted his master's idealist philosophical method.

> By adopting the progressive part of the Hegelian method, namely, the dialectic, Marx not only cut himself off from Hegel's successors; he also split Hegel's philosophy in two. He took the historical tendency in Hegel to its logical extreme. . . . In this sense Marx's critique of Hegel is the direct continuation and extension of the criticism that Hegel himself levelled at Kant and Fichte. So it came about that Marx's dialectical method continued what Hegel had striven for but had failed to achieve in a concrete form [Lukacs, 1971:17].[1]

This reading of an essential continuity underlying the Hegelian and Marxian dialectics leads us to the methodological interpretation of a second school, Soviet Marxism, in which Marx is seen as having appropriated the *idealist* Hegelian dialectic and stood it on its head, or reversed it, creating a *materialist* dialectic (Plekhanov, 1940, 1969, 1973; Cornforth, 1953, 1954, 1955, 1965; Lenin, 1967, 1971; Konstantinov and Kelle, n.d.; Glezerman and Kursanov, 1968; Frank, 1969).

George Plekhanov states:

> In general, one of the greatest services rendered to materialism by Marx and Engels is their elaboration of a *correct method* . . . Dialectics, which with Hegel was of a purely idealist character and had remained so with Proudhon (so far as he had assimilated it), was placed on a *materialist foundation* by Marx. [Plekhanov, 1969:43–44]

The emphasis is now placed upon Marx's alleged philosophical materialism – opposed to Hegelian idealism in every respect but that it is still a *dialectical* materialism. His method, however, is no longer seen as being the inheritance of, or being in essential continuity with, the Hegelian dialectic, but is rather its mirror opposite. It is to this phase of 'Marxism' that we owe Engels' 'scientific' dialectics, 'dialectics of nature,' etc. (see Engels, 1970, 1940).

In both of the above schools of interpretation, the definition of precisely what constitutes this dialectical method is left exceedingly vague. We are given instead such general formulations as Engels' three laws of dialectics: the law of the transformation of quantity into quality, the law of the interpenetration of opposites, and the law of the negation (Engels, 1940:26). Or, on the other hand, there is the more explicitly Hegelian formulation of Lefebvre:

> This dialectical movement with its three fundamental concepts of truth, going beyond, and disalienation characterizes every aspect of Marx's writings, the order in which they were written, their inner Logic, the very movement of his thought. [Lefebvre, 1968b:9–10]

3

It is clear that here we are a long way from any recognizable social science methodology. We are also a long way from Marx, at least in his later formulations.

In recent years this three-sided relationship of Marxian method-Hegelian dialectic-Engels' dialectical materialism has been markedly clarified by a series of studies which have shattered conclusively the myth that Marx was the originator of a dialectical materialist philosophy and directed attention back to the more sociological focus of Marx's own thought (Jordan, 1967, 1971; Jones, 1973; Hodges, 1965; Meyer, 1959; Sedgwick, 1966; Bottomore, 1964, 1973; Nicolaus, 1970 – see also Hook, 1940, 1962).[2] As Z. A. Jordan has stated this theme:

> The emphasis given by Engels to Marxian thought consists in viewing it as a monistic system concerned with the ultimate constituents and laws of the universe rather than as an application of a unified method. Thus, for instance, Engels gave final currency to the belief that *Capital* was an exposition of a system of political economy, and not a critical, sociological, and historical analysis of a particular socio-economic formation ... In philosophy, a similar shift was accomplished, for Marx, who, after his break with Hegel, was uninterested in academic metaphysics and the theory of knowledge, was presented by Engels as a supporter of dialectical materialism and naive realism. ... These doctrines are incompatible with the views to be found in Marx's works. [Jordan, 1967:9]

One result of this re-examination of the philosophical origins of Marx's thought has been the more careful restatement of the dialectical theme in Marx's work by a number of scholars who still wish to salvage the Hegelian link, who have done so in a more rigorous fashion than the earlier school of dialecticians (Korsch, Lukács) whose work primarily dated from the 1920s–1940s (see Fromm, 1961; McLellan, 1969, 1970; Schmidt, 1971; O'Neill, 1972; Mészáros, 1970; Petrovic, 1967; Ollman, 1971; Goldmann, 1969; Avineri, 1971 – for a critical assessment, see Fernbach, 1969; Glucksmann, 1969).

Their Marx is the Marx of alienation and the estrangement of man in society, which is to say the young Marx, and the textual references for their theoretical exegeses of Marx's work inevitably draw heavily upon such early works as the 1843 *Critique of Hegel's Philosophy of Right*, the 1844 'Introduction,' and the 1844 *Paris Manuscripts*. Thus, while these scholars and their works are of great interest in understanding the philosophical (Feuerbachian) humanism of the young Marx, they are of less help in deciphering the sociological content of Marx's later, mature works.

Another consequence of this recent interest in the analysis of the

4

Marxism dialectic has been the attempt within academic sociology to reconcile the Hegelian-Marxian dialectic with neo-functionalist 'consensus theory,' and the debate within the discipline which this attempt has sparked (see van den Berghe, 1963; Dahrendorf, 1958, 1959; Lockwood, 1964; Frank, 1969; Cole, 1966; Horton, 1966; Williams, 1966; Weingart, 1969; Turner, 1973).

The thesis of a convergence between Marxian and functionalist theory is most directly stated by van den Berghe:

> Functionalism and the Hegelian-Marxian dialectic each stress one of two essential aspects of social reality, and are thus complementary to one another. . . . Our central contention is that the two major approaches which have dominated much of social science present partial but complementary views of reality. [van den Berghe, 1963:695, 704–705]

But here, too, the analysis of Marx's sociology goes little beyond the platitudes of dialectical materialism: functionalism gives us a social statics, Marxian dialectics gives us a social dynamics – each therefore has what the other lacks. The mating of the two methods should then yield a comprehensive social theory, in the same manner that the addition of two numbers yields a unified sum.

More pertinent to the present discussion than the shallow eclecticism of this approach, however, is the extent to which it still fails to look within Marx's work for the unified methodology which is indeed there. Despite the overt interest in the contribution of Marx to scientific sociology, the old equation of Marxian method = Hegelian dialectics is still preserved.

Against the many theoretical weaknesses of these several historically dominant 'dialectical' readings of Marxism, I would like in this introduction and the readings which make up this text to introduce and examine the contributions of a more sociologically oriented tradition of European Marxism which, although largely overlooked, has been much more perceptive in its appreciation of the scientific character of Marx's theoretical work. Throughout the 19th and 20th centuries there has existed a strong tradition of European scholarship which has succeeded in going well beyond the formulations of both Hegelian dialecticians and dialectical materialists in unraveling the scientific basis of Marx's thought. The theoretical basis for this reconstruction of Marx's thought was laid during the late 19th and first half of the 20th century by such scholars as Antonio Labriola, Max Weber, Vilfredo Pareto, Nikolai Bukharin, Karl Korsch, Sidney Hook, Galvano della Volpe, and the Austro-Marxian school of Max Adler, Karl Renner, Otto Neurath,

5

Otto Bauer, and others.[3]

The work of these scholars has provided a constant counterpoint to the dialectical, or philosophical interpretation of Marx's work. Labriola, for example, first initiated discussion of Marx's work as a theoretical sociology in 1897 (see Plekhanov, 1940 for an 'orthodox' Marxist-Leninist appraisal of Labriola's work). Neurath, a member of the positivist Vienna Circle, attempted to demonstrate a strong positivist element within Marx's work in a series of essays written during the 1920s and 1930s. This work was paralleled by Bukharin in his 1921 *Historical Materialism*, subtitled 'A System of Sociology,' in which he attempted to restate Marx's general theory in the light of contemporary sociological research. More recently, della Volpe's work in the 1940s and 1950s is important for the emphasis which he has placed upon Marx's methodologically crucial and recently published 1857 'Introduction to Political Economy' in the interpretation of Marx's thought.

The work of these scholars has been taken up in recent years by a number of others who have continued the tradition of interpreting Marx's work as a theoretical sociology (see Zeitlin, 1967, 1968; Bottomore, 1966, 1973; Bottomore and Rubel, 1964; Giddens, 1971; Colletti, 1972; Jordan, 1971; Hobsbawm, 1969; Meyer, 1963; Needleman and Needleman, 1969; Althusser and Balibar, 1970; Godelier, 1970, 1972).

Especially pertinent to this discussion of Marxism and sociology has been the work of the French Marxist Louis Althusser. Althusser has emphasized the scientific character of Marx's later work (from *The German Ideology* to *Capital*) by introducing the concept of an 'epistemological break,' or rupture, within Marx's work which separates his earlier, more philosophical writings, composed under the intellectual influence of Hegel and Feuerbach, from his later scientific writings (Althusser, 1970: 32–38). What, among other things, defines the character of this epistemological break, is Marx's characteristic focus in his later works on the 'mode of production' – a theoretically defined scientific object – as the subject of his sociology. According to Althusser, it was this development which marked Marx's break with Hegelian metaphysics, and indeed with all forms of 'humanist' philosophy. From the philosopher of man's alienation from his own human 'essence,' Marx developed into the theorist of the 'laws of motion' of the capitalist mode of production, the founder of a new science. As is the case in the development of every new science, Marx's theoretical innovation was accompanied by and expressed through the elaboration of a new technical vocabulary: forces of production, relations of production, infrastructures, superstructures, contradiction, political conjuncture, etc. (see Althusser and Balibar, 1970: 145–157).

6

This Althusserian theme has been independently developed in the work of the Italian Marxist philosopher Galvano della Volpe, mentioned above, and his student Lucio Colletti. Della Volpe characterized Marx's method as one of 'determinate abstraction' or the use of historically specific theoretical concepts which are abstracted from empirical concrete social formations (see della Volpe, 1974:246–254). Colletti has extended this discussion to include an appreciation of the role the concept 'mode of production' plays in Marx's method as an ideal model of the concrete social formation. Yet Colletti does not wish to reduce Marxism to an idealist method, and insists upon the empirical nature of Marx's 'determinate abstractions' as opposed to the Weberian 'ideal type.'

> Hence the need for a new method, a new type of abstraction. More precisely, on the one hand the need for an approach which can encompass the *differences* presented by one object or species with respect to all the others – for example bourgeois society as against feudal society – and which does not, therefore, arrive at the *generic*, idealist nation of society 'in general,' but rather hangs on to this 'determinate society,' the particular object in question. (The need for a method which does not give us abstractions, but facts.) [Colletti, 1972:8]

The French structuralist Maurice Godelier (whose article is included in this volume) has gone even farther in identifying the congruence between Marx's work and recent methodological innovations in the social sciences. Viewing Marx's work as essentially a theory of social structures and their correspondence, Godelier focuses upon the incongruity in Marx's work between the everyday, taken-for-granted, 'visible' functioning of social relations and the 'hidden' nature of the social laws which govern and 'explain' these relationships. 'For Marx, then, the scientific model corresponds to a reality which is hidden beneath the visible reality' (Godelier, 1970:340). Working in the rather more empiricist tradition of Anglo-American social science, Irving Zeitlin and T.B. Bottomore have both contributed major works continuing the elaboration of Marx's sociology as a general paradigm for the analysis of social structure – Bottomore provocatively posing the question Karl Marx – Marxist or Sociologist? (Bottomore, 1966). The general position of this group of scholars on the interpretation of Marx's thought is adequately summarized by a brief passage from Irving Zeitlin's *Marxism*, which expresses the tone of this volume as well:

> Karl Marx thought of himself as a scientist as well as a revolutionary. He conceived of much of his work as providing both a scientific account of the nature of capitalism and a scientific basis for the socialist movement of his time. He advanced his general theory in

7

order to guide the revolutionary action of the working class, the main agency through which the capitalist system was to be changed and ultimately superseded. The possibility of revolution rested in certain objective economic and political conditions which could be grasped through a careful study of the structure and tendencies of capitalism. In these terms, Marx's theory is empirically based and informed by the spirit of scientific inquiry. [Zeitlin1967:iii]

In the selection of essays which make up this volume, I have drawn upon the contributions of these scholars, and others where appropriate. Their achievements have provided a theoretical beginning and orientation without which this present study would not have been possible.


## INTELLECTUAL FOUNDATIONS

As a result of the distortions, gaps, and misunderstandings in the secondary literature discussed above, Marx has all too often been denied his place as one of the founders of social science method and theory, and placed instead in the category of a 'forerunner,' or 'influence' on the development of the field. His sociology has been dismissed as a philosophy of history, distorted by partisanship – fundamentally unscientific. However, far from belonging to the pre-history of social science, Marx in fact engaged in a serious early attempt to construct a 'positive' science of society, which he conceived as at once being a sociology, or theory of society, and a theory of history. This 'science of man,'[4] as formulated by Marx, was to consist in the search for law-like uniformities governing the various stages in human history, their 'hidden laws of motion,' which were to be derived from and tested by empirical data. In this way, philosophy would be transformed into the objective, exact empirical study of society (see Marx, 1968a:118–119). In his discovery and adaptation of a scientific methodology to the needs of the social sciences, Marx constructed a model whose theoretical structure departed radically from the efforts of both his predecessors and contemporaries.[5]

Through the period 1845–1847, in what Louis Althusser (1970) has called the 'works of the break' (*The Holy Family, The German Ideology*, 'Theses on Feuerbach,' *Poverty of Philosophy*), Marx's early interest in Hegel, Feuerbach, and German philosophy – the dominant influence in his early (1840–1844) works – was slowly replaced, through a series of joint studies carried out by Marx and Engels, with an interest in French social thought, first studied at secondhand through the works of August Cieszkowski, Lorenz von Stein, and Marx's close friend Moses Hess, and later through the study of Pierre-Joseph Proudhon, Charles Fourier, and especially the great socialist thinker Henri de Saint-Simon.[6]

8

It was from the writings of Saint-Simon that Marx was inspired to his mature work: formulating a scientific sociology, a 'science of man,' which, along with Saint-Simon (and his close collaborator and disciple Auguste Comte), he envisioned as being both a social statics and dynamics – a theory capable of explaining both social structures and their evolution. At this same time, Marx threw himself into the study of European biology, physics, chemistry, mathematics (in fact, discovering a transformation in calculus which to this day carries his name), and in particular English political economy (see Mehring, 1962:227; Ollman, 1971:53; Sedgwick, 1966:191; McLellan, 973:141–142; Bottomore and Rubel, 1964:11–12; Struik, 1964:42–43; Gerratana, 1973; Struik, 1948).

From these studies emerged the first fruits of Marx's efforts at formulating the Saint-Simonian 'science of man,' starting with the 'Theses on Feuerbach' and *The German Ideology*, in which Marx finally settled his accounts with his former companions, the Young Hegelian school of radical German philosophers, and the *Anti-Proudhon* (or, as it is better known, *The Poverty of Philosophy*), Marx's early critique of French political economy and utopian socialist thought. This science of man, as formulated by Marx, was to consist in the search for law-like uniformities governing the various stages in human history, their 'hidden laws of motion,' which were to be derived from and tested by empirical data. In this way, philosophy would be transformed into the objective, exact, empirical study of society (see Marx, 1968a:118–119).

The theoretical foundations of Marx's attempt to construct a science of society lie in his original insight into the central role of historical and material conditions in molding human life. In the preface to the *Critique of Political Economy*, discussing his own intellectual biography, Marx explained the source of his break with Hegelian philosophy as follows:

> My inquiry led me to the conclusion that neither legal relations nor political forms could be comprehended whether by themselves or on the basis of a so-called general development of the human mind, but on the contrary they originate in the material conditions of life. [Marx, 1970a:20]

Since the foundations of social life are to be discovered, according to Marx, not in the elevated spheres of speculative philosophy, but in earthly fact, he proposed that the study of human history be approached in a scientific manner; that the study of history be transformed from metaphysics (ideology) to science, and pass from the simple apparent description of phenomena to their 'hidden' laws of motion. This 'natural science about man,' or 'science of man' would

9

comprise both history and present-day social science, and would be subject to validation by historical and social evidence gathered through empirical study (cf. Jordan, 1967:304). As early as the 1844 *Economic and Philosophic Manuscripts* Marx wrote:

> Sense experience must be the basis of all science. Science is only genuine science when it proceeds from sense experience. Natural science will one day incorporate the science of man, just as the science of man will incorporate natural science; there will be a *single* science (Marx, 1964:142–143).

Thus, Marx urged that human history is not an accidental aggregate of events, but a unified realm of phenomena marked by regularity of occurrences like the regularity of the occurrences in nature. There are ascertainable objective forces which govern civilization. In each of the historical epochs they play a major part in shaping man's motives, ideas, and institutions, governing the relationship of man to man and directing the flow of events to predictable goals. These forces are to be investigated in a *scientific* manner and are to be discovered in the *empirical* study of history itself (Bober, 1962:3–4).

## VALUE COMMITMENT AND OBJECTIVITY

This view of Marx as a man centrally preoccupied with these specific questions of science and scientific method, or rather the adaptation of the methods of natural science to the study of human history, has been seriously disputed by several recent scholarly interpretations of his work. The emphasis of such writers as Erich Fromm (1961), Gajo Petrovic (1967), Robert Tucker (1961 and 1969), Shlomo Avineri (1971), Alan Ryan (1967), and John O'Neill (1972) – drawing extensively on such early Marxian works as the 1843 *Critique of Hegel's Philosophy of Right*, the 1844 'Introduction,' the 1844 *Economic and Philosophical Manuscripts*, and the 1845 *Holy Family* – has been upon the earlier, philosophical component of Marx's writings, and especially the revolutionary (Feuerbachian) humanism of Marx's early unpublished manuscripts.

An extreme statement of this general tendency is found in Robert Tucker's analysis of Marx's work, *Philosophy and Myth in Karl Marx*. Tucker writes:

> It seems fair to say that a change in the generally accepted view of Marx has been taking place in the twentieth century. In the new image he appears not as the scientist of society that he claimed to be but rather as a moralist or a religious kind of thinker. The old assumption that 'scientific socialism' is a scientific system of thought has tended

more and more to give way to the notion that it is in essence a moralistic or religious system. . . . It was not 'real positive science' at which he had arrived out of Hegelianism. Instead, he had gone beyond philosophy into that out of which philosophy ages ago, originated – myth. [Tucker, 1961:12,219]

The conclusion of this analysis of Marx's break with Hegel is not, then, a movement *forward* to the foundation of social science, but rather a *regression* from philosophy to myth. That this thesis will not stand up to any analysis of Marx's mature works will, I believe, be adequately demonstrated in the following discussion (see Bottomore, 1964:xii–xv for a further discussion of Tucker's work). However, the question of Marx's conception of the nature of scientific research, especially in relation to the charge of political *partisanship*, has long been a source of unwarranted confusion and criticism in Marxian scholarship.

There is no question that Marx's earlier writings are replete with formulations similar to the following concerning the relationship of theory to the revolutionary movement:

> Just as philosophy finds its *material* weapons in the proletariat, so the proletariat finds its *intellectual* weapons in philosophy . . . [Marx, 1970c:59]

However, in his later sociological works, Marx had come to a rather more complex conceptualization of the nature of scientific knowledge and the relationship of scientific research to the labor movement. In a crucial passage from *Theories of Surplus Value*: vol. II, reviewing the various 18th and 19th century schools of political economy, Marx contrasts the scientific objectivity of the British economist David Ricardo against the alleged partisanship of Thomas Malthus and then follows with a discussion of the consequences of this for the reliability of the two men's research in political economy.

Marx regarded Ricardo as the greatest of the 18th century political economists (see Marx, 1963a:49; Dobb, 1968), and while he realized that Ricardo '. . . regards the capitalist mode of production as the most advantageous for production in general' and furthermore found him to be 'ruthless' with respect to the plight of the working class under capitalism, Marx continues: 'Ricardo's ruthlessness was not only *scientifically honest* but also a scientific *necessity* from his point of view' (Marx, 1968a:118).

Ricardo's 'ruthlessness' toward the condition of the working class is not merely *understandable* to Marx because of his (Ricardo's) class position as a bourgeois political economist (a question of ideology) or *excusable* because of his conclusions, which may be turned to Marx's

11

advantage (a matter of dialectics, or unintended consequences), but is also, according to Marx, a matter of 'scientific necessity.' Marx explains:

It is not a base action when Ricardo puts the proletariat on the same level as machinery or beasts of burden or commodities, because (from his point of view) their being purely machinery or beasts of burden is conducive to 'production' or because they really are mere commodities in bourgeois production. This is stoic, objective, scientific. [Marx, 1968a:119]

Furthermore, Ricardo's 'ruthlessness' toward the working class is an even-handed ruthlessness. Where he conflicts with the taken-for-granted world of bourgeois ideology he is equally harsh.

Where the bourgeoisie comes into conflict with this he is just as *ruthless* towards it as he is at other times toward the proletariat and the aristocracy. [Marx, 1968a:118]

But as for Malthus:

This wretch only draws such conclusions from the given scientific premises (which he invariably *steals*), as will be 'agreeable' (useful) to the aristocracy against the bourgeoisie and to both *against* the proletariat. [Marx, 1968a:118]

Malthus seeks only to bolster the claims of a given political class and is thus unwilling to strictly draw the conclusions of his own research. It is important to note here that what Marx is criticizing is *not* Malthus' allegiance to a reactionary social class – the epithet 'bourgeois science' did not originate with Marx – or even the politically objectionable consequences of social research which reinforces the ideological claims of the ruling capitalist class. For Ricardo was equally guilty of both of these 'sins' and yet Marx praises him for his 'scientific honesty.'[7]

This 'scientific honesty' is, in fact, the very spirit of Weber's insistence that research be 'ethically neutral,' or value-free, which lies at the very crux of the problems of verification, reliability, and replication in every science (see Weber, 1949). There is no need here to go into an extended discussion of the various ramifications of the doctrine of ethical neutrality. However, what is essential here, for Marx as well as Weber, is not some prohibition against theoretical generalization or even a certain intellectual partisanship (of which Weber was certainly as guilty – in the specifically political sense – as Marx) but rather a prior agreement upon basic procedures and methods for testing the empirical adequacy of those theories – for these remain a convention wholly determined by solely *scientific* criteria.

And so, Marx concludes:

But when a man seeks to *accommodate* science to a viewpoint which is derived not from science itself (however erroneous it may be) but from *outside, from alien, external interests,* then I call him 'base' [gemein]. [Marx, 1968a:119]

This is not an isolated incident, an aberration in the context of Marx's mature work. It is precisely this spirit of strict adherence to the canons of scientific research which informed the elaboration of Marx's important sociological and economic studies. Indeed, Marx showed himself just as quick to turn his scorn upon those self-styled 'proletarian' scientists who broke with the laws and spirit of scientific research as with the ideological representatives of the bourgeoisie.

Proudhon begins by taking his ideal of justice, of 'justice éternelle,' from the juridical relations that correspond to the production of commodities: thereby, it may be noted, he proves, to the consolation of all good citizens, that the production of commodities is a form of production as everlasting as justice. Then he turns round and seeks to reform the actual production of commodities, and the actual legal system corresponding thereto, in accordance with this ideal. What opinion should we have of a chemist, who, instead of studying the actual laws of the molecular changes in the composition and decomposition of matter, and on that foundation solving definite problems, claimed to regulate the composition and decomposition of matter by means of the 'eternal ideas,' of 'naturalité' and 'affinité'? Do we really know any more about 'usury,' when we say it contradicts 'justice éternelle,' 'équité éternelle,' 'mutalité éternelle,' and other 'verités éternelles' than the fathers of the church did when they said it was incompatible with 'grâce éternelle,' 'foi éternelle,' and 'la volunté éternelle de Dieu'? [Marx, 1967a:84–85n]

On the other hand, however, there is no evidence in Marx's writings that he regarded the construction of a positive science of society to be incompatible with the practical activity of changing society. While Marx considered himself a scientist, his conception of science was pragmatic.[8] He wished to furnish a 'scientific basis' for socialism, which he regarded not as a *science* in itself, but as the social and political struggle of the working class to bring about a new, more equalitarian system of human relations – a movement in the realm of politics and ideology. Thus, in the *Poverty of Philosophy* Marx referred to 'the theorists of the proletarian class' who no longer need, as did the Utopian socialists '. . . to improvise systems . . . and seek science in their own minds; they have only to take note of what is happening before their eyes and to become its vehicle of expression' (Marx, 1963a:125).

Their conclusions are to be derived from the empirical study of historical and social facts and do not form a new 'scientific socialism,' but rather constitute a science *of* socialism, an analysis of the existing proletarian movement and the specific empirical conditions in which it develops (Bottomore and Rubel, 1964:15–16). These conclusions should not be taken to form a dogmatism, moreover, but must always remain *tentative* – open to question and qualification from the results of further research. From his earliest to his last writings, Marx maintained a consistent position on this point. In an 1843 letter, he wrote:

> I am not at all in favor of raising our own dogmatic banner. Quite the contrary . . . We do not confront the world in doctrinaire fashion with a new principle, saying: Here is the truth, bow down before it. [Marx to Ruge, 1843 – quoted in Padover, 1971:516–518]

Indeed, Marx noted, the creation of a science of man, or social science, must necessarily differ from the formation of the natural sciences since, as he quotes Giambattista Vico, '. . . human history differs from natural history in this, that we have made the former but not the latter.' Elaborating upon this point, Marx continued:

> The weak points in the abstract materialism of natural science, a materialism that excludes history and its process, are at once evident from the abstract and ideological conceptions of its spokesmen, whenever they venture beyond the bounds of their own speciality. [Marx, 1967a:372–373n]

Human history is, above all, the history of man's activity as a specifically *social* being, and it is this which separates man from the theoretical objects of a natural science. This viewpoint of a strictly social, that is, of an historical and anti-reductionist science, dominates the entire system of Marx's sociology and forms a distinct, independent alternative to both contemporary materialist and idealist schools of thought.

The existence of physical man and the external natural world in which he moves, governed by the operation of regular law-like forces – these are, of course, real suppositions for Marx as for *natural* science. They do not, however, appear as *theoretical* premises of the new system of a *social* science which starts from its own heuristic principles defined in historical and social terms (Korsch, 1938:192–193).

THE HIDDEN NATURE OF SOCIAL LAWS

For Marx, the construction of a science of man began with the establishment of two irreducible premises, or methodological assumptions, which were consequences of the special nature of his subject for scientific study. These premises, concerning (1) the character of social laws, and (2) the definition of his theoretical object were dictated for Marx by

14

the very nature of his attempt to apply a scientific method of analysis to human history.

The first of these premises lies in Marx's characterization of the 'hidden' nature of social laws – the way in which a scientific understanding of social life takes place at a level which *underlies* the commonplace everyday understanding of social actors.[9] A note of warning should be sounded here that this reflection on the nature of social laws by Marx in no way was derived from or corresponded to the Hegelian distinction between *phenomenon* and *essence*. Rather, Marx's conception was derived from the distinction, common to all of the physical sciences, between *manifestation* and *cause*.

According to Marx, this is the objective of *all* science – the passage from the simple apparent motion of phenomena (manifestation) to their real, internal motion (cause). On the treatment of the subject of competition by political economy, he wrote:

> A scientific analysis of competition is not possible, before we have a conception of the inner nature of capital, just as the apparent motions of the heavenly bodies are not intelligible to any but him who is acquainted with their real motions, motions which are not directly perceptible by the senses. [Marx, 1967a:316]

The supposition of 'hidden' social forces which operate with law-like regularity beyond the consciousness of social actors may, Marx noted, appear paradoxical and contrary to everyday observation. However, Marx insisted, there would be no need for science at all if one held fast to appearance and took it for the ultimate word (Marx to Kugelmann, 1868 – in Marx and Engels, 1955:209–210).[10]

> It is also a paradox that the earth moves about the sun, and that water consists of two highly inflammable gases. Scientific truth is always paradox, if judged by everyday experience, which catches only the delusive appearance of things. [Marx, 1968d:209]

It is this specific character of the social laws belonging to a science of man – their 'hidden,' non-apparent nature – which formed the basis for Marx's distinction between science and ideology. If science lays bare the 'hidden' character of social life, the *real* relations within a given society, then ideology is precisely the un-real apparent everyday manifestation of these social relations in which the real relations between 'men and their circumstances appear upside down as in a *camera obscura*' (Marx and Engels, 1970:47).

Just as scientific analysis requires that the real motions of the heavenly bodies be differentiated from the apparent ones, so the necessary forces or tendencies underlying human behaviour and thought must be

15

distinguished from their forms of manifestation. These necessary tendencies should not be explained on the basis of what people say about the sources of their views and the motives of their actions but rather on the basis of rigorous empirical experimentation and study of the concrete material conditions of their lives (Marx and Engels, 1970:42; cf. Jordan, 1967:316).

Thus Marx writes in *Capital*: vol. I, concerning the 'hidden' relationship between wages and profit revealed in the concept of surplus value:

> This form of wage, which is merely an expression of the false visible appearance of paid labour, renders *invisible* the *real* relationship between capital and labour and gives an *impression* which is in fact the opposite of the truth; it is from these false appearances that all the legal notions of the wage-earner and the capitalist are derived, as are all the myths which surround capitalistic production. [Marx, 1967a:540 – translation modified by Godelier, 1970:342]

So long as, as in traditional political economy, wages are thought of as the fair 'price' of labor there can be no question of profit being understood as unpaid labor. Each side to the transaction between capital and labour seems to be drawing from production the revenue to which it is entitled. There is no visible exploitation of one class by another. But underneath this 'visible' transaction lies the 'hidden' relationship between the two classes – the production and expropriation of surplus value.

Marx writes:

> In present bourgeois society as a whole, this positing of prices and their circulation, etc. appears as a surface process, beneath which, however, in the depths, entirely different processes go on, in which this apparent individual equality and liberty disappear. [Marx, 1973a:247]

Without going any further into a discussion of the place of this key economic concept in Marx's analysis of the capitalist mode of production we can see that, for Marx, the conceptual distinction between appearance and reality is simply a general requirement for arriving at scientific knowledge – part of the method which he has taken over to political economy from the other sciences where this distinction has long been established. Thus, the various economic categories of wages, profits, interest, etc. which express the visible relations of the day-to-day practice of business affairs, while they are of some *practical* use to us, are the productions of a given false, *ideological* awareness and as such can be of no *scientific* value whatever (cf. Geras, 1971:70–71; Godelier, 1970:342–343). And so, Marx continues, any so-called science based on these categories is no more than

... a systemization of the claims and pretensions of agents of production who are themselves prisoners of bourgeois relationships of production and merely constitutes an apology of these ideas . . . It is therefore hardly surprising that the popular notions of economics appear perfectly self-evident and that the relationships seem the more obvious for their internal structure remaining hidden. [Marx, 1967b:168,313]

## THE SOCIAL NATURE OF MAN

For Marx, the construction of a science of man began with the second irreducible premise of man's own activity as a member of a social collectivity, or what Marx called *social practice* or *production*. Here, at once, Marx (1) rejected positing society as a separate entity partaking of any reality over and beyond the summation of its individual human components, and yet (2) still insisted upon the specifically *social* nature of man.

Above all we must avoid postulating 'Society' again as an abstraction vis-a-vis the individual. The individual *is the social being*. [Marx, 1964:137–138]

Throughout his life Marx never swerved from this strict rule of nominalism (the rejection of methodological realism) – that the real referents of any general proposition or statement can be nothing other than individual concrete objects. Society is nothing more than 'man himself in his social relations' (Marx, 1971:149).

Society for Marx thus refers to individuals in their interrelations, or interactions, and it is precisely this interaction among individuals which is the theoretical object of the science of man.[11] Marx writes:

The premises from which we begin are not arbitrary ones, not dogmas, but real premises from which abstraction can only be made in the imagination. They are the real individuals, their activity and the material conditions under which they live, both those which they find already existing and those produced by their activity. These premises can thus be verified in a purely empirical way. [Marx and Engels, 1970:42][12]

This activity of real individuals does *not*, however, presuppose the existence of so many solitary, isolated men who have created society by means of a *contrat social*, establishing a relationship and connection between subjects that are by nature independent and separate (Marx, 1970b:124). Marx rejected any theorizing based upon an individualistic model of human existence or behavior, such as was common to 18th century political economy, which started with the premise

17

of the isolated individual producing for his own needs. He argued that such an individualistic model dealt with undifferentiated human entities, improperly abstracting from the individual's concrete social status and condition. Instead of discussing real individuals as they appeared in real, human relations, the model divested the individual of precisely those social attributes which make his existence real, positing an unnatural solitary 'Robinsonesque'[13] existence (cf. Avineri, 1968:82–83).

To the contrary, Marx insisted, the fundamental activity of empirical men is precisely their *socially* mediated action and interaction; what he labelled their *social practice*, that is, socially productive – rather than individualistic – activity or labor. Marx repeatedly insisted upon the specifically social nature of man and the social character of his productive activities. 'All production is the appropriation of nature on the part of an individual within and through a specific form of society' (Marx, 1973a:87 – see also Marx, 1968b:81).

Production is always a social, not an individual activity. Indeed, according to Marx, it is this productive activity of man which strictly defines his social nature – a view shared by Weber, Durkheim, and Pareto, and one which served as one of the major premises of late 19th and early 20th century European sociology.

> Individuals producing in a society, and hence the socially determined production of individuals, is of course the point of departure. The solitary and isolated hunter or fisherman, who serves Adam Smith and Ricardo as a starting point, is one of the unimaginative fantasies of eighteenth-century romances *la* Robinson Crusoe . . . Man is a *zoon politikon* in the most literal sense: he is not only a social animal, but an animal that can individualize himself only within society. Production by an isolated individual outside society – a rare event, which might occur when a civilized person who has already absorbed the dynamic social forces is accidentally cast into the wilderness – is just as preposterous as the development of speech without individuals who live *together* and talk to one another. [Marx, 1970b: 124–125]

Production, for Marx is not simply a process in which man expropriates and works on the natural wealth of nature as an individual but is essentially a process carried on *between* men, a social process. Indeed, the socially productive activity in which men collectively produce and reproduce the very conditions and circumstances of their existence is the constitutive fact of society itself. For Marx, this social process of production is the core of the social process *per se*.

Marx writes:

> Men can be distinguished from animals by consciousness, by religion, or anything else you like. They themselves begin to distinguish

18

themselves from animals as soon as they begin to *produce* their means of subsistence. [Marx and Engels, 1970:42]

Here and elsewhere in Marx's writing, the term 'production' is not meant to refer to merely material, or economic production, but actually includes a much wider range of human activity. As Maurice Dobb has noted, the term 'production' generally – and more specifically the term 'mode of production' – has a connotation in the writings of Marx and Engels which is in fact a great deal wider than most interpreters of their work have taken it to be. Dobb writes:

> The notion that this term refers only to the technique of production (and hence implies a purely technological interpretation of history) may well have contributed to the view, which we have discussed, that historical materialism dethrones men as makers of history and puts some mechanistic demiurge in their place. For Marx, however, the mode of production was evidently a more precise development of Hegel's 'civil society' (of which he once spoke as 'the true source and theater of all history'). [Dobb, 1951:9–10]

In fact, the term 'mode of production,' as used by Marx, refers to the *totality* of social relations and human interaction within any given society, encompassing the diverse aspects of both 'society' and 'culture' (Marx, 1968b:81).[14] Marx writes:

> The mode of production must not be considered simply as being the production of the physical existence of the individuals. Rather it is a definite form of activity of these individuals, a definite form of expressing their life, a definite *mode of life* on their part. As individuals express their life, so they are. What they are, therefore, coincides with their production, both with *what* they produce and with *how* they produce. [Marx and Engels, 1970:42]

The mode of production, then, is analyzed by Marx as the site, or the unity, of so many distinct social practices (productions) in which individuals conduct the everyday activities and interactions through which they define and express their lives as social beings. This, for Marx, is the theoretical starting point of the construction of a science of society – the analysis of the different specific levels of social production. This analysis is to include both *what* is produced (the level of production, or distinct productive practice *per se* – economic production, political production, intellectual production, etc.) and *how* it is produced – the *mode* of production.

The elaboration of productions includes not only material economic production, strictly speaking, but all of the various social practices of man.

Religion, family, state, law, morality, science, art, etc., are only

19

*particular* forms of production, and fall under its general laws. [Marx, 1964:136]

Man 'produces' mentally as well as materially. As a worker he engages in the 'material production of life' while as an intellectual he engages in 'mental production;' he is a 'producer of the concept' (Marx and Engels, 1970:42, 64–68).

Indeed, science itself was considered by Marx to be a specific form of production, or particular practice, and its development was to be explained in the same terms as any other form of human productive activity. Marx writes:

> *The development of science,* of this ideal and at the same time practical wealth, is however only one aspect, one form, of the *development of human productive forces.* [Marx, 1971:120 – see also Marx and Engels, 1970:63]

Thus the entire range of man's social life is encompassed, for Marx, by the concept of social production, interpreted in its widest sense. It is this concept which forms the focus of Marx's theoretical science.

## THE MODE OF PRODUCTION AS A THEORETICAL MODEL

Marx's historical materialism is not, as it is so often taken to be, a succession of universal stages of economic-social formations ruled by implacable laws which carry them irresistibly forward to capitalism and thence to socialism and communism. As we have just seen, however, neither is it a simple classificatory schema, a series of pigeon-holes for conveniently locating various historical societies. In approaching historical materialism and appraising Marx's general theory it is essential to see that Marx's theoretical interest in pre-capitalist history was in relation to capitalism. What specifically interested him was the appearance in preceding formations of the conditions which made possible the emergence of capitalist society in Western Europe (Hobsbawm, 1964:19–20; 43; Rodinson, 1966:98).

Yet despite this narrowly empirical interest, the starting point for Marx's methodology was the derivation and statement of propositions (first approximations) at a high level of theoretical abstraction. In the 1859 preface to the *Critique of Political Economy* Marx attempted to reconcile the strict requirements of his methodology with the (self-acknowledged) limited nature of his historiographic interest and knowledge to produce what remains the basic statement of his general theory, historical materialism, in semi-propositional form – unsatisfactory, fragmented, and incomplete though it may be (although Marx was to modify his 1859 theses considerably in later years, as we shall see).

In the social production of their existence, men inevitably enter into definite relations, which are independent of their will, namely relations of production appropriate to a given stage in the development of their material forces of production. The totality of these relations of production constitutes the economic structure of society, the real foundation, on which arises a legal and political superstructure and to which correspond definite forms of social consciousness . . . At a certain stage of development, the material productive forces of society come into conflict with the existing relations of production or – this merely expresses the same thing in legal terms – with the property relations within the framework of which they have operated hitherto. From forms of development of the productive forces these relations turn into their fetters. Then begins an era of social revolution. [Marx, 1970a:20–21]

Here, concrete social relations among individual human actors have been replaced by a number of *abstract* terms – 'forces of production,' 'social relations of production,' etc. – which, at first glance, give the appearance of reification. However, as we have seen, the abstract character of these various theoretical elements is inextricably tied to the very nature of Marx's scientific method.[15]

To return to Marx's statement of his methodology in the preface to *Capital:* vol. I, he has chosen England as the 'classic ground' of the development of the capitalist mode of production. England, then, the country in which the process of capitalist development was most advanced, has been appropriated by Marx as his *laboratory* in which to study 'the capitalist mode of production, and the relations of production and intercourse corresponding to that mode,' just as the physicist who studies the processes of nature observes them where 'they occur in their most typical form and most free from disturbing influence' (Marx, 1967a:8).

England alone can serve as the *lever* for serious *economic* revolution. It is the only country where there are no longer any peasants and where landed property is concentrated in a few hands. It is the only country where the *capitalist* form – that is, labor combined on a large scale under capitalist entrepreneurs – has taken over practically the whole of production. It is the only country where *the great majority of the population consists of wage laborers*. It is the only country where the class struggle and organization of the working class by trade unions have attained a certain degree of maturity and universality. It is the only country where, thanks to its domination of the world market, every revolution in economic relationships must directly affect the whole world. [Marx, letter to the Swiss Romansh Federal Council – quoted from Padover, 1973:171–172].

21

The original process always takes place in England; it is the demiurge of the bourgeois cosmos. The different phases of the cyclical motion of bourgeois society occur on the continent in a secondary and tertiary form. [Marx, *The Class Struggles in France* – in Marx, 1973b:130–131; see also Marx to Meyer and Vogt, 1870 – in Marx and Engels, 1955:237; Marx to 'Otechestvenniye Zapiski,' 1877 – in Marx and Engels, 1955:313]

Yet even this 'classic' or 'ideal' example is subjected to a further 'purification,' or abstraction, since on his own admission Marx analyzes it on the assumption that (1) there are only two classes in his object of study (a situation which has never existed anywhere), and that (2) the world market is entirely subject to the capitalist mode of production, which is just as far from reality (Marx, 1968a:492–493; Marx, 1967b:885,110; Marx, 1963b:409–410).[16]

The reason for this further 'purification' is that the English example, however classical and pure it may be, *is not the theoretical object of Marx's study – Capital –* but is only an example. England does indeed enter into the analysis but, as Marx has said, for a particular reason, as the 'classic' or 'typical' ground of something else, as the laboratory of his scientific analyses. 'Their classic ground is England. That is the reason why I have taken the chief facts and examples which *illustrate* the development of my theories from England' (Marx, translation from Roy's 1872 French text of *Capital*: vol. I – authorized and approved by Marx, with several corrections and additions to the original German text – from Althusser and Balibar, 1970:194).

This statement puts into correct perspective the immediately preceding sentence in the preface to *Capital* in which the methodology of physics was evoked in a way that might suggest that Marx, like the physicist, was investigating a 'pure' object, 'free from disturbing influences.' In this respect England, however, is an impure perturbed object, but these 'impurities' and 'disturbances' cause no theoretical trouble since the object of Marx's study is not any empirical subject but rather a theoretical abstraction, not England but the capitalist mode of production in its 'Kerngestalt' [ideal or core form] (Marx, 1967a:8; Marx, 1967b:83; cf. Althusser and Balibar, 1970:196).

'Intrinsically,' Marx immediately continues:

. . . it is not a question of the higher or lower degree of development [in different countries] of the social antagonisms that result from the natural laws of capitalist production. It is a question of *these laws themselves* [emphasis added]. [Marx, 1967a:8]

But what is this capitalist mode of production, which Marx has determined to investigate in its 'ideal form': something oppressively real and yet at the same time invisible, i.e. abstract.

The Chilean sociologist Theotonio dos Santos has written in respect of Marx's analysis of social class:

> The starting point of Marx's analysis is the study of a determinate mode of production. At any given moment social classes appear as 'personifications,' the volitional, personal, active content of certain relations that are described abstractly. This does not mean that at a more concrete level it will be impossible to describe the classes of society as social groups that can be studied sociologically [i.e. empirically]. However, this empirical study of classes has a definite theoretical sense only when it is located within the framework of an abstract analysis. That is, it is only possible to arrive at an explanatory level of analysis when the empirical descriptive level is inserted into an abstract theoretical picture. This gives a more precise form to the problem of levels of abstraction, by clearly defining the theoretical starting point of the analysis. [dos Santos, 1970:173]

This abstract 'theoretical starting point,' the mode of production, is conceived by Marx as a *theoretical model* of the empirical society, ideally isolated in its essential parts as an organic interacting social whole (Marx, 1963a:110; Marx and Engels, 1970:58).

The abstract concept of the capitalist mode of production is contained, then, in the theoretical construct of the mode of production as a *system* composed of so many basic *elements* – the economic forces of production and relations of production, and the political and cultural, or ideological superstructures, each of which forms a sub-system composed of its own basic structural elements.

This whole is a totality, a unity, but it is a unity of *heterogeneous* parts, a synthesis of analytically *distinct* elements and is therefore susceptible to theoretical analysis at the level of its component elements as well (cf. Colletti, 1972:14). The various elements of the theoretical system do not actually exist in any pure 'ideal' or abstract form, even in the 'classic ground,' England, but are rather theoretical variables abstracted from concrete phenomena. They are the theoretical representation of 'certain essential features' abstracted from a given series of concrete social formations which 'in spite of their motley diversity of form . . .' are held 'in common' (Marx, 1968c:331). Thus, they are abstract and artificial but not arbitrary. Concerning this particular point, Marx wrote:

> The simplest economic category, say, exchange-value implies the existence of population, population that is engaged in production within determined relations; it also implies the existence of certain types of family, class, or state, etc. It can have no other existence except as an abstract *one-sided relation* of an already *given and living*

23

*aggregate.* [Marx, 1970b:141 – translation modified by Ollman, 1971:12–13]

Nevertheless, the investigation which Marx undertakes in *Capital* is not the analysis of any concrete social formation ('concrete and living aggregate'), but the investigation of a general (theoretical) model embracing a number of social formations which share the common central characteristic of capitalist production. Throughout *Capital* there is an *apparent* contradiction or tension between the abstract nature of the model and the idealized, tentative nature of its economic laws on the one hand and, on the other, the continual invocation by Marx of empirical statistics, examples, and data taken from industry reports, government 'blue books,' etc., illustrating the operation of the idealized model in its 'classic ground,' England. But the appearance and use of the British example causes no contradiction in the abstract nature of Marx's method. England does indeed enter the analysis but, as Marx says, for a *particular* reason: only because and insofar as within it, at a certain historical moment, an empirical situation was produced to approximate the 'laboratory conditions' of the abstract model.

Marx writes:

> In a general analysis of this kind, it is nearly always assumed that the actual conditions correspond to their concept, or, what is the same, that actual conditions are represented only to the extent that they are typical of their own general type. [Marx, 1967b:143]

Within the systems-model, the various components of the model exist in a state of mutual dependence. In Marx's view, the relationship between the components is an *internal* one, that is, a change in one of the factors leads to a change in the other elements of the system. For example, if wage-labor disappeared, that is, if the workers' connection to capital radically changed, capital would cease to exist and a whole series of secondary changes in the structure of the state, cultural forms, etc. would then follow. The opposite proposition would also be true (Ollman, 1971:15).

This is the meaning of Marx's famous aphorism: 'The handmill gives you society with the feudal lord; the steam-mill, society with the industrial capitalist' (Marx, 1963a:109). The means of social production of existence – economic, intellectual, political, cultural, etc. – all form an interconnected organic whole.

The existence of a given system of economic relationships at the same time *presupposes* and *preconditions* a concomitant constellation of social and cultural institutions and arrangements. These institutions and arrangements, being mutually conditioned expressions of men's social and historical situation, must change to reflect or react to changes in the conditions under which they have arisen. Marx continues: 'The same men who establish their social relations in conformity with their material productivity, produce also principles, ideas, and categories, in conformity with their social relations' (Marx, 1963a:109).

If the social relations in a society using a handmill are different from those prevailing in a society making use of a steam-mill, then the political systems, religious organizations, law, science, and philosophy must also be different in the two societies.

> Assume a particular state of development in the productive faculties of man and you will get a particular form of commerce and consumption. Assume particular stages of development in production, commerce, and consumption and you will have a corresponding organization of the family, or orders or of classes, in a word, a corresponding civil society. Assume a particular civil society and you will get particular political conditions which are but the official expression of civil society. [Marx to Annenkov, 1846 – in Marx and Engels, 1955:35]

For Marx, this principle assumes the stature of an abstract social law, useful both in the 'postdiction' (see Hempel, 1965:173–174) and prediction of empirical historical events.

> Robespierre, Saint Just, and their party fell because they confused the realistic democratic common-wealth of antiquity, which rested on the basis of real slavery, with the modern spiritualist-democratic representative state based on the emancipated slavery of bourgeois society. [Marx, 1957:164]

> If the proletariat destroys the political rule of the bourgeoisie, that will only be a temporary victory, only an element in the service of the *bourgeois revolution* itself, as in 1794, so long as in the course of history, in its 'movement,' the material conditions are not yet created which make necessary the abolition of the bourgeois mode of production and thus the definitive overthrow of bourgeois political rule. [Marx, article from the *Deutscher-Brusseler Zeitung* – quoted from Bottomore and Rubel, 1964:240]

The economic factor plays the leading role. But 'superstructural' elements, growing out of and along with changing economic conditions and the various 'material' (technological) factors determining these conditions, in their turn react upon and exert a decisive influence on the structure of economic life. In either case, there is no doubt, in Marx's work, of a simultaneous reverse process at work. A constant process of mutual cause and effect is in operation between the various categories of social phenomena (Marx and Engels, 1970:58; Marx, 1967c:791–792; Marx, 1963b:228; Engels to Bloch, 1890 – in Marx and Engels, 1955:417; cf. Lopreato and Hazelrigg, 1972:40).

Like all its predecessors, the capitalist mode of production proceeds under definite material conditions, which are, however, simultaneously the bearers of definite social relations entered into by individuals in the process of reproducing their life. Those conditions, like these relations, are on the one hand prerequisites, on the other hand results and creations of the capitalist process of production; they are produced and reproduced by it. [Marx, 1967b:818–819]

In his exposition of Vilfredo Pareto's use of this same theoretical concept of system, the Harvard chemist and physiologist L. J. Henderson wrote:

The parts and forces of the social system, like those of analogous systems, are conceived as in a state of mutual dependence. They interact. Once again this arises from the fact that it is, in general, impossible to explain the phenomena in terms of ordinary cause and effect. Therefore, such an explanation gives place to the type of description previously found necessary for dynamical, thermodynamical, physiological, and economic systems. So it comes about that *the central feature of Pareto's use of his theory is the analysis of mutually dependent variations of his variables* [emphasis added]. [Henderson, 1935:17–18]

This was *precisely* the theoretical position taken earlier by Marx, although Pareto, having done a doctoral dissertation in engineering on the equilibrium of elastic bodies along lines analogous to the mathematical discoveries of J. Willard Gibbs, was in a position to be more formally explicit about it (see Lopreato, 1973:451–452). This often misunderstood concept of the effect of a system on its elements lies at the very heart of Marx's method.

The result at which we arrive, is not that production, distribution, exchange, and consumption are identical, but that they are all elements of a totality, distinctions within a unity. Production predominates . . . From it, the process continually recommences . . . but there is interaction between the various elements. This is the case in every organic whole. [Marx, 1973a:99–100 – translation by Bottomore and Rubel, 1964:18]

Marx's position may now be summarized as follows: Within a given theoretical system, certain elements, or structures, are associated in a *determined* state of *mutual dependence*. This determined state is the designation of a given mode of production – the capitalist mode of production, for example. This determinate condition is not a stable state of equilibrium, however, but is constantly altering due to a process of

26

immanent change arising from the internal contradiction, or dialectic, both *within* and *between* the various system elements.

## SOCIAL STRUCTURE AND SOCIAL EVOLUTION

Marx viewed the entire question of the successive evolution of various stages in human society as extremely complex, devoting himself to detailed historical studies which led him to engage in continuous re-examination and revision of his basic theoretical principles. Marx, himself, insisted that he had not formulated a general theory of history but rather a materialist methodology which had no general use except in application to particular concrete historical phenomena (Marx to the *Otechestivenniye Zapiski*, 1877 – in Marx and Engels, 1955:312–313).

Indeed, Marx argued that the discovery of the laws governing a given social formation requires a patient and minute scientific study of concrete evidence and not the projection of an *a priori* scheme.

> By studying each of these forms of evolution separately and then comparing them one can easily find the clue to this phenomenon, but one will never arrive there by using as one's master key a general historico-philosophical theory, the supreme virtue of which consists in being super-historical. [Marx to the '*Otechestvenniye Zapiski*.' 1877 – in Marx and Engels, 1955:313]

> But our conception of history is above all a guide to study, not a lever for construction after the manner of the Hegelians. All history must be studied afresh, the conditions of existence of the different formations of society must be examined individually before the attempt is made to deduce from them the political, civil-law, aesthetic, philosophic, religious, etc., views corresponding to them. [Engels to Schmidt, 1890—in Marx and Engels, 1955:416]

Marx's application of his general model to the study of human history and societies yielded a series of successively modified and refined classifications of modes of production, each representing a particular stage in the organization of economic and social life. Each of these theoretical stages corresponds to certain historical social-economic formations in which a particular mode of production predominates.

> The relations of production in their totality constitute what are called the social relations, society, and specifically, a society at a definite stage of historical development, a society with a peculiar, distinctive character. *Ancient* society, *feudal* society, *bourgeois* (or capitalist) society are such totalities of production relations, each of which at the same time denotes a special stage of development in the history of mankind. [Marx, 1968b:81]

27

To be more precise, the various modes of production are abstract idealizations – defined by a certain level of technology, development of economic surplus and the division of labor, pattern of property relations, class structure, form of the state, and configuration of cultural and intellectual life. They were abstracted by Marx from his readings in and studies of the varied complex types of economies and social orders known throughout history.

Furthermore, these various modes of production constitute abstract, analytical models in a double sense. First, they will only rarely, if ever, empirically occur in their 'pure' form, but will normally be analytically applied to societies exhibiting many additional characteristics and deviations from the 'normative' model. (Remember, within the abstract model, Marx has only undertaken to analyze the interaction of a limited number of 'crucial variables.') And secondly, these various abstract models will commonly be found in their concrete form, or application, in a 'mixed' state of coexistence, side by side and intertwined with one another – particularly in those transitional stages occurring between such historically neighboring types as feudalism and capitalism (Wesolowski, 1967:59).

Thus the capitalist mode of production dominating an entire society such as contemporary England is to be distinguished from capitalist relations which may exist in a number of social and historical formations while not actually dominating those societies, such as the capitalist market relations in the late Roman or Inca Empires (Marx to the *Otechestvenniye Zapiski*, 1877 – in Marx and Engels, 1955:313; Marx, 1973a:102–103; Marx, 1970a:60).

The slave, feudal, and capitalist modes of production are ideal types, abstract models of social relations that have seldom, if ever, been applicable to the whole of a population of a given society. Next to the slave-worked latifundia of the Roman aristocracy existed small peasant farms; next to the medieval manors, factories and artisan workshops thrived. Marx writes:

> We are only concerned here with striking and general characteristics; for epochs in the history of society are no more separated from each other by hard and fast lines of demarcation, than are geological epochs. [Marx, 1967a:371]

Consequently, Marx argued that in the application of the ideal model to empirical societies one can only speak of the *preponderance* of a given mode of production in any particular concrete social formation. 'Modern capitalist society,' then, whether in England, Holland, or France, is simply '. . . the form of society in which the capitalist mode of

28

production predominates' (Marx, 1963b:409). In this way Marx avoided the inextricable difficulties which would have followed from the attempt to pigeon-hole every historical formation into the mode of production.

Similarly, Marx recognized that past forms of society may survive the specific social conditions which gave birth to them and linger on into a radically changed social climate. Such social anachronisms may be either historically 'progressive' such as the 'trading nations' which 'existed in the ancient world only in its interstices' or they may be historical 'survivals,' remnants of earlier modes of production such as the independent handicraftsmen and rural peasants of Marx's own time about whom he wrote: 'although they are producers of commodities, . . . their production does not fall under the capitalist mode of production' (Marx, 1967a:79; Marx, 1963b:407 – see also Marx and Engels, 1970:87–88).

In short, in his application of the method of successive approximations to a dynamic systems model of social order, Marx was in fact pursuing what Lopreato and Alston (1970) have termed an 'idealization strategy,' with a theoretical model at the highest level of abstraction yielding a set of 'pure' or 'ideal' types, or representations of actual historical formations – the various modes of production in their 'ideal average,' (Marx, 1967b:143, 831) which are then subject to subsequent revision and qualification through a series of particular, detailed, historical studies.

The laws and 'tendencies' of the Marxian model are therefore of an abstract (i.e. ideal) nature, but indeed, these are the types of formulations required by any scientific theory that aims at more than a simple enumeration of empirical data. For Marx, the abstract nature of his theoretical model was not pursued as an end in itself; the model itself served as a *heuristic* device through which Marx attempted to approach the complex phenomena of empirical social life in a series of successive approximations. As such, the theoretical models of Marxian analysis, the historical modes of production in their 'ideal average,' constitute merely the first– but necessary – step toward the elaboration of concrete theoretical propositions.

Concerning Marx's use of this methodology, Max Weber wrote:

> We will only point out here that naturally all specifically Marxian 'laws' and developmental constructs – insofar as they are theoretically sound – are ideal types. The eminent, indeed unique, *heuristic* significance of these ideal types when they are used for the assessment of reality is known to everyone who has ever employed Marxian concepts and hypotheses. [Weber, 1949:103]

Marx's theoretical writings comprise, then, not a unilinear scheme of social evolution, as is commonly believed, but rather form primarily a theory of structures and their correspondence within the abstract, 'ideal' conditions or limits of the 'mode of production,' considered as a predictive systems model for the empirical social formation. The discovery and definition of the necessary relationships between the various factors within a system of social production and exchange constitutes the starting point of Marx's sociological inquiry. Social change thus occurs through time as *a consequence of the reproduction of a given system of social productions*, or practices – the manifestation of latent structural contradictions (a concept which plays a similar role in Marx's model to the concept of friction in physics).

Thus, Marx insisted that it would be 'inexpedient and wrong' for social science to adopt its categories in a sequence determined by their 'natural succession' or historical evolution. Marx writes:

> The point at issue is not the role that various economic relations have played in the succession of various social formations appearing in the course of history; even less is it their sequence 'as concepts' (Proudhon) [a method derived from Hegel] (a nebulous notion of the historical process), but their articulation within modern bourgeois society. [Marx, 1970b:147]

Marx then does not follow the Hegelian procedure of the deduction of each historical category from its temporal predecessor. Neither does his model reflect the radical social evolutionism endemic to 19th century European sociology – the evolution of Reason (Comte), the struggle for survival (Spencer), etc. Rather, Marx prefers to describe the functions of one element within a structure, or of one structure within a system, and then advance to the application of this theoretical model to the concrete social-economic formation. It is this which forms the essence of the Marxian method, and not the recourse to some supra-evolutionary scheme of history.

In not making the question of the origin or the history of social relations the principal task for social science, as did the social evolutionists and cultural diffusionists of the nineteenth century, Marx's thinking on this point converged with that of Radcliffe-Brown, Lévi-Strauss, Pareto, and other modern 'structuralists.' He writes:

> History is nothing but the succession of the separate generations, each of which exploits the materials, the capital funds, the productive forces handed down to it by all preceding generations, and thus, on the one hand, continues the traditional activity in completely changed circumstances and, on the other, modifies the old circumstances with a completely changed activity. This can be speculatively

30

distorted so that the later history is made the goal of earlier history, e.g. the goal ascribed to the discovery of America is to further the eruption of the French Revolution. Thereby history receives its own special aims and becomes 'a person ranking with other persons' (to wit: 'Self-Consciousness, Criticism, the Unique,' etc.) while what is designated with the words 'destiny,' 'goal,' 'germ,' or 'idea' of earlier history is nothing more than an abstraction formed from later history, from the active influence which earlier history exercises on later history. [Marx and Engels, 1970:57–58]

In no sense does Marx treat the Asiatic, Ancient, Feudal, and various other pre-capitalist modes of production as merely so many 'preliminary stages' of contemporary society. Marx's own historical research (notably the section of the 1857–1858 *Grundrisse* manuscript entitled 'Pre-Capitalist Economic Formations') rather stresses the radical *discontinuity* of these historical formations, which are theoretically treated as independent, historically discrete entities, to be separately analyzed on the basis of their own categories and social laws.

The notion that socialism is bound to evolve as the inevitable 'synthesis' of primitive communism and its opposite, private property, is sheer nonsense on the assumptions of Marx's own theoretical model. In any event, Marx himself – unlike some of his followers – deduced the 'necessity' of socialism not from any general theory of history but from his analysis of the capitalist mode of production and its internal contradictions and crises, to which, Marx proposed, socialism offered the only rational alternative to the eventual regression of the capitalist system to chaos and 'barbarism.' Whether one accepts or rejects this, it is clear that Marx is not here proclaiming a universal 'law' of social evolution and progress. George Lichtheim has noted:

> Unlike Hegel, Marx does not treat history as the unfolding of a metaphysical substance and unlike Comte, he does not claim to be in possession of an operational key which will unlock every door . . . The 'relentless onward march of civilization' is a Comtean, not a Marxian postulate. If the second generation of his followers understood Marx to have expounded a kind of universal optimism, they thoroughly misunderstood the meaning and temper of his message. [Lichtheim, 1967a:13–14; see also Marx to Domela-Niuwenhuis, 1881 – in Marx and Engels, 1955:337–339]

CONCLUSION

In summary, I have attempted to isolate a number of key methodological steps utilized by Marx in his analysis of capitalist society. These may be summarized under three general headings. First, and perhaps most striking, is Marx's characteristic focus upon the antagonistic, or conflict side of social relationships. This is the element of Marx's work most readily identified with the contemporary Marxian, or 'conflict' perspective in sociology. However, it reflects, in Marx's thought, not so much a concern with the analysis of conflict, *per se,* as the belief that (1) conflict between individuals and social groups over rival and incompatible claims to scarce resources, to wealth, power, or prestige are an inevitable factor of social life (an inheritance of Marx's grounding in classical political economy); and (2) indeed, these conflicts are the primary source of social change and progress. The absence of conflict – at least short of the achievement of socialism – indicated, for Marx, not health, but social pathology – a stagnating, stationary society.[17]

Secondly, we can credit Marx with raising the concept of society as a system composed of interdependent parts – which had been a commonplace of social thought at least since Plato – to the level of serious scientific analysis. We can credit Marx with initiating discussion in the social sciences of the conceptual and methodological problems arising from the postulate of interdependence which underlies his analysis of the various historical modes of production. Marx's work in this respect clearly anticipates the later analyses of Vilfredo Pareto and modern systems theorists.

Finally, we can credit Marx with the contribution made to the theoretical study of whole societies by his conceptualization of the various modes of production as analytically distinct models, subject to independent analysis and therefore subject to varying 'historical' laws.[18] This abstract systems analysis, coupled with Marx's application of the method of successive approximations – the utilization of an idealization strategy by which an abstract systems model is applied, tested, and modified through successive stages of empirical experimentation and study – served to yield a powerful unified methodology and programmatic paradigm for the establishment of a social science, or 'science of man.'

Although it is precisely this feature of Marx's work which has been the most consistently misunderstood and neglected by both Marxist and Western sociologists; it is clear that this – Marx's methodological program – as much as any of his substantive achievements in the field of economic or social theory, deserves to be considered the site of one of Marx's most important contributions to social science and one of his most lasting accomplishments.

A NOTE ON THE SELECTIONS

The essays in this volume have been selected from a large secondary literature on Marx and his work (see the bibliography at the end of this volume). They are, for the most part, recent contributions to the discussion on Marxism and the social sciences. Although the reader will quickly discover that there is no unanimity of opinion on a number of crucial issues among the authors represented here, he will find that all of the selections do reflect some degree of commitment to the proposition that Marx's writings form the starting point for the construction of scientific theory in the area of social studies. In this sense, all of the authors represented here may be called Marxists, although several would resist the title of orthodox Marxist. Their work is part of a general resurgence of interest in Marxism in the 1960s and 1970s which has led to the publication of a number of scholarly articles and monographs dealing with Marx's work and its relationship to contemporary social science theory and research. Together, this work necessitates a major reappraisal of the scientific nature and content of Marx's theoretical writings.

In drawing together a number of the most important contributions of recent years, this volume, it is hoped, has helped this process of reappraisal along. It is a testament to the intellectual strength and vitality of Marx's work that it continues to inspire such important commentary and critical elaboration today. It will doubtless continue to do so in the future.

I would like to thank Ms Ruth Seligman for her aid in typing portions of the manuscript and the editors at Quartet Books in London for their patience.

## NOTES TO THE INTRODUCTION

1. One result of this reading of Marx has been to lead members of this school to attempt a major effort at the reinterpretation of Hegel in which, just as Marx has now been 'Hegelianized,' Hegel becomes more and more to look like Marx (see Hyppolite, 1969; Kojeve, 1969; Marcuse, 1960; Lukács, 1973 – for a critical assessment, see Lichtheim, 1971; Colletti, 1973).

2. The materialist ontology, or dialectical materialism was rather elaborated by Engels in the period immediately preceding and following Marx's death. This expansion of Marxism from its original historical-sociological focus to the level of a general philosophy of being, or ontology, was carried out by Engels in an effort to both systematize Marx's work and combat certain neo-positivist interpretations, such as that of Eugen Duhring – see Engels, 1970.

3. See Labriola, 1966; Weber, 1949, 1964; Pareto, 1926, 1935; Bukharin, 1969; Neurath, 1959; Korsch, 1938, 1972; Renner, 1949; Hook, 1933; Schumpeter, 1954, 1962; della Volpe, 1974; Hoffman, 1972.

4. The term 'science of man' was borrowed by Marx in the 1844 Philosophical and Economic Manuscripts from the French socialist Henri de Saint-Simon (Jordan, 1971:9 – See Saint-Simon, 1964; Marx, 1964).

5. In this study, I shall be focusing fairly exclusively on Marx's later more sociological works: especially the recently published *Grundrisse* manuscript, the *Theories of Surplus Value,* and the three volumes of *Capital*. I wish to stress here that much of what shall follow cannot and should not be applied to Marx's earlier 'humanist' writings, such as the 1844 *Paris Manuscripts*, etc. In these works, as well as others, Marx was concerned with different objectives and may be said to have used different methodologies in pursuit of those aims.

6. See Bottomore and Rubel, 1964:9–10; Jordan, 1967:111–148; Lichtheim, 1967c:15–16; Jordan, 1971:9; Mehring, 1962:60; McLellan, 1973:16, 25, 103, 113 – see also Bernstein, 1948; Simon, 1956; Mengelberg, 1961; Hepner, 1952; Manuel, 1965; Manuel and Manuel, 1971; Lichtheim, 1969.

7. This important point cannot be stressed too much in assessing Marx's careful distinction between *science* and *ideology*. Marx never dismissed any serious theoretical view merely on the ground that it expressed a non-proletarian ideology. From his early criticism of German philosophy in *The Holy Family* and *The German Ideology*, through the critique of Proudhon in *The Poverty of Philosophy*, up to the critical examination of political economy in *Capital* and *Theories of Surplus Value*, Marx always undertook first to show by theoretical argument and appeal to empirical evidence that the views he opposed were false, and only later, if at all, to demonstrate their ideological, or class source.

8. Paul Lafargue, in his 'Personal Remembrances' (published in 1890), quoted Marx's remark that: 'Science should not be an egoistic pleasure. Those that are fortunate enough to be able to devote themselves to scientific work should be the first to apply their knowledge in the service of humanity' (Bottomore and Rubel, 1964:14).

9. Engels writes: 'Historical events thus appear on the whole to be likewise governed by chance. But where on the surface accident holds sway, there actually it is always governed by inner, hidden laws and it is only a matter of discovering these laws' (Engels, 1968:623; see also Marx, 1967b:209).

10. Marx writes: 'But all science would be superfluous if the outward appearance and the essence of things directly coincided' (Marx, 1967b:817).

11. This also holds in the discussion of such terms as 'productive forces,' 'productive relations,' etc. According to Marx, 'productive forces' are not objective facts external to human consciousness and activity. They represent rather the social organization of human consciousness and human activity. For example, Niagara Falls does or does not constitute a 'productive force' not because of its natural, objective attributes *per se*, but because *men* do or do not view it as a productive force or do or do not harness it to purposive human action. And, again, the 'relations of production' are, precisely, relations between

men, not bloodless abstractions (Avineri, 1968:76).

12. Although *The German Ideology* was written in 1845–1846 as a joint work, the important first part (pp. 39–95), from which the above quotation is taken, was written entirely by Marx himself under the title 'Feuerbach: Opposition of the Materialist and Idealist Outlook' (Tucker, 1961:177). This section, which marks a radical break from Marx's earlier 'philosophical' (Feuerbachian) writings, forms the first systematic statement of Marx's mature sociology (Althusser, 1970:33–38; Mandel, 1971:37; Arthur, 1970:21).

13. 'Robinsonesque' – after Daniel Defoe's character Robinson Crusoe, a favorite example of 18th century political economists of the economically productive individual, and a favorite target of Marx's ridicule (see Marx, 1970b:124–125).

14. To be more precise, the term 'mode of production' refers to the totality of social relations within a given *model* of society – but this is a distinction which will be made later. For now, the definition given above will stand as a first approximation.

15. 'My analytical method does not start from man but from the economically given social period' (Marx, 1882 Marginal Notes on Wagner – quoted in Fleischer, 1973:25).

16. Marx writes: 'We do not examine the competition of capitals, nor the credit system, nor the actual composition of society, which by no means consists of only two classes; workers and industrial capitalists' (Marx, 1968a:492–493).

17. This conclusion is indicated by Marx's analysis of the Asiatic mode of production. This Asiatic model was analyzed by Marx as a static, traditional society in which the historical rule of a paternalistic centralized government over a population consisting almost entirely of a supine, dispersed peasantry had created a social climate so devoid of social strain and conflict that the society literally lacked any social class, group, or stratum capable of initiating any social change. Marx writes: '[Asian] society has no history at all, at least no known history. What we call its history, is but the history of the successive intruders who founded their empires on the passive basis of that unresisting and unchanging society (Marx, 'The Future Results of the British Rule in India' – in Marx and Engels, 1972:81; see also, Lichtheim, 1967b; Turner, 1974). Whether or not Marx's statements are of any relevance to the analysis of Asiatic societies as they really existed is another question entirely from that of the role which the theoretical construct of the Asiatic mode of production played in Marx's thought.

18. Actually, to be more precise, the laws themselves are unchanging and unhistorical; as Popper (1950; 1957) has clearly shown, to claim otherwise would be foolish. It is rather the conditions of those laws, as specified in their antecedents, which are held by Marx to obtain only in a limited historical period. For example, the law of the tendential fall of the rate of profit is perfectly atemporal; it is held by Marx to hold as a general law under any condition of capitalist production. But precisely this condition is itself historical; the law does not apply to and will not explain the functioning of a primitive barter economy. Nicholas Lobkowicz (1971:243) has written: 'One might object that social laws *should* be

construed so as to be applicable to all historical epochs. To my knowledge neither Marx nor any Marxist ever denied that there might be such laws. But Marx felt that such laws, first, will be too trivial to be of any real use in social science and, secondly, will not be social laws properly speaking. They will be biological, physiological, and perhaps behavioral laws, but not social laws in the proper sense of the term. He might have added that the tendency to find biological or social laws that apply to *any* organism or to *any* society, respectively, furthers a sort of reductionism. For it is to be expected that laws equally applicable, say, to ants and to men will make it possible to explain human phenomena only to the extent that men are, among other things, similar to ants; and that laws common to a primitive and to a highly developed society will suggest explanations that treat a modern nation or political party as if it were a variety of cannibal tribe. This does not exclude of course that there are laws applying to all animals or all societies. But these laws either will concern a stratum that is ontologically more basic – for example, the phenomena studied by biologists, physiological psychologists or ethnologists – or else will be nothing more than the conceptual paradigm within which social science has to move.'

# SECTION I

## MARX'S SOCIOLOGY

# INTRODUCTION TO SECTION I

As I have attempted to show in the introduction to this volume, the theoretical content of Marx's writings may be said to form the outlines of a scientific sociology. While this conclusion is shared by a wide variety of Marxist and non-Marxist scholars, the precise content of this contribution remains an issue of contention. Does Marx's contribution lie mainly in his methodological approach to theory construction, his analysis of social structure and change, his analysis of social classes, his concept of praxis, or his refinement of the Hegelian dialectic? Different scholars give different answers.

The first of the three authors making a contribution to this section is Karl Korsch, best known for his critical study *Karl Marx* (1938) and his earlier political manifesto *Marxism and Philosophy* (1970). This latter work, upon its original publication in Germany in 1923, had an effect upon the German Social Democratic Party, of which Korsch was at the time a left-wing member, similar to that of George Lukács' more well-known *History and Class Consciousness*. Korsch, like Lukács, stresses the importance of the materialist dialectic in Marx's work and emphasizes its revolutionary nature. For Korsch, there is a fundamental opposition between revolutionary Marxian science and all forms of bourgeois ideology. In the current essay, originally published in 1937, Korsch begins by examining the Hegelian sources of the young Marx's critique of 'civil society,' contrasting this critique to the 'escapist' attitude adopted by Auguste Comte and his followers. This leads Korsch to a discussion of the important principle of historical specification in Marx's work, that is, the comprehension of all social relations ' . . . in terms of a definite historical epoch.' The general concepts of 'value' and 'commodity' are given meaning in Marx's work only when embedded in treatment of empirically verifiable and historically specific social relationships. This principle of historical specificity according to Korsch, radically separates Marxian laws from the more general and historically indeterminate abstractions of all other forms of academic sociology.

In the second essay in this section Loyd Easton approaches the problem of the relationship of rationalism and empiricism in Marx's work. The deeper issue at stake here is to what extent Marx wrote under the influence of the Hegelian dialectic and to what extent he was a scientific materialist. Different interpreters of Marx's work have stressed one aspect of Marx's method, oftentimes to the complete exclusion of the other. Thus, the image of Marx as an Hegelian dialectician has been popularized in a number of recent works by European scholars (see, for example, Lefebvre, 1968b; Hyppolite, 1969). However a number of other scholars, such as Irving Zeitlin (1967), have convincingly documented the empirical and inductive nature of Marx's later scientific work.

Easton's view on the subject is somewhat more complex than either of the positions suggested above. He finds an ambivalence throughout Marx's work on this matter which was never wholly resolved. However, Easton suggests that Marx's thought increasingly tended toward scientific empiricism, as he gradually liberated himself from what Martin Nicolaus, in another paper in this volume has called 'the spell of the Hegelian choreography.' This scientific empiricism shows through in *Capital* in Marx's thorough-going philosophical 'materialism' (or, more technically, naturalism) and his preoccupation with uncovering the 'laws of motion' of capitalist society through the application of a research program based upon the model of the natural sciences. The precise effect of the Hegelian dialectic in Marx's later work remains a research problem which badly needs explication. However, it is clear that in the long run, Hegel's influence upon Marx's thought diminished, rather than increased.

Perhaps the most ambitious attempt to formalize Marx's work into a systematic sociology in recent years has been made by the loosely grouped school of French structuralist-Marxists. Some of the important figures here include Louis Althusser, Étienne Balibar, Nicos Poulantzas, Manuel Castells, and Maurice Godelier. Of this group, Godelier has been the most consistent in his reading of Marx's theoretical work as a form of structuralism. In the controversial essay reproduced here he presents the outlines of a profoundly anti-Hegelian, anti-historicist reading of Marx, arguing that Marx's work provides a solution to the long-standing antinomy of social structure and change.

For Marx, Godelier argues, social reality presents itself as a multiplicity of layers, or structures. The role of social science is to peel back the surface layers of taken-for-granted ideological representations of everyday life and penetrate to the 'hidden' forms of social relations, the internal structures which underlie and determine more 'visible' social relationships. Thus, for example, the wage-exchange, which on the surface appears to be a 'fair' exchange of equivalents, is shown to conceal an unequal exchange – the exploitation of surplus value. This 'equal exchange' in fact establishes the precondition for the subjugation of one class by another. Godelier concludes that it is here, in the study of social structures and their 'hidden' and multiple evolution, that Marx made his most important contribution to the development of the human sciences.

# LEADING PRINCIPLES OF MARXISM:
## A RESTATEMENT*

KARL KORSCH

### MARXISM VERSUS SOCIOLOGY

What is the relationship between Marxism and modern sociological teaching? If we think of the sociology originated by Comte, and first named by him, as a special section in the system of constituted sciences, we shall find no link between it and Marxism. Marx and Engels paid no attention to either the name or content of this ostensibly new branch of knowledge. When Marx felt himself compelled to take terse notice of Comte's *Cours de Philosophie Positive*, thirty years after its appearance, 'because the English and French make such a fuss about the fellow,' he still spoke of 'Positivism' and 'Comtism' as of something to which he was 'thoroughly opposed as a politician' and of which he had 'a very poor opinion as a man of science.'[1] Marx's attitude is theoretically and historically well founded. The science of socialism, as formulated by Marx, owed nothing to this 'sociology' of the nineteenth and twentieth centuries which originated with Comte and was propagated by Mill and Spencer. It would be more correct to say that 'sociology' is a reaction against modern socialism. From this standpoint only is it possible to understand the essential unity of the diverse theoretical and practical tendencies which during the last hundred years have found their expression in this science. As with Comte in his relation to Saint Simon, his 'great master,'[2] so have the later bourgeois 'sociologists' opposed another way of answering the questions first raised by the rising proletarian movement to the theory and thus also to the practice of *socialism*. To these issues, which modern historical development has put on the agenda of present-day society, Marxism stands in a much more original and direct relationship than the whole of the so-called 'sociology' of Comte, Spencer and their followers. Fundamentally, then, there exists no theoretical relationship between those two doctrines of society.

* Originally published in *Three Essays on Marxism* by Karl Korsch, London: Pluto Press, 1971 and New York: Monthly Review Press, 1972. Reprinted with permission of the publishers.

Bourgeois sociologists refer to the revolutionary socialist science of the proletariat as 'an unscientific mixture of theory and politics'. Socialists, on the other hand, dismiss bourgeois sociology as mere 'ideology'.

The position of Marx, however, is quite different toward the first 'Enquirers into the Social Nature of Man,' who in the preceding centuries, in the radical struggles of the rising bourgeois class against the obsolete feudal order, had first set up the new idea of *Civil Society* as a revolutionary slogan, and had even unearthed, in the new science of *Political Economy*, the material foundations of this new 'civilized' form of society.[3]

According to Marx's own statement, made in 1859, in the preface to his *Contribution to the Critique of PoliticalEconomy*,[4] he had begun the development of his materialistic theory of society sixteen years earlier with a critical revision of Hegel's *Philosophy of Law*. This was a task he had set himself because of certain grave doubts which had recently assailed him in regard to his Hegelian idealistic creed. Previously, as an editor of the *Rheinische Zeitung* (1842–1843), he had for the first time found himself called upon to discuss 'so-called material interests.' He had already begun to study 'economic questions' and had become vaguely acquainted with the ideas of 'French Socialism and Communism.' His criticism of Hegel led him to the conclusion that 'legal relations as well as forms of state cannot be understood out of themselves nor out of the so-called general development of the human mind, but on the contrary, are rooted in the material conditions of life, the aggregate of which Hegel, following the precedent of the English and French of the eighteenth century, grouped together under the name of 'civil society' – and that the anatomy of civil society is to be sought in political economy.'

We see here the decisive significance which the notion of 'civil society' had gained for the young Marx who was at that time just completing his transition from Hegelian idealism to his later materialistic theory. While still formally basing his materialistic criticism of Hegel's idealistic glorification of the state on the realistic conclusions (unexpected in an idealist philosopher) regarding the nature of civil society which he had found embodied in Hegel's *Philosophy of Law*,[5] Marx now definitely abandoned Hegel and all his idealistic philosophy. Instead he associated himself with those earlier investigators into the nature of society who had arisen in the period of revolutionary development of the English and French bourgeoisie, when the name 'sociology' had not yet been invented, but 'society' had already been discovered as a special and independent realm of knowledge.

Hegel, indeed, had not derived that deep realistic knowledge of 'civil society', which stands in such sharp relief to the rest of his book,[6] from an independent study of the then extremely backward state of German society. He took both the name and content of his 'civil society' ready-made from the French and English social philosophers, politicians and economists. Behind Hegel, as Marx said, stand the 'English and French of the eighteenth century' with their new discoveries of the structure and movement of society, who in their turn reflect the real historical development which culminated in the Industrial Revolution in England after the middle of the eighteenth century and in the great French Revolution of 1789 to 1815.

Marx, then, in developing his new socialist and proletarian science, took his cue from that early study of society, which, although it was first communicated to him by Hegel, had really been born in the revolutionary epoch of the bourgeoisie. In the first place he took over the results of 'classical political economy' (from Petty and Boisguillebert through Quesnay and Smith up to Ricardo) consciously developing them as that which the great bourgeois investigators had already more or less unconsciously taken them to be, i.e. the basic structure or, as it were, 'the skeleton' of civil society. Even this basic importance of political economy, to which Marx alludes in calling it the 'anatomy of civil society', had before him been recognized by his immediate predecessors, the German idealist philosophers, Kant, Fichte and Hegel. In the philosophical system of Hegel, 'civil society' is based on the 'system of needs' explored by the new science of political economy, and the philosopher had, in an earlier work, even expressly described the 'system of needs' as the 'first form of government', as opposed to such higher developed forms as the state and the law.

The very pungency with which Marx in his later writings repeatedly emphasized that post-classical bourgeois economy (the so-called 'vulgar economy') had not advanced beyond Ricardo in any important points,[7] and scornfully dismissed the new socio-scientific synthesis of Comte's Positivism for the infinitely greater achievement of Hegel,[8] only shows once more the lasting influence of that early phase of economic and social thought on the theory of Marx. This is true even though his analysis of the new development of society and the new needs and aims of the proletariat, now emerging as an independent class, far transcended the results of those older theories. The proletarian class guided by the Marxist theory is therefore not only, as Friedrich Engels put it, 'the inheritor of German classical philosophy',[9] it also is the inheritor of classical political economy and social research. As such it has transformed the traditional classical theory in accordance with the changes in historical conditions.

Marx no longer regards bourgeois society from the standpoint of its first phase of development and its opposition to the feudal structure of medieval society. He is not only interested in the static laws of its existence. He treats bourgeois society as historical in all its traits and therefore merely a transitory organization of society. He explores the whole process of its historical genesis and development, and the inherent tendencies which, in their further development, lead to its revolutionary overthrow. He finds these tendencies twofold: *objective* in the economic basis of bourgeois society, *subjective* in the new division of social classes arising out of this same economic basis and not out of politics, law, ethics, etc. Thus civil society, which until then had constituted a homogeneous whole, opposed only to feudalism, is now torn into two opposed 'parties.' The assumed 'civil society' is in reality 'bourgeois society,' i.e. a society based on the cleavage of classes, in which the bourgeois class controls other classes economically and therefore politically and culturally. So at last *la classe la plus laborieuse et la plus misérable* enters the widened horizon of social science. Marxist theory recognizes the class war of the oppressed and exploited wage labourers of present-day society to be a war for the supersession of the present structure of society by a more highly developed form of society. As a materialistic science of the contemporary development of bourgeois society, Marxist theory is at the same time a practical instrument for the struggle of the proletariat to bring about the realization of proletarian society.

The later artificial detachment of sociology as a special branch of learning, whose scientific origin dates from Comte, and, at the best, allows the great original thinkers who have done the real productive work in this field to stand as its 'forerunners,' represents nothing more than an escape from the practical and, therefore, also theoretical tasks of the present historical epoch. Marx's new socialist and proletarian science, which further developed the revolutionary theory of the classical founders of the doctrine of society in a way corresponding to the changed historical situation, is the genuine social science of our time.

### THE PRINCIPLE OF HISTORICAL SPECIFICATION

Marx comprehends all things social in terms of a definite historical epoch. He criticizes all the categories of the bourgeois theorists of society in which this specific character has been effaced. Already in his first economic work we find him reproaching Ricardo for having applied the specifically bourgeois concept of *rent* to 'landed property of all epochs and of all countries. This is the error of all economists who represent bourgeois production relations as eternal.'[10]

46

The scope of the principle of historical specification is clearly demonstrated in this example. *Landed property* has been widely different in character and has played very different roles in the various historical epochs of society. Already the different ways in which primitive communal property in land had been broken up, directly influenced the varied forms of the later development of society based upon private property.[11] Up to the middle ages *landed property* (agriculture) constituted, according to Marx, the central category, dominating all the other categories of production, just as *capital* does in present-day bourgeois society.[12] The different ways in which, in different countries, after the victory of the capitalist mode of production, feudal property in land was subjected to capital; the different ways in which rent was transformed into a part of capitalist surplus value, and agriculture into an industry – all retain their importance for the capitalist systems which arose therefrom, for the different forms of the labour movement which subsequently developed within them, and for the different forms in which the transition to the socialist mode of production will ultimately be effected in each of the different systems. For this reason Marx investigated with particular care, to the end of his life, the history of landed property and rent as shown on the one hand in the *United States*, and on the other hand in *Russia*. In the same way, at the end of the nineteenth century, Lenin, in his *Development of Capitalism in Russia*, analysed particularly the specific historical forms of this transition process.[13] Yet all this comprehensive study of the various historical forms serves, with both Marx and Lenin, only as a base for the working out of the specific character of *capitalist* rent in fully developed *bourgeois society*.

In the fundamental analysis of the modern capitalist mode of production, which forms the subject matter of the first book of *Capital*, Marx does not deal with the category of rent at all. What is discussed there, in addition to the general function of the soil as an element of the labour process itself,[14] is only the different ways by which the transition to the modern capitalist mode of production reacted upon the conditions of the agricultural proletariat, first, in developed capitalist countries,[15] second, in such countries as Ireland that had fallen behind in the process of industrialization, and finally in the colonial countries.[16]

Marx discusses 'rent' in the proper place, in a section of the third book of *Capital*, in which the special forms of capitalist *distribution* are analysed as they arise from the special historical forms of capitalist *production*.[17] Even here, there is no room for an independent exposition of earlier historical forms. Only a few scattered remarks throw a flash of light on the contrast between the modern bourgeois form of landed property and past historical forms; and only an additional closing chapter – and indeed, of that only a part – is devoted to the historical *Genesis of Capitalist Rent*.[18] Indeed, as Marx says in the opening phrase of this whole section, 'the analysis of landed property in its various historical forms lies beyond the scope of this work.'[19]

The concept of 'rent', then, as discussed in the Marxist theory, is in no way a general term referring to landed property of all epochs. The form of landed property which is considered in *Capital* is 'a specifically historical one; it is that form into which feudal land ownership and small peasants' agriculture have been *transformed* through the influence of capital and of the capitalist mode of production.'[20] In this sense, and in this sense only, an analysis of modern capitalist rent, or of that portion of the surplus value produced by industrial capital which falls into the hands of the capitalistic landowner, is a necessary part of the complete analysis of the process of capitalist production which is embodied in the three books of *Capital*.

The application of the principle of historical specification is further demonstrated by the way Marx deals with the different historical forms of capital itself. Just as in the present epoch *industrial capital* appears as the standard form, so did *merchants' capital* and its twin brother, *interest-bearing capital*, and the various sub-forms of these (more exactly described by Marx as 'capital for trading in goods,' 'capital for trading in money,' 'capital for lending money') occupy an independent and, in certain respects, a predominating position in the epochs preceding capitalist society, and, indeed, in the first phases of capitalist society itself. Even in present-day fully developed capitalist economy the merchant and the banker, though not involved in actual production like the industrial capitalist, still perform a definite function in the circulation of capital. They also participate in the distribution of the total 'surplus value', a considerable part of the yearly amount as the disposal of the capitalist class falls to their share as 'commercial profit' and 'interest' – just as we have seen another part of it going in the form of 'rent' to landed owners of property who have as little to do with actual production. Moneylenders' capital has even recaptured an important position – though not, as many Marxists have believed, a definite supremacy – in its new form as an integral part of the modern so-called 'finance capital,' i.e. a system of highly concentrated capital created by the fusion of private and state-controlled bank capital with trust and state-controlled industrial capital.[21]

The Marxist analysis of modern capitalist production starts from the assumption that the previously independent forms of trading-capital and money-capital have been *transformed* into mere accessories of the new prevailing form. It is true that capitalist production even today bears the stamp of its historical origin – the intrusion of the merchant into the sphere of feudal production. All capitalist production remains essentially a *production for sale*. Every article resulting from capitalist production is to be sold as a commodity, whether it is sold to another industrial capitalist who needs it for carrying on his own process of production or, ultimately, to the immediate consumer. Again the very way in which 'capital' first arose and gained control of production in the shape of *money*, as supplied by wealthy individuals, merchants, usurers, etc., constantly repeats itself under the present condition of fully developed capitalist production. Every new aggregate of capital, even today, 'enters upon the stage, i.e. comes into the market – the commodity market, the labour market or the money market – still in the form of money that by a definite process has to be transformed into capital.'[22]

Nevertheless the 'secret,' not only of 'how capital produces' but also of 'how capital *is* produced' – and incidentally the key to the abolition of all capitalist exploitation and wage-slavery – can in no way be theoretically discovered by an analysis of the functions performed by those 'accessory' forms of capital in the process of circulation, or of the revenues which accrue to the capitalists concerned, in consideration of the 'services' they perform in this sphere. 'One will therefore understand,' says Marx, 'why in our analysis of the basic form of capital, of the form in which it determines the economic organization of modern society, its popular, and as it were, antediluvian forms, "trading capital" and "usurers capital," are for the present (viz. in the analysis of the actual process of capitalist production in the first book of *Capital*) entirely ignored.'[23]

Even when, in the second and third books of *Capital*, Marx comes back to these 'antediluvian forms' in his analysis of capitalist circulation and distribution,[24] he takes as his main theme, not their historical development, but only the specific form into which they have been transformed by the action of modern industrial capital. Just as with rent, the historical analyses which run through the whole of Marx's work, and both the concluding chapters added to the sections concerned, under the headings *Historical data concerning merchants' capital* and *Precapitalistic conditions*,[25] merely serve to illuminate that great historical process through which, in the course of centuries and millennia, *trade* and *money transactions* lost more and more of their originally dominating position until they assumed their present place as mere detached and one-sidedly developed modes of existence of the various functions which industrial capital sometimes adopts and sometimes discards within the sphere of its circulation.

There is one aspect alone, under which rent as well as trading-capital and money-capital might have been treated as a proper subject in Marx's analysis of the modern capitalist mode of production and of the economic form of society based thereon. According to an original and more comprehensive plan, Marx would have followed up the discussion of the more strictly economic questions of production, circulation and distribution, social classes etc., as contained in the three books of *Capital*, by an investigation of what may be called 'economic questions of an higher order' such as the relation between *town and country* and the *international relations of production*.[26]

Only with these later researches would Marx's analysis have reached the point where the antagonism of landed property to *capital*, as well as that of trade and money-capital to *industrial capital* survives in present-day society; the former as a relation between agricultural and town industry and as an international relation between primarily agrarian and industrial countries – the latter as a relation between trading cities and factory towns, and on an international scale between commercial and industrial states.

The principle of historical specification as illustrated by the preceding examples (landed property and the various forms of capital) is strictly adhered to by Marx in all his economic and socio-historical researches. He deals with all categories in that specific form and in that specific connection in which they appear in modern bourgeois society.[27]

The contrast which exists in this respect between Marx and his fore-runners, comes out most strikingly in a comparison. While the work of the last representative of classical bourgeois economy, David Ricardo, is devoted to the *Principles of Political Economy*, Marx strictly limited his economic research to 'modern bourgeois production,'[28] and finally gave the work which contains the whole of his analysis and critique of all traditional political economy the plain and definite name *Capital*. Ricardo begins the exposition of his system with the general concept of 'value;' Marx commences his critical investigation of the theory and the facts underlying modern bourgeois economy with the analysis of an external object, a palpable thing – 'commodity.' Again, Ricardo frees the traditional economic concept of value from the last earthly impurities that were still attached to it by his predecessors; while Marx, on the contrary, regards even the concept of 'commodity' in its isolation, as it applies also to conditions other than those of present-day bourgeois production, as too abstract a category, and defines it specifically as an element of 'bourgeois wealth'[29] or as the 'wealth of those societies in which the capitalist mode of production prevails.'[30] Only in this specific definition does 'commodity' form the subject matter of his investigation. Only as properties of such a commodity do the general concepts of 'value in use' and 'value in exchange,' and the other terms of the classical economic system derived from these fundamental concepts, interest him. He does not treat them as eternal categories. Nor does he for that matter transform himself into an historian. While fully aware of the fact that many economic categories of modern bourgeois society occurred, in other specific relations to the whole of the mode of production, also in earlier epochs, he does not go into the history of 'money,' of 'exchange of commodities,' of 'wage-labour,' or that of 'co-operation,' 'division of labour,' etc. He discusses the different stages of the historical development of all these economic concepts only in so far as it is necessary for his main theme: the analysis of the specific character assumed by them in modern bourgeois society.

All the economic terms of Marx, then, as opposed to those of the classical bourgeois economists, refer to a specific historical epoch of production. This applies even to that most general term, *value*, which, according to Marx, must still be distinguished from 'value in exchange' – the latter being only the external form in which the intrinsic 'value' of a given commodity manifests itself in the ratio of exchange of such commodities.[31] This most abstract term, which Marx adopted from the later classical economists, has been highly suspect to some well-meaning but superficial interpreters of Marx who found that the concept of an intrinsic 'value,' distinct from exchange-value, reeks of scholasticism, metaphysical realism, Hegelian idealism and what not, and for this reason does no credit to a 'materialistic' science. As a matter of fact, Marx discussed just these fundamental concepts of his economic theory in a somewhat obscure language, thereby avowedly 'coquetting' with the 'modes of expression peculiar to that mighty thinker, the idealist philosopher Hegel.'[32] However, there is no point in accepting the term exchange-value, as taken by Marx from his forerunners, the founders of classical political economy, and rejecting that of intrinsic 'value' which was used by Marx only as a means to work out more clearly the true content of the 'value' concept of the classical writers and to expose critically what he called the 'fetishism' underlying the whole of their economic theory.[33]

Marx was fully conscious of the fact that all concepts of 'value' are strictly relative terms. They either denote an immediate relation between objects and man (which becomes a reality by actual use or consumption), or a relation of a different order (realized by the exchange of such objects), viz. the quantitative relation in which use-values of one sort are exchanged for those of another sort whenever they are exchanged. The relations of the latter order had been regarded by the later classical economists as the only 'value' to be dealt with in a strictly economic science, and had been styled by them *value in exchange* or *value* proper, as distinguished from mere utility or *'use-value'*. Marx easily agreed with the classical writers when they established the difference in kind prevailing between *value* as a quantitative relation arising through the exchange of commodities, i.e. by a social process; and *use-value* as a merely qualitative relation between external objects and man. But he did not agree with them in the ultimate location of the social relations manifesting themselves in the 'value' relations of the commodities as established by their exchange. A closer investigation of the economic concept of 'value' shows that this concept expresses a relation arising not between the commodities as exchanged on the market, but rather a relation previously established between human beings cooperating in the production of such commodities, *a social relation of production arising between man and man*. Indeed, the main result of Marx's criticism of the traditional theory of political economy consists in the discovery and description of these fundamental social relations of men – relations which, for a definite historical epoch, appear to the subjects concerned in the disguised and, as it were, perverted form of relations of things, viz. as 'value-relations' of the commodities cooperatively produced by them and mutually exchanged on the market.

'Value,' then, in all its denominations, just as other economic things or relations such as 'commodity,' 'money,' 'labour-power,' 'capital,' means to Marx a *socio-historical fact* or something which though not physical is still given in an *empirically verifiable manner*.[34] 'As in general, with every socio-historical science, we must always keep in mind when considering the progress of economic theory, that the subject matter, here modern bourgeois society, is given in the mind of the observer just as it is in reality, and that its categories express, therefore, forms of being, modes of existence, and often only single aspects of this definite society or subject matter.'[35]

We shall later in another connection study the far-reaching theoretical and practical implications of this apparently minor difference between the scientific method of Marx and that of the classical bourgeois economists. We here confine ourselves to one most important result. The concept of *commodity*, in the specific form and context in which it appears under the conditions of the present system of 'capitalistic commodity production,' includes from the very beginning a commodity of a peculiar nature, incorporating the flesh and blood in the hands and heads of the wage-labourers – the *commodity labour-power*. 'These labourers who have to sell themselves piecemeal, are a commodity like every other article of commerce, and are consequently exposed to all the vicissitudes of competition, to all the fluctuations of the market.'[36]

Further, the sellers of this peculiar commodity, under the very conditions of its sale, are never in the position of free agents,[37] for they 'live only so long as they find work, and find work only so long as their labour increases capital.'[38]

Only by bearing in mind this specific sense in which for Marx 'commodity production' or *'general' commodity production* becomes entirely equivalent to present-day *'capitalist' commodity production*[39] can we understand the importance of that general analysis of 'commodity' which in Marx's book precedes all further analysis and critique of the capitalist mode of production. Marx is aware of the 'definite historical conditions' which are necessary in order that a product may become a 'commodity' and that, in its further development, 'money' should appear as the general commodity, for the purpose of exchange. 'The appearance of products as *commodities* presupposed such a development of the social division of labour, that the separation of use-value from exchange-value, a separation which first begins with barter, must already have been completed.' Again, 'the peculiar functions of *money* which it performs, either as the mere equivalent of commodities, or as means of circulation, or means of payment, as hoard or as universal money, point to very different stages in the process of social production.'[40] Yet we know by experience that a relatively primitive development of society suffices for the production of all these forms. It is otherwise with capital.

> The historical conditions of its existence are by no means given with the mere circulation of money and commodities. It can spring into life only when the owner of the means of production and subsistence meets in the market with the free labourer selling his labour-power. And this one historical condition comprises a world's history. Capital therefore, announces from its first appearance a new epoch in the process of social production.[41]

At this stage only are we able to grasp the full importance of *industrial capital* as the only form of existence of capital which adequately represents the nature of modern capitalist production. 'Industrial capital,' according to an express assertion of Marx which we may safely take to be his final and most complete statement on this matter,

> gives to production its capitalistic character. Its existence includes that of class antagonism between capitalists and labourers. To the extent that it assumes control over social production, the technique and social organization of the labour process are revolutionized and with them the economic and historical type of society. The other kinds of capital, which appear before industrial capital amid past or declining conditions of social production, are not only subordinated

to it and suffer changes in the mechanism of their functions corresponding with it, but move on it as a basis; they live and die, stand and fall, as this, their basis, lives and dies, stands and falls.[42]

NOTES AND REFERENCES

1. See Marx's letter to Engels of 7 July 1866, *Marx-Engels-Gesamt Ausgabe* (MEGA III, 3; p. 345); also Marx's letter to Beesly of 12 June 1871, and further the letter to Engels of 23 May 1869 in which Spencer's name is curtly mentioned along with some other contemporary writers (MEGA III, 4; p. 58). See also the ironical dismissal of 'Comtist recipes for the cook-shops of the future' in Marx's reply to the reviewer of *Capital* in the Paris *Revue positiviste* in the preface to the second edition of *Capital*, 1872–73, and Engels' letter to Tönnies of 24 January 1895 quoted in G. Mayer's *Biography of Friedrich Engels* (1934) vol. II, p. 552. Letters of 7 July 1866 and 12 June 1871 in Marx-Engels, *Selected Correspondence*, Moscow n.d., pp. 217–218, 322.

2. See Lévy-Bruehl, *La Philosophie d'Auguste Comte* (1900), p. 8.

3. See, for example, Adam Ferguson, *An Essay on the History of Civil Society*, 1767, and Adam Smith, *An Inquiry into the Nature and Causes of the Wealth of Nations*, 1776.

4. Hereafter referred to as *Preface*, 1859. In English in Marx-Engels *Selected Works* (1-vol. ed.), London, 1968, pp. 181–185.

5. See the comprehensive manuscripts of 1843 now published in MEGA I, 1, 1; pp. 401–553. q.v. Marx, *Critique of Hegel's Philosophy of Right*, Cambridge, 1970.

6. See Hegel, *Philosophy of Law*, Part III, Section 2 (Civil Society), esp. § 188 *et seq.* (System of Needs), §230 *et seq.* (Police).

7. See *Capital*, I Moscow, 1959, p. 80, footnote 2, and *Theories of Surplus Value*, III, pp. 571–576 (German ed.).

8. See letter to Engels of 7 July 1866.

9. See the concluding sentence of *Ludwig Feuerbach and the End of Classical Philosophy*, 1888. A similar statement, with an amplifying reference to the equal importance of the 'developed economic and political conditions in England and France', is found in the preface to the first German edition of Engels' *Socialism, Utopian and Scientific*, 1882.

10. See *Poverty of Philosophy*, Moscow, n.d., p. 154.

11. See *Contribution to the Critique of Political Economy*, 1859, translated by N. I. Stone, Charles Kerr, Chicago 1904, p. 29, footnote 1.

12. See the ms of a 'general introduction' to the *Critique of Political Economy* dated 25 August 1857, first printed in *Neue Zeit*, XXI, 1, 1903 – hereafter referred to as *Introduction* 1857. Available in English in Stone translation (note 11 above) and in C. J. Arthur's edition of Marx-Engels, *The German Ideology*, London 1970, pp. 124–152. Page references are to the Arthur edition.

13. Lenin began to write this book in 1896 while he was in prison and went on with it during his exile in Siberia. The first Russian edition appeared in 1899, the second in 1907. English edition in *Collected Works*, III.

14. See *Capital*, I, pp. 178 *et seq.*
15. *Ibid.*, pp. 639 *et seq.*; *ibid.*, pp. 664 *et seq.*
16. *Ibid.*, Chapters 32 and 33 dealing with 'so-called original accumulation' and the 'modern colonial system.'
17. See *Capital*, III, Moscow edition, pp. 614–812.
18. *Ibid.*, pp. 782–812.
19. *Ibid.*, p. 614.
20. *Ibid*, pp. 614 *et seq.*
21. See Hilferding's *Finance Capital*, 1910, and Lenin's *Imperialism, the Newest Stage of Capitalism*, 1917.
22. See *Capital*, I, p. 146, and for a more detailed analysis of the various forms which capital assumes in its different stages, *Capital*, II, Chapter 1.
23. See *Capital*, I, p. 163.
24. See *Capital*, II, Chapters 1–4; III, Chapters 16–20, 21–36.
25. *Ibid.*, III, Chapters 20 and 36.
26. See *Introduction*, 1857, p. 148, and *Capital*, I, p. 352 where Marx expressly states that he cannot here go further into the topic of the cleavage between town and country, although 'the whole economic history of society is summed up in the movement of this antagonism'. See also the more detailed discussion of the later changes in the plan of *Capital* in the introduction to my edition, Berlin, 1932, pp. 8 *et seq.* (reprinted in this collection of essays).
27. See *Introduction*, 1857, pp. 140 *et seq.*
28. *Ibid.*, p. 125.
29. See *Contribution to the Critique of Political Economy*, opening sentence.
30. See *Capital*, I, opening sentence.
31. See *Capital*, I, pp. 36–38.
32. See postscript to second edition of *Capital*, 1872–1873 – hereafter referred to as *Postscript*, 1873. In Moscow edition, pp. 12–20.
33. See *Capital*, I, pp. 71–83.
34. See Marx's letter to Engels, 2 April 1858, in which he says that this concept of value 'although an abstraction, is an *historical abstraction* which, therefore, could not only be made on the basis of a particular economic development of society'. See *Selected Correspondence*, p. 127.
35. See *Introduction*, 1857, p. 146. See also the preceding remark on p. 141 where Marx opposing his own 'theoretical' method to that hitherto applied by the classical theorists, emphasized the same point: 'Even when applying a theoretical method we must bear in mind the subject, society, as our real presupposition.'
36. See *Communist Manifesto*.
37. See the Report of the Inspectors of Factories of the six months ending 30 April 1850, p. 45 – quoted by Marx in *Capital*, I, p. 302 footnote.
38. See *Communist Manifesto*.
39. See *Capital*, I, p. 170 footnote 1; see also *Capital*, II, pp. 31, 33 *et seq.*, 116–117 etc.
40. See *Capital*, I, p. 170.

41. *Ibid.*; see also *Capital*, II, p. 35.
42. See *Capital*, II, p. 55.

# ALIENATION AND EMPIRICISM
# IN MARX'S THOUGHT*

LOYD D. EASTON

Like his thought on democracy and the state Marx's view of knowledge is a battleground of competing and conflicting interpretations. Some interpreters have found him to be essentially an empiricist holding that knowledge is based on and tested by data of observation and sense-perception following the inductive pattern of natural science. Others have taken him to be primarily a rationalist who regards the basic relations of events to be those that Hegel found in concepts – 'dialectic' and 'necessity' – apprehended by reason independently of sense-perception. Still other interpreters have found Marx to be a particular kind of empiricist, a pragmatist who holds that ideas and concepts are instruments to guide and be tested by perceptible practice as in scientific experiment.

These diverse interpretations result largely from the fact that Marx never systematically devoted himself to a theory of knowledge. He wanted to write a treatise on dialectic but never did, so his views on knowledge and science are scattered among unfinished manuscripts, aphoristic theses, personal letters, and prefatory remarks on methodology. In such conditions his views, not unexpectedly, abound in ambiguities that encourage diverse interpretations. The diversity of interpretation also reflects the diversity of interests and purposes of his interpreters.

The major purpose of this paper is not to achieve a unique interpretation of Marx's views on knowledge but to examine precisely his major statements on the subject in their development, starting from the concept of 'alienation' in his early writings. The main aim is to pinpoint what he was asserting, the relations of his assertions to one another, their ambiguities, and their possible preponderance of direction in respect to the issue of empiricism vs. rationalism.

*Originally published in *Social Research*, 37:3, Autumn 1970. Reprinted with permission of the Graduate Faculty, New School for Social Research, New York.

In Marx's early writings from 1843 to *The Communist Manifesto* he prominently and widely used the idea of 'alienation' to refer to projections and externalizations of human experience which are either mistaken in respect to knowledge or harmful in respect to man's integral self-development. In the first sense, alienation was a part of Marx's view of knowledge, our main interest here. In the second sense, alienation was a central issue in his moral and political philosophy, his commitment to the wholeness and sovereignty of man emphasized in Feuerbach's humanism, a cornerstone of Marx's commitment to democracy and socialism. This form of alienation has been explored many times in relation to Marx's view of labor and socialism in his *Economic-Philosophic Manuscripts* of 1844 and other early writings.[1]

Marx's earliest use of the idea of alienation appeared in an extensive paragraph-by-paragraph criticism of Hegel's *Philosophy of Law* written in the summer of 1843. Marx attacked Hegel's method as abstract and speculative from the standpoint of an empiricism derived from Ludwig Feuerbach, from the position that genuine knowledge, truth, is based on sense-perception rather than being a purely logical or formal development of concepts. In the classical statement of his historical materialism sixteen years later, the Preface to *A Contribution to the Critique of Political Economy,* Marx traced his 'guiding thread' to this first criticism of Hegel. It was a turning-point in his thought, his first radical objection to the philosophy he had followed at important points since 1837 when he became active in the Doctors' Club at the University of Berlin and resolved to seek 'the Idea in the real itself.'[2]

In his doctoral dissertation Marx had applied Hegel's thought to a neglected aspect of Greek philosophy and committed himself to 'criticism,' to measuring existing actuality against the Idea and to seeking out 'the deficiency of the world to be made philosophical.'[3] Further, his dissertation had criticized Democritus' more directly empirical view of atomism as being inferior to Epicurus' because it lacked an 'energizing principle.' Marx's essays in Ruge's *Anekdota* and in the *Rheinische Zeitung* followed Hegel in main points or defended politically liberal positions from Hegel's premises. For example, he opposed easier divorce laws on the basis of Hegel's view of the ethical nature of marriage. In defending freedom of the press, he saw the state as 'the great organism' in which reason – not reason in the individual but 'reason in society' – is actualized as law and freedom.[4] But this identification with Hegel, qualified in the direction of liberal democracy, was breached in 1843 over Hegel's theory of the state.

In his analysis of paragraphs 261 to 269 of Hegel's *Philosophy of Law* Marx charges that with Hegel the 'dependence' of family and civil society on the state is a relationship not in experienced actuality but only in something external and alien to them. 'Actuality,' says Marx, 'is not experienced as it is but as another actuality. Common experience is not subject to the law of its own spirit but to an alien spirit.' The 'dependence' Hegel finds is an 'alienation within unity.' His mistake is a result of reversing subject and predicate in relation to the Idea and its content while 'development takes place on the side of the predicate,' on the side of the content which is the real meaning of the Idea. So Hegel, Marx objects, 'does not develop his thinking from the object but he develops the object by a sort of thinking he manages, and manages in the abstract sphere of logic.' As a result, Hegel's method is through and through a 'mystification' involving the alienation of abstract concepts from the concrete connections of experience.[5]

Here Marx was following Feuerbach's attack on speculation which had appeared in the *Anekdota* with his first published essay on censorship. The speculative philosopher, Feuerbach charged, sees nature, religion, and philosophy itself as mere predicates of the Idea, but 'we need only to convert the predicate into the subject to get at the pure, undisguised truth.' Feuerbach saw Hegel's idealism as the apotheosis of abstraction which 'alienates man from himself' because it inverts the real relation of thought to its object.[6] Following Feuerbach's criticism of Hegel, Marx would look to 'empirical actuality' and 'common experience' for the content of the Idea. He would be an empiricist to avoid Hegel's mystification, his way of connecting things 'in the abstract sphere of logic.' In relation to other paragraphs in his criticism of Hegel, however, Marx firmly adhered to the 'liberal party' in criticism, to 'the party of the Concept,' to use his identification of 1840 in his doctoral dissertation. From this position he accused Hegel of uncritically accepting the *status quo* as the truth of the Idea, as being a genuine state.[7] This was internal criticism of Hegel from the premise of Hegel's own rationalism. It was criticism of 'empirical actuality,' of the observable social world of 'common experience,' in terms of its failure to measure up to 'the Concept' and thus fulfill the 'demands of Reason.'

Marx's first discussion of knowledge and reliable thinking thus expressed an ambivalence. On the one side, with Feuerbach, he affirmed empiricism, the control of ideas and concepts by their reference to experienced objects. From this perspective he rejected self-sufficing speculation, thinking managed by the thinker in the abstract sphere of logic, as a form of alienation. On the other side, his view of 'criticism' involved adherence to Hegel and to rationalism to find the truth about the observable social world in the 'demands of Reason,' 'the Concept.' In subsequent developments of his views on knowledge to be examined below, Marx increasingly abandoned the Hegelian terminology of 'Reason' and 'the Idea.' But their substance reappeared in 'historical development' as dialectical, the 'rational kernel' of Hegel's philosophy that Marx admittedly retained in his mature thought, as noted in the second preface to *Capital*. Marx was well aware that Hegel had identified 'the Idea' with 'process' as development in a pattern of dialectical necessity. This is what Hegel meant by 'Reason.'[8] So the ambivalence between empiricism and rationalism that Marx expressed in 1843 serves as an appropriate frame of reference for examining his more mature views on knowledge and science.

2

In Marx's published writings that immediately followed and utilized his unpublished 'Critique' of 1843, his rationalism came to the fore in his view of the proletariat and the proper procedure of political criticism. To be sure, Marx learned much about the proletariat empirically, indirectly through study of Lorenz Stein's book on the French proletariat and directly through association with French workers. But his view of the special role of the proletariat in achieving 'full human emancipation' and democracy was justified as a logical corollary of Hegel's dialectic. He had read in Hegel that with development of industry 'a great mass of people sink down below a certain subsistence and thus suffer a loss of a sense of right and of the honor to exist by one's own activity and labor.' This 'produces the proletariat [*Pöbel*] which in turn further promotes the concentration of riches in a few hands.'[9] The special role of the proletariat exemplifies Hegel's dialectic – namely, a class in chains will destroy all chains, a particular class will end classes, the complete loss of humanity will redeem humanity. Furthermore, the proletariat, in Marx's words, is a sphere of civil society, i.e., of the economic order, having a universal character and a universal human title. It is, Marx concluded, the 'realization of philosophy.' In such terms it is what Hegel called a 'concrete universal' and thus the truth of society's development in history. With such a line of thought Marx's main conclusions about the proletariat and the pattern of class struggle were grounded on the 'demands of Reason,' the dialectic of reason in history and social life, which he had imbibed from Hegel.

Marx's rationalism stands out in his view of the proper procedure of political criticism. In Marx's words:

Reason has always existed but not always in rational form. The critic, therefore, can start with any form of theoretical and practical consciousness and develop the true actuality out of forms inherent in existing actuality as its ought-to-be and goal. As far as actual life is concerned, the political state contains in all its modern forms the demands of Reason, even where the political state is not yet conscious of the socialistic demands. . . . We develop new principles for the world out of the principles of the world.[10]

Here Marx was saying, in opposition to the 'utopian' views of Weitling and Proudhon, that socialism is the extension of existing forms of social life as the realization of reason, the fulfillment of the 'demands of Reason' and 'principles' already operative in society. Further, Marx suggests that such realization not only gives us the truth about 'existing actuality,' what that actuality really amounts to, but also establishes its desirability, its value or worth. This is a step well beyond making socialism and the overcoming of man's secular self-alienation a response to 'the categorical imperative' – Kant's 'ought' – 'to overthrow all conditions in which man is a degraded, enslaved, neglected, contemptible being.' It is a step that identifies the 'ought' with the projection of forms and principles 'inherent in existing actuality.' Such identification will be touched upon later. Here it raises the logical problem of how any 'truth' about existing actuality can determine what 'ought-to-be,' a problem implicit in the ambiguity of 'Reason' inherited from Hegel. In any case Marx's rationalism is apparent in what he thinks 'criticism' should do.

In the *Economic-Philosophical Manuscripts* of 1844 Marx revived his earlier definition of alienation. He vigorously opposed Hegel's speculative method as 'the alienation of man's nature,' enthusiastically followed Feuerbach as 'the true conqueror of the old philosophy,' and adopted Feuerbach's empiricism as the remedy for speculative alienation. As opposed to self-sufficing speculation, genuine thought, Marx agreed with Feuerbach, is rooted in sense-perception, the object, or nature, and such perception involves the social relation of man-to-man. In contemporary terms, Marx seemed to be insisting that the objectivity of sense-perception is to be found in its intersubjectivity. Further, he seemed to anticipate recent 'logical empiricism' and its demand for 'unity of science.' 'Natural science,' wrote Marx, 'will in time include the science of man as the science of man will include natural science: There will be one science.'[11] He referred to this position as 'naturalism or humanism.' It is to be distinguished, he pointedly indicated, from both idealism and materialism but unites the truth of each. This distinction is noteworthy in view of Marx's subsequent reference to his position as 'materialism,' a topic to which we shall return.

Some interpreters of Marx's view at this point have seen his empiricism, his rooting of genuine knowledge in sense-perception, as showing that he was committed to a thoroughly positivistic science of sociology that decisively eclipsed the rationalism he had appropriated from Hegel. Such a conclusion, however, is over-hasty. The *Manuscripts* of 1844 go beyond Feuerbach to insist that sense-perception and man's varied needs are functions of the history of industry and society, a point Marx later develops against Feuerbach in *The German Ideology*. Further, this history is to be understood as a dialectical development. The 'great thing' Marx finds about Hegel in the *Manuscripts* is his insight that man is the historical product of his own work in a dialectical process of alienation and resolution.[12] Marx objected to Hegel's treatment of that process speculatively, as a purely conceptual development rather than as a dialectical development in perceptible historical practice, namely, in labor and production. Thus Marx was groping for an empirical dialectic, a conception of 'dialectical development' wedded to sense-perception and observation. Major problems in such a marriage will be considered later in regard to Marx's treatment of the empirical data of history, classes, and 'necessity' in historical development.

3

In *The Holy Family*, Marx is more explicit than in previous writings concerning the dialectic and 'necessity' in historical development and the consequences of empiricism. He praises Proudhon, with whom he often discussed Hegel's dialectic, for his elaboration of the continuous contradictions in the movement of political economy. Extending Proudhon's insight, Marx finds a dialectical connection between property and poverty by virtue of their internal movement. Proletariat and wealth are antitheses, poles of a dialectic. Both manifest private property and depend on one another. They represent the same human self-alienation, but the propertied class is comfortable in this alienation. It is driven to destroy the antithesis. Marx sees this dialectical movement as 'a development [of private property] which does not depend on it, of which it is unconscious, which takes place against its will, and which is brought about by the very nature of things.'[13] The action of the proletariat in this process 'is prescribed, irrevocably and obviously, in its own situation in life as well as in the entire organization of present civil society.' For such a view Marx was obviously indebted to Hegel's conception of Reason, the Idea, in history. Marx's conception of class struggle, the resolution of man's alienation, the pattern of necessity in historical action, were simply applications of Hegel's dialectic. But Marx saw this dialectic not as a movement of concepts 'in the abstract sphere of logic' so much as a movement of actual perceptible events and relationships, a deliverance of observation and experience. Again the problem of fusing dialectic and empiricism arises. 'Contradiction,' 'antitheses,' 'necessity' can be given clear meanings as functions of interrelations of concepts within the 'sphere of logic.' How can they be deliverances of observation and experience? If they cannot be, as empiricists have long insisted, they are evidence of Marx's rationalism.

On the other side, Marx strongly affirmed empiricism in writing on 'The Mystery of Speculative Construction,'[14] a criticism of speculative metaphysics that would please the most ardent practitioners of 'analytical philosophy' among us today. In six or seven pages of careful linguistic surgery Marx showed how the notion of 'Fruit' as true 'Substance,' 'Self-activity of the Absolute Subject,' or 'inner Process' was only a devious conceptual invention that renamed the ordinary, experienced properties and relations of ordinary apples, pears, and strawberries. Marx allowed, however, that Hegel himself, in contrast to his followers, very often gave 'an actual presentation, a presentation of the *matter* itself, within his speculative presentation.'[15] This concession suggests that dialectical Reason is *in* things as their pattern of development, a point on which Hegel always insisted even though he might treat that pattern apart from its embodiment in order to write books on logic.

With his discussion of French materialism in *The Holy Family* Marx further indicated his debt to Feuerbach's empiricism which rooted genuine thought in sense-experience. Marx noted that Feuerbach, like Pierre Bayle, had regarded speculative metaphysics as the last prop of traditional theology. The radical enemy of both theology and metaphysics is materialism, and materialism, Marx further indicated, is the view that 'our knowledge and ideas originate from the world of the senses' as Bacon, Hobbes, and Locke had insisted. This is a crucial point. In this first designation of his philosophy as 'materialism' Marx was not espousing a theory of the substance or stuff of things. He was not talking about ultimate causes or facts. Rather he was indicating his adherence to a particular theory of knowledge, empiricism, derived from Feuerbach. Marx went on to link this position with communism. If man forms all his knowledge from the world of sense, it follows, said Marx, that the empirical world must be so arranged that man experiences what is truly human in it. 'If man is formed by circumstances, his circumstances must be made human.' In this way, Marx concluded, Fourier, Babeuf, and Owen 'developed the doctrine of materialism as a doctrine of *real humanism,* the logical basis of communism.'

In using 'materialism' as equivalent to 'empiricism' Marx was following Feuerbach and a common usage of his day. He was not referring to an ontology, a theory of the stuff or substance of things, but rather to a theory of knowledge. A year earlier he had refused to identify his position with materialism, and he was probably well aware, or should have been from his university studies, that the rootage of knowledge in sense-experience did not imply for Locke or Berkeley that everything is matter in its substance. Like Feuerbach, who professed to have 'no philosophy' in relying on the results of empirical natural science, and like contemporary thinkers who identify materialism with scientific, behavioral explanation, Marx treated materialism primarily as a declaration of his adherence to empiricism.

Marx's direct derivation of communism from empiricism, however, is logically questionable even though it significantly indicated his moral commitments. The rootage of knowledge in sense-perception does not logically imply that the perceptible world ought to be changed and made more humane. Actuality or what 'is' as sensuous fact does not directly imply what 'ought to be.' Marx's conclusion did indicate that along with his empiricism there was a moral commitment to socialism as involving the dignity and preciousness of every man and thus a moral commitment to democracy. While Feuerbach had a similar moral commitment, he did not see it as directly implied by empiricism. In the preface to *The Essence of Christianity,* with which Marx was intimately familiar, Feuerbach separated the 'is' from the 'ought,' theoretical matters from moral commitments. For the former he relied on 'materialism,' i.e., empiricism (including the independence of the object of sense but not its unrelatedness to the perceiving subject). For the latter, he saw the Hegelian Idea as signifying moral faith in the future, as having 'only a political and moral significance.' But Marx made no such separation. For him 'criticism,' fulfillment of the 'demands of Reason,' as we have seen, had both theoretical and moral significance. Later, particularly in *The Poverty of Philosophy* (1847), the substance of 'demands of Reason' appears in the dialectic of 'historical development.' In this way for Marx the 'is' or 'will be' as fact did imply and guarantee 'the ought,' so his rationalism provided an essential prop for his socialism and revealed the depth of his debt to Hegel.

4

In his well-known 'Theses on Feuerbach'[16] Marx continues with the theme of alienation in relation to empiricism. In spite of their fame and suggestiveness the 'Theses' are so highly aphoristic and truncated that they must be related to writings that preceded and followed them to bring out Marx's meaning. At the outset Marx discusses Feuerbach's 'materialism' but finds it lacking in the active element he had earlier found in Hegel's idealism. But Marx also rejects Hegelian 'activity' as 'abstract,' detached from sensuous objects and perceptible events. He was thus objecting to what he earlier called the alienation in Hegel's self-sufficing speculation, his movement in abstractions. Now, however, he refers to the solvent of such alienation as 'sensuous human activity' equated with *praxis* as 'practical-critical' and 'revolutionary' activity. His loose allegations against Feuerbach in regard to *praxis* and social relations will be examined below, but here it should be noted that he specifically objects to Feuerbach's 'man' as sundered from 'historical process.' Thus in the 'Theses' practical-critical activity in history, historical *praxis*, becomes the fulcrum of Marx's view of knowledge.

Some interpreters of Marx's thought have taken his emphasis on 'practical-critical activity' as a rough but nonetheless definite anticipation of pragmatic empiricism, particularly the experimentalism of John Dewey in which ideas and theories are 'plans of action' that actively mediate experience in observation and experimentation. Such an interpretation was advanced by William English Walling in 1913 and figured prominently in Sidney Hook's writing in the 1930s, such as *From Hegel to Marx.*[17] It can be supported from other sources besides the 'Theses on Feuerbach' – for example, *The German Ideology,* which will be considered next, Marx's subsequent designation of his theory of history as his 'guiding thread,' his recognition of the historically conditioned and thus tentative character of all scientific theories, and Engels' view of the test of knowledge by action in *Socialism, Utopian and Scientific.*[18]

But in one of its main aspects Marx's view moved in the opposite direction from pragmatic empiricism toward the rationalism we have already found at a number of points. This direction is implicit in his linkage of *praxis* with 'criticism.' By 'criticism' he meant not ordinary critical-mindedness as the analytical assessment of some idea or theory. Rather, as noted earlier, he meant 'the measuring of particular actuality against the Idea' to 'grasp the deficiency of the world to be made philosophical.' Further, criticism was to make the world philosophical, fulfill the 'demands of Reason,' actualize 'the principles of the world,' and hence transcend philosophy as thought *per se,* as alienation. Thus Marx regarded 'critical-practical activity' as realization or fulfillment of an antecedently real principle rather than instrumental projection of thought as in Dewey's pragmatism. Writing on Hegel's philosophy of law in 1844, Marx held that 'it is not enough that thought should seek its actualization.' This is the direction of empiricism and what Marx two years later called 'real, positive science.' But, said Marx, 'actuality must itself strive towards thought.'[19] Such striving, he indicated, is to be found in the dialectic of history and the movement of the proletariat which actualizes philosophy. '*Praxis*,' 'criticism,' and 'revolution' were thus rooted in the rationalism Marx appropriated from Hegel.

5

The fuller meaning of the aphoristic 'Theses on Feuerbach' in regard to the overcoming of alienation in abstract concepts on speculation through sense-perception in 'historical *praxis*' is to be found in *The German Ideology* (1845) and *The Poverty of Philosophy* (1847). The former was written in collaboration with Engels who later noted, however, that Marx had already arrived at the main features of his view in the spring of 1845, so the theory 'rightly bears his name.' Its foundational first part was never finished and was left unpublished, with little regret, 'to the gnawing criticism of the mice,' literally to the gnawing. Its unfinished character should at least be a warning against taking it as a fully reliable statement of Marx's views. *The Poverty of Philosophy,* however, was a finished publication, and Marx regarded it as the first 'scientific' presentation of his theory aiming at a final settlement with German philosophy.

In *The German Ideology* Marx deals with alienation in its moral and political aspects but also introduces empiricism as the basis for his conclusions about communism. The remedy for man's alienation in government, wealth, and culture is 'communism' or a 'real community' which overcomes the contradiction between the individual family and the general interest, between production and consumption arising from division of labor in industry. As this contradiction is resolved, the seemingly independent bonds of state, class, and religion are brought under man's control so there is nothing independent of self-active, associated individuals. But this 'communism,' Marx warns, is not a speculative conclusion. Quite the opposite. Its foundation is 'real individuals, their activity, and the material conditions under which they live,' and such premises can be verified 'in a purely empirical way.' But this 'purely empirical way' derived from Feuerbach does not save him from criticism. Marx accuses him of having an 'abstract' view of human nature. Earlier Marx had praised and adopted Feuerbach's view of man as a 'species-being.' He had agreed with Feuerbach that 'the essence of man exists only in community, in the unity of man with man.' Feuerbach, as

66

Marx may have known, had even based human nature and human thinking on 'universal history itself.'[20] What, then, was the deficiency which led Marx to proclaim that he did not 'deal with history,' did not view men 'under their existing condition of life which made them what they are?' We must conclude, in view of Marx's later criticism of Feuerbach, that he lacked a dialectical view of man's development in relation to industry and labor. Hence Feuerbach could only find remedy for man's alienation in an ideal 'ought' as suggested in the preface to *The Essence of Christianity* and discussed earlier in this essay. But for Marx the overcoming of man's alienation through communism was 'the *real* movement which abolishes the present state of things.' That is, it was the dialectic of reason in history manifest in the movement of labor, industry, and social classes. Thus Feuerbach's deficiency was corrected by the 'rational kernel' from Hegel that Marx acknowledged in his preface to *Capital* in 1872.

Further, Marx directly analyzes Feuerbach's empiricism, his appeal to sense-perception, and finds it as defective as his view of human nature. In the exchange of letters that opened the *Deutsch-Französische Jahrbücher* two years earlier Feuerbach had insisted that philosophy must be purged by yoking theory under *praxis* so thought can live humanly on the shoulders of active men.[21] *Praxis* unites men and has a mass effect in the world. Now, in *The German Ideology*, Marx calls such views mere 'isolated surmises,' 'embryos capable of development,' and proceeds to develop them. He finds Feuerbach's empiricism confined to 'mere perception' and 'mere sensation.' Feuerbach does not see that the sensuous world is 'not something directly given and the same from all eternity but the product of industry and of the state of society in the sense that it is an historical product.' Feuerbach rests his thought on natural science but does not see that even 'pure natural science receives its aim, like its material, only through commerce and industry, through the sensuous activity of men' which is an historical and not merely a natural process.[22]

Thus Marx was insisting that 'mere perception' or sensation is not enough to get at the truth of things. In addition there is the historical element, the element of cumulative practical activity. Without this element, Marx insists, empiricism is 'abstract,' a collection of dead facts. In contrast, 'real positive science' which can correct speculation and the illusory, inverted relations of ideas to actual life – the 'false conceptions' men have of themselves – in ideology, is 'the representation of the practical activity and practical process of the development of men.' The abstractions of such 'real positive science' are 'derived from observation of the historical development of men' and have no value apart from such

derivation. Whether these abstractions are themselves any less historical products, and thus any less historically relative and transitory than
those of the '"pure" natural science' on which Feuerbach relied, is a
question to which we shall later return. What is clear, however, is that
Marx's empiricism – which he also called 'materialism' – was an historical empiricism in contrast to Feuerbach's 'abstract' empiricism. It was
an empiricism wedded to history as cumulative practical activity, not
the empiricism of the eighteenth century which derived ideas from pas-
sively received atomic sensations. For this emphasis on history Marx
was heavily indebted to Hegel, and his immediately subsequent, more
finished writing in *The Poverty of Philosophy* indicates that the 'historical development' he observed with 'real positive science' was a dialectical process. Thus the deficiency Marx found in Feuerbach's empiricism
as well as in his view of man was corrected by the 'rational kernel' from
Hegel.

6

Marx's first 'scientific' and finished presentation of his theory, *The
Poverty of Philosophy,* continues his attack on what was earlier called
'alienation' and more recently 'ideology,' namely, the speculative abstractions of independent philosophy, by criticizing Proudhon's
method, an adaptation of Hegel's dialectic with which Marx had admittedly infected Proudhon. Marx finds Proudhon transforming historical
relations of production into a dialectic of abstract categories and pre-
existing eternal ideas. Proudhon does not see, Marx charges, that the
same men who change their social relations as they change their mode of
production also produce ideas and categories that are historical products, no more eternal than the relations they express. In this criticism
Marx was proceeding from the objections to speculative philosophy he
had developed in *The German Ideology* with his method of 'historical
empiricism.' And here he clearly and explicitly uses Hegel's dialectic –
of which Proudhon 'has nothing but the language' – to formulate in
detail 'the real movement of things' in history as dynamic antitheses and
contradictions within feudal and bourgeois production.[23] Such a movement foreshadows socialism which is not utopian but rather the outcome of observable developments leading to a new society, an
'association' without class antagonisms or a separate political power. In
subsequent letters of 1865 and 1868 Marx criticized Proudhon for not
having grasped 'the secret of scientific dialectic,' and called Hegel's dialectic 'the basic form of all dialectic.' 'Feuerbach,' wrote Marx, 'has
much to answer for' in the disrepute of Hegel's dialectic, in its being

treated as a 'dead horse.'[24] With all his criticism of Hegel, then, Marx retained an essential aspect of his thought – the dialectic of reason in history – and used it to amend the empiricism he had found in Feuerbach.

Marx's fusion of empiricism with the 'rational kernel' of historical dialectic leads to a specific, even a fateful, answer to the problem of how to 'unmask' ideology through objective knowledge. For Marx, as we saw, ideology involves 'false conceptions,' distorted and inverted ideas, as in the 'independent philosophy' he had earlier characterized as 'alienation' or abstract speculation. To many of Marx's readers the correction of ideology and the elimination of 'false' conceptions has seemed to be simply a matter of following the method of natural science, deriving our conceptions from and testing them by observation and sense-perception. Marx himself seems to give such an answer in a later classic reference to ideology in the *Critique of Political Economy* of 1859. There Marx contrasts 'ideological forms' to ascertainment of the economic conditions of production 'with the precision of natural science.'

But the matter is not so simple. For Marx, as we have seen, 'natural science receives its aim, like its material, only through commerce and industry.' He thus seemed to hold that not only the external uses of natural science but its purpose and content as well were determined by the historical development of conditions of production. He viewed that development as a dialectical movement of classes, observably exemplified, to be sure, in the society around him but nonetheless a dialectical and thus rational development.

It would seem to follow, then, that genuine knowledge or truth is not to be found in the immediate deliverances of natural science but rather in the dialectic of reason in history on which science itself depends, in the fulfillment of the 'demands of Reason' in history, to use an earlier formulation. In 1844 Marx saw the proletariat as that fulfillment. The first 'scientific' statement of his view in *The Poverty of Philosophy* similarly assigns such a special role to the proletariat. The theoreticians of the proletariat, Marx claims, do not have to 'seek science in their minds' but 'have only to give an account of what is happening before their eyes and give voice to it.' Hence science, 'produced by the historical movement and linking itself to that movement in full consciousness, has ceased to be doctrinaire and has become revolutionary.'[25] It has ceased to be ideological and is thus substantively true, Marx seems to be saying, because it is identified with the proletariat. Knowledge becomes a function of the dialectic of reason in history, and Marx's 'rational kernel' from Hegel provides support for the view that truth manifests the consciousness and thought of the proletariat as the dialectically emergent, and thus progressive, social class. From here it is a short step to the doctrine of *partijnost,* party-mindedness, as fulfilling the 'demands of Reason.' *The Communist Manifesto* makes the party the vanguard of the proletariat, a vanguard that is 'theoretically clearer' in grasping the 'line of march' and outcome of the proletarian movement.

## 7

Marx's rationalism, prominent and apparent in his early thought, remained in his mature thought after *The Poverty of Philosophy* and *The Communist Manifesto.* We have noted several times his appropriation of the 'rational kernel' of Hegel mentioned in the second preface to *Capital.* That 'rational kernel' was dialectic, involving 'affirmation' of the existing situation followed by a 'negation' that is 'inevitable.' This movement, says Marx, in terms identical with Hegel's, 'lets nothing impose on it.'[26] As involving negation it is 'revolutionary.' Marx further asserts, however, that his dialectic is the opposite of Hegel's in that it views the process of thinking not as inherent in an independent subject, demiurge, or Spirit but as belonging to the human mind reflecting the material world and translating it into the forms of thought. But even with this difference, dialectic was for Marx a movement of thought or reason involving 'necessity' and 'inevitability,' and as such it was also a movement reflecting the material world.

The 'rational kernel' of dialectic appears at many points throughout *Capital* where Marx speaks of 'contradictions' in economic development, and is particularly prominent in Chapter 32 on the 'Historical Tendency of Capitalist Accumulation.' In terms virtually identical with those of *The Communist Manifesto* Marx argues that capitalist production 'begets, with the inexorability of a law of Nature, its own negation. It is the negation of negation.' The prominence of dialectical rationalism in *Capital* provides more than a little justification for Lenin's claim in his *Notebooks* that it is impossible to comprehend *Capital* without studying and understanding Hegel's *Logic.*

With the 'rational kernel' of dialectic from Hegel, Marx was led to view social developments, and natural processes as well, as 'necessary' and 'inexorable.' While Engels found the views of Pierre Tremaux on evolution to be 'pure construction,' Marx favored them as an advance over Darwin, 'a demonstration of the evolution of species according to "necessary law."'[27] But no induction or generalization from sense-perception and observation, empiricists have long argued, can 'demonstrate' a conclusion as 'necessary.' Though Marx's contemporaries may have loosely assumed that observation-based science could demonstrate necessity, Marx's education had exposed him to the sharpest critique of this notion ever to appear in philosophical literature. At the University of Berlin he had closely studied and copied excerpts from Hume's *Treatise*, including the sections that analyzed necessity into constant conjunction in experience to conclude that such conjunction is never demonstrable but can support only contingent truths or probability statements.[28] But apparently this lesson in empiricism did not sink very deeply into Marx's thought and was easily displaced by his subsequent reading in Rosenkranz's *History of Philosophy*, particularly the section on the *Überwindung* of Kant who had confined knowledge to the perceived world and dismissed the dialectic of reason as 'illusion.'

Further, the 'rational kernel' of dialectic is often apparent in Marx's treatment of history, resulting even in such a priori 'trimming' by a 'recipe or schema' as he condemned among his contemporaries in *The German Ideology*. To be sure, Marx's empirical conscience is often evident in historical writings such as *Class Struggles in France* and *The Eighteenth Brumaire*. In these works he reported a detailed diversity in social class structure and complex movements of events, so diverse and devious as to be immediately 'bewildering.'[29] But in the end such data dropped into place as required by the dialectic of reason in history. Ultimately Marx viewed social facts through the spectacles of a dialectical movement of 'contradictions' in civil society – 'poverty' and 'wealth,' 'proletariat' and 'bourgeoisie.' His 'rational kernel' from Hegel thus supported oversimplifications about class conflict and the dialectical 'cunning' whereby intensification of the power of the centralized state, as in *The Communist Manifesto*, can make it wither away.

Marx's rationalism in regard to thought and knowledge is further apparent in his repeated negative criticisms of empiricism, or 'positivism,' as it was called in his day. We have already seen how he amended and qualified Feuerbach's empiricism. Later he condemned the views of Auguste Comte as 'positivist rot,' miserable in comparison with Hegel. When Joseph Dietzgen, whom Marx introduced to the International Workingmen's Association as 'our philosopher,' developed from Feuerbach a view of knowledge which strikingly anticipated Ernst Mach and recent logical positivism, Marx criticized it precisely for not having absorbed Hegel.[30] In a recent discussion of Marx's views on knowledge and ideology, George Lichtheim has argued that Marx's thought moves in the opposite direction from empiricism and positivism toward a rationalism implying that there is a 'logic in history' grasped by 'an act of intellectual intuition.' Marx's criticism of Feuerbach, Lichtheim concludes, 'left intact the rationalist principle which Marx shared with Hegel: namely, the belief that cognition gives access to universal truths not present in immediate experience.'[31] Again,

Marx's rationalism in opposition to empiricism is developed and documented in detail by Herbert Marcuse in *Reason and Revolution* where the socialist 'realm of freedom' is seen as 'reason determining itself.' Here socialism has become virtually 'a chapter in logic,' to use Marx's invidious phrase of 1843, a chapter in dialectical logic.

Yet at numerous important points Marx's mature thought moved against rationalism to reaffirm and develop the empiricism he had adopted from Feuerbach as a corrective for 'alienation' in speculative thought and ideology. This direction supports the frequent claims that Marx basically adhered to the inductive, empirical procedure of the natural sciences and sought to apply that procedure to social phenomena. From an examination of Marx's view of ideology T. B. Bottomore concludes: 'His theory of knowledge was implicitly that of the natural sciences.'[32] Similarly, I. M. Zeitlin asserts in his recently published *Marxism: A Re-examination* that Marx's characteristic conclusions were all 'empirical' and 'inductive,' so his views on classes and dialectic must be understood as 'working hypotheses' or 'heuristic' general ideas. A similar interpretation, we noted earlier, is prominent among pragmatists, particularly those who find Marx's views on knowledge reaffirmed and elaborated in John Dewey's experimentalism.

Marx's bent towards empiricism is particularly apparent in his introduction to the unfinished *Critique of Political Economy* of 1857. There he finds Hegel's supposedly concrete concept to be the result only of 'self-coordinating, self-absorbed, and spontaneously operating thought.' A genuinely concrete concept, however, is 'the working-up, the elaboration, of perception and presentation into conceptions.' This way of grasping the world, Marx insists, is *not* to be identified with 'the artistic, religious, or practical-minded' way. Further, it does not make the perceived world a product of mind or thought. Why not? Because, Marx argues, it is only a tautology to say that a concrete whole as thought of is the product of thought, so *what* is perceived, the concrete subject matter, continues to exist independently of our thinking about it.[33]

This discussion of 'genuinely concrete concepts' is notable in several respects. It reiterates Marx's objection from 1843 on to Hegel's 'self-sufficing speculation' as 'alienation' from data of sense-perception. It indicates that a genuine concept is derived from data of perception and, presumably, is to be tested for its truth in relation to such data. The derivation, furthermore, is an active process involving 'elaboration' and working-up of what is given in perception. Yet this activity, Marx warns, is not to be identified with 'practical-mindedness,' so it apparently is not to be absorbed into or squared with historical *praxis* involving dialectic and the 'demands of Reason,' the point at which

Marx previously amended Feuerbach's empiricism. While the separation of genuine knowledge from practical-mindedness undercuts the 'pragmatism' some interpreters have found in Marx's 'Theses on Feuerbach,' it also implicitly retracts the view that scientific truth is a function of the dialectic of historical *praxis* and ultimately of the consciousness of the proletariat. This separation, moreover, points towards a distinction between theoretical matters and moral commitments, the 'is' and the 'ought-to-be' – a distinction, we have noted, that Marx obliterated in 'criticism' but Feuerbach pointedly affirmed in opposition to Hegel.

Further, Marx's description of a 'genuinely concrete concept' reveals his specific ground for believing that the activity of thought in knowing does not make the world into thought, as with idealism. His argument from 'tautology' is closely akin to recent arguments of analytical philosophers who assert a common-sense realism in opposition to idealism. Marx's discussion, of course, leaves many questions unanswered. What exactly is involved in the 'elaboration' and 'working up' of what is given in perception? How does such 'elaboration' escape the idealists' conclusion that the world as grasped in true concepts embodies the activity of thought? But regardless of the incompleteness of Marx's discussion, his intention seems to be clear. He aimed to show that 'genuinely concrete concepts' are derived from and tested by what is given in perception and such presentation consists of real objects that are independent of our thinking about them.

A decade later in *Capital* a number of Marx's statements about his method lean towards empiricism and against the rationalism we earlier found him endorsing and using in the same context. For example, he makes a point of distinguishing between his method of inquiry and his method of exposition, suggesting that the former must 'appropriate the material in detail,' much as in the working up of a 'genuinely concrete concept,' while the exposition 'may appear as if we had before us a mere a priori construction' as it occasionally coquets with 'modes of expression' peculiar to Hegel.[34] Here Marx's words – 'a mere a priori construction' – epitomize his opposition to rationalism, an opposition long evident in his defense of empiricism against Hegel's 'self-sufficing speculation.' Marx further suggests that his dialectic method is to be understood empirically, not as adherence to Hegel's rationalistic formula of 'affirmation' and 'negation.' After quoting from a reviewer who says that *Capital* presents phenomena analogous to the history of evolution in biology and discloses laws of the origin, development, and death of a given social organism, Marx asks: 'What else is he picturing but the dialectic method?' Here Marx suggests that dialectic is identical with empirical description of social development involving laws as statements of functions in such development. Marx pointedly identifies his method of inquiry with the method of the natural sciences in which conclusions are based on observation of phenomena directly or through experimentation, thus reiterating his earlier claim that natural science and the science of man should be seen as 'one science.' In 1844 he had seen the 'unity of science' as a corollary of Feuerbach's empiricism, and in this respect Feuerbach was 'the true conqueror of the old philosophy,' i.e., Hegel's philosophy.

Marx not only verbally endorsed empirical method but widely used it in his research. While his writings on labor and production prior to the 1850s were largely based on inference from social and political theories, supplemented by general observation and Engels' reports on factory conditions, the conclusions of *Capital* were widely and massively supported by specific facts and figures gathered by Parliamentary commissions or cited in current literature on industrial development in England. Further, Marx's commitment to empirical method is apparent in a 'questionnaire' he prepared in 1880 to circulate among French workers. Though 25,000 copies were distributed, the results were never published. The very preparation of the questionnaire, however with its 101 pointed and specific questions, many of them quantitative, indicates Marx's view of the basis of reliable knowledge. Applying empirical method, he aimed at '*exact* and *positive* knowledge' of the conditions of labor.[35]

## 8

What may be concluded, on the whole and in the end, about Marx's view of knowledge in respect to the issue of rationalism versus empiricism? One thing seems to be clear. There was always an ambivalence in his thinking on this matter. If it be objected that this ambivalence was implicitly resolved in dialectic, we must at least conclude that Marx never pointedly or clearly explicated the resolution. To do so would have required an analysis of 'necessity' that would show its precise relation to and compatibility with inductions from observation and perceptual data. It would also have required an analysis of 'criticism' and 'reason' in relation to such induction. Without such philosophical work Marx's view of knowledge and science is 'open' as being a thicket of ambiguities and unanswered questions.

Our survey of Marx's thought, however, does suggest that his ambivalence on the issue of rationalism versus empiricism was not evenly balanced. His thought seems to have generally and somewhat increasingly inclined toward empiricism – which he also identified as 'materialism' – and the application of the empirical methods of natural science to social phenomena. But it was still freighted with the rationalist elements from Hegel we have noted, elements involving the 'self-sufficing speculation' he sharply rejected as forms of 'alienation' and 'ideology.' Perhaps the immense problems dealing with such freight in relation to a more thoroughgoing empiricism was what deterred Marx from undertaking the systematic treatise on dialectic he intended to write but never did.

NOTES AND REFERENCES

1. For a recent and particularly thorough instance of such exploration, see Shlomo Avineri, *The Social and Political Thought of Karl Marx* (Cambridge: University Press, 1968).
2. 'Letter to His Father,' in *Writings of the Young Marx on Philosophy and Society,* trans. and ed. by Loyd Easton and Kurt Guddat (New York: Doubleday, 1967) [hereafter referred to as *Writings*], p. 46.
3. 'Philosophy After Its Completion,' *Writings,* pp. 61–63.
4. 'The Leading Article in No. 179 of the *Kölnische Zeitung,*' *Writings,* p. 130.
5. 'Critique of Hegel's Philosophy of the State,' *Writings,* pp. 155–157, 163–164.
6. Ludwig Feuerbach, *Kleine philosophische Schriften* (Leipzig: Meiner, 1950), pp. 56, 59, 144, 149; *The Essence of Christianity,* trans. G. Eliot [M. Evans], (New York: Harpers, 1957), ch. 1 § 2.
7. 'Kritik des Hegelschen Staatsrechts,' *Marx-Engels Werke* (Berlin: Dietz, 1961), Bd. 1, pp. 241, 266.
8. *Cf.* Hegel, Introductions to 'The Philosophy of History' and 'The Science of Logic,' in C. J. Friedrich, ed., *The Philosophy of Hegel* (New York: Random House, 1954), pp. 4–5, 191–196.
9. 'Philosophy of Law and Right,' § 244 in Friedrich, *op. cit.,* pp. 278–279.
10. 'An Exchange of Letters (1843),' *Writings,* p. 213.
11. *Writings,* p. 312.
12. *Ibid.,* p. 321.
13. *Ibid.,* p. 367.
14. *Ibid.,* pp. 369–374.
15. *Ibid.,* pp. 391–395.
16. *Ibid.,* pp. 400–402.
17. Cf. W. E. Walling, *The Larger Aspects of Socialism* (New York: Macmillan, 1913), pp. 373–385; Sidney Hook, *From Hegel to Marx* (New York: Humanities Press, 1950), pp. 281–285.
18. Friedrich Engels, *Socialism, Utopian and Scientific* (New York: International, 1935), pp. 13–14.
19. *Writings,* p. 259.
20. *Writings,* pp. 305–306; Feuerbach, *Kleine philosophische Schrif-*

*ten*, p. 168; G. Plekhanov, *Fundamental Problems of Marxism* (New York: International, 1928), p. 136, quoting from Feuerbach on history.

21. *Writings*, p. 211.

22. *Ibid.*, pp. 416–419.

23. *Ibid.*, pp. 477–487.

24. Karl Marx and Friedrich Engels, *Selected Correspondence*, trans. D. Torr (New York: International, 1942), pp. 175, 233.

25. *Writings*, p. 494. Cf. Friedrich Engels, *Ludwig Feuerbach* (New York: International, 1941), p. 60: 'The more ruthlessly and disinterestedly science proceeds the more it finds itself in harmony with the interests and efforts of the workers.' Georg Lukács's development of this 'historicist' view of knowledge in opposition to scientific empiricism and as implying *partijnost* is well summarized and documented from *Geschichte und Klassenbewusstsein* (1923) by George Lichtheim in *The Concept of Ideology* (New York: Vintage Books, 1967), pp. 35–40.

26. Marx, *Capital* (Chicago: Kerr, 1906), vol. I, pp. 25–26. Cf. Hegel, *Logic* (from the *Encyclopedia*), trans. Wallace (Oxford: Clarendon Press, 1892). Pt I, Ch. VI, § 81 (p. 150).

27. *Marx-Engels Historische-Kritische Gesamtausgabe,* hgn. V. Adoratskij (Berlin: Marx-Engels Verlag, 1931), [hereafter MEGA], Abt. III, Bd. 3, pp. 355–363.

28. MEGA, Abt. I, Bd. 1², pp. 112–113.

29. Cf. L. Krieger, 'Marx and Engels as Historians,' *Journal of the History of Ideas,* 14 (1953), pp. 383–384, 392–393.

30. Cf. Marx and Engels, *Selected Correspondence,* pp. 210, 252–253; L. Easton, 'Empiricism and Ethics in Dietzgen,' *Journal of the History of Ideas,* 19 (1958), pp. 77–83.

31. Lichtheim, *op. cit.,* pp. 18, 32, xvi. Cf. H. Marcuse, *Reason and Revolution* (New York: Humanities Press, 1954), pp. 271, 315–330 *et passim.*

32. T. B. Bottomore, 'Some Reflections on the Sociology of Knowledge,' *British Journal of Sociology,* 7 (1956), p. 54. Cf. I. M. Zeitlin, *Marxism: a Re-examination* (Princeton, N. J. Van Nostrand, 1967), pp. 7–8, 14, 121–123.

33. Marx, *Grundrisse der Kritik der politischen Ökonomie (Rohentwurf) 1857–1858* (Berlin: Dietz, 1953), p. 21. The Introduction to the *Grundrisse*, with Marx's views on method and 'genuinely concrete concepts,' was first published in *Die Neue Zeit* in 1903 and appeared as an appendix to *A Contribution to a Critique of Political Economy* (Chicago: Kerr, 1904), but the translation by N. I. Stone is confusing and sometimes misleading.

34. Marx, *Capital,* Vol. I, pp. 25–26. Cf. Alfred Schmidt, 'Zum Erkenntnisbegriff der politischen Ökonomie,' in G. Mann *et al., Karl Marx 1818–1868* (Bad Godesburg: Inter Nationes, 1968), pp. 104–106, holding that 'exposition' implies, as in Hegel, knowing through dialectic the 'concrete unity' of 'isolated' results of inquiry – further evidence of Marx's rationalism.

35. 'Marx's Enquête Ouvrière' in Karl Marx, *Selected Writings in Sociology and Social Philosophy,* edited by T. B. Bottomore and M. Rubel (Harmondsworth: Penguin Books, 1963), pp. 210–218.

# SYSTEM, STRUCTURE AND CONTRADICTION IN *CAPITAL**

MAURICE GODELIER

Is it possible to analyse the relations between an event and a structure, or to explain the genesis and evolution of that structure, without being forced to abandon a structuralist viewpoint? These two questions are topical, and some have already hazarded an affirmative reply. A new situation is emerging, one of the aspects of which is the resumption of a dialogue between structuralism and Marxism. This is hardly surprising, as Marx himself, a century ago, described the whole of social life in terms of 'structures,' advanced the hypothesis of the necessary existence of correspondences between infrastructures and superstructures characterizing different 'types' of society, and, lastly, claimed the ability to explain the 'evolution' of these types of society by the emergence and development of 'contradictions' between their structures.

But the appearance of the word 'contradiction' might seem to cut short this resumed dialogue, for we all remember the dialectical 'miracles' of Hegel and many more or less well-known Marxists. But can the question be so simply answered; is Marx's dialectic the same as Hegel's? Marx's own statements on this point are equivocal: it sufficed to 'turn the dialectic right side up again' to make it 'scientifically useful,' and to strip off all the mystifications with which Hegelian idealism had surrounded it.

I should like to reconsider this question by returning to the text of *Capital*. In fact, I think I can show that, in basic principles, Marx's dialectic has nothing to do with Hegel's, because they do not depend on the same notion of contradiction. Traditional exegeses of Marx then collapse, giving place to a Marx largely unknown even to Marxists, a Marx capable of providing unexpected and fruitful elements for the most up to date scientific reflection.

* This essay first appeared in *Les Temps Modernes*, No. 246, November 1966. The translation is by Ben Brewster. Originally published in English in *The Socialist Register*, 1967, (eds.) Ralph Miliband and John Saville. Reprinted with permission of Merlin Press, London.

## 1. FROM THE VISIBLE FUNCTIONING OF THE CAPITALIST SYSTEM TO ITS HIDDEN INTERNAL 'STRUCTURE'

What does Marx mean by an economic 'system'? A determined combination of specific modes of production, circulation, distribution and consumption of material goods. In this combination, the mode of production of goods plays the dominant rôle. A mode of production is the combination of two structures, irreducible to one another: the productive forces and the relations of production. The notion of productive forces designates the set of factors of production, resources, tools, men, characterizing a determined society at a determined epoch which must be *combined* in a specific way to produce the material goods necessary to that society. The notion of relations of production designates the functions fulfilled by individuals and groups in the production process and in the control of the factors of production. For example, capitalist relations of production are relations between a class of individuals who have private possession of the productive forces and of capital, and a class of individuals without this property who must sell to the former the use of their labour power in exchange for a wage. Each class complements and presupposes the other.

For Marx, the scientific understanding of the capitalist system consists in the discovery of the internal structure hidden behind its visible functioning.

Thus, for Marx, as for Claude Lévi-Strauss,[1] 'structures' should not be confused with visible 'social relations' but constitute a *level of reality* invisible but present behind the visible social relations. The logic of the latter, and the laws of social practice more generally, depend on the functioning of these hidden structures and the discovery of these last should allow us to 'account for all the facts observed.'[2]

A very crude summary of Marx's thesis might go as follows: in the practice of the capitalist system everything *occurs as if* the wage were paid for the worker's labour, and as if the capital had of itself the property of automatic growth and of rendering a profit to its owner. In day to day practice there is no *direct* proof that capitalist profit is unpaid workers' labour, no *immediate* experience of the exploitation of the worker by the capitalist.

For Marx, profit is a fraction of the exchange value of commodities which remains in the hands of their owner after deducting prime costs. The exchange value of commodities presupposes a unit of measurement which makes them commensurable. This common unit cannot be the utility of the commodities since there is nothing in common at the level of use value between vegetables and a fountain pen. . . . The exchange value of commodities can only derive from what they have in common as products of labour. The substance of value is therefore the socially necessary labour for the production of these commodities. Profit is a fraction of the value[3] created by the use of workers' labour power which is not paid as wages. Profit is thus unpaid labour, free labour. But in practice, in the eyes of capitalists and workers, everything takes place as if the wages were paid for all the labour provided by the worker (bonuses, piece rates, overtime rates, etc.). Wages thus give the workers' unpaid labour the appearance of paid labour: 'This phenomenal form, which makes *the actual relation invisible*, and, indeed, *shows* the direct opposite of that relation, forms the basis of all the juridical notions of both labourer and capitalist, of all the mystifications of the capitalistic mode of production.'[4]

In fact, once wages appear as the price of labour, profit can no longer appear as unpaid labour. It necessarily appears as the product of capital. Each class seems to draw from production the revenue to which it has a right. There is no visible exploitation of one class by another. The economic categories: wages, profits, interest, etc., thus express the visible relations of day to day business and as such they have a *pragmatic utility*, but no scientific value. Once economic science bases itself on these categories it, in fact, does no more than '*interpret, systematise and defend* in doctrinaire fashion the conceptions of the agents of bourgeois production who are entrapped in bourgeois production relations. It should not astonish us, then, that vulgar economy feels particularly at home in the estranged outward appearances of economic relations . . . and that these relations seem the more *self-evident* the more their internal relationships are concealed from it. . . .'[5] The intelligibility and coherence introduced by this systematization of the current conceptions of members of the society can only result in mythology. 'To talk of the price of labour is as irrational as to talk of a yellow logarithm.' Myth here consists of a coherent theory of appearances, of what *seems* to happen in practice. The scientific conception of social reality does not 'arise by abstraction' from the spontaneous or reflected conceptions of individuals. On the contrary, it must destroy the obviousness of these conceptions in order to *bring out* the hidden internal logic of social life. Therefore, for Marx, the model constructed by science corresponds to a reality concealed beneath visible reality. But he goes even further; for him this concealment is not due to the inability of consciousness to 'perceive' this structure, but to the structure itself. If capital *is not* a thing, but a *social relationship*, i.e. a non-sensible reality, it *must inevitably disappear* when presented in the sensible forms of raw materials, tools, money, etc. It is not the subject who deceives himself, but *reality* which deceives *him*, and the appearances in which the structure of the capitalist production process conceals itself are the starting-point for individuals' conceptions. For Marx, a determined mode of *appearance* corresponds to each determined structure of the real, and this mode of appearance is the starting-point for a kind of *spontaneous* consciousness of the structure for which neither consciousness nor the individual are responsible. It follows that the scientific understanding of a structure does not abolish the spontaneous consciousness of that structure. It modifies its rôle and its effects, but it does not suppress it.[6]

When Marx assumes that structure is not to be confused with visible relations and explains their hidden logic, he inaugurates the modern structuralist tradition. And he is fully in accord with this tradition when he proposes the priority of the study of structures over that of their genesis and evolution.

## 2. THE PRIORITY OF THE STUDY OF STRUCTURES OVER THAT OF THEIR GENESIS AND EVOLUTION

This priority is apparent from a simple glance at the architecture of *Capital*. The work does not start with the theory of capital, but by setting out the theory of value, i.e. by the definition of a group of categories necessary to the study of any system of commodity production, whether this is based on the labour of a free peasant, a slave, a serf, or a wage labourer, etc. This group of categories is developed from a definition of the exchange value of a commodity. Money is then introduced as a special commodity with the function of expressing and measuring the exchange value of other commodities. Coin is defined as a form of money. Coin ceases to function as a simple means of circulation of commodities and begins to function as capital when it brings in coin, when its use adds value to its initial value. The general definition of capital whatever its form – commercial, financial or industrial – is that it is value that makes value and brings in surplus value.

By the end of the second section of volume I of *Capital* Marx thus has at his disposal the theoretical instruments necessary to identify the specific structure of the capitalist economic system, the capital-labour relation, and to construct the theory of capital. Before this theory could be undertaken, a rigorous definition of the notion of commodity was essential, for within the capital-labour relation labour power appears as a commodity. This makes possible an analysis of the internal structure of the capitalist system, i.e. a study of the mechanism of the production of surplus value through the capital-labour relation. Volume I analyses at length the two forms of surplus value: absolute surplus value (obtained by lengthening the working day without increasing wages) and relative surplus value (obtained by decreasing the costs of employing the worker, by increasing the productivity of labour in the branches producing the means of subsistence of the workers and their families).

Only at the end of volume I does the reader find Marx setting out the problem of the *genesis* of the capitalist production relationship via a discussion of what the classical economists called 'the problem of primitive accumulation.' Marx's procedure thus marks a break with any historicism or reliance on events. The genesis of a structure can only be studied under the 'guidance' of a pre-existing knowledge of that structure. To study the genesis of the specific structure of the capitalist system is to determine the particular historical circumstances of the emergence of individuals who are free in person, but deprived of the means of production and of money and forced to sell the use of their labour power to other individuals who possess the means of production and money but are forced to buy others' labour power to set these means of production in motion and breed their money. But Marx only sketches this genesis in a rapid perspective of some of the conditions, forms and stages of the appearance of capitalism in Europe, and this does not constitute a history of capitalism. Among these stages we might mention the disbanding of feudal retinues in England, the expropriation and partial expulsion of cultivators, the 'enclosures' movement, the transformation of merchants into merchant-manufacturers, colonial trade, the development of protectionism. All these appeared in the fifteenth, sixteenth, and seventeenth centuries here and there in Portugal, Spain, France and England, and generally resulted in the emergence of a large number of producers without means of production and their use in a new structure of production.

'The capitalist system *presupposes* the complete separation of the labourers from all property in the means by which they can realize their labour. As soon as capitalist production is once on its own legs, it not only *maintains* this separation, but *reproduces* it on a continually extending scale. The process, therefore, that clears the way for the capitalist system, can be none other than the process which takes away from the labourer the possession of his means of production; a process that transforms, on the one hand, the social means of subsistence and of production into capital, on the other, the immediate producers into wage labourers. The so-called primitive accumulation, therefore, is nothing else than the historical process of divorcing the producer from the means of production. It appears as primitive, because it forms the prehistoric stage of capital and of the mode of production corresponding with it. The economic structure of capitalistic society *has grown out of* the economic structure of feudal society. The dissolution of the latter sets free the *elements* of the former.'[7]

Thus to analyse the historical genesis of a structure is to analyse the conditions of emergence of its internal elements and the way they come into relation with one another. In its constitution, economic history pre-supposes that these elements and this relation are already identified, so it presupposes economic theory. In Marx's text the genesis of one system is described simultaneously with the dissolution of another, and these two effects depend on the same process, the development of in-ternal contradictions within the old system (which must also be theor-ized).

This general progress from the identification of the structure to the study of its genesis might seem to founder on an obstacle that Marx himself considered. For how can the hypothesis of the appearance of in-ternal contradictions inside a system be reconciled with the thesis that the functioning of this system necessarily *reproduces* its conditions of functioning? For example, the capitalist system's functioning mechan-ism ceaselessly reproduces the capital-labour relation on which it is built. The mechanism of profit and wage always allows the capitalist class to accumulate new capital and to reproduce itself as the ruling class, while on the other hand it forces the working class to put its labour power up for sale again, and to reproduce itself as the ruled class.[8] The capital-labour relation appears as the *constant element* in the capitalist economic structure throughout all the latter's variations: the passage from the capitalism of free competition to private or state monopoly capitalism, the appearance of new productive forces, changes in the composition of the working class, in its forms of trade union and political organization etc. The discovery and definition of this con-stant constitute the necessary point of departure for the scientific study of the system, of its genesis and evolution. The latter appears as the study of *variations compatible* with the reproduction of the constant element of the system structure. At this level the passage from political economy to economic history is once again set out. Synchronic and diachronic studies are possible (analyses of the various *states* of a structure corresponding to various *moments* in its evolution). But diachronic analysis of the variations which are com-patible with the reproduction of a constant relation does not produce any structural incompatibles, any conditions of change.[9]

But can incompatible variations be produced *within* the function-ing of a system if the very maintenance of the system proves that they are compatible with its reproduction? Before I analyse Marx's notion of contradiction in detail, I should like to develop further that of 'structural compatibility,' for it plays a decisive double role which illuminates the whole method and plan of *Capital*. It allows Marx to account for the visible forms of the functioning of the capitalist system which he had initially rejected. It also allows him to explain the new role and new forms which the 'antediluvian' forms of capital[10] – commercial capital and finance capital – take on when they function in the framework of modern capitalism. I shall summarize these two points briefly so as to be able to deduce their methodological consequences. As we have seen, Marx first of all analysed the production mechanism of surplus value and showed that it consisted of production from unpaid labour. He then showed that the internal and necessary connection between surplus value and labour disappears once surplus value is put into relation with all the capital advanced by the capitalist rather than with the wage paid to the worker, i.e. it disappears once surplus value appears as profit. The results of volume II allow him, in Part 1 of volume III, to analyse the complex conditions for the realization of a maximum profit by the capitalist entrepreneur. I can leave aside these problems – those of the relations between value and price, price and profit, normal profit and super profit, rate of profit in various branches and at the level of the national economy, etc. – without loss for our purposes. What is essential is that we should remember Marx's conclusions. From his profit, which at the limit seems to have little relation to the real exploitation of his own workers, the capitalist must subtract a portion for the ground rent of the proprietor of the land on which his factory stands, another which goes as interest to a lender or to a bank, another which he owes to the State as taxes. The remainder constitutes the profit of his enterprise. By showing that the mechanism of the production of surplus value is the common origin of the visible forms of capitalist profit even though certain categories of capitalists seem to have no direct link with the production process, Marx made possible the analysis of the articulation of the internal structure of the system to the visible forms which he avoided on principle at the outset of his work.

Marx returns to these visible forms by defining at one and the same time their real function in the system and their internal compatibility with the essential structures that were given priority in his study. In modern terms, his progress would constitute a kind of ideal genesis of the various elements of a system on the basis of its laws of internal composition. Marx defined it himself in respect to money:

> Everyone knows, if he knows nothing else, that commodities have a value-form common to them all, and presenting a marked contrast with the varied bodily forms of their use-values. I mean their money-form. Here, however, a task is set us, the performance of which has

never yet even been attempted by bourgeois economy, the task of tracing the *genesis* of this money-form, of developing the *expression* of value implied in the value-relation of commodities, from its simplest, almost imperceptible outline, to the dazzling money-form. By doing this we shall, at the same time, *solve* the riddle presented by money.[11]

But I must avoid a misunderstanding which might arise from what I have called the ideal genesis of economic categories. For if an object becomes a commodity once it is produced for exchange, this exchange could be by barter and thus not imply the existence of any money. The exchange of commodities necessitates the specialization of a commodity in the function of expressing and measuring the exchange value of other commodities only in determined concrete conditions (whether this commodity be cocoa, sea-shells, cattle or gold does not alter its function). Other precise conditions are necessary if a precious metal is to be imposed as the general form of money. Marx is thus not working as a Hegelian by the 'deduction' of one category from another. He makes explicit the functions of one element within a structure, or of one structure within a system and explains the ranking of these functions. There is therefore no need to wait for the discovery of where and how the first money was invented to solve the 'riddle presented by money.' The object of economic theory is to render explicit these functions and their ranking in a given structure, and thus to articulate one to the others in a kind of logical genesis. But this genesis is not the real genesis and does not replace it. Once more economic theory, without being confused with economic history, provides it with the guide line for its analyses while developing thanks to its results. Here Marx totally rejects any historicism and any priority of the historical study of a system over its structural study, and anticipates by more than half a century the crises of linguistics and sociology which led de Saussure and Lowie to reject 19th century evolutionism.

Rent *cannot* be understood without capital, but capital *can*, without rent. Capital is the all-dominating economic power of bourgeois society. It must form the starting point as well as the end and can be developed before land-ownership is. After each has been considered separately, their mutual relation must be analysed. It would thus be *impractical* and *wrong* to arrange the economic categories in the *order* in which they were the *determining* factors *in the course of history*. Their order of sequence is rather determined by the *relation* which they bear to one another in modern bourgeois society, and which is the exact *opposite* of what seems to be their natural order or the order of their historical development. *It is not a matter of* the *place* which economic *relations* occupy in the *historical succession* of different *forms of society*. Still less is it a matter of the order of their succession 'in the Idea' (Proudhon) (a nebulous conception of historical movement). It is a matter of their *articulation* within modern bourgeois society.[12]

This explains why the functioning of a structure must be compatible with the functioning of other structures, or must become so if they are to belong to the same system. It illuminates the status of the analysis of commercial and financial capital in *Capital*. Commodity production is not, in fact, exclusively characteristic of modern capitalism. To the extent that an important exchange of commodities existed in some societies with as different relations of production as the great states of the ancient East, Greek and Roman slave societies and the feudal societies of the Middle Ages, the functions of commerce and to a certain extent those of credit had also to exist. But in both cases the forms and importance of these commodity relations changed. Marx shows, for example, that the rates of usury in money trade and the immense gains from international commodity trade characteristic of many precapitalist societies were incompatible with the development of industrial capital, and that this last imposed the creation of new forms of credit and the establishment of much lower interest rates. This profoundly altered the proportion of the value of commodities returned to commercial or financial capital.

> The credit system develops as a reaction against usury. But this should not be misunderstood. . . . It *signifies* no more and no less than the *subordination* of interest-bearing capital to the *conditions and requirements* of the capitalist mode of production.[13]

Thus the appearance of new structures modifies the conditions of existence and role of older structures which are obliged to transform themselves. Our analysis closes with the emergence of the notion of a *limit* to the functional compatibility of different structures. We have once again arrived at the problem of the genesis of new structures and of Marx's notion of contradiction.


## 3. TWO NOTIONS OF CONTRADICTION IN 'CAPITAL'

I shall start by listing the various contexts in which we find Marx talking of contradiction. First of all there is the contradiction between workers and capitalists. Then there are the economic 'crises' in which contradictions appear between production and consumption, between the conditions of production of value and surplus value and the conditions of their realization, and basically between productive forces and relations of production. Finally there are the contradictions between capitalism and small peasant or artisan property, capitalism and socialism, etc. This simple list reveals differences of nature and importance among these contradictions, of which some are internal to the system, and others exist between the system and other systems. They must therefore be analysed theoretically.

The first contradiction presented is that between capital and labour, between the capitalist class and the working class. One owns the capital, the other is excluded from ownership of it. One's profit is the unpaid labour of the other. What characterizes this first contradiction? It is inside capitalist 'relations of production.' It is thus an *'internal contradiction of a structure.'*

This contradiction is *specific*[14] to the capitalist mode of production. It characterizes it as such, distinguishing it from other, slave-based, feudal, etc., modes of production. As it is specific, it characterizes the system *from the beginning*, and the functioning of the system continually *reproduces* it. It is therefore original, in the sense that it is present from the beginning, and remains until the disappearance of a system. It develops with the development of the system, it is transformed by the evolution of capitalism from free competition to monopoly and by the evolution of the trade union and political organization of the working class. This contradiction is antagonistic: the function of one class is to exploit the other. It reveals itself in the class struggle. It is visible to and to some extent deciphered by the psychologist and sociologist, who distinguish individuals by their different functions and statuses, by the economist and the historian; finally, the philosopher may take it as his object when reflecting on justice, inequality, etc.

Is this basic antagonism, which would seem to occupy the forefront of the historical stage in fact the basic contradiction of capitalism? No. For Marx, the latter is the contradiction between the development and the socialization of the productive forces and the private ownership of the means of production.

> The contradiction, to put it in a very general way, consists in that the capitalist mode of production involves a tendency towards absolute development of the productive forces, regardless of the value and surplus-value it contains, and regardless of the social conditions under which capitalist production takes place; while, on the other hand, its aim is to preserve the value of the existing capital and promote its self-expansion to the highest limit (i.e. to promote an ever more rapid growth of this value).[15]

How is this contradiction visible? 'This collision appears partly in periodical crises.'[16]

In a crisis, the basic contradiction appears in the contradictions be-

86

tween production and consumption and between production and circulation of commodities. More profoundly, it appears in the tendency for the rate of profit to fall.

What are the characteristics of this contradiction?

It is not a contradiction within a structure, but *between two structures*. It is thus not directly a contradiction between individuals or groups, but between the structure of the productive forces – their ever greater socialization – and the structure of the relations of production – the private ownership of the productive forces.

Now the paradox is that this contradiction, which is basic because it explains the evolution of capitalism and its inevitable disappearance, *is not original*. It appears at 'a certain stage' of evolution,[17] at a 'certain stage of maturity'[18] of the system. And this stage is the stage of large-scale industry, i.e. a certain state of development of the productive forces. Marx clarifies this in a letter to Kugelmann: 'He would have seen that I represent *large-scale industry* not only as the *mother* of the *antagonism*, but also as the *creator* of the material and spiritual *conditions* necessary for the *solution* of this antagonism.'[19]

In the beginning, on the contrary, far from contradicting the development of the productive forces, capitalist relations of production pushed it ahead and gave it its impetuous progression from the organization of manufacture to the appearance of mechanization and heavy industry. Mechanized industry, completing the separation of agriculture and domestic rural industry (which is annihilated), 'for the first time, conquers for industrial capital the entire home-market' and gives it 'that extension and consistence which the capitalist mode of production requires,' the latter having become 'combined and scientific'[20] with the progress of the division of labour. Before machinery, manufacturing production could not achieve this 'radical transformation.'

Thus, initially, far from there being a contradiction between capitalism and the development of the productive forces, there was a correspondence, a functional compatibility which was the basis for the dynamism of technical progress and the capitalist class. But this very structural correspondence between capitalism and the forces of production means a non-correspondence of these forces of production and feudal relations of production. And for Marx this non-correspondence is the foundation of the objective contradiction between feudal and capitalist relations, between the seigneurial class and the capitalist class. For as we have seen, if there are to be capitalists, there must also be labourers facing them, free in their person, forced to put their labour power up for sale, i.e. excluded from ownership of the means of production.[21]

The immediate producer, the labourer, could only dispose of his own person after he had ceased to be attached to the soil and ceased to be the slave, serf or bondman of another . . . Hence, the historical movement which changes the producers into wage-workers, appears, on the one hand, as their emancipation from serfdom and from the fetters of the guilds. [The industrial capitalists'] conquest of social power appears as the fruit of a victorious struggle both against feudal lordship and its revolting prerogatives, and against the guilds and the fetters they laid on the free development of production and the free exploitation of man by man.'[22]

Thus the basic contradiction of the capitalist mode of production is *born* during the development of the mode of production, and *is not present* from the beginning of the system. This contradiction appears without anyone wishing to make it appear. This contradiction is therefore *unintentional*. It is a result of the action of all the agents of the system and of the development of the system itself, and is never the project of any consciousness, is never anyone's goal. Marx is therefore drawing attention to *aspects of reality which cannot be referred to any consciousness nor explained by consciousness*. It is the mode of production itself, the valuation of capital, which produces this result 'unconsciously.'[23]

But this basic, unintentional, non-original contradiction is not the opaque involuntary residue of intersubjective action. It is unintentional and without teleology, but transparent to *science* because it is 'significant.' It signifies the *limits* within which it is possible that capitalist relations of production, based on private property, may correspond to the development of the productive forces to which they have given birth.

These limits are 'immanent' to capitalist relations of production, and cannot be 'overcome,'[24] since the valuation of capital depends on the exploitation of the great mass of producers; they are thus limits expressing *objective properties* of the capitalist mode of production (not of capitalists or workers as individuals or economic agents).

'The entire capitalist mode of production is only a relative one, whose barriers are not absolute. They are absolute only for this mode, i.e. *on its basis.*'[25]

These limits are the limits within which the relations of production can remain constant, allowing for gigantic variations in the productive forces. These limits are thus objective properties of the system and these properties establish the necessity for its evolution and disappearance. They can act on the system itself and are the *causality* of the structure on itself. 'The *real barrier* of capitalist production is *capital itself.*'[26]

This causality acts everywhere, but it is impossible to localize its effect anywhere. It intervenes everywhere between one event and another to give each all its dimensions, whether conscious or not, i.e. the field of its effects, whether intentional or not. For Marx, the set of properties of the structure always comes between a cause and its effects, giving the action its objective dimensions.

Thus, while ceaselessly developing the productive forces, capital '*unconsciously* creates the *material* requirements of a higher mode of production,'[27] and necessitates the transformation of capitalist conditions of large-scale production based on private property into 'general, common, social conditions.'[28] The development of capitalism makes possible and necessary the appearance of a socialist economic system, of a 'higher' mode of production. But what does 'higher' mean here. What is the criterion on which this value-judgement is based?

The criterion is the fact that the *structure* of socialist relations of production *corresponds* functionally with the conditions of rapid development of the new, gigantic, more and more socialized productive forces created by capitalism. The criterion thus expresses the possibilities, the objective properties, of a historically determined structure. This correspondence is totally *independent* of any a priori idea of happiness, of 'true' liberty, of the essence of man, etc. Marx demonstrates the necessity and superiority of a new mode of production, thus establishing a value-judgement *without starting with* an *a priori* criterion of rationality.[29] This value-judgement is not a judgement of 'people,' it does not demonstrate any progress in 'morality,' any victory of 'ethical principles' in socialist society as against capitalist society. It is a judgement of the 'properties' of a structure, of the particular conditions of its appearance and functioning.

The necessity for the appearance of a new mode of production no longer derives from a teleology concealed in the mysteries of the essence of man as revealed to the philosopher alone, be he materialist or idealist, for it is no longer possible to read into the historically determined contradiction of capitalist relations of production with a determined level of the productive forces the philosophical drama of the revolt of the 'true essence' of man against the 'dehumanized existence' imposed on the workers by the bourgeoisie.

In *Capital*, the analysis of the contradictions of the capitalist system radically separates economic science from any ideology, and Marx has nothing more to do with the young Marx. For ideology consists precisely of transforming the 'merely historical transitory' necessity of the mode of production into a characteristic attributable to 'Nature.'[30] Marx's analysis rejects all the 'humanist' justifications which might be given for the superiority of socialism. This does not mean that he rejects the real problems that may be expressed in a humanist ideology if it is materialist. But to analyse these problems theoretically is to determine the new possibilities for social evolution specific to socialist structures.[31] By suppressing capitalist relations of exploitation and domination, the socialist society creates new conditions of social evolution just as the capitalist system did by destroying the earlier feudal society and its forms of slavery.

I have distinguished two types of contradiction in *Capital*, and shown that the basic contradiction illuminating the evolution of the system is the contradiction *between* its *structures*, and that this contradiction is born of the objective *limits* to the relations of production maintaining themselves constant while the productive forces vary in certain proportions. Now I can attempt a definition of the theory of contradiction which is implicit in Marx, and, which I think, radically opposes Marx's dialectic to that of Hegel.

## 4. THE RADICAL OPPOSITION BETWEEN MARX'S DIALECTIC AND HEGEL'S DIALECTIC

The terms which still obscure Marx's and Engels' presentation of this problem are well known. On the one hand, Marx declares that his dialectical method is the 'direct opposite' of Hegel's, Engels that the dialectic was 'useless in its Hegelian form' and that only Marx's dialectic is 'rational.' But at the same time, Marx adds that it suffices to put the Hegelian dialectic 'right side up again' to find its 'rational form,' and to set it right side up again is to remove the 'mystifying side' introduced by Hegel's absolute idealism. The matter seems simple and reassuring. But in recent articles[32] Louis Althusser has torn off this veil of words and forced us to see the unlikely absurdity of this hypothetical 'inversion of Hegel.'

> It is inconceivable that the essence of the dialectic in Hegel's work should not be contaminated by Hegelian ideology . . . that the Hegelian ideology could cease to be Hegelian and become Marxist by a simple, miraculous 'extraction.'

For Althusser the specific difference of Marx's dialectic is to be found in the fact that the latter's contradictions are 'overdetermined' in principle. This answer does not seem to me to grasp the essential point, although it provides valuable positive elements at another level. To take up the problem from another angle, Marx describes two kinds of contradiction. One of these, within the structure of the relations of production, appears before the other which is produced little by little between *the two structures* of the capitalist mode of production, the relations of production and the productive forces. The first contradiction appears and disappears with the mode of production. The second appears with the development of the system as an effect of the functioning of the first contradiction, but it is this second one which creates the material conditions for the disappearance of the system; it is the fundamental contradiction. The relation between the two contradictions thus shows that the *first* contradiction, within the relations of production, *does not contain within itself the set of conditions for its solution*. The material conditions of this solution can only exist outside it as the productive forces are a *reality completely distinct* from the relations of production and *irreducible* to them, a reality which has its own internal conditions of development and its own temporality.

The other conditions of solution of the contradiction in the relations of production are found at the level of the political, cultural superstructures, and these structures are equally irreducible to the relations of production and have their own modalities of development. For Marx the solution to an internal contradiction of the structures of the relations of production is not created solely by the internal development of this contradiction. The greater part of the conditions of this solution is outside the contradiction, and irreducible to its content.

On the other hand, the possibility of resolving the second contradiction, between the structures of the economic system, is born of the internal development of the system (and, as we shall see, from the movement of all the structures of the society). The solution to this second contradiction is a change in the structure of the relations of production *to make them correspond* with that of the productive forces. This change implies the exclusion of private ownership of the means of production, thus suppressing *the very basis of the internal contradiction* in capitalist relations of production. But this suppression is only possible at a certain moment in the development of the mode of production, a moment in the development of the productive forces. The class contradictions within the relations of production may 'simmer' but no solution will emerge necessarily, unless there is development of the productive forces (on the contrary, there may be a cyclical reproduction of social conflict, stagnation, etc.).

Our analysis definitely excludes the possibility that Marx could have held a theory of the 'identity of opposites.' This hypothesis was, in fact, invented by Hegel to show that there is an *internal solution* to *the internal contradictions of a structure*. If such a solution is possible, each of the elements contradicted within the structure must at the same time be its own opposite. The thesis must be itself and its opposite the antithesis if

91

the synthesis is already contained in their contradiction. Marx's work radically excludes this possibility, for neither the elements in contradiction within a structure, nor the structures in contradiction within a system *are reducible to one another*, identical to one another.

This shows that the identity of opposites, the basic structure of the Hegelian dialectic *is only necessary* to provide 'proof' of absolute idealism and *to establish Hegelianism* as the absolute knowledge of the absolute spirit, a totality which itself contradicts itself in the exteriority of nature and the interiority of the Logos, maintaining its identity through all its contradictions. The identity of opposites is, in fact, the magical operator which Hegel had to provide himself to build the palace of ideas[33] which is absolute knowledge, and to give a rational appearance to the ideological sleight of hand which serves as the unprovable point of departure for absolute idealism. Thus Hegel's philosophical idealism determines the specific internal content of this notion of contradiction, and this structure, based on the principle of the identity of opposites, is the direct inverse of Marx's, making the dialectic 'useless for science.'[34] In fact anything, i.e. nothing, can be proved with the hypothesis of the identity of opposites.

It is now easy to understand why Marx declared from the *Contribution* on: 'Hence, *it is the simplest matter* with a Hegelian to treat production and consumption *as identical* . . .'[35] and added: 'The result we arrive at *is not* that production, distribution, exchange and consumption are identical, but that they are all members of one totality, differences within one *unity*.'[36]

And in *Anti-Dühring*, Engels defended Marx's dialectical method by showing that it could not be reduced to 'these dialectical . . . mazes . . . this mixed and misconceived idea (according to which) *it all amounts to the same thing in the end*,'[37] where the negation of the negation serves 'as the midwife to deliver the future from the womb of the past,' and consists of 'the childish pastime of . . . alternately declaring that a rose is a rose and that it is not a rose.'[38]

Here Althusser's analyses are really relevant. The postulate of the identity of opposites guaranteed Hegel at any time an imaginary internal solution to the internal contradictions to be analysed, and this solution is usually a magical ideological operation within a 'simple' dialectic.

How then can we explain the impotence of Marx's commentators in the localization of the radical differences between Marx and Hegel? The answer is hardly complex. The *theoretical distinction* of the two kinds of contradiction (within and between structures), and the clarification of their reciprocal articulation were never explicitly stressed or developed by either Marx or Engels. This being so, the 'eye-catching' contradiction was that between capitalists and workers, and the second contradiction was confused with this one, i.e. with the structure's internal contradiction. Analysis thus slid over into the sphere of Hegel's mystified and mystificatory dialectic, the fascinating dialectic of the identity of opposites, the internal solution, etc. And Marx's and Engels' equivocal formulations did not help to dispel this fascination, nor did the antiscientific habits of dogmatic Marxism:

> The capitalist mode of appropriation, the result of the capitalist mode of production, produces capitalist private property. This is the first negation of individual private property, as founded on the labour of the proprietor. But capitalist production begets, with the inexorability of a law of Nature, its own negation. It is the negation of the negation.[39]

But what is for Marx no more than a metaphor, a way of expressing the movement of capital, becomes for Engels 'an extremely general – and for this reason extremely far-reaching and important – law of development of nature, history and thought.'[40]

In fact, to the extent that the specific character of Marx's notion of contradiction remained unanalysed, the notion of the negation of the negation was the only general Hegelian concept which still *seemed rational* when the mystification of the identity of opposites had been got rid of.

As I understand it, Marx's analysis of the basic notion of contradiction between structures tallies with the most recent scientific practice.[41] The notion makes explicit certain objective properties of structures, the objective *limits* to their possibilities of reproduction, to their remaining *essentially constant*, given the variations of their internal and external conditions of functioning, and, more *profoundly*, to their reproducing their relations, their *connection* with other structures. The appearance of a contradiction is, in fact, the appearance of a limit to the conditions of invariance of a structure. Beyond this limit a change in structure becomes necessary. In this perspective, the notion of contradiction I am putting forward would perhaps be of interest to cybernetics. This science explores the limit possibilities and internal regulation that allow any system, physiological, economic or whatever, to maintain itself in spite of a determined range of variation of its internal and external conditions of functioning. This analysis brings together the sciences of nature and the sciences of man. To give a frivolous example, I could suggest that if a glaciation caused the disappearance of the dinosaur from the face of the earth, this species did not perish through the spontaneous development of its internal contradictions, but through a contradiction

93

between its internal physiological structure and the structure of its external conditions of existence.

My theory of contradiction should therefore be able to restore to the dialectic its scientific character, and, for the same reasons, this scientific dialectic can only be materialist. For if the dialectical method no longer depends on the hypothesis of the 'identity of opposites' and if the contradictions born of the functioning of a structure express its 'limits' and are partially conditioned in appearance and resolution *outside* that structure, there is *no internal teleology* regulating the evolution of nature and history.

On this basis it should be possible to establish a new dialogue – centering on the hypothesis of the necessary correspondence of structures – between the sciences and Marxism and between structuralism and Marxism. I should like to close this essay with a confrontation of this hypothesis and another of Marx's theses which might seem to contradict it, or at least to reduce its importance by ideological sleight of hand: I mean the thesis of the determinant role played 'in the last instance'[42] by economic structures in the evolution of social life.

Everyone is familiar with the famous sentence from the *Preface* to *A Contribution to the Critique of Political Economy*:

> [The] relations of production correspond to a definite stage of development of (the) material powers of production. The set of these relations of production constitutes the economic structure of society – the real foundation, on which legal and political superstructures arise and to which definite forms of social consciousness correspond . . . The mode of production of material life determines the general character of the social, political, and spiritual processes of life . . . With the change of the economic base the entire immense superstructure is more or less rapidly transformed.[43]

The peculiar causality that Marx grants to the economic in the interplay of the set of all the reciprocal causalities of infrastructure and superstructures has generally been misinterpreted. We have seen that even within the infrastructure Marx distinguishes between relations of production and productive forces, and never confuses these two structures. This irreducibility of structures cannot be confined to the economy, and we must start from the fact that each social structure has for Marx its own content and mode of functioning and evolution. This irreducibility immediately excludes two kinds of interpretation of the determinant causality of the economy.

On the one hand, non-economic structures cannot 'emerge' from economic relations; the causality of the economic cannot be the genesis of the superstructure from within the infrastructure. On the other hand, non-economic structures are not simple 'phenomena' accompanying economic activity with only a passive reaction on social life while the economic relations are the sole active causality with more or less 'automatic'[44] effect. In either case, it is hard to see by what bizarre alchemy the economy becomes, say, kinship, or for what mysterious reason it should be (badly) hidden behind kinship. We must therefore look elsewhere for an answer, and study the notion of 'correspondence' of structures more closely.

For example, let us examine the process of production in our capitalist society. The relations of production between capitalists and workers and the latter's obligation to work for the former seem largely independent of the religious, political or even familial ties which they may have among themselves. Each social structure seems broadly 'autonomous,' and the economist tends to treat non-economic structures as 'exogenous variables,' and to look for a rationality that is economic 'in itself.' The correspondence of structures therefore seems mainly 'external.' In an archaic society, this is not the situation. The Marxist economist, for example, easily distinguishes between the productive forces of these societies (hunting, fishing, agriculture, etc.), but he cannot distinguish their relations of production 'in isolation.' Or at best, he can distinguish them in the functioning of the kinship relations themselves. The latter determine the rights of individuals to the land and its products, their obligations to work for others, to receive or to give. They also determine the authority of certain individuals over others in political and religious matters. In such a society, kinship relations dominate social life. How, within Marx's perspective, can we understand both the *dominant* role of kinship and the *determinant* role of the economy in the last instance?

This is impossible if economy and kinship are treated as base and superstructure. In an archaic society kinship relations *function* as relations of production, just as they function as political relations. To use Marx's vocabulary, kinship relations are here *both* infrastructure and superstructure[45] and it would be a fair guess that the complexity of kinship relations in archaic societies relates to the multiple functions they take on in such societies.[46] It could also be suggested that the dominant role and complex structure of kinship relations in archaic societies are related to the general structure of the productive forces and their low level of development, which impose the co-operation of individuals and therefore group life for subsistence and reproduction.[47]

In this abstract example, the economy-kinship correspondence no longer appears as an external relation, but as internal correspondence,

95

without for all that confusing economic relations between kinsfolk with their political or sexual relations, etc. Thus, to the extent that kinship in this kind of society really functions as relations of production, the determinant role of the economy does not contradict the dominant role of kinship, but is expressed through it.[48]

This perspective makes it possible to predict one of the contributions Marx will make in the future to the scientific study of social structures and their multiple evolution, a contribution profoundly different from those his exegesists attribute to him, or deny him. For what are, in fact, irreducible are the functions and evolution of structures, so their differentiation should be explained by the transformation and evolution of their functions. It would be possible, for example, to guess that the appearance of new conditions of production in archaic societies will modify their demography, demand new forms of authority, and bring with them new relations of production. It is a fair guess that beyond a certain limit the old kinship relations will no longer be able to fulfil these new functions. The latter will develop outside kinship and will bring forth distinct political and religious social structures which will in their turn function as relations of production. It is not the kinship relations that are transformed into political relations, but the political function of the old kinship relations which develops on the basis of new problems. The kinship relations will shift into a new role with a different social importance, and the political and religious relations, charged with new functions (both infra- and super-structural), will come to occupy the liberated central place.

To explain the determinant role of the economy is at the same time to explain the *dominant* role of non-economic structures in a given type of society, and societies distinct in time and space belong to the same 'type' if their *structure as a whole* is comparable, i.e. if the *relation* between their social structures determined by the *functions* and the *importance* of each of them is comparable. This perspective makes it possible to reconcile the usual oppositions: structure-event (anthropology-history) and structure-individual (sociology-psychology) in a new way.

An event – whether from outside or inside – always acts on the whole structure by acting on one of its elements. The set of known and unknown properties of one or several structures always intervenes between a cause and its effects. This structural causality gives an event all its conscious and unconscious dimensions and explains its intentional and unintentional effects. It is therefore incorrect to abandon the structuralist viewpoint or to *leave structure aside to account for events*. When, by their acts, men create the conditions for the appearance of new structures, in fact, they open up the way to new fields of objective

96

possibility of which they are largely ignorant, which they discover through events and whose limits they submit to necessarily when the conditions of functioning of these structures vary, and when these no longer fulfil the same function and are transformed. The intentional behavioural rationality of the members of a society is always inscribed within the basic unintentional rationality of the hierarchical structure of the social relations characterizing that society. Instead of starting from the individuals and their hierarchies of preference to explain the role and relation of the structures of a society, it is necessary rather to explain this role and this relation in all their aspects, known or unknown by the society, and look in this hierarchy of structures for the basis of the hierarchy of 'values,' i.e. the social norms of prescribed behaviour. This hierarchy of 'values' could then illuminate the hierarchy of needs of individuals playing a given role with a given status in the society.

This would make it impossible to challenge history with anthropology[49] or anthropology with history, to set psychology and sociology or sociology and history in sterile opposition. The possibility of human 'sciences' would definitely depend on the possibility of discovering the laws of the functioning, evolution and internal reciprocal correspondence of social structures. And one day these human sciences could give the lie to Aristotle by becoming sciences of the 'individual' as well. The possibility of human 'sciences' depends on a generalization of a method of structural analysis which has become capable of explaining the conditions of variation and evolution of structures and their functions. This generalization is today very unevenly developed, depending on whether the study is economics, kinship, politics or religion. Perhaps Marx's work, purged of equivocation, could help accelerate this development.

NOTES AND REFERENCES

1. Claude Lévi-Strauss: 'On Structure' in *Structural Anthropology*, Ch. XV, p. 279.
2. *Ibid.*, p. 280. [This is a direct translation of the French text used by Godelier (*Anthropologie Structurale*, p. 306); Lévi-Strauss' (original) English version reads: 'make immediately intelligible all the observed facts' – *Translator's note*.]
3. This is a deliberate simplification, for profit may or may not correspond to the surplus value really produced in an enterprise.
4. *Capital*, I, p. 540 (Moscow 1961). Emphases N.G. unless otherwise stated.
5. *Capital*, III, p. 797.
6. In the same way for Spinoza knowledge of the second kind

(mathematical knowledge) does not suppress that of the first kind (everyday experience).

7. *Capital*, I, pp. 714–715.

8. This is not weakened by the phenomenon of social mobility which allows certain workers to become capitalists, or which is produced by competition and the ruin of certain capitalists or category of enterprises.

9. This diachrony seems to be always recreated in the synchrony or at least to show the multiple modes of existence of the same structure, once given the local variations of its conditions of functioning. Cf. Marx: '. . . the same economic basis – the same from the standpoint of its main conditions – due to innumerable different empirical circumstances, natural environment, racial relations, external historical influences, etc., (is not prevented) from showing infinite variations and graduations in appearance, which can be ascertained only by analysis of the empirically given circumstances.' (*Capital*, III, p. 772)

10. *Capital*, III, p. 580.

11. *Capital*, I, pp. 47–48.

12. *A Contribution to the Critique of Political Economy*, trans. N. I. Stone (Chicago 1904), pp. 303–304. [Corrected – *Translator's note*]

13. *Capital*, III, p. 586.

14. *Capital*, III, p. 856.

15. *Capital*, III, p. 244.

16. *Capital*, III, p. 258.

17. *Capital*, III, p. 237.

18. *Capital*, III, p. 861.

19. Letter to Kugelmann, 17th March, 1868.

20. *Capital*, I, pp. 748–749.

21. *Capital*, I, p. 168.

22. *Capital*, I, p. 715.

23. *Capital*, III, p. 254.

24. *Capital*, III, p. 245.

25. *Capital*, III, p. 252.

26. *Capital*, III, p. 245, Marx's emphasis.

27. *Capital*, III, p. 254.

28. *Capital*, III, p. 259.

29. Engels writes, in a letter to Paul Lefargue, 11th August, 1884: 'Marx rejected the "political, social and economic ideal" you attribute to him. A man of science has no ideals, he elaborates scientific results, and if he is also politically committed, he struggles for them to be put into practice. But if he has ideals, he cannot be a man of science, since he would then be biassed from the start.' (*Correspondance Engels-Lafargue*, Éditions Sociales, Paris, p. 235.)

30. *Capital*, III, p. 237.

31. See Marx's whole discussion of the Gotha programme and his savaging of its humanist declarations of 'equal rights,' justice for labour, etc.

32. 'Contradiction et Surdétermination' and 'Sur la Dialectique Matérialiste,' re-edited in *Pour Marx*, Paris 1965; 'Contradiction and Overdetermination,' *New Left Review*, 41, January–February 1967.

33. In *The Concept of Dread*, Kierkegaard takes issue with Hegel and rationalism over this point, opening the way to existentialism.

34. When Lenin declares that the dialectic is 'the theory of the identity of opposites' or 'the study of the contradiction in the very essence of things,' I suggest that he is proposing a false equivalence between these two definitions.

In the same way, Mao Tse-tung constantly confuses the unity of opposites with their identity: 'How . . . can we speak of identity or unity [of opposites]? The fact is that a contradictory aspect cannot exist all by itself. If there is not the opposite aspect, each aspect loses the conditions of its existence . . . Without landlords, there would be no tenant-peasants; without tenant-peasants, there would also be no landlords. Without the bourgeoisie there would be no proletariat; without the proletariat there would also be no bourgeoisie . . . All opposite elements are like this: Under certain conditions they are on the one hand opposed to each other and on the other hand interconnected, interpenetrated, interpermeated and interdependent; that is what we mean by identity.' (*On Contradiction*, Peking, 1960, p. 47; and in *Selected Works*, I.)

35. *A Contribution to the Critique of Political Economy, op. cit.*, p. 282.

36. *Ibid.*, p. 291. [Corrected, *Translator's note*]

37. *Anti-Dühring*, p. 169.

38. *Ibid.*, p. 195. As Marx and Engels well knew, the dialectical method did not lead Hegel to confuse all opposites in their identity, nor to incoherence in his philosophical discourse. No doubt the identity of opposites is both *the principle and the object* of this discourse, and therefore, its *imaginary basis*, the speculative foundation of the theoretical validity of absolute idealism. But it is not the sole principle invoked by Hegel since the principle of the identity of opposites *a fortiori* establishes the principle of their unity. There can therefore be positive islands in the sea of Hegel's speculative discourse, induced from a reflection on the unity of opposites. For example, in the *Phenomenology of Mind*, the master-slave relation, within the speculative identity of master and slave (the master is the slave of his slave, the slave the master of his master), the relation of master and slave is constituted by two asymmetrical relations, that of master to slave, and that of slave to master, which are not superimposed or confused. The master-slave relation is polarized by this fact, and evolves in a determined, irreversible direction.

Perhaps what Marx meant by the positive 'nucleus' (*Kern*) of Hegel's dialectic is the following group of properties: the unity of opposites, the asymmetry of the relations within this unity, a relation oriented in a certain direction and animated with an irreversible movement. Perhaps certain Hegelian analyses, of secondary importance, could be added to this group of properties: for example, the hypothesis of the transformation of quantity into quality.

This illuminates the two metaphors used by Marx to indicate the relations of his dialectical method with that of Hegel: the metaphor of the 'nucleus' and that of the 'inversion.' For it was not sufficient to put the Hegelian dialectic back onto its feet to give it a completely 'rational' air, since it was first necessary to amputate the principle of the identity of opposites which was both its first methodological principle and the last basis of absolute idealism. Such nuclear fission shows that the nucleus itself was not preserved intact within Marx's dialectic as the metaphor pretends.

But it is difficult to imagine that Marx, the only nineteenth or twentieth century thinker to revolutionize both philosophy and a domain of scientific knowledge, could be *completely* mistaken about his relations to Hegel. Probably what Marx conceived as his theoretical debt to Hegel, as the positive heritage handed down to him, was this fragment of the nucleus: the concept of the unity of opposites and the group of attached properties. In that case it has to be stated – as Marx himself did – that as an *explicitly developed theory* of the unity of opposites, the dialectical method has as yet no scientific, i.e. no real existence. This is even more true if, as we shall see, the various kinds of contradiction should perhaps be linked to the concept of the 'limit,' which means that there were already – as the very existence of *Capital* proves – as many *implicitly* dialectical analyses as there were scientific practices elucidating the limits of functioning in domains of 'objects' investigated by the sciences. But nothing ensures *a priori* that, once explicit, the methodological principles of each of these practices (whose operational norms work in the shadow of the scientific exploit) will take their places in one unique, unifying dialectic.

39. *Capital*, I, p. 763.

40. *Anti-Dühring*, p. 193; cf. p. 190, the fifteen-line sketch of the dialectical evolution of humanity from primitive communism to real communism via private property.

41. And within this practice, mathematics and cybernetics have a privileged place in the exploration of the notion of the 'limit.' This is one of the reasons their use is becoming more and more general in the social sciences. But the real effectivity of mathematics is circumscribed in principle within the limited set of problems which can already be formalized and for whose treatment mathematics has sufficient operational power.

For more complex problems of structural analysis – for example the analysis of the *modalities* of the *connection* of the structures of a system (whether social or not) so as to be able to explain why these modalities induce a *dominant function* within these connected structures – the scientific concept of structure is apparently still too narrow. Further, to use the concept of a limit is to determine the set of relations *allowed* between the structures of a system, the set of variations compatible with these structures. It is also to determine the set of incompatible variations which would provoke the elimination of one of the connected structures and change the system. If the first already seems to have been partially explored (for example, the mathematical concept of a *category* of sets takes as its object a set of things *and* the system of functions allowed between these things), we are still largely ignorant as far as the second is concerned.

As soon as mathematics is applied to a field of problems for which it is still too weak, there is a risk of creating illusory knowledge, scientific phantoms. There is also a risk that without knowing or wishing it, i.e. *with no ideological intent*, the invisible but real line which always

100

separates scientific knowledge from ideology will have been crossed.

42. Engels: letter to Joseph Bloch, 21st September, 1890: 'If somebody twists this into saying that the economic element is the *only* determining one, he transforms that proposition into a meaningless, abstract, senseless phrase.' (Marx-Engels: *Selected Works* II, p. 488.)

43. *A Contribution to the Critique of Political Economy, op. cit.*, pp. 11–12; Marx-Engels: *Selected Works*, I, p. 363. [Corrected, *Translator's note*]

44. Engels: Letter to Starkenberg, 25th January, 1894.

45. In *The Origin of the Family, Private Property and the State* (Marx-Engels: *Selected Works* II, p. 170, Preface to the First Edition), Engels, by declaring that 'the determining factor in history is, in the last resort, the production and reproduction of immediate life,' implies that kinship plays a determinant role *alongside* the economy, whereas in these societies it is really an element of the economic infrastructure.

46. This plurifunctionality of kinship has led Beattie and other anthropologists to claim that kinship has no content of its own, but is a container or symbolic form in which the content of social life is expressed (economic, political, religious relations and so on), i.e. that kinship is merely language, a means of expression. While not quarrelling with the notion that kinship functions as a language symbolizing social life, Schneider objects that kinship also has its own content which can be brought out by *subtracting* from its functioning the economic, political and religious *aspects*. The set of relations of consanguinity and alliance which serve as the means of expression of social life and serve as the *terms* of the symbolic language of kinship will then appear. Here kinship is both a particular content of social life and serves as the mode of appearance and expression of all other contents.

But when he sets out to rediscover a content for kinship in this way, Schneider hardly evades the biologism for which he condemns Gellner. Everyone knows that the set of biological relations of consanguinity and alliance is not kinship, as kinship is always a particular 'group' of these relations within which descent and alliance are socially regulated. Because these relations are selected and 'retained,' real kinship is not a biological fact, but a *social* one.

Schneider and Beattie have in common the error of looking for the content of this kind of kinship *outside* the economic, the political and the religious, since kinship is neither an external form nor a residual content but functions *directly* and internally as economic and political relations and so on, and therefore functions as a mode of expression of social life and as a symbolic form of that life.

The scientific problem thus becomes the determination of why this is so in many types of society, and, in the methodological sphere, the conclusion would seem to be that the conceptual couples: form-basis, container-content are not the right ones for an account of the functioning of social structures.

Gellner: 'Ideal Language and Kinship Structure,' *Philosophy of Science*, vol. XXIV, 1957; Needham: 'Descent Systems and Ideal Language,' *Ibid.*, vol. XXVII, 1960; Gellner: 'The Concept of Kinship,' *Ibid.*, vol. XXVII, 1960; Barnes: 'Physical and Social Kinship,' *Ibid.*, vol. XXVIII, 1961; Gellner: 'Nature and Society in Social Anthropology,' *Ibid.*, vol. XXX, 1963; Schneider: 'The Nature of Kinship,' *Ibid.*, vol. XXXI, 1964.

47.  On this see Claude Lévi-Strauss: 'The situation is quite different in groups for which the satisfaction of economic needs rests entirely on conjugal society and the sexual division of labour. Not only are man and woman differently specialized technically, and therefore depend on one another for the construction of the things necessary for daily tasks, but they devote themselves to the production of different kinds of food. A complete, and above all a regular diet thus depends on that veritable "production cooperative," the household . . . Particularly in primitive societies, where the harshness of the geographical environment and the rudimentary state of technique make hunting and gardening, collecting and gathering equally hazardous, existence is almost impossible for an individual left to himself.' (*Structures Élémentaires, op. cit.*, p. 48.)

48.  Marx wrote of the 'rank and influence' of social structures in a society characterized by a determined production: 'It is the universal light with which all the other colours are tinged and are modified through its peculiarity. It is a special ether which determines the specific gravity of everything that appears in it.' (*A Contribution to the Critique of Political Economy*, Introduction, *op. cit.*, p. 302.)

49.  Cf. Roland Barthes: 'Les Sciences Humaines et l'Oeuvre de Lévi-Strauss,' *Annales*, November–December 1964, p. 1086.

# SECTION II

# SOCIAL CHANGE AND EVOLUTION

# INTRODUCTION TO SECTION II

A fundamental concern in Marx's sociology is the attempt to account for social processes of structuration and decay. Since history is conceived by Marx as a progression of historically specific forms of social relations (modes of production), the explication of the transformation of these modes of production becomes a central problematic for Marxist social science. There are two important questions here. First, the process of social change demands explanation – its forms, causes, consequences. Marx's attempt to grapple with this question resulted in the general theory of social change presented schematically in the preface to the *Critique of Political Economy* (1970:20–21). Social change occurs through time as a consequence of the reproduction of a given system of social relations in which latent structural contradictions become manifested in open class conflict. The forms that these struggles take are historically specific, but the *logic* of this general model is universal, deriving from Marx's analysis of the centrality of the productive process and the antagonistic nature of all pre-socialist forms of productive relations.

Second, this processual model of social change gives rise to the question of historical periodization, or a taxonomy of social relations. Marx never gave a definitive solution to this problem of the number and types of historical modes of production, in part because he was centrally preoccupied with the emergence and transformation of a specific mode, the capitalist, and in part because he considered the taxonomy of modes of production to be a question which was to remain open to modification by empirical research. As a consequence, this has remained an area of intense debate within contemporary Marxism. The structure and historical role of the Asiatic mode of production, the nature and universality of primitive communism, the specific form of class relations in the Eastern European Bloc, the character of neo-colonial and peasant societies, the transitions to capitalism and socialism; all of these important topics remain unsettled and work in these areas is still inconclusive, despite a great deal of recent scholarship exemplified by Barry Hindness' and Paul Hirst's excellent *Pre-Capitalist Modes of Production* (1975).

105

The four articles in this section all touch upon this important category of social change in Marx's sociology. The first essay, by the Italian sociologist Franco Ferrarotti, examines the role of technological change within Marx's general theory. Observing that Marx was not a simple technological determinist, Ferrarotti nonetheless stresses the importance of the history and development of productive technique in Marxist theory and concludes that a return to Marx is indispensable for a comprehensive understanding of modern problems of technical change.

The second paper, by Nicholas Lobkowicz, contains a subtle and penetrating analysis of the character of Marxian historical laws. Rejecting Karl Popper's (1950;1957) well-known attempt to interpret Marxism as a form of historicism radically opposed to the logic of the natural sciences, Lobkowicz finds the conception of historically limited developmental laws presented by Marx (i.e. the laws of capitalist development) to be fully intelligible as well as compatible with the strictest canons of the philosophy of science. This conclusion leads Lobkowicz to call for a re-evaluation of Marx's contribution to contemporary social science in the analysis of historical change.

The question of the relation between the natural and social sciences and their intersection in Marx's work is the focus of the contribution by Valentino Gerratana. Whereas Lobkowicz approaches this problem through an examination of Karl Popper's critique of Marx's alleged historicism in terms of the rules of scientific method, Gerratana proceeds through a comparison of the two greatest thinkers of the nineteenth century in the social and natural sciences, Marx and Charles Darwin. Specifically, he is concerned with the extent of Darwin's influence on Marx's theoretical work in the two realms of the relationship between natural evolution and human history and the question of a unitary method for the sciences. Here, Gerratana carefully reviews Marx's appreciation of Darwin's *Origin of Species* as an exemplary application of the same materialist method which Marx was attempting to introduce into the study of human history, while not omitting crucial points of difference. He concludes with a re-examination of the interconnection between these two areas of scientific research, admitting that the problem of the relationship between the natural and social sciences, or between the natural sciences and philosophy, is necessarily complex and does not submit to easy solution.

The final contribution to this section, by Norman Levine, takes us directly to the discussion on the Asiatic mode of production inaugurated by Karl Wittfogel's idiosyncratic work *Oriental Despotism* (1964) and to the even more fundamental debate over the unilinear (universal)

106

versus multilinear (particularistic) nature of Marx's historical materialism. At issue here is whether Marx saw a necessary historical succession of modes of production occurring, in the nature of a universal evolution, or whether the progression Ancient society – feudalism – capitalism was historically specific and unique to the development of Western Europe.

Levine undertakes to answer this question through an examination of Marx's writings on the *mir*, the ancient Russian rural community. Representing a pre-capitalist form, Levine argues, the communal *mir* formed a hindrance to the development of rationalized capitalist agricultural production in nineteenth century Russia. Yet he finds convincing evidence in Marx's writings that Marx saw the *mir*, because of its collectivist principles of communal organization, as providing the organizational means by which Russia could develop directly from agrarian feudalism to socialist industrialism, by passing the stage of capitalist industrialization altogether. Levine concludes that the interpretation of historical materialism as a dogma of historically inevitable laws governing the unilinear development of all societies marks a serious deformation of Marx's thought.

# NOTES ON MARX AND THE STUDY
# OF TECHNICAL CHANGE*

FRANCO FERRAROTTI

Present day industrial sociology shows an increasing inability to cope with the problem of technical change. This inability shows itself in full with regard to the methods for the collecting and processing of empirical data as well as with regard to the question of general interpretation. Despite foundation money and considerable research effort, technical or, as some sociologists prefer to say, 'technological' change remains an essentially elusive phenomenon. 'In the past decade,' it has been aptly remarked, 'there has been a proliferation of published works on the subject of technological change and its consequences for society, industry and individual. This exchange of ideas, however, has not produced a commonly accepted definition of "technological change." Indeed, in general, it is questionable whether the public discussion has even resulted in a widely accepted terminology for many aspects of the subject.'[1] This is paradoxical and disturbing at the same time: an apparently advanced society, which likes to think of itself in terms of instrumental activism and technical know-how, is ignorant of the very basis of its own self-definition and self-image.

It is my contention that a careful rereading of Marx (in particular *The Poverty of Philosophy* and the first volume of *Capital*) still is of great relevance to a comprehensive understanding, and to an eventual integrated explanation of technical change. This does not mean that Marxism amounts to nothing more than a special variety of technological determinism, although it should be clearly recognized that Marx was, in his time, a thoroughly up-to-date student of the evolution of industrial machinery in the most painstakingly analytic sense. A construction of Marxism as technological determinism can, undoubtedly, be made to appear largely plausible through the recognition of a privileged position, within the system, for the technical variable. This reduc-

* Originally published in *Marx and Contemporary Scientific Thought*, (ed.) The International Social Science Council, The Hague: Mouton & Co. 1969. Reprinted with permission of International Social Science Council and International Council for Philosophy and Humanistic Studies.

tive operation has been tried by J. H. Hallowell[2] among others. He capitalizes on some terminological ambiguities of Marx especially in the *Critique of Political Economy*, following a lead by Hans Kelsen according to which there is, in Marx, a strange ambiguity in the meaning of the relationship between reality and ideology, which makes very uncertain the foundation of Marx's theory of knowledge.[3] Hallowell expands this kind of criticism to involve, in a similar set of strictures, the Marxian dichotomy between the technical mode of production and the social being, or *gesellschaftliches Sein*, as a determining factor of consciousness for human beings, and finally concludes that, for Marx, history is intelligible because it is the history of technology; tools are in fact man-made, and what is man-made is intelligible.

Here the reductive interpretation becomes apparent: the determining factor is reduced simply to the 'mode of production' conceived in purely technical terms regardless of the more historically and sociologically relevant concept of 'social being.' Certainly Marx attributes great importance to technological development. The bitter polemic with Proudhon, whose peasant and anarchistic, anti-mechanization attitude must have clashed with and irritated his urban, cosmopolitan outlook, is there to prove it. But the great modernity and value of Marx's standpoint lies precisely in the fact that he does not attribute any dogmatic priority to any single component or dimension of the social process. On the contrary, he insists on the necessity of viewing the social system as a system (although not in the reified meaning of the term). The social system is conceived as a dynamic and historically determined globality which is susceptible of scientific analysis on four different levels: (a) the stage of development of productive forces; (b) the prevailing mode of production and exchange; (c) the social structure or, as Marx puts it in *The German Ideology*, the 'civil society'; (d) the specific political and general intellectual conditions.

These four levels are certainly interrelated and interacting in any given historical situation. They condition each other but their determining power is not obviously the same; to ensure for the social process its driving force against total or relative stagnation, they are active at different levels with respect to the global social structure and have a differential weight with respect to historical development as a whole. A superficial interpretation could perhaps attribute to level (a), that is to the productive forces in the narrow, technical sense, the role of a (relatively) independent variable, but then it would be impossible to avoid a definitely technocratic bias which is essentially alien to Marxism. For Marx and Engels the basic connotation by which a society may be defined, is not, in fact, its technology but its 'social structure,' or in other words its 'class structure.' The concept of 'class' and 'class structure' is the fundamental concept. Were the technological factor to play a determining and really crucial role in historical development, the first relevant consequence would necessarily amount to the dropping of the dialectical approach, since technological development cannot be analysed by it or, more simply, does not permit that approach. *Its character is cumulative and evolutionary, not dialectical.* Its analysis rests on sociological and experimental research, and eludes a dialectical historical approach.

In this connection it is perhaps useful to mention another recent attempt to see Marx as a 'thinker of technics.'[4] Axelos' intent is clearly stated as aiming at an analysis of Marxian thought as 'a descriptive and dialectical interpretation' of technics as a human, voluntaristic initiative: 'men were naturally prone to division of labor; in the future, they will be in a position to devote themselves *voluntarily* to social activities, going beyond the suffocating framework of the division of labor . . . One should never lose sight of the very strict connection which binds division of labor to property and the different forms of division of labor to the different forms of property' (italics in the text). This attempt has merits. In a cultural situation in which Marx is usually interpreted and commented upon *sub specie philosophica* it underlines the peculiar nature of Marxian analysis which is not deduced from Platonic ideas or neo-Kantian categories but is rather outlined and set forth in its day-to-day unfolding through practice and the instruments of practice: 'neither *politics* nor *religion* nor *art* nor *philosophy* are for him (Marx) constitutive forces of man's history (even alienated) of the ways in which man and the world are bound together. Practice alone is the source of truth and reality; it is practice which binds man to the world . . .' (italics in the text).

This is very well and convincingly put: practice with its instruments or, in other words, technology. More than a comment on Marx, it is an inspired repetition. In fact in the first volume of *Capital*, we read:

Technology discloses man's mode of dealing with Nature, the process of production by which he sustains his life, and thereby also lays bare the mode of formation of his social relations, and of the mental conceptions that flow from them. Every history of religion even, that fails to take account of this material basis, is uncritical. It is in reality much easier to discover by analysis the earthly core of the misty creations of religion than, conversely, it is to develop from the actual relations of life the corresponding celestialised forms of those relations. The latter method is the only materialistic and therefore the only scientific one. The weak points in the abstract materialism of natural science, a materialism that excludes history and its process, are at once evident from the abstract and ideological conceptions of its spokesmen whenever they venture beyond the bounds of their own speciality.[5]

In other words, the problem does not consist of opposing *Unterbau* and *Überbau*, as many of Marx's disciples, beginning with Engels, would do in a naturalistic fashion. For Marx, what is most important is to look hard at the 'practical basis,' to observe phenomena scientifically according to precise heuristic procedures and definite methodological controls. There is a whole literature on the subject of the 'dialectical impatience' and 'messianic spirit' of Marx, which is not entirely unfounded. But it is a fact that Marx, as we noted earlier, provides strikingly accurate descriptions of industrial machinery, and of the major technical operations of the stage of the industrialization process of his day. It would be enough to read Chapter 15 of the first volume of *Capital* to be convinced *ad abundantiam*. It is difficult to understand how one can talk about the sociology of work and industry without going back to it specifically. For instance, with one sentence Marx disposes of the hard-dying legend of the steam engine as the mother of the 'industrial revolution,' and certainly he does not consider substituting for it the 'watch,' as Lewis Mumford would have it. Marx sees with astonishing perceptiveness that the revolutionary machine is actually the machine tool; this is the machine that made a revolution in the form of steam engines necessary. As soon as man, instead of working with an implement on the object of his labor, becomes merely the motive power of an implement machine, it is a mere accident that motive 'power takes the disguise of human muscle: and it may equally well take the form of wind, water or steam.'[6]

In my opinion the importance of Marx as a sociologist lies in this capacity for empirical, factual observation essentially guided by a formidable apparatus of historical-predictive hypotheses at the macrosociological level. No doubt most of these hypotheses do not appear to be easily operationalized; that is, they are not easily linked with significant empirical indicators, but one can build only with the bricks available if he is seriously interested in building. Social science methodology has in some respects progressed since Marx, but his lesson for substantive social theory is still important. Axelos sees this point, it seems, but he does not realize that Marx's 'technics' are something more than the external application of an explicatory scheme of Hegelian ascendancy. It is interesting to note that Axelos always writes about 'technics' in general, in a typically metaphysical perspective in which Heidegger's suggestions become transparent. One should see in particular Heidegger's note on 'the eternal return of the identical.'[7]

What is the essence of a 'modern' machine – Heidegger asks himself – if not a new form of the eternal return of the identical? Expressed in these terms, the problem of technics cannot escape a decadentistic approach; that is to say one which would confuse important analytic observations with purely suggestive propositions. The main shortcoming of such propositions is that they cannot be verified and necessarily lead to the elaboration of the myth of technics – a myth which stems from an equivocal experience because it expresses an evaluation of technics, as if technics were completely alien to us; like the entomologist who talks of the life of ants and speaks of a society with absolute central power and strict division of labor. These may be interesting opinions, but they are hardly relevant to the world of ants.

It is, to say the least, curious that Axelos never clarifies in what sense Marx speaks of man's work (from a technical point of view) as a 'metabolic process' which involves man and nature. The fact is that in Marx there is no metaphysical construction of practice. Practice is not an *absolute* point of departure, a *pre-categorical postulate*. It is simply the specific life situation, the immediate social process with its multidimensional inter-acting aspects. Marx never talks about 'technics' in general, as more or less conscious technocrats like to do. When he says 'technology,' or 'machinery and big industry,' he means 'factory system,' and he says it explicitly.

In other words, he sees things in a sociologically relevant perspective; he does not look at machines as if they were mythical monsters but rather as a situation resulting from 'the cooperation of many homogeneous machines,' from a 'machines system.' What Marx has in mind therefore is not abstractly conceived technics, but the 'factory system' with its social norms and regulations; that is to say *technics as a power structure* which upsets the traditional social framework according to a specific dialectic of its own, which Marx foresees but which he is not in a position to make explicit. He says in fact:

Modern Industry had therefore itself to take in hand the machine, its characteristic instrument of production, and to construct machines by machines. It was not till it did this that it built up for itself a fitting technical foundation and stood on its own feet. Machinery, simultaneously with the increasing use of it, in the first decades of this century, appropriated, by degrees, the fabrication of machines proper. But it was only during the decade preceding 1866 that the construction of railways and ocean steamers on a stupendous scale called into existence the cyclopean machines now employed in the construction of prime movers.[8]

And later:

113

Machinery also revolutionises out and out the contract between the labourer and the capitalist which formally fixes their mutual relations. Taking the exchange of commodities as our basis, our first assumption was that capitalist and labourer met as free persons, as independent owners of commodities; the one possessing money and means of production, the other labour-power. But now the capitalist buys children and young persons under age. Previously the workman sold his own labour-power, which he disposed of nominally as a free agent. Now he sells wife and child. He has become a slave-dealer'[9]

There is an important lesson here for social scientists, which should be made clear. In the first place, Marx explodes the fallacy of the use, good or bad, of technics. Technology has a human weight, a social impact, a power structure which it makes necessary to adopt, and one which reasoning in terms of good or bad use completely overlooks. Secondly, he stresses the vital interconnection between technical change, power structure, workers' family life, relationships within the family, the labor market, and the political system. *This feeling for the interconnectedness of the various aspects of the life process has been largely lost.* Each aspect is studied as if it bore within itself its meaning and justification. A social phenomenon is therefore reduced and broken down into a series of isolated discrete units. It is perhaps true to say of present day industrial sociology, as Marx used to remark about the political economy of his day: that here is a science which employs rigid dogmatic concepts as if they had sprung, ready-made, *ex capite Jovis*. These static concepts cannot cope with the unfolding dialectic reality of the social process and in fact they tend to obscure the very nature of the process they are intended to explain. Here we find the reason why the suggestion put forth by Marx, in a famous footnote in the first volume of *Capital*, has gone to this day substantially unanswered. Darwin – Marx remarks – called attention to the history of natural technology; that is to say, to the formation of vegetal and animal organs as instruments of production for the life of plants and animals. Is not the same attention deserved by the history of the formation of the productive organs of social man, which are the material basis of any social organization? We do not yet have a critical history of technology. Sociologists of work and industry do not seem, as a rule, to be history-oriented. They assume that the problems they explore are everywhere essentially the same. Thus the inadequacy of a static, piece-meal, approach is less apparent. Those problems are seen as related to the social and human concomitants of the same phenomenon, i.e. the organizational framework and productive techniques of modern industrial work. They overlook an important fact:

that of historical variability. The organizational framework is in fact far from being always and everywhere the same. In the West the factory system has passed through various stages of development (family capitalism, scientific management, functional decentralization of authority, restructuring and concentration of decision-making power), each accompanied by a special technology (universal or 'flexible' machines, special machines, assembly line, repetitive jobs, transfer machines, automation) and its evolution has certainly not reached its final phase.

For this reason, as I have remarked elsewhere, although the problems might be basically the same, their main features and the way they emerge vary according to the differences in the specific environment and in the variables at work in it: degree of industrialization, historical background, cultural patterns, natural and economic resources, political institutions, shared goals and social values, demographic situation and labor market. Industrialization is a global process. It cannot be properly studied by limiting the perspective of the investigation to the small work group or even to the industrial plant conceived *separately* as a social system, and therefore without making explicit reference to the rest of society.

With few exceptions, this is a common defect of research in industrial sociology and in sociology of work. The evolution of industrial machinery is analysed as if it had taken place in a social vacuum; secondly, and this is no wonder once the larger society is deliberately overlooked, the issues are reduced to their purely psychological connotation (whether the worker likes or dislikes technical change; whether he is afraid of it; whether he thinks he is going to get higher or lower pay as a result of it, and so on; in a word: *structural problems are reduced to a personal headache*). These studies are entirely preoccupied with the worker's intrinsic satisfaction in his job but they fail to ask themselves why the worker should consider the job as sacred and desperately try, with the help of sociologists, to adapt to it.

The studies conducted by J. Woodward, A. Touraine and R. Blauner,[10] among others, are more directly concerned with the ascertainable social characteristics which appear to be associated with each type of production system. Thus, Woodward constructs a scheme which includes nine stages of technical development and two mixed types of production system and is essentially based on criteria relating to technical complexity and the degree to which it is possible to exercise control over manufacturing operations and to reduce areas of uncertainty. Touraine develops a three-stage typology of technical evolution which according to him is characterized by the decomposition and fragmentation of the worker's skill and at the same time by an increasing integration of productive operations from a mechanical point of view. Blauner, finally, describes four major types of technology: (a) craft industries; (b) machine-minding industries; (c) assembly line industries; (d) process industries, on the basis of increasing mechanization and standardization of the product.

The attempt to relate, problematically, certain technical characteristics to a particular social structure makes these studies valuable. A reservation must be made, however, with regard to the rigidity of the various typologies outlined, and to some sort of implicit ideological commitment which seems to act as a mechanism of self-censorship whenever the research touches on the systemic characteristics of the work situation. Another reservation concerns a lack of diachronic perspective, especially as regards the great transition from a 'natural' to a 'technical' environment. The fact is that any technical change, which has relevance to the daily worker's job performance, has an impact upon his entire work life, his family life and his general view of life. Even at the elementary level of the factory or shop floor, a coordinated analysis is necessary to comprehend different levels of experience simultaneously. A modification in the job performance caused by a technical innovation is always accompanied by a corresponding change in the worker's attitude toward his job, his fellow-workers and his supervisors, not to mention the broader implications for community and society. This change necessarily calls for a period of personal adjustment to the new situation during which the worker revises his personal outlook toward work, management, company, union organization, and finally society as a whole, as a 'system.'

This process of 'adjustment through revision of his outlook' has an *objective* basis in the worker's feelings of unrest and uneasiness which are due both to the objective consequences of technical innovation (for instance, changes in his pay packet, or in his potential occupational mobility) and to the diffuse feelings of being carried further and further away from a 'natural environment' and immersed in a deeper and less personally controllable 'technical environment' where stability and security are lacking and change seems to be the rule.

On the basis of this leading idea, a set of specific working hypotheses could be formulated with respect to the following aspects:

1. The impact of technical innovation on the psychological security of the industrial worker (frustration, feelings of alienation, anxiety, etc.).
2. The impact of technical change on actual working conditions.

116

3. The manner of personal and work-group adjustment to the experienced process of technical change and its perceived consequences, with particular reference to:
   (a) the fragmentation of professional skills and their increased interchangeability;
   (b) the breaking down of previous and customary occupational careers;
   (c) the tendency to reduce autonomy in the decision-making process concerning job performance;
   (d) the increased formalization of worker-supervisor relationships.

In all these areas researchers might expect to find widespread unfavourable attitudes among workers. The rationale for this general hypothesis could be complementary with the class struggle idea and summarized in terms of *isolation*, that is in terms of physical, mental and social isolation at the place of work. The worker might experience physical isolation because of a lower density ratio between men and machinery; mental isolation because of insufficient information concerning the necessity of technical innovation, and finally social isolation because of the breaking down of customary interpersonal relationships and consequently of work-group solidarity.

In this respect the only way to escape the shortcomings of psychologism seems to be a return to Marx – so far as the single firm is also concerned. In fact, in the modern industrial company, the decision-making power is not so much distributed on the basis of a criterion of a technical division of labor (differentiated needs to operate discretionally). The fact that power at the company level is not allocated according to a *technical* division of functions and tasks but according to organizational needs makes the manipulative nature of the company and the essential contrast between supraordinates and subordinates very clear. The contradictory nature of the company as a system both of cooperation and of domination also becomes apparent. In regard to the workers, Davydov has aptly remarked by literally following *The German Ideology*:

Social power, i.e. the multiplied productive force which originates through the cooperation of various individuals and is determined by the division of labour, appears to these individuals, since the cooperation itself is *not voluntary but natural*, not as their own unified power, but as an alien force external to themselves, whose origins and destination they do not know, and which, therefore, they have no means of controlling – on the contrary, it follows its own succession of phases and stages of development, a succession which is independent of the willed actions of these individuals and indeed actually directs their willed actions'[11] (my italics).

117

Undoubtedly in the *Manuscripts* (1844), the process of alienation is seen from a philosophic point of view and it involves both the worker and the capitalist. In *Capital* only the worker is alienated. There are also noticeable changes of terminology: we find words such as 'alien power,' 'alien will,' 'alien force,' but not the term 'alienation.' However, it can be plausibly argued that Marx coherently applies, in his later works, the connection he has established in the *Manuscripts* between alienation from activity and alienation from man. The value of man's work and its meaning lead to the analysis of the social structures of cooperation. This analysis makes it possible to impute the loss of meaning of work activity to social factors which are empirically relevant.

Thus, the criterion of the worker's alienation conceived in terms of subordination to the employer-capitalist allows one to assemble in one category different historical phases with a different stage of development as regards the productive forces, but it also has the advantage of giving us the possibility of describing and interpreting the specific changes in the worker's situation during the transition from one phase to another of the capitalistic work organization; from simple co-operation (in which the worker is still essentially an artisan and retains a certain amount of free choice in his work operations) to the manufacturing phase (in which the work still has a definite meaningful content but the worker is permanently assigned to a given machine), and finally to the phase in which the work operation no longer has any independent content, and workers, through the homogenization of the flux of production, become essentially interchangeable. The subsumption of the worker under the capitalist, at first only formal, tends in this way to become substantive. The interesting thing to observe, in this respect, is that, in a parallel way, the evolution of the work instrument, *while* it is being transformed and incorporated in the machine, accompanies and corresponds to an increasing alienation on the part of the worker. In this sense Marx goes beyond any mechanistic interpretation of technical change. On the one hand, he shows that the solutions adopted on the basis of the productive transformations are referred to the technical requirements of the work process; while on the other, he constantly analyses these solutions, also referring them to the specific, historically determined power structure which is characteristic of any given phase of capitalistic cooperation. This is the dialectical relationship which is usually missing in the current studies of industrial sociology, and of sociology of work, and which is mainly responsible for the uncritical nature of those studies.

## NOTES AND REFERENCES

1. S. D. Anderman (ed.), *Trade Unions and Technological Change*, London: Allen & Unwin, 1967, p. 39.
2. J. H. Hallowell, *Main Currents in Modern Political Thought*, New York: Holt, Rinehart & Winston, 1950, pp. 723 *et seq.*
3. H. Kelsen, *The Communist Theory of Law*, London: Stevens, 1955.
4. K. Axelos, *Marx penseur de la technique: L'aliénation de l'homme à la conquête du monde*, Paris: Éd. de Minuit (Collection Arguments), 1961.
5. K. Marx, *Capital: A Critical Analysis of Capitalist Production*, Moscow: Foreign Languages Publishing House, 1960, pp. 372 *et seq.*
6. Marx, *Capital*, p. 375.
7. M. Heidegger, *Vorträge und Aufsätze*, Pfullingen: Neske Verlag, 1967.
8. Marx, *Capital*, pp. 384–385.
9. *Ibid.*, p. 396.
10. See in particular: J. Woodward, *Industrial Organization, Theory and Practice*, Oxford University Press, 1965; A. Touraine, *L'évolution du travail ouvrier aux usines Renault*, Paris: C.N.R.S., 1955; R. Blauner, *Alienation and Freedom*, University of Chicago Press, 1964.
11. Y. N. Davydov, *Trud i svoboda*, Moscow, 1962.

# HISTORICAL LAWS*

NICHOLAS LOBKOWICZ

In this paper,[1] I should like to make a few remarks concerning the Marxist notion of 'historical law;' and, by implication, the Marxist notion of science. This is a rather tangled subject, mainly for three reasons. First, it is far from clear what exactly it is that Marx and his followers do hold by claiming that there are such laws; in fact, there is considerable disagreement about this point among Marxists themselves. Secondly, even provided that one can with some precision say what it is that Marxists claim, it is rather difficult to decide to what extent this claim is meaningful; Popper and others have argued to the contrary. Finally, the issue is further complicated by an involved discussion of historical explanation among (this time) analytical philosophers, a discussion that was provoked in 1942 by Hempel's article on 'The Function of General Laws in History' and later continued by authors such as Michael Scriven, William Dray, and Arthur C. Danto. What I should like to do here, then, is to try to clarify at least some aspects of this issue, first, by stating the Marxist claim as clearly as I can, secondly, by briefly discussing the question as to whether and to what extent this claim is a meaningful one, and finally, by relating this Marxist claim to the more recent analytical discussion of the role of general laws in the study of history.

As far as the Marxist claim goes, the general idea would seem to be:

1. Both nature and society are governed by laws. But while the laws of nature, for all we know, do not change, laws of society are historical. This may mean a number of different though related things which neither Marx nor his followers cared to distinguish. In order to clarify the Marxist claim, I shall introduce three different meanings of the expression 'historical law.'

When speaking about scientific laws we ordinarily feel that they hold irrespective of historical developments. For example, we do not expect someone to ask about Galileo's law of falling bodies, or Maxwell's laws

* Originally published in *Studies in Soviet Thought*, vol. II, 1971. Reprinted with the permission of the publisher.

of electromagnetism, a question such as when they began, or how long we should expect them to hold. But it is of course conceptually quite possible that there are laws with respect to which such questions might be meaningfully asked – laws, that is, which hold only for a certain span of time. Hume, for example, seems to have entertained the logical possibility that the whole complexion of the world might change some day, after which none of our general laws would hold but, presumably, would be replaced by others. If we assume that such a change, not of the whole but only of a part of the complexion of the world, would fall within the span of mankind's history, the laws both of the old and of the new era would be historical in the sense that they would hold only for a limited historical period; accordingly, one might want to call such laws 'historically limited laws.'

A second, less unambiguous, sense in which laws might be historical is the following. Suppose that there are laws that hold only for a limited period after which they are replaced by new ones; and suppose moreover that the old and the new laws have enough in common to permit one at a relatively high level of abstraction to express them by one law which, then, holds for both periods. If the relation between this general law and the two historically limited laws is similar, not to the relation between genus and species, but rather to the relation between an expression and the various meanings that this expression acquires in the course of history, then the general law is historical in the following sense: although it holds for both periods, its concrete meaning varies from period to period. Accordingly, one might call it a 'historically varying law.'

A third, by far the most ambiguous, sense in which a law might be called 'historical' is this. Suppose that we discover a law to which events in the real world only approximate; and suppose moreover that this approximation increases as history goes on. Such a law would be historical in the sense that strictly speaking it does not hold today but will hold some time in the future; and that in the meantime reality gradually adjusts itself, as it were, to this law. Such a law one might call a 'tendential historical law,' since history 'tends' to make this law hold.

Now I can state what Marxists mean by saying that social as opposed to natural laws are historical. They mean first that all specific empirical social laws are historically limited. They mean secondly that general social laws which constitute the framework of social science are historically varying. They mean thirdly that some historically limited social laws are tendential. And they mean fourthly that laws that are neither historically limited nor historically varying nor tendential are of no use in social science.

121

**2.** Thus far I have only spoken of laws that are historical as opposed to historical laws; and it must be emphasized that, at least in principle, laws of nature no less than laws of history could be historical in this sense. However, a law might be historical still in another sense, namely, that – just as there are laws of nature – there are laws of history. As we have seen, Marxists claim that all social laws are historical in the sense just mentioned; but they claim moreover that a significant number of social laws are historical in the sense that they are laws of the *history* of society, that is, laws expressing regular patterns in the development of societies.

Now the claim that human history is governed by laws is of course not peculiar to Marxism. Vico argued as early as 1725 that all nations pass inevitably through certain distinguishable and enumerable stages of development. In 1784 Kant suggested that at least some aspects of historical developments – he mentions population growth – are governed by natural, if statistical, laws. The same point has been argued by thinkers as radically different as Comte, Condorcet, Hegel, Herder, and Mill; and in the sixties and seventies of the past century the idea of such laws of history became almost a general obsession.

What makes the Marxist claim that there are laws of history unique is the fact that Marxism speaks of *historical laws* of history. By this I mean that it claims that there are laws of the historical development of human society, which are historically limited, historically varying, or tendential, or possibly even all this at the same time.

It is often overlooked that, with the exception of a few passages in which he tries to sketch his approach, Marx speaks almost exclusively of laws proper to capitalist society. Even Marxists themselves often have overlooked this. And yet Marx was very explicit about it. Thus in a letter to a Russian newspaper, written in 1877 and first published in Russia in 1886, he explicitly says that he did not intend to advance 'a historico-philosophic *(geschichtsphilosophische)* theory of the general course of the development every people is fated to tread' but only the 'inexorable laws' of the capitalist system. And he adds: 'Events strikingly analogous but taking place in different historical surroundings lead to totally different results. By studying each of these developments by itself and then comparing them one can find the clue to the phenomenon, but one will never arrive there by using as one's master key a general historico-philosophical theory, the supreme virtue of which consists in being supra-historical.'[2] Four years later, in a letter to a Russian lady, who later became Marxist, Marx even explicitly states that the historical inevitability about which he had spoken in

*Das Kapital* is 'limited to the countries of Western Europe.'[3] This does not mean of course that Marx believed that only capitalist countries of Western Europe were governed by, as he put it, 'iron developmental laws.' There are many passages in his writings that make it clear that he believed it possible to discover such laws in any society of any age. But these laws will be different from age to age, in fact even different for different cultural fields of the same age, since societies of different ages may happen to be contemporaneous. The reader will perhaps object that at least in some texts Marx clearly seems to speak of developmental laws that hold for all societies in all ages. The most striking example is the famous preface to *A Contribution to Political Economy* of 1859 in which Marx traces the development of his ideas and then presents what is the most concise statement of his materialistic conception of history. The crucial passage runs thus: 'At some stage of their development, the material forces of production of a society come to contradict the given relations of production or which is but another expression for the same, the property relations within which the forces of production had acted. What hitherto were developmental forms of the forces of production turn into their fetters. There follows a period of social revolution.'[4] In this passage Marx clearly tries to express a developmental social law that is so general that it holds for the whole development of all societies in which there is private property. However, it is equally clear that Marx has here in mind what I have described as a historically varying law. It is not a law properly speaking but rather a sort of an abstract summary of a number of more specific laws that widely differ among each other.

**3.** The historically limited developmental laws of societies are in turn historically connected with each other. That is to say, the laws of the development of a given society, say of capitalistic society in France, are themselves the outcome of the lawful development of the society immediately preceding it. This idea is intimated several times in Marx's major writings, although neither Marx nor any of his followers have ever tried to elaborate on it. What is meant, might perhaps be sketched as follows. Suppose four successive societies $A$, $B$, $C$, and $D$, for example France during the Roman empire, medieval France, France during the Renaissance, and early capitalistic France. Each of these societies develops in conformity with a set of developmental laws some of which might in turn be tendential; say the set $L_a$, the set $L_b$, and the set $L_c$. Now some laws of the set $L_a$ do not only concern the development of $A$ but also the passage of $A$ to $B$, that is, the emergence of a society governed by the set $L_b$; $L_b$ in turn contains laws that predict the genesis of a society developing in conformity with $L_c$; and so on. Thus, for example, the developmental laws of capitalism mention the emergence, in the womb of bourgeois society, of a new class which will overthrow capitalistic society and establish communist society.

This entails that not only the development of a particular society but also its emergence from the preceding society is governed by laws, somewhat as the development of a butterfly is determined by its having been a caterpillar, although the developmental laws of caterpillars and butterflies differ. Accordingly, just as ideally it is possible to construe the development from an egg through the caterpillar to the butterfly as lawful, it is in principle possible to construe a law that governs the development from the most primitive to the most developed society. This law will of course be discovered only at the end of history. However, once this end is given, it is possible to construe either a law of the sequence of developmental laws such as $((L_a \supset L_b) \supset L_c) \supset L_d$ or a law of the development $A–B$ itself, say, $((A \supset B) \supset C) \supset D$. The implication sign of course stands for an empirical, not for a logical connection; it is not possible to deduce $A$ from $B$, although it is possible to say that if society $A$ occurs society $B$ will follow.

At present I am not interested in the question as to what exactly the laws mentioned would be; as I have said already Marx never even as much as tried to formulate laws other than those of capitalist society in Western Europe. Instead, I now should like briefly to discuss another question, namely, whether and to what extent the Marxist claim as hitherto sketched is meaningful. In *The Poverty of Historicism*, Karl Popper argues, in Chapter 22, that, although it may be true that biological evolution or social development are governed by a number of causal laws, the very notion of *a* law of evolution or *a* law of history is preposterous. Reduced to the essentials, Popper's objections to such notions amount to the following three points:

First, the evolution of the species or of human history as the sequences of organic or of socio-economic formations are *unique events*. Accordingly, the sentence stating that animals developed from a protozoon to man, or the sentence stating that mankind developed from a primitive classless society to a capitalist society cannot possibly be a law. Rather, it is what Popper calls a 'singular historical sentence,' similar to a sentence such as 'Darwin and Galton had a common grandfather.' Such a sentence may indeed be a hypothesis. But although all laws have to be construed as hypotheses and moreover all hypotheses presuppose laws for both their explanatory function and their verification (or rather, falsification), not all hypotheses can meaningfully be construed as laws. In order that a hypothesis be a law, it is necessary, among other things, that the events with respect to which the law is said to hold be numerous. A law is by definition universal. The claim that an event is governed by such a universal law entails that it is possible to distinguish between this event and the law that governs it. This, however, does not seem possible if the event is unique; in this case, one cannot distinguish what is merely a fact from what is lawful.

Secondly, the very notion of a developmental law is an illegitimate extrapolation of the physical notion of a 'law of motion.' The difference between a developmental law, whether biological or social, and a law of motion is that the latter does not speak of the development of a system but only specifies how within a given system bodies may move with respect to each other. It is of course possible to deduce from a physical law of motion predictions concerning the development of the system; but this requires statements about initial conditions which are not part of the law. In other words, a physical law never entails predictions about real facts except in connection with statements about what the present facts are; a developmental law, on the contrary, presumes *to be* a prediction, that is, to anticipate *qua* law future developments.

Finally, notions such as that of a law of evolution or a law of history confuse laws with trends. The difference between these is as follows: a law is not a statement of facts but a statement about which facts are impossible; a sentence that states a trend, on the contrary, concerns facts and says nothing about the impossibility of other facts. This amounts to saying that a law but not a trend-sentence permits one to predict. In the development of species or in the course of history one may indeed discover trends; but these do not permit one to make predictions except on the assumption that the trend will continue – an assumption that is sound only if one knows of laws that explain the trends as hitherto observed. But these laws will not be developmental laws. To give an example: that the earth cools off is a trend that we can explain in terms of laws of thermo-dynamics or thermochemistry; but a sentence describing the cooling of the earth is not a law. And even our knowledge of thermodynamic or similar laws permits us to predict the future temperature of the earth only on the assumption that the conditions presently given will not change, for example, that the earth will not move significantly closer to the sun.

To these three objections I should like to add a fourth one which Popper advances mainly in Chapter 26 and which would seem to contain the major premise of the other objections. It amounts to saying that the very notion of scientific law entails that such a law be ahistorical. A law is a conditional proposition which states that if certain conditions obtain certain events will occur. Now the antecedent of this conditional proposition must not contain any reference to a particular time, for otherwise we will be forced to say that laws can change. But if we allow for laws that undergo change, we no longer can explain change by laws. In case of unexpected observations we would not be forced to revise our theories; it would suffice to advance the *ad hoc* hypothesis that the laws changed – which would of course be the end of scientific progress.

So much for Popper's objections. Now I am not convinced that these objections are valid. More precisely, although everything that Popper says is perfectly true, it does not necessarily seem to affect the essentials of the Marxist claim. I say: the *essentials* of the Marxist claim, for there can be no doubt that Marx and his followers usually wrap up their ideas in a terminology which is by no means immune to objections such as those of Popper. But contrary to most Marxists I feel that this terminology (and the same applies to the so-called dialectical method) is not essential to the Marxist claim. In a word, I am of the opinion that what Marx is trying to say may be rephrased in perfectly analytical terms and rephrased in such a way that Popper's objections do not affect it.

Let me begin with the question as to whether a law may be historically limited. Popper is of course right when he argues that if we admit laws that hold today but not tomorrow, no satisfactory explanation of change will be possible. But suppose I rephrase the notion of a historically limited law as follows: though the law itself is unchanging and ahistorical, the conditions specified in its antecedent obtain only in a limited historical period. Take as example the famous law of progressing pauperization of the proletariat as stated in the 23rd and 24th chapters of *Das Kapital*: with the accumulation of capital the difference between the living standard of the capitalists and the living standard of the workers increases, or as Marx puts it: 'Along with the constantly diminishing number of the magnates of capital, who usurp and monopolize all advantages of the process of transformation, grows the misery, oppression, slavery, degradation.' In a sense, this law is perfectly atemporal: it holds wherever and whenever there is accumulation of capital; that is, under the conditions of private property, the national income is reinvested into production. But precisely this condition is historical: it occurs only in capitalist societies which are only a few centuries old.

The Marxist claim that all social laws are historically limited would then amount to saying that the conditions that make social laws applicable are historically limited. Something similar, incidentally, applies to physiological, behavioral and psychological laws: the organisms, animals and intelligent beings to which these laws apply emerged at a

126

definite point in evolution. In a sense, the same applies to many physical laws as well: prior to the emergence of a planet whose average pressure was 760 mm mercury, the law concerning the boiling point of water did not apply. However, while physics and chemistry easily can disregard this fact, biology cannot and still less can social science. To use behavioral laws for the explanation of events prior to the rise of animals is an anachronism; and so is the use of the laws of capitalist society in the explanation of, say, ancient Greece or medieval Italy.

Now I am not saying that this proves that social laws *are* historically limited. It proves, however, that the Marxist claim is by no means as meaningless as it might seem at first sight. Moreover, it proves that Popper, not the Marxists, extrapolates physical laws to society. For Popper seems to suggest that the conditions specified in the antecedent of a scientific law must be such that at least in principle they may occur at any time. Except for some cosmological problems, this is, in physics, a quite reasonable assumption. But it is not a reasonable assumption in biology; it does not seem overly reasonable to assume that tomorrow conditions will obtain, or events occur, that would permit one to apply laws concerning the blood pressure or the behavior of dinosauria. And it certainly is at least worth discussing whether sociological laws applicable to contemporary American society applied to Indian tribes of several centuries ago or will apply to American society in the 25th century A.D.

One might object that social laws *should* be construed so as to be applicable to all historical epochs. To my knowledge neither Marx nor any Marxist ever denied that there might be such laws. But Marx felt that such laws, first, will be too trivial to be of any real use in social science and, secondly, will not be social laws properly speaking. They will be biological, physiological, and perhaps behavioral laws, but not social laws in the proper sense of the term. He might have added that the tendency to find biological or social laws that apply to *any* organism or to *any* society, respectively, furthers a sort of reductionism. For it is to be expected that laws equally applicable, say, to ants and to men will make it possible to explain human phenomena only to the extent that men are, among other things, similar to ants; and that laws common to a primitive and to a highly developed society will suggest explanations that treat a modern nation or political party as if it were a variety of cannibal tribe. This does not exclude of course that there are laws applying to all animals or all societies. But these laws either will concern a stratum that is ontologically more basic – for example, the phenomena studied by biologists, physiological psychologists or ethnologists – or else will be nothing more than the conceptual paradigm within which social science has to move. These paradigms are what I have described as historically varying laws: they are little more than the conceptual framework within which social science, as Marxists understand it, operates.

Finally, as to the tendential historical laws, they may now be sketched as follows: there are, both in evolution and in history, trends that gradually establish conditions for some law to apply. These trends are of course not laws (it cannot be denied that Marxists often overlook this); but they can be explained by laws – and this means that their future development *can* be predicted. Popper is of course right when he argues that a trend as such does not permit one to deduce any predictions; but it seems equally clear that if the trend can be explained by referring to laws, predictions are possible as they are on the basis of laws anyway.

As to Popper's claim that there are no developmental laws, I submit, first, that almost any law can be construed as developmental, and, secondly, that biology constantly operates with developmental laws. In most laws the expression 'then' in 'If $x$, then $y$' suggests a temporal sequence, that is, a development; otherwise we would be forced to say that all laws are definitions, a claim that would lead to the conventionalism that Popper himself opposes. And is not the statement that frogs lay eggs out of which come tadpoles out of which come frogs at least a law-like statement? Of course it is true that Marxists, like all historicists, tend to overlook the fact that laws are conditional propositions and consequently phrase their laws in such a way that the difference between conditional and unconditioned predictions threatens to disappear. But I think Popper takes this obvious weakness more seriously than it deserves. When Marx, for example, phrases laws as if they would be predictions of future events he simply takes it for granted that the conditions presently given will not disappear overnight. In this respect, he speaks like a geologist announcing that the volcanoes of a South Sea island will continue to be active for another three hundred years. Of course it is possible that these volcanoes will be extinguished by some unexpected catastrophe; but no serious geologist will refrain from making predictions because of such eventualities. And though societies are not as lasting as geological phenomena, it does not seem unreasonable to expect that the basic frame of a social formation such as capitalism lasts long enough to make predictions about its future development meaningful. After all, it has outlived Marx – and most of his predictions.

What I am driving at is this: as important as it may be, from the point of view of philosophy of science, to distinguish between laws that are conditional propositions and predictions that are deduced from laws by a *modus ponens*, as little relevant is this distinction for the practice of those sciences which deal with phenomena that are longlasting and relatively stable. To speak of developmental laws of volcanoes on South Sea islands is of course a thorn in the flesh of a philosopher of science. But as it is relatively easy to rephrase the geologist's way of speaking in a more adequate terminology – for example, by saying that these laws apply to phenomena that are relatively stable – the philosopher's noisy protests smack a little of pedantry.

But what about Popper's objection that the history of mankind is a unique event? I think that this objection might be countered as follows: Marx tacitly assumes that there are a number of societies that develop according to the same laws. Thus he repeatedly says that a country $A$ shows to the country $B$ what its future path will be; or that country $B$ has anticipated in theory what the country $A$ has already reached in practice. As far as I see, Marx never speaks of a law of human history as a whole as if this unique history were the only exemplification of that law; he speaks of developmental laws, not of capitalism, but of capitalist societies in the plural. An evolutionary biologist might speak in the same way when comparing the biological evolution on different continents.

However, here emerges an objection that is rather serious after all. When, in the Marxist spirit, we compare primitive tribes in, say, South America, Australia, and Africa, and discover that their development follows the same course, we may argue that we have three independent instances that justify the assertion of a law hypothesis. When, however, as Marx did, we compare the development of England, France, and Germany in modern times, we obviously are not concerned with three independent instances; the fact that these countries develop along the same lines may easily be explained by their influencing each other. Thus in the case of the subject-matter that Marx analysed there emerges the difficulty after all that it is virtually impossible to say to what extent we are confronted with several developments governed by the same laws or with a trend which spreads, as it were. That Germany has developed along the same lines as England before it may be explained perfectly well by the fact that English trends had influenced Germany.

There is another point that needs emphasizing. I have been trying to defend the Marxist idea of historical explanation against Popper's objections. But there is one point in which Popper is obviously correct: this kind of explanation does not allow reliable predictions. But it is not the fact that the notion of historical laws of the history of societies is meaningless or that Marxists, and historicists generally, have an untenable notion of law, that prevents them from making reliable predictions; rather, this is due to the fact that their explanations are no more, and probably cannot be more, than what Hempel has called 'explanation sketches'.

It is well known that explanations of facts are deductions whose two premises are, on the one hand, one or several laws, and, on the other hand, statements about initial conditions, and whose conclusions are descriptions of the fact to be explained. Put in this way, explanation and prediction seem perfectly symmetrical: to the extent to which I can explain the phenomenon $P$, I can also predict under which conditions $P$ will occur again. This notion of explanation that was advanced by Hempel and Oppenheim in 1948 and on the whole accepted since, has led to many discussions as to whether explanations and predictions are really as symmetrical as the Hempel-Oppenheim schema suggests. I cannot discuss this issue in detail; it may suffice to point out that Hempel himself has indicated that this symmetry might not be as perfect as it seems, because many explanatory analyses are only explanation sketches which consist of a more or less vague indication of the laws and initial conditions considered as relevant. Most explanations of empirical events (as opposed to abstract states of affairs) ultimately are of this kind: we can explain the events, but not enough in detail to be able to make precise predictions. Marx's simplistic view of science undoubtedly prevented him from noticing this, although he occasionally made a tremendous effort to specify the possible reasons why a prediction might not come true. Thus in his famous treatment of the law of the tendential fall of the profit rate in the third volume of *Das Kapital* he belabors no less than six 'counteracting causes' permitting to explain why capitalism may, at least in the near future, not develop in conformity with this law.

Hempel puts great emphasis upon the distinction between explanation sketches, on the one hand, and what he calls pseudo-explanations, on the other. While a scientifically acceptable explanation sketch is incomplete in that it needs to be filled out by more specific statements but at the same time clearly points in the direction where these statements are to be found, a pseudo-explanation subsumes the phenomena under some general idea which in principle is not amenable to empirical tests and therefore cannot indicate in which direction concrete research should turn. It has often been suggested that the Marxist historicist theory of society is such a pseudo-explanation rather than an explanation proper. I do not believe that this is the case. Concrete research may not, and in fact did not, corroborate many of the laws by which Marx was trying to explain capitalist development; but the fact that research is at all relevant to the Marxist theory indicates that the latter is not a pseudo-explanation.

Of course, there is a peculiar difficulty with empirical tests of a social theory such as Marxism. Take Marx's law, already mentioned, that in capitalist societies capital accumulates in fewer and fewer hands and thus the difference between the capitalist's and the worker's living standard increases. Many, among them Marxists themselves, feel that this law has not been corroborated by the actual development: capital did not accumulate in significantly fewer hands and the living standard of the wage-laborer increased so much that since about 1890 it would be ridiculous to speak even of a relative pauperization of the proletariat. This development may be interpreted in two different ways: it may be argued that Marx was wrong when he believed his law to hold; or it may be argued that he was correct, but that unexpected developments prevented his predictions from becoming true.

This leads me to a difficult but crucial issue which I should like at least to mention before I conclude. Confronted with an experiment contradicting the predictions deduced from a hypothesis, a scientist may take two attitudes: he may reject the hypothesis or call into question the experiment. Popper has often argued as if a single falsification would force the scientist to revise his theory. But although this is logically correct, it certainly is not what usually happens in science. I do not think that it is an exaggeration to say that scientists on the whole distrust their experiments and observations more than their hypotheses and theories. There is a good reason for this. A scientist is interested in the progress of knowledge; and a theory that is false or doubtful serves this progress more than no theory at all. This is the reason why theories often are upheld for decades and even centuries although everybody knows that something is wrong, since they entail predictions which are not corroborated or even are contradicted by observation. As Kuhn has convincingly argued in his book on scientific revolutions, theories in general are not given up until an alternative theory turns up that is comparable in explanatory power to the one that creates trouble. In the meantime, one will try to explain away experiment and observation – for example, by additional hypotheses.

The situation with Marxism is similar. Most of Marx's predictions did not come true. But as Marxism is the only developmental theory of society that claims to be empirically testable, that is, as no serious alternative of the same caliber ever showed up, many social scientists continue to adhere to it while trying to explain why Marx's predictions failed to materialize. There are of course other reasons as well why scholars remain Marxists. But it should not be overlooked that it is possible to agree with most of Marx's ideas while admitting that his predictions did not materialize. There is first the possibility of saying that the conditions from which Marx deduced his predictions no longer obtain. The laws were correct but the conditions changed before the events predicted could take place. There is secondly the possibility of saying that the laws are correct and the original conditions still obtain, but the predicted events are hindered from taking place by purposeful countermeasures. There is thirdly the possibility of saying that Marx was much less concerned with prediction than with explanation – and that his predictions were not thought through carefully enough.

That the latter is the case, is obvious. There are a number of developments that Marx did not anticipate. Among other things, he did not anticipate that his predictions might be self-defeating, that is, that capitalists, after hearing his predictions, would actively prevent what he had predicted. One might even argue that it was the growing social-democrat movement that prevented some of Marx's predictions from becoming true: for this movement forced the capitalists to give in to a degree that Marx did not and could not foresee. But all this does not exclude the possibility that Marx was correct in the sense that he discovered laws that really were operative; and it does not exclude the possibility that his basic idea as to how social science should look was to a large extent correct.

In other words: that Marx's predictions did not materialize only proves that Marx was wrong in making them. It does not prove that his theory was false. If we assume that his theory is an explanation sketch, it simply does not lend itself to predictions but rather is a guide to research. And I want to go further and say: even if Marx was completely wrong – which to my mind he was not – his theory of society was and still is an enormous incentive to research that would never have come about without his ideas. And even if Marx was completely wrong: his idea that social science has to try to uncover developmental social laws that are historically limited in the sense explained still can be taken seriously. In this respect, Marxism is a challenge to social science: it offers an alternative, first, to a haphazard search for empirical social laws and, secondly, to an idea of social science that sees its ideal in physics, a science that legitimately ignores what social science probably cannot ignore, namely, history.

NOTES AND REFERENCES

1. This paper is a revised version of the first of four lectures presented at the Carnegie Summer Institute, University of Notre Dame, in July 1970.

2. Karl Marx and Friedrich Engels, *Werke*, vol. XIX, Berlin: Dietz Verlag, pp. 108–112.
3. *Werke*, vol. XXXV, p. 166.
4. *Werke*, vol. XIII, p. 9.

# MARX AND DARWIN*

VALENTINO GERRATANA

In the middle of the 19th century, no one could at the time have discerned any relationship between Marx and Darwin, when there appeared almost simultaneously, a few months apart, two works which were in fact to become fundamental for all modern culture: *Zur Kritik der politischen Ökonomie* (June 1859) by Karl Marx and *On the Origin of Species* (November 1859) by Charles Darwin. In particular, Marx's work at first found virtually no response, whereas Darwin's work achieved an overwhelming success, which started on the very day *On the Origin of Species* appeared in the bookshops (as is known, the first edition sold out within twenty-four hours), and lasted for the remainder of the century. Even in the following decades, when Marx's reputation broke through the barriers of isolation within which socialist thought had been confined after 1848, and finally came into wider public circulation, it was Darwin, not Marx, who dominated the cultural scene and influenced every sector of it. Admittedly, the depth of this influence was not equal to its extent. Darwinism was essentially a diffuse cultural atmosphere that imbued the most diverse, and even opposite, tendencies with its hues. Thus, for example, both socialists and anti-socialists, democrats and reactionaries, in those years called themselves Darwinian, and disputed at length who was more legitimately so. Not only the majority of natural scientists, but also philosophers and literati, sociologists and artists, drew sustenance from his doctrine and received direct or indirect inspiration from it. It will suffice here to cite the testimony of a great Italian man of letters, brought up in a completely different intellectual tradition, but sensitive to the new ferments in the culture of his time: 'There are men who may never have heard of the books or even the name of Darwin, but despite themselves live within the atmosphere created by him and feel its influences,' wrote the critic Francesco De Sanctis in a lecture in the last year of his life, entitled *Darwinism in Art*.[1]

This lecture starts with an apology for Darwin, but then develops into a manifesto for a literary poetics that has at bottom only a fortuitous

* Originally published in *New Left Review*, 82, November/December 1973. Reprinted with the permission of the editors.

connection with the theory of the scientist of Down House. It is not without significance, however, that De Sanctis had read Darwin with enthusiasm ('those were fine days of my life that I spent reading the works of Charles Darwin'), whereas it does not appear that he ever read a page of Marx or was struck by him in any way. On the other hand, there is one element in this apology by De Sanctis for Darwin which is of particular interest to us here: the passage in which he presents the limitation of the scientist as one of his titles to glory: 'the scientist's pride did not prevent him, in that marvellous chain of beings he conceived, from bowing before the Supreme, the Unknowable.' In reality this limitation was not so much Darwin's – he merely submitted ultimately and reluctantly, after many vacillations, to the anti-scientific suggestion of an unknowable – as that of later Darwinism, which in keeping with all positivist culture of the age ended up by making gnoseological agnosticism into a new philosophical dogma. This indeed was to be one of its weakest links, which was precisely breached towards the turn of the century by the irruption of a new wave of spiritualism, to which Darwinism proper was gradually to yield. Darwinism thus eventually faded away as a general cultural atmosphere, while an aberrant outgrowth from it, *Social Darwinism*, survived and even acquired new virulence. In this situation the whole problem of the developmental relationship between Marxism and Darwinism, as it had been posed and discussed in the last decades of the 19th century, finally came to seem stale and superseded. We shall consider whether and to what extent this epilogue was justified, once we have examined the more specific, and necessarily prior, question of the historical relations between Marx and Darwin.

## 1. HUMAN HISTORY AND NATURAL HISTORY

De Sanctis's lecture on *Darwinism and Art* was given in Rome on 11 March, 1883. A few days later in London, on 17 March, in his speech at the graveside of Marx, in the presence of a few intimate friends (including two natural scientists, the chemist Schorlemmer and the Darwinian biologist Ray Lankester), Engels publicly linked for the first time the name of his great dead friend with that of Darwin: 'Just as Darwin discovered the law of development of organic nature, so Marx discovered the law of development of human history.'[2] This verdict of Engels on the fundamental parallelism between Marx and Darwin was later taken up again and again,[3] and eventually became a commonplace of Marxist literature.

But the problem cannot be exhausted in these terms; even if those who have tried to advance beyond them have typically run the risk of becoming entangled in the most extreme confusions.[4] It remains a fact, however, that before the idea of any parallelism arose, Marx and Engels were themselves preoccupied with another question: that of establishing the significance, importance and limits of Darwin's work for their own conception of the world. It is therefore appropriate to begin by considering the judgments on Darwin and Darwinism expressed directly by the founders of scientific socialism.

The first pronouncement on Darwin came from Engels, in a letter to Marx of 12 December, 1859. He had in his hands, still fresh from the press, one of the 1,250 copies of the first edition of *On the Origin of Species* (which had been published on 24 November of that year). For some time Engels had already been engaged in studying with some assiduity the natural sciences, in which he had discovered various elements which seemed to confirm a line of thought which he had hitherto in certain respects been able to pursue only speculatively.[5] It is therefore not surprising that a reading of *On the Origin of Species* delighted him, not because of the novelty of its conclusions – for which he was in a sense prepared – but on the contrary because they offered a *new* confirmation and a scientific demonstration of certain general principles which until that time had not enjoyed much credit, but which he, along with Marx, had never doubted. 'The Darwin, which I am just reading,' he wrote to Marx, 'is really stupendous. Teleology in one respect had still not been finished off hitherto: it is now. Moreover, there has never yet been such a magnificent attempt made to demonstrate historical development in nature, or at least not so happily. Of course, you have to pass over the crude English method [*die plumpe englische Methode*].'[6]

Marx, at that period absorbed with other work and preoccupations, had not had the chance to read *On the Origin of Species* right away, but when about a year later he had occasion for the first time to appraise Darwin's work, his verdict did not differ from that of Engels, except in so far as it was expressed in a more laconic but even more categorical fashion: 'However grossly unfolded in the English manner' – wrote Marx to his friend on 19 December 1860 – 'this is the book which contains the natural-historical foundation [*die naturhistorische Grundlage*] of our outlook.'[7] Shortly afterwards, in a letter to Lassalle on 16 January 1861, Marx repeated the same judgement virtually verbatim, expressly reiterating the anti-teleological motif already emphasized by Engels: 'Darwin's book is very important and serves me as a natural-scientific basis for the class struggle in history [*als naturwissenschaftliche Unterlage des geschichtlichen Klassenkampfes*]. One has to put up with the gross English mode of development, of course. Despite all deficiencies, not only is the death-blow dealt here for the first time to "teleology" in the natural sciences, but its rational meaning is empirically explained.'[8]

## The 1857 Introduction

These assessments may, however, be easily misunderstood if they are not situated within the general framework of the theoretical positions at which Marx and Engels had by then arrived. If the whole way in which the materialist conception of history gradually took shape is not borne in mind, it might seem that it was only with *On the Origin of Species* that historical materialism acquired a basis that it formerly lacked; indeed that it was only now that the problem of the relationship between human history and natural history, and thus between science of society and science of nature, was posed for Marxism. In fact, of course, it is plain that Marx and Engels did not wait for Darwin in order to postulate a historical and anti-teleological development of nature in close relation with their materialist conception of history. The very idea of the evolution of animal species – which, as is well known, did not originate with Darwin[9] – was anything but extraneous to their range of interests, even before 1859. There is a significant hint in this respect in the 1857 draft introduction to *A Contribution to the Critique of Political Economy*. Describing bourgeois society as a superior form of social organization compared with the historical formations which preceded it – 'out of whose ruins and elements it built itself up' – Marx resorted precisely to an analogy with the evolution of animal species: the bourgeois economy, as the highest phase of development of an anterior historical process, furnishes the key for understanding the economy of past societies, just as 'human anatomy contains a key to the anatomy of the ape.'[10] On the other hand, he adds immediately, continuing the analogy, 'the intimations of higher development among the subordinate animal species can only be understood after the higher development is already known.' In other words, Marx was already not only taking for granted the principle of the historical evolution of animal species and of nature in general, which found little favour in the science of the time, but also tending to exclude from that evolution any finalist assumption. Admittedly, it could be said that for a consistently anti-teleological conception of nature there cannot be anything in a lower species which *intimates* as such something higher, in the sense (for example) of that internal tendency towards perfection postulated by Lamarck. Nothing of the kind, however, can be found in Marx's statement, despite the finalistic overtones of the metaphor he employed; on the contrary, his stress that a higher development of a less evolved antecedent form can only be

137

understood *a posteriori*, implicitly denies any preordained design in nature, any internal rationality of the real which precedes the material process of its external formation.

## The Problem of the Unity of Science

These and other passages might, however, seem merely casual or fortuitous if they are not situated within the framework of the general conception of the world which presided over the birth of historical materialism. It is therefore necessary to recall the way in which the problem of the relation between man and nature was treated by Marx as early as the *Economic-Philosophic Manuscripts* of 1844. The traditional antithesis of man and nature was not there overcome by a new philosophical solution, but for the first time found its explanation in a process of practical origin, and its solution consequently became a problem of historical practice, 'a *real* task of life,' and no longer a purely theoretical aim, as it had always been for speculative philosophy. Effective and complete unity of man with nature can only be realized through society and within society, and this will be the accomplishment of communism, which 'as fully developed naturalism, equals humanism, and as fully developed humanism, equals naturalism.'[11] Such a perspective, on the other hand, can only be meaningful if a real analysis of the laws of development of human society has at least been started, and if this analysis has shown a non-extrinsic link between human history and natural history. In the *Manuscripts*, in fact, Marx had already discovered that the productive activity of men is the basis of their history and at the same time the indispensable substratum of the history of nature, hence too of the natural sciences, which from the dawn of human history have developed step by step with human productive activity. 'Industry,' says Marx, 'is the *actual*, historical relationship of nature, and therefore of natural science, to man.'[12] The same theme is taken up again and developed in *The German Ideology*: nature, the sensible world which surrounds us, is not 'a thing given direct from all eternity, remaining ever the same, but the product of industry and of the state of society; and, indeed, in the sense that it is an historical product, the result of the activity of a whole succession of generations, each standing on the shoulders of the preceding one, developing its industry and its intercourse, modifying its social system to the changed needs'; thus 'the celebrated "unity of man with nature" has always existed in industry, and has existed in varying forms in every epoch according to the lesser or greater development of industry . . . but where would natural science be without industry and commerce?'[13] This historical relation of man to nature has, however, been realized hitherto through a contradictory process; for the more society tightens and extends its bonds, the more it accentuates social antagonisms and isolates its members, while humanity prepares its emancipation by multiplying the elements of its own dehumanization.

For the same reason, the ever deeper unity of man with nature itself produces the separation of man from nature, and consequently of the human sciences from the natural sciences. All this was already emphasized by Marx in the *1844 Manuscripts*, where he describes the various dimensions of alienation: 'natural science has invaded and transformed human life all the more *practically* through the medium of industry, and has prepared human emancipation, although its immediate effect had to be the furthering of the dehumanization of man.'[14] It is in these circumstances that there develops between philosophy on the one hand (and between 'human sciences' in general) and natural sciences on the other a relation of reciprocal estrangement: 'The *natural sciences* have developed an enormous activity and have accumulated an ever-growing mass of material. Philosophy, however, has remained just as alien to them as they remain to philosophy. Their momentary unity was only a *chimerical illusion*. The will was there but the means were lacking.'[15] Only the unfolding practical process of this contradiction can lead to its real supersession, when natural science would eventually become the real 'basis of *human* science, as it has already become the basis of actual human life, albeit in an estranged form';[16] so clear did that truth appear which the phenomenon of alienation had hitherto hidden – namely, that 'history itself is a *real* part of *natural history*, of nature developing into man.' 'Natural science,' Marx therefore concluded, 'will in time incorporate into itself the science of man, just as the science of man will incorporate into itself natural science: there will be *one* science.'[17]

## Insights and Limits of the Young Marx

If these texts, in their specific philosophical terminology (from which Marx, of course, was very soon to distance himself), seem momentarily to have diverted us away from the theme of Darwinism, they may nonetheless help us to understand why the development of the natural sciences could not leave the founders of scientific socialism indifferent. For they show that it was not a chance interest, but a much deeper need, rooted in the very origins of the materialist conception of history, that was expressed by Marx when he defined *On the Origin of Species* as a book which contained the natural-historical foundations of the human science on whose construction he was at work. In reality, from 1844 to

1846, in the *Economic-Philosophic Manuscripts* and in *The German Ideology*, these foundations still appeared in many ways too slim and scientifically too approximate to sustain a conception of the world which advanced the perspective of the unity of all sciences. It is clear that within the postulated coincidence of humanism and naturalism, of historical nature and natural history, Marx's accent fell, and could not help falling, on that *part* of natural history constituted by human history. Since this was not just 'any part' but the very centre of natural history, of the process leading to the humanization of nature, yet which had hitherto lain outside the domain of scientific inquiry and been consigned to the abstract speculations of the philosophy of history, Marx's scientific endeavour could find no more appropriate object. The historicity of nature could not, however, have only this anthropological sense, could not be exhausted in that unity of man with nature which is a result of the productive activity of men; for in that case there would still remain room above and beyond this *historical nature* for an original act of creation, in other words for the restoration of the old spiritualism beyond the limited confines of our material world. Although in the *Manuscripts* of 1844 Marx still to some extent indulged in the naturalistic anthropologism of Feuerbach (which he superseded and criticized shortly thereafter in *The German Ideology*), he was aware of the danger of this restoration and did not hesitate to confront it with the most radical arguments against creationism. 'The creation of the earth,' writes Marx, 'has received a mighty blow from geogeny – i.e. from the science which presents the formation of the earth, the further development of the earth, as a process, as a self-generation. *Generatio aequivoca* is the only practical refutation of the theory of creation.'[18] This reference to a 'nature preceding human history,' which is yet never conceived as given directly from eternity, always equal to itself, reappears in *The German Ideology*, in the passages already cited in which the historicity of nature is presented as the result of human productive activity. 'Of course,' Marx adds, 'in all this the priority of external nature remains unassailed, and all this has no direct application to the original men produced by *generatio aequivoca*.'[19]

For our purposes here, it is not of great importance to what extent, in these allusions to *generatio aequivoca*, Marx had directly in mind the disputes that had raged within the natural sciences since the 17th century over the hypothesis of spontaneous generation, in which the idea had rebounded in a curious fashion from the vitalists to the mechanists. In any case, the notion of *generatio aequivoca* had passed from scientific debates into the philosophical systems of the time, where it is to be found for example as the general mode of the origin of life in the natural philosophies of Schelling and of Hegel. However, there is no specificity of reference in the way Marx alludes to this hypothesis; he takes from it only one element, the concept of self-formation, of generation as a *process of development*, which therefore excludes any act of creation. The function of the idea of *generatio aequivoca* is therefore equivalent in the writings of the young Marx to the idea of evolutionism itself. Its most serious limitation is not that it rests on an ambiguous theory, later to be scientifically discredited,[20] but above all that it remains only an *idea*, which in fact is marginal to Marx's youthful outlook. In this way, however, the task of linking human history with the whole of the rest of natural history into a unitary conception of the world, was entrusted to a mere rational hypothesis, not empirically verified – indeed not even speculatively developed. On the other hand it must be acknowledged, however paradoxical it may seem, that this very limitation is an index of the seriousness and greatness of Marx right from the outset of his scientific activity. Once he had arrived at a conception of the development of society as a *process of natural history*,[21] and was therefore convinced of the need to apply the rigour of the scientific method, based on rational reconstruction of facts empirically investigated, to the analysis of the laws of social development, he could not then for mere love of system invert the method and integrate the new materialist *science* of society with the old materialist *philosophy* of nature. Only parallel progress of scientific research in all fields could have brought nearer in a real and not illusory way that prospect of a unitary science, whose full realization moreover presupposed for Marx, as we have seen, not only an advance of knowledge but also a further progress of social relations. We shall, in fact, see how the step forward in the direction of this prospect represented by the work of Darwin was immediately to be followed by two steps backward, with the active collaboration of Darwinist culture itself.

## 2. THE MATERIALIST METHOD

*On the Origin of Species* finally gave the idea of evolutionism, the conception of nature as an historical process, for the first time an entirely scientific, that is both rational and empirical, basis. Both purely rational hypotheses and collection, classification and analysis of empirical data are integral elements of the history of science, as constituent moments of its development. But the objective result of its movement of knowledge, *scientific truth*, is reached only when empirical research and rational interpretation coincide, without extraneous residues. Before

Darwin this coincidence had not yet been attained in the theory of evolution. While the idea of evolution had been worked out on a speculative basis, above all by the materialist philosophers of the 18th century (Diderot, Maupertuis, Holbach and others), empirical research had been accumulating data which could not easily be squared with traditional conceptions. Thus from Buffon onwards there had been no lack of natural scientists who had attempted a new systematization of empirical data by relating them to evolutionist ideas. But the connection between the two always remained at least partly extrinsic. Even Lamarck, unquestionably the most gifted of Darwin's naturalist predecessors, could surmount the difficulties of the theory of evolution only by extravagant hypotheses with no support in empirical analysis, and which consequently had to resort on the one hand to naïve mechanistic crudities and on the other to the *deus ex machina* of finalism. Nevertheless, it was these attempts, for all their approximation and improvization, which made Darwin's work possible. The idea of evolution, as a rational hypothesis to explain facts observed and data gathered, was certainly in Darwin's mind (he says the idea 'pursued' him) long before he managed to demonstrate it scientifically; it was therefore, as an *idea* or *rational hypothesis*, no less a presupposition than his empirical research, of the *scientific theory* of evolution. Darwin then had to undertake more than twenty years' work to rediscover in the facts, and only in the facts, the rationality of this hypothesis, in order for empirical research and rational interpretation to coincide.

For this purpose, however, it was not enough to combine all the possible arguments in favour of the theory of evolution with all the actual modifications of species. Darwin realized that no argument could have the full value of proof if it did not provide an empirical explanation of the *mode* of evolution as well, the mechanism whereby species underwent modifications.[22] The traditional models of the evolutionary mechanism (the principle of use and disuse, and the influence of the external environment through the inheritance of acquired characteristics) did not seem to him to be adequate; for however derivable from empirical observation, they had no explanatory self-sufficiency, and in fact always led back in one way or another to a teleological interpretation of nature. Darwin never intended to deny the value of these traditional models.[23] Instead he made a deeper examination of the conditions in which they became operative, and eventually found in the principle of natural selection the *principal* agent of the mechanism of evolution, the most important fact round which all other facts could be rationally coordinated, the guiding thread which unravelled the tangle of apparent accident and reciprocal influence in which empirical observation always risked becoming lost. Any finalist explanation thus became superfluous, finally receiving, as Marx was to say, 'the death-blow.'

## Marx's Comments in Capital

*On the Origin of Species* was thus bound to attract the attention and interest of Marx, not merely for its results, but also for its thoroughly materialist – that is, scientific – method. If in his first enthusiastic judgments, already recorded, Marx's positive appreciations seem to concern only the overall conclusions of the work, he subsequently came to emphasize its methodological significance, along with the most controversial aspects of Darwinism. It is revealing, for example, that in an important footnote to *Capital*, which raises questions of method essential to the materialist conception of history in connection with the problem of the historiographic importance of technology, Marx uses precisely Darwin as the starting-point of his argument, citing his work as an exemplary application of the materialist method: 'Darwin has interested us in the history of Nature's Technology, i.e. in the formation of the organs of plants and animals, which organs serve as instruments of production for sustaining life. Does not the history of the productive organs of man, of organs that are the material basis of all social organization, deserve equal attention?'[24] It is no less significant, however, that at the end of this note to *Capital*, Marx felt it necessary to warn against a materialism 'abstractly modelled on the natural sciences.' The defects, he writes, of such a materialism, 'that excludes history and its process, are at once evident from the abstract and ideological conceptions of its spokesmen, whenever they venture beyond the bounds of their own speciality.'[25] We must be careful to avoid any misunderstanding here. Marx does not warn us against the materialism of the natural sciences, but against *a materialism abstractly modelled on the natural sciences*. The distinction is fundamental: for him, in fact, materialist method and scientific method are equivalent, are two terms for the same concept (in fact, a little earlier in the same note, he speaks of 'the only materialistic, and therefore only scientific method').[26] Nor does he think that the natural sciences necessarily exclude all historical development: the very example of Darwin shows the contrary. When, however, on this occasion he speaks of 'history and its process,' the context makes it clear that he is referring to the historical process specific to human forces of production and to social relations that correspond to them: that is, the historical process outside which scientific knowledge of society is not possible, and in the name of which, therefore, we speak of *historical materialism*. It is *this* historical process which remains excluded from any type of materialism 'abstractly modelled on the natural sciences,' with unhappy consequences when its advocates venture beyond the bounds of their own speciality. Marx, on the other hand, is careful not to conclude by inviting scientists to shut themselves up within the confines of their own respective disciplines. If he had done so, he would have had to start by setting an example himself and abstaining from frequent references to the natural sciences, Darwin included. What then is the relation between the various sciences, and in particular between natural sciences and social sciences, between natural sciences and philosophy? The problem is indubitably a complex one, but examination of the ulterior relations between Marxism and Darwinism may help to clarify it.

## 3. DARWIN AND MALTHUS

We have seen that the first enthusiastic judgements of Marx and Engels on Darwin were always tempered by a reservation about the 'crude English method,' the 'gross English mode of development.' In general this reservation was marginal in character, since it concerned not the method of investigation but the method of exposition. That the latter was not always up to the standard of the former, that the scientific rigour of his method of research was often not matched by an equal rigour in his exposition, is a verdict to which Darwin himself would probably have found no objections. For in his *Autobiography* he was the first to admit the difficulties he had always experienced in expressing himself with clarity and concision, and candidly regretted his shortcomings: 'There seems to be a sort of fatality in my mind leading me to put at first my statements and propositions in a wrong or awkward form.'[27]

The reservation of Marx and Engels, however, becomes less marginal when we pass from Darwin's general method of exposition to consideration of certain substantive questions where the inexactitude of his formulations reveals a flaw in his reasoning. This is the case, for example, with the relation of Darwin to Malthus. However little Darwin, unlike his followers, was generally inclined to venture outside his speciality, in this particular instance he did so, abandoning his well-known caution as a scientist. The resultant confusion was not confined to Darwin's own understanding, for even today Malthus's theory of population is commonly mentioned as one of the principal sources of Darwin's theory of evolution. Darwin himself, when he invoked Malthus, was not preoccupied with deepening his comprehension of the latter's thought: he merely stopped at the first chance impression he received from a *casual* reading of the *Essay on the Principle of Population*. In turn, none of the later interpreters of Darwin took the trouble to check the original texts, which are nevertheless well-known and easily accessible, to establish the exact value of Darwin's reference.[28]

## The Two Proportions

In his introduction to *On the Origin of Species*, in which he described the plan of the work, Darwin wrote the following passage: 'In the next chapter the Struggle for Existence among all organic beings throughout the world, which inevitably follows from the high geometrical ratio of their increase, will be treated of. This is the doctrine of Malthus, applied to the whole animal and vegetable kingdoms.'[29] The scientific validity of any attempt to transfer a doctrine elaborated for society to the field of biology is disputable on principle, of course. But a methodological discussion would in this case anyway be superfluous, since Darwin, at the very moment when he says he wants to apply the 'doctrine of Malthus' to the whole animal and vegetable kingdom, empties that doctrine of everything that defines it and finds himself with something quite different on his hands, which bears only a nominal relation to the former. Neither the principle of the struggle for existence, nor that of the natural increase of population in geometric proportion, in fact serve to justify the theory of Malthus, who himself – despite his propensity to plagiarism, noted by Marx and other economists – appealed in turn explicitly to other authors to validate these principles. Malthus' 'discovery,' the pillar on which his whole *Essay on the Principle of Population* rests, was the supposed *divergence*, the catastrophic pincer, between a human population which in each period of twenty-five years grew naturally in *geometric proportion*, and means of subsistence which, whatever efforts were made ('in the most favourable conditions of human industry,' said Malthus, in so far as he could foresee them) could not in the same period grow at more than *arithmetical proportion*. This divergence between the two proportions has a meaning only for human society, outside of which it is not, in fact, possible to speak of a continuous increase, even in arithmetical proportion, of the means of subsistence; whereas for plants and animals, according to Malthus, the problem does not even arise, since the matter would proceed 'very simply,' by the mere automatic elimination of superfluity.[30] While claiming to apply Malthus' theory, Darwin in reality belied it; he was in fact to spend his whole career showing how complex, rich and multiform the problem was which had appeared so 'simple' to Malthus.

Probably a latent doubt as to whether he was forcing the meaning of Malthus's theory somewhat did occur to Darwin. For he later introduces a variant of his first formulation, to cover the objection which must have struck him; in the same section, under the heading 'geometrical powers of increase,' he writes: 'It is the doctrine of Malthus applied with manifold force to the whole animal and vegetable kingdoms; for in this case there can be no artificial increase of food and no prudential restraint from marriage.'[31] But with this nonchalant logical leap, Darwin failed to realize that, lacking the premise of an arithmetical progression of the means of subsistence, Malthus' theory does not apply 'with manifold force,' it ceases to apply at all – losing any specific meaning to become a completely arbitrary metaphor devoid of content, a mere literary reminiscence. In reality, what interested Darwin was not the 'geometric progression' but the struggle for existence, as an indispensable presupposition of natural selection. But this struggle for existence was not in fact related to any 'rapid rate of increase in geometric progression' of all living beings, as Darwin wrote in formal reference to Malthus, but simply to the fact that – as he himself immediately added – in each species 'more individuals are produced than can possibly survive.' But for this phenomenon, the type of proportion in the rate of increase is irrelevant, and the struggle for existence would proceed indifferently – in the case of living beings not capable of producing and increasing their own conditions of existence – whether the proportion was geometrical or arithmetical (and in fact the rate of reproduction is more or less rapid depending on the different species of animals and vegetables).

Malthus' theory can thus be seen to have been superficially interpolated into Darwin's thought, to which it remains substantially foreign. The fortuitous and haphazard character of Malthus' influence on the author of *On the Origin of Species* is, moreover, manifest from the passage of his *Autobiography* in which the scientist records the circumstance in which he thought he had contracted his curious debt of gratitude to the famous economist. After alluding to the first stages of his investigations, when he had still not managed to work out 'how selection could be applied to organisms living in a state of nature,' Darwin writes:

In October 1833, that is, fifteen months after I had begun my systematic enquiry, I happened to read *for amusement* Malthus on *Population*, and being well prepared to appreciate the struggle for existence *which everywhere goes on from long-continued observation of the habits of animals and plants*, it at once struck me that under these circumstances favourable variations would tend to be preserved, and unfavourable ones to be destroyed. The result of this would be the formation of new species. Here, then, I had at last got a theory by which to work . . .[32]

The merits of Malthus for Darwin are therefore only indirect, and can

146

be reduced to the fact that Malthus had called his attention to the principle of the struggle for existence – a principle which on the one hand Malthus himself made no claim to have fathered, and on the other hand Darwin had already obtained directly from empirical observation. It should be added that with the acquisition of the notion of the struggle for existence, he was still not even half-way towards his goal: for the eventual discovery of a 'theory by which to work' he had to reach the conclusion – for which Darwin certainly got no help from Malthus – that in the conditions of struggle for existence favourable variations tended to be conserved and unfavourable ones to be eliminated.

We can therefore understand the reaction of Engels, when faced with those who like Dühring criticized Darwin's theory of the struggle for existence on the grounds of its presumed Malthusian origins. 'Now Darwin,' Engels remarks,

> would not dream of saying that the *origin* of the idea of the struggle for existence is to be found in Malthus. He only says that his theory of the struggle for existence is the theory of Malthus applied to the animal and plant world as a whole. However great the blunder made by Darwin in accepting the Malthusian theory so naïvely and uncritically, nevertheless anyone can see at the first glance that no Malthusian spectacles are needed to perceive the struggle for existence in nature – the contradiction between the countless host of germs which nature so lavishly produces and the small number of those which ever reach maturity; a contradiction which in fact for the most part finds its solution in a struggle for existence – often of extreme cruelty. Just as the law of wages has maintained its validity even after the Malthusian arguments on which Ricardo based it have long been consigned to oblivion, so likewise the struggle for existence can take place in nature, even without any Malthusian interpretation.[33]

### The Deeper Link between Malthus and Darwin

It still remains to be explained why Darwin let himself be influenced by a reading of Malthus up to the point of accepting uncritically a doctrine he could very well have done without. In fact, the extrinsic and superficial link between Darwin's thought and Malthus' work reveals a deeper relationship of *On the Origin of Species* with something much more serious and important: precisely with the reality to which the *Essay on the Principle of Population* brutally drew attention, even if it then tended to mystify it in the interests of the dominant classes. It is not so much the *social doctrine* of Malthus which was applied, as Darwin stated, to the plant and animal world, as the *social reality* which inspired the doctrine that found in the eyes of the natural scientist a singular reflection in the reality of the vegetable and animal nature which was the subject of his

147

research. This double aspect of the relationship between Darwin and Malthus (where the superficiality of the direct relation was redeemed by the profundity of the indirect relation) was pointed out by Marx in a letter to Engels in 1862.

Darwin, whom I have looked up again, amuses me when he says he is applying the 'Malthusian' theory *also* to plants and animals, as if with Mr Malthus the whole point were not that he does *not* apply the theory to plants and animals but only to human beings – and with geometrical progression – as opposed to plants and animals. It is remarkable how Darwin recognizes among beasts and plants his English society with its division of labour, competition, opening up of new markets, 'inventions,' and the Malthusian 'struggle for existence.' It is Hobbes's *bellum omnium contra omnes*, and one is reminded of Hegel's *Phenomenology*, where civil society is described as a 'spiritual animal kingdom' while in Darwin the animal kingdom figures as civil society.[34]

The amused and ironic tone of these comments should not mislead us; Marx is not satirizing Darwin, for whom his admiration – as we shall see – never waned, but registering an objective satire on bourgeois society that is reflected even in the disinterested work of a great natural scientist. It is in this sense that the same theme was to be taken up again later by Engels in the preface to the *Dialectics of Nature*:

Darwin did not know what a bitter satire he wrote on mankind, and especially on his countrymen, when he showed that free competition, the struggle for existence, which the economists celebrate as the highest historical achievement, is the normal state of the *animal kingdom*. Only conscious organization of social production, in which production and distribution are carried on in a planned way, can lift mankind above the rest of the animal world as regards the social aspect, in the same way that production in general has done this for men in their aspect as species.[35]

For his part Darwin did not even reach the threshold of these problems. Not only did he never surpass the limits of bourgeois society, he did not even succeed in imagining a way in which it would be possible to apply to the study of society the same scientific methods which he himself had coherently employed to investigate the laws of development of organic nature. It is true that Darwin was not the author of the Social Darwinism which was to infest the positivist culture of the end of the 19th century, and basically had minimal responsibility for this by-product of his theories. But to the extent to which he could not avoid at least touching on the field of social problems, even he was not exempt from a methodological decadence. Thus, for example, his conclusions in *The Descent of Man* on the 'progress of the well-being of the human race' are of some significance. It is, he says, a problem 'difficult to solve' (but the more difficult, of course, the less scientifically founded the terms of the problem). Although Malthus is not named in this passage, his theory of population remains Darwin's only available point of reference; on the other hand he is so intellectually casual here that after having claimed to apply Malthus' social theory to the whole of organic nature, he ends by rejecting the conclusions of Malthusianism in the social field itself. However, the reason with which he justifies his anti-Malthusian theses are just as unscientific as those customarily used to support the opposite Malthusian theses. Thus, the restriction of marriage proposed by Malthus to combat the phenomenon of over-population is criticized by Darwin, on the grounds that without over-population the prerequisite for the struggle for existence would be lacking, and without the struggle for existence Darwin cannot conceive the possibility of progress.[36] The descent at this point from the materialism of the natural sciences to a *materialism abstractly modelled on the natural sciences* is patent. As a scientist, Darwin drew from empirical observation of the animal and plant world the principle of the struggle for existence, and used it concretely to investigate the processes of development of organic nature and thus to discover their mechanisms and laws; but as far as the processes of society were concerned, it did not even occur to him that he should follow the same scientific method of research, and he confined himself instead to an abstract extension of results obtained from natural science to another science – that of society – where he supposed it possible to draw valid conclusions without any concrete or specific research. The result is the strange paradox that the scientist who more than any other contributed by his theory of evolution to demonstrating the historicity of nature, ended by denying and excluding the historical process in the very part of natural history that is human history. The struggle for existence, which conditions the development of the plant and animal world, becomes an eternal law of nature from which man can never escape, not only a stimulus but at the same time an insurmountable barrier of evolution. This conclusion remains even if Darwin adds, with eclectic caution, that he does not mean the struggle for existence to be taken as the sole or even the principal instrument of progress in human history. The signal for a methodological inversion was now given: denial of the eternity of natural laws, and their reinterpretation as historical laws, lapsed back into affirmation of historical laws of social development as eternal laws of nature.

This methodological inversion – which in Darwin himself is only suggested, remaining on the margins of his work as a sign of the bourgeois limits of his thought – was to become central to Darwinist culture, not only indicating its limits, but determining the fundamental character of its influence. However, this shift was to be possible because Darwin, despite the step he accomplished towards bringing the natural sciences and the historical sciences together, had already left the problem of the unity of science in a new impasse.

## 4. SCIENCE, PHILOSOPHY AND RELIGION

An indispensable condition, though not the only one, for overcoming this impasse is that each science should not shut itself up within its own concerns and ignore all the other sciences. But it cannot be denied that this desirable goal is confronted with a practical obstacle in the increasing specialization of research; nor can it be asked that this specialization be sacrificed for the sake of broadening the horizon of the individual knowledge of each scientist. However, lack of intellectual curiosity outside his own field of research will never be the mark of a scientist's greatness. This does not mean, of course, that a great scientist cannot have intellectual limits which he fails to surmount, nor that his value as a scientist is inversely proportional to these limits; it may, however, be said that the less they impinge on his research the more he will acknowledge them as such, as personal limits, and not pretend to justify them as limits of science. An acknowledgment of this kind can also be found in Darwin, in that measured and frank self-criticism which is one of the finest passages of his *Autobiography*, a moving document of scientific probity and scholarly humanity.[37]

Clearly, Marx too could not hope to deal simultaneously – on the plane of research – with both social and natural sciences, nor did he ever imagine resolving the problem of the unity of science by a utopian omniscience. A scientist like Marx, not only could not help being interested in the impetuous development of the natural sciences of his time, but was particularly obliged to ask himself what were the overall intellectual perspectives into which the new scientific discoveries should be inserted. The need to acquire critical and more than superficial information about them thus became an imperative task, which could not be eluded. Engels, as we have seen, had been the first to move in this direction, and Marx did not fail to recall this when he in turn felt the need to follow the same path. In a letter to Engels on the 4 July 1864 – which shows him immersed in works on physiology, histology and anatomy of the nervous system – after having noted with pleasure a certain correspondence between a point in Hegel's *Phenomenology* and the critique of phrenology in Lord's *Popular Physiology*, he added: 'You know that (1) I get round to everything late; and (2) I always follow in your footsteps. So it is likely that now in my free time I will devote myself a lot to anatomy and physiology, and also that I will attend courses (with demonstrations *ad oculos* and dissections).'[38] Of course, we should not take this declaration from Marx about his relations with Engels literally; the affectionately joking exaggeration – which would have been out of place had Marx not been sure of the complete lack of any intellectual vanity in his great friend and collaborator[39] – should not, however, be allowed to conceal the real significance of these expressions. From them it is clear that (1) Engels acted as an important intellectual stimulus to Marx and (2) Marx attributed great value to the field which was later systematically developed by Engels in *Anti-Dühring* and the *Dialectics of Nature*.

## Huxley's Agnosticism

We should not, on the other hand, be surprised that in this period of natural scientific apprenticeship the judgement of Marx and Engels on individual questions of detail is sometimes unfounded, and that their opinions do not always coincide.[40] What is more important, however, is to evaluate fundamental questions of scientific orientation, and it is about them – where the agreement between Marx and Engels is always complete – that the principal themes of the cultural debate set off by the spread of Darwinism in fact crystallized. At the centre of this debate was the problem of the relationship between science and philosophy, between science and religion. It is true that even here the issues did not concern only Darwin, and not even principally Darwin (who, as Labriola observed, 'was not the philosopher of his science'[41] and remained on the side-lines, leaving to his supporters, led by Huxley – 'the attorney-general of Darwinism' – both the responsibility for more general theorization and the onus of public polemics). The intellectual revolution which started with the publication of *On the Origin of Species* all of a sudden found its first battle-field on the terrain of religion. Yet it was a conflict which did not last long, at least in its sharpest forms, soon tending to find a basis for partial accommodation. Engels, in a letter of April 1863 drawing Marx's attention to some writings of Lyell and Huxley wrote: 'They are making a great fuss here with violent attacks against the old beliefs, and from all sides,' but he added the warning that there would inevitably be a search to prepare some diluted form of rationalism for the defense of religion.[42] A few years later, in 1868, it was Marx who pointed out a contradictory symptom of the attitude of Darwinist culture:

Huxley, in his last talk at Edinburgh, in which he showed himself more materialist again than in the last few years, still left himself a back door for retreat. So long as we effectively observe and think, we can never get away from materialism. But this merely resolves into a relation of cause and effect, and 'your great countryman Hume' has already shown that these categories have nothing to do with things in themselves. *Ergo* you are free to believe what you want. QED.[43]

Later, as is well known, Huxley was to coin the happy term 'agnosticism' for this position, and Engels in turn was doing no more than taking up Marx's remarks again when he spoke of this as a 'materialism that is ashamed of itself.'[44]

## Darwin's Doubts

There is no doubt that this mantle of agnosticism enabled the scientific spirit of Darwinism to mollify and deflect the obstacles to it, making its success quicker and easier, but at the same time preparing the conditions for its later collapse. The way in which this process occurred seems tortuous in many respects, but it is not difficult to reconstruct its essential outlines. Darwin, for example, was personally an unbeliever (or at least became so at a certain point), but he did not want this to be publicly known, and thus preferred to continue to let it be believed that evolutionism was compatible with religion. In private he professed himself an 'agnostic,' but his agnosticism, unlike Huxley's, was innocent of any philosophical emphasis; it was basically no more than a new way of acknowledging his own personal limits, at which he considered it honest, as well as prudent, to stop. On the other hand, the content of his agnosticism indubitably represented an advance on his previous positions. In one passage of his *Autobiography* he records that in the period when he was writing *On the Origin of Species* he had come to theist conclusions: since it was impossible to explain 'this immense and wonderful universe, including man with his capacity for looking far backwards and far into futurity, as the result of blind chance or necessity,' he was inevitably compelled to have recourse 'to a First Cause having an intelligent mind in some degree analogous to that of man.' This conclusion was, however, after many vicissitudes eventually shaken by doubt:

Can the mind of man, which has, as I fully believe, been developed from a mind as low as that possessed by the lowest animal, be trusted when it draws such grand conclusions? May these not be the result of the connection between cause and effect which strikes us a necessary one, but probably depends merely on inherited experience? Nor must we overlook the probability of the constant inculcation in a belief in

God on the minds of children producing so strong and perhaps an inherited effect on their brains not yet fully developed, that it would be as difficult for them to throw off their belief in God, as for a monkey to throw off its instinctive fear and hatred of a snake.[45]

Huxley himself would never have dared to advance such an impious argument against religion. It was not, however, mere caution or simple tactical prudence, but above all an awareness of the unscientific characters of these ideas, that prevented Darwin from exposing them publicly. In substance he limited himself in this field to proposing conjectures, to which however he did not seek to attribute greater value than to any other conjecture. The passage just cited from the *Autobiography* in fact concludes: 'I cannot pretend to throw the least light on such abstruse problems. The mystery of the beginning of all things is insoluble by us; and I for one must be content to remain an Agnostic.'

Darwin's agnosticism therefore has a more modest tone than Huxley's, betraying a perplexity which leaves a door open to all solutions. If human reason does not deserve to be relied upon when it speculatively deduces the idea of God, it is not apparent why in Darwin's eyes it should merit greater confidence when it speculatively denies it, given that in neither case can there be any experimental proof. Content with having wrested away from speculation another portion of its domain, the scientist falls back on himself, not daring to destroy that domain completely. To do so, however, would have necessitated not only an acknowledgment of the social character of all speculative thought, starting with religious speculation (and Darwin, as we have seen, approaches this acknowledgment) but a passage back from the critique of speculation to the critique of society; it would have involved, in other words, a rendezvous with Marx.

## The Correspondence between Marx and Darwin

But while Marx was in a position to understand and appreciate in all its importance the work of Darwin, by contrast Darwin was not capable of broadening his intellectual horizon to perceive at least the significance of the work of Marx, and in fact let fall the opportunities he was offered to acquaint himself with it. The two letters which Darwin wrote to Marx provide in this respect a significant testimony. The first, dated 1 October 1873, was occasioned by Marx's dispatch of a complementary copy of *Capital*, the second edition of which had just been published. It reads:

Dear Sir,
I thank you for the honour which you have done me by sending me

your great work on Capital; and I heartily wish that I was more worthy to receive it, by understanding more of the deep and important subject of political economy. Though our studies have been so different, I believe that we both earnestly desire the extension of knowledge, and that this in the long run is sure to add to the happiness of Mankind.

I remain, Dear Sir, Yours faithfully
Charles Darwin

Despite the courteous tone of this letter, it was clearly Darwin's intention to stay clear of a science which was not his own, and it seems in fact that the copy of *Capital* remained uncut in the library of Down House.[46] It would not, however, be fair to attribute this fact to bias or ill-will: after all, Marx's work is not suitable reading for 'amusement,' like Malthus' *Essay*, and demanded an intellectual effort that Darwin's mind, virtually devoid of economics or philosophy, was not equipped to undertake. Other preoccupations, however, must have come into play when Darwin unexpectedly found himself faced with a proposal to link his name publicly with that of Marx. In 1880, in fact, Marx asked Darwin by letter for permission to dedicate volume II of *Capital* to him.[47] Unfortunately, Marx's letter has not been found, and we lack some of the essential data for clarifying the significance of this interesting episode in full. Darwin's reply, declining Marx's offer, has however been preserved.[48] The letter is dated 13 October 1880:

Private

Dear Sir,
I am much obliged for your kind letter and the enclosure. The publication in any form of your remarks on my writings really requires no consent on my part, and it would be ridiculous in me to give consent to what requires none. I should prefer the Part or Volume not to be dedicated to me (though I thank you for the intended honour) as this implies to a certain extent my approval of the general publication, about which I know nothing. Moreover though I am a strong advocate for free thought on all subjects, yet it appears to me (whether rightly or wrongly) that direct arguments against christianity and theism produce hardly any effect on the public; and freedom of thought is best promoted by the gradual illumination of men's minds, which follows from the advance of science. It has, therefore, been always my object to avoid writing on religion, and I have confined myself to science. I may, however, have been unduly biassed by the pain which it would give some members of my family, if I aided in any way direct attacks on religion. I am sorry to refuse you any request, but I am old and have very little strength, and looking over proof-sheets (as I know by present experience) fatigues me much.

I remain, Dear Sir, Yours Faithfully,
Ch. Darwin

Although in this letter Darwin seems preoccupied solely with the relations between science and religion, it is probable that the reasons for
his negative reply to Marx's request, as also the reasons for the request
itself, are to be sought in other circumstances which are not explicitly
apparent here. To start with, it should be noted that in 1880, although
Marx had recommenced working on the continuation of *Capital*, the
publication of volume II was anything but near. There was not yet a
final draft (nor, of course, would there ever be), nor were any printer's
proofs in preparation. The problem of a possible dedication, with the
proposal to send Darwin in due course the proofs to read, was not therefore posed in an immediate way. Marx's inquiry had in all probability a
less contingent purpose. For the possibility of establishing on scientific
ground the relations between Darwinism and socialism, if accepted by
Darwin, would have finally discouraged the dilettante polemic which
was developing in those years, and was to continue for several decades,
with equal superficiality on the part of scientists and socialists.[49] The
onset of this polemic went back to 1877 when Virchow, in order to justify his hostility to Darwinism in the most vehement way at the Munich
Congress of German naturalists, did not hesitate to warn that it 'led
directly to socialism.' To defend Darwin from the superficial and ma-
licious criticism of Virchow, another great scientist like Haeckel found
no better solution than to attack socialism, eventually advising right-
thinking statesmen to spread Darwin's theory of evolution 'as the best
antidote to the absurd egalitarian theses of the socialists.' The political
tendency of Darwinism was, he claimed, in fact neither socialist nor
even democratic, but aristocratic. 'The theory of natural selection
teaches,' said Haeckel, 'that in the life of humanity, as in that of plants
and animals, it is only a small privileged minority that always and everywhere manages to live and grow; the immense majority, on the contrary,
suffers and succumbs more or less prematurely.' This was the ideological road that was promptly taken by the most reactionary 'Social
Darwinists' to justify imperialist wars and the exploitation of the majority by a minority.[50] But even the Darwinian socialists showed little
sense or judgement. Imbued with positivist culture, even when they professed themselves Marxists, they would not abandon the bad habit of
finding new proofs for socialism in the natural sciences, an aberration
deplored by Engels.[51] Appropriating the Virchow-Haeckel polemic,
they had no hesitation in mechanically inverting the terms of the controversy and basing themselves on the scientific authority of Virchow to

use in favour of socialism the arguments advanced by the German scientist against Darwinism.[52]

Compared with this superficiality, Darwin's caution appears subjectively justified. On the other hand, knowing Marx only by name, he must have feared that if he accepted the dedication of a book by a socialist, he would nourish new misunderstandings. Yet in this way Darwin's very prudence and his tendency to agnosticism – which affected not only the problem of religion, but all other questions outside his own field of research – objectively encouraged the superficial eclecticism of Darwinist culture in general. Thus it proved possible in turn to combine Darwinism with religion,[53] with imperialism and racism, with socialism, with the tritest positivist banalities, with the most contrary ideological and philosophical tendencies, with Spencer or with Nietzsche. The scientific spirit, which in the second half of the 19th century had seemed destined to penetrate all fields of knowledge, could not but be finally compromised by such eclecticism. Thus was revealed the illusion into which Darwin had fallen when he trusted in the spontaneity of intellectual progress, in the 'gradual illumination of men's minds which follows from the advance of science.' While scientific advance in fact continued to be rapid, the cognitive value of science was at the same time increasingly questioned, until eventually the 'eternal values of the spirit' were allowed to return to the fray and to celebrate new triumphs, while scientists, sequestered within their specializations, were relegated to a subordinate function within early 20th century culture.

The sole alternative to this process of involution was seen by Marx and Engels in a return to the best philosophic tradition, understood as the 'experimental history' of thought: of the real thought necessary to the art of operating with concepts (Engels). Hence their partial revaluation of the Hegelian dialectic, indicated very explicitly by Marx and developed by Engels in ways which can seem excessive if we do not bear in mind this historical need to reassert the rigour of rational thought, without which science is degraded to a purely instrumental value, available for all uses. Today, the interest of the theme of the relationship between Marxism and Darwinism in the superficial traditional terms of eclectic integration (as formulated by Bebel and Kautsky, by Bernstein and Lafargue, as well as by our own Enrico Ferri) has naturally expired. But at a time when new scientific advances risk following the same parabola as those of the 19th century, with the aid now of neo-positivist agnosticism, there is every reason for us to ponder once again this first historical example of a new conception of the relations between philosophy and science, between natural sciences and social sciences.

NOTES AND REFERENCES

1. F. De Sanctis, *Saggi Critici*, vol. III, Bari, 1953, pp. 355–367.
2. Marx-Engels, *Selected Works* (London, 1968), p. 435. Engels repeats the same comparison in his 1888 preface to the English translation of the *Communist Manifesto*.
3. 'An analogous case,' said Antonio Labriola (*Saggi sul Materialismo Storico*, Rome 1964, p. 236), while in the same period Edward Aveling was writing of the 'twin theories of evolution and surplus value' ('Charles Darwin und Karl Marx – eine Parallele,' *Die Neue Zeit*, 1897, vol. II, pp. 745–757). Turati, in a polemic of 1892 over the relations between Marxism and Darwinism, had noted in the same sense that 'Marx is precisely the Darwin of social science' (*Critica Sociale*, II, p. 135).
4. See, for example, the essay by the Russian scientist Timiryazev, 'Darwin and Marx,' written in 1919 and included in D. Ryazanov (ed.), *Karl Marx: Man, Thinker and Revolutionary* (London, 1927), which contains some interesting observations so long as it remains on the plane of parallels and analogies, but promptly lapses into a positivist eclecticism when it broaches problems common to the two doctrines: Marx is thrust into the company not only of Darwin, but also of John Stuart Mill and Comte. Much the same can be said of an article by Howard Selsam, 'Charles Darwin and Karl Marx' (*Mainstream*, New York, vol. 12, 6, 1959, pp. 23–36), where finally even peaceful competition between capitalism and socialism becomes an example of Darwin's law of natural selection – little to the advantage of either the notion of peaceful competition or an understanding of Darwin.
5. Especially interesting in this respect is Engels' letter to Marx of 14 July 1858: see Marx-Engels, *Werke*, vol. 29, pp. 337–339.
6. *Werke*, vol. 29, p. 524.
7. *Werke*, vol. 30, p. 131: 'obgleich grob englisch entwickelt . . .'. Contrary to Liebknecht's claim in his memoir of Marx, there is no evidence that Marx 'discerned the innovatory importance' of Darwin before the publication of *On the Origin of Species*.
8. *Werke*, vol. 30, p. 578; *Selected Correspondence* (Moscow, 1965), p. 123.
9. For the precursors of evolutionism, see especially the interesting essay of P. Omodeo, 'Centocinquant'anni di evoluzionismo', *Società*, XV, No. 5, 1959, pp. 833–883.
10. *Grundrisse* (Penguin/NLR edition) (London, 1973), p. 105.
11. *Economic and Philosophic Manuscript of 1844* (London, 1970), p. 135.
12. *Ibid.*, pp. 142–143.
13. *The German Ideology* (London, 1965), pp. 57–58.
14. *Economic and Philosophic Manuscripts of 1844*, p. 142.
15. *Ibid.*, p. 142.
16. *Ibid.*, p. 143.
17. *Ibid.*, p. 143.
18. *Ibid.*, p. 144.
19. *The German Ideology*, p. 58.

20. For the dispute over the notion of *generatio aequivoca*, see Engels' remarks in *Dialectics of Nature* (Moscow, 1966, pp. 296–297), and for the history of the theory, A. I. Oparin, *L'Origine della Vita sulla Terra* (Turin, 1956), pp. 7–44.

21. This conception, which as we have seen was an achievement of the young Marx, remains a methodologically operative principle in all his scientific work. In his preface to the first edition of *Capital* (and indirectly in his postscript to the second edition), Marx explicitly stated his view of human history as natural history: 'My standpoint, from which *the evolution of the economic formation of society is viewed as a process of natural history . . .*' (Our italics), *Capital*, vol. I (Moscow, 1961), p. 10.

22. This methodological imperative was emphasized by Darwin in his Introduction to *On the Origin of Species* (London, 1903, p. 8): 'In considering the Origin of Species, it is quite conceivable that a naturalist, reflecting on the mutual affinities of organic beings, on their embryological relations, their geographical distribution, geological succession, and other such facts, might come to the conclusion that each species had not been independently created, but had descended, like varieties, from other species. Nevertheless, such a conclusion, even if well founded, would be unsatisfactory, until it could be shown how the innumerable species inhabiting this world have been modified, so as to acquire that perfection of structure and coadaptation which most justly excites our admiration.'

23. The invalidity of the current view that counterposes Darwin to Lamarck over the problem of the inheritance of acquired characteristics, is demonstrated in the essay by P. Omodeo, 'Darwin e l'Ereditarietà dei Caratteri Acquisiti', *Scientia*, 54, December 1959.

24. *Capital*, vol. I, p. 372. The passage continues: 'Would not such a history be easier to compile, since, as Vico says, human history differs from natural history in this, that we have made the former, but not the latter?' We have seen, however, that this distinction should not be understood in any rigid sense, since for Marx the history of humanity is none other than a part of natural history. For other suggestions of similar methodological value taken by Marx from the writings of Darwin, see *Capital*, I, p. 341, and *Theories of Value*, vol. III, London 1972, pp. 294–295.

25. *Capital*, I, p. 373. (The phrase rendered as 'a materialism abstractly modelled on the natural sciences' by Gerratana is *abstrakt naturwissenschaftlichen Materialismus* in the German original; see *Werke*, vol. 23, p. 393.)

26. *Capital*, I, p. 373.

27. *The Autobiography of Charles Darwin* (edited by Nora Barlow), (London, 1958), p. 137.

28. It is regrettable that natural scientists make this mistake, but easily explicable, since the problem is of only incidental interest to them. It is much more surprising that the same uncritical attitude is to be found among social scientists; see, for example, D. G. MacRae, 'Darwinism and the Social Sciences,' in S. A. Barnett (ed.), *A Century of Darwin* (London, 1958), pp. 296 *et seq*.

29. *On the Origin of Species*, p. 9.

30. See Malthus, *Essay on the Principle of Population* (London, 1803), pp. 2–3: 'In plants and irrational animals the view of the subject is simple. They are all impelled by a powerful instinct to the increase of their species; and this instinct is interrupted by no reasoning or doubts about providing for their offspring. Wherever, therefore, there is liberty, the power of increase is exerted; and the superabundant effects are repressed afterwards by want of room and nourishment, which is common to plants and animals; and among animals, by their becoming the prey of each other.'

31. *On the Origin of Species*, p. 33.

32. *The Autobiography of Charles Darwin*, p. 120. (Our italics.)

33. Engels, *Anti-Dühring* (Moscow, 1947), p. 86. These considerations were developed by Engels in a passage of the *Dialectics of Nature* which stresses the complexity of the relationship between animal and vegetable over-population and the principle of natural selection (*Dialectics of Nature* (Moscow, 1966), pp. 306–307). Marx for his part confined himself to remarking that the idea of the 'struggle for life' becomes a mere phrase if used as an explanatory principle or natural law of all history. Thus he commented in a letter to Kugelman on 27 June 1870: 'Herr Lange, you see, has made a great discovery. The whole of history can be brought under a single great natural law. This natural law is the *phrase* (in this application Darwin's expression becomes nothing but a phrase) "the struggle for life", and the content of this phrase is the Malthusian law of population, or rather, over-population. So, instead of analysing the struggle for life as represented historically in varying and definite forms of society, all that has to be done is to translate every concrete struggle into the phrase "struggle for life", and this phrase itself into the Malthusian population fantasy. One must admit that this is a very impressive method – for swaggering, sham-scientific, bombastic ignorance and intellectual laziness.' Marx-Engels, *Selected Correspondence*, pp. 239–240.

34. Marx-Engels, *Selected Correspondence*, p. 128. In his historical analysis of theories of surplus value, Marx expressly emphasized the importance of Darwin's work as a scientific 'refutation' of Malthus' theory: *Theories of Surplus Value*, vol. II (London, 1969), p. 121.

35. *Dialectics of Nature*, p. 35. See also *Anti-Dühring*, pp. 324, 333; and Engels' letters to Lange of 29 March 1865 and Lavrov of 12–17 November 1875, *Selected Correspondence*, pp. 171–173 and 301–304.

36. Darwin, *The Descent of Man* (London, 1901), p. 945: 'Man, like every other animal, has no doubt advanced to his present high condition through a struggle for existence consequent on his rapid multiplication; and if he is to advance still higher, it is to be feared that he must remain subject to a severe struggle. Otherwise he would sink into indolence, and the more gifted men would not be more successful in the battle of life than the less gifted. Hence our natural rate of increase, though leading to many and obvious evils, must not be greatly diminished by any means.' Malthus was also preoccupied with 'indolence' in his *Essay on the Principle of Population*, and to avoid it he wanted the limitation of births to be entrusted exclusively to the means 'indicated by reason and sanctioned by religion,' so that 'the desire for marriage should conserve

all its force, quicken activity and impel the celibate to acquire by his labour the degree of comfort he is wanting;' and he therefore rejected with contempt 'any means artificial and foreign to the laws of nature which might be adopted to restrict population, both as an immoral means and as tending to suppress a necessary stimulus for inciting men to work. If in every marriage the number of children were to be subjected to a voluntary limitation, one would have to fear an increase of indolence.'

37. *The Autobiography of Charles Darwin*, pp. 136–142.

38. *Werke*, vol. 30, p. 418.

39. It is easy to imagine the way in which his letter might have been used by another man; but when after Marx's death a tendency developed to overestimate Engels' contribution to the construction of scientific socialism, Engels himself felt the need to 'settle this point' by stating publicly: 'What I contributed – at any rate with the exception of my work in a few special fields – Marx could very well have done without me. What Marx accomplished I could not have achieved.' Marx-Engels, *Selected Works*, p. 618.

40. See, for example, the polemical exchange between Marx and Engels over a book by Pierre Trémaux (*Origine et Transformations de l'Homme et des Autres Bêtes*, Paris 1865), whose scientific accuracy Engels judged severely, while Marx was inclined to overestimate it, immediately hailing it as 'a notable advance on Darwin.' In fact, this work disappeared without a trace in the history of biological science. See the letters from Marx of 7 August, 13 August and 3 October 1866, and from Engels of 10 August, 2 October and 5 October 1866; *Werke*, vol. 31, pp. 247–252, 256–261.

41. Labriola, *Saggi sul Materialismo Storico*, p. 218.

42. *Werke*, vol. 30, p. 338.

43. *Werke*, vol. 32, p. 229.

44. See the preface to the English translation of *Socialism: Utopian and Scientific*, in Marx-Engels, *Selected Works*, pp. 384–386.

45. *The Autobiography of Charles Darwin*, pp. 93–94. In earlier editions of the *Autobiography*, the last part of this passage was suppressed at the direct instance of Darwin's wife, as emerges from her letter to her son Francis, mentioned in a footnote in the Barlow edition. For Darwin's attitude to religion, see the whole section of the *Autobiography* on this topic (pp. 85–96), together with chapter nineteen of the biography by Arthur Keith, *Darwin Revalued*, London 1955.

46. See Barnett's preface to the symposium, *A Century of Darwin*, p. xv.

47. See *Karl Marx – Chronik seines Lebens in Finzeldaten* (Moscow, 1934), p. 379.

48. Darwin's first letter to Marx in 1873 was published by Edward Aveling in 1897 in his article in *Neue Zeit*, 'Charles Darwin und Karl Marx – eine Parallele' (which appeared simultaneously in *New Century Review* and *Devenir Social*). Darwin's second letter of 1880 was published for the first time in the Soviet journal *Pod Znamenem Marxizma*, 1931, Nos. 1–2. The originals of both letters are now kept at the Institute of Marxism-Leninism in Moscow. Keith, in his *Darwin Revalued*, cites

the second letter in another version that is probably a retranslation into English from a previous translation into another language.

49. The literature on the problem (ill-conceived) of the relationship between socialism and Darwinism is extremely large. The weightiest, although somewhat dubious, volume is Ludwig Woltmann, *Die Darwinische Theorie und der Sozializmus* (Düsseldorf, 1899).

50. For the reactionary character of Social Darwinism, see Rudolf Gottschalk, 'Darwin und der Sozialdarwinismus,' in *Deutsche Zeitschrift für Philosophie*, 1959, No. 4, pp. 521–539. Some information is also provided in O. Barie, *Idee e Dottrine Imperialistiche nell' Inghilterra Vittoriana* (Bari, 1953), pp. 248 *et seq.* There is a very broad and penetrating – if incomplete – analysis of German Social Darwinism in George Lukács, *Der Zerstörung der Vernunft* (Neuwied, 1962), pp. 591–605.

51. See also Engels' comments on Büchner, *Dialectics of Nature*, pp. 202, 205.

52. See, for example, Bebel in his popular work *Woman and Socialism* (London, 1904), and the Italian Enrico Ferri in *Socialismo e Scienza Positiva (Darwin-Spencer-Marx)*, (Rome, 1894), p. 19. Labriola's comment that Ferri's work had encountered 'little response' (*Saggi sul Materialismo Storico*, p. 232) was not wholly accurate. It was translated into numerous languages, and was praised by Bebel himself in a subsequent edition of his own book, in which he declared himself in 'complete agreement' with Ferri. Some criticisms of Ferri's work can be found, however, in the journal *Der sozialistische Akademiker*, as well as in the two reviews mentioned by Labriola. In any case, Ferri did not invent the 'Trinity Darwin-Spencer-Marx;' it was already widely current in the socialist culture of the period, and was introduced and defended in Italy by Napoleone Colajanni in a book (*Il Socialismo*, Catania, 1884) which directly inspired Ferri.

53. In Italy, for example, Darwinism was first introduced in a guise that reconciled it with religion, which provoked mistrust on all sides. See the amusing description of the lecture given at Turin in 1864 by De Filippi, a professor of zoology at that university, cited by Montalenti in his introduction to the recent Italian edition of *On the Origin of Species* (Turin, 1959). Later, this presumptive reconciliation was more or less tacitly accepted by virtually all religious confessions, including Catholicism, while the fiercest anti-evolutionist zeal continued to be typical of their propaganda for 'simple people.'

# DIALECTICAL MATERIALISM AND THE *MIR**

NORMAN LEVINE

The *mir* was an ancient Russian rural community. An institution of local self-government, the *mir* practiced communal ownership of agrarian property. Communal officials had jurisdiction over local forests, fisheries, hunting grounds and vacant lands. In the 19th century, the authority of the *mir* was enlarged. In 1838, it was given the power to redistribute arable land so that a direct relation could be established between the size of a household and the amount of land that it possessed. After the emancipation of the serfs in 1861, primitive democracy was established and a village assembly was empowered to manage all internal affairs. Consequently, the *mir* was a symbol of primitive village communism. Communal landholding promoted a sense of equality and mutual aid within the community, and the decisions of the *mir* possessed indisputable authority.

During the 19th century, the Russian Populists regarded the *mir* as the seed of Slavic rejuvenation. Alexander Herzen, Nicholai Bakunin, and the Russian Populists in general, saw the *mir* as the guardian of Slavic virtues against the ravages of Western materialism and scientism. The Populists romanticized the *mir*, seeing in it the uniqueness of the Russian spirit. Economic cooperation, religious faith, brotherliness, were all parts of this Russian spirit. Using the *mir* as a foundation, the Populists believed, Russia would rebuild itself in a unique fashion, and not imitate the pattern of development of Western Europe.

On the other hand, the Russian Social Democrats thought the *mir* a hindrance to the further progress of Russia. Progress for the Social Democrats entailed the industrialization and capitalization of Russia and, with rural capitalism, the destruction of the communal *mir*. Lenin, a member of the Social Democratic Party before its split into Bolshevik and Menshevik wings, predicted in *The Progress of Capitalism in Russia* that the *mir* would collapse before the advance of industrialization and capitalization. To Lenin, the *mir* was a romantic fantasy and the Popu-

* Originally published in the *Berkeley Journal of Sociology,* vol. 18, 1973–1974. Reprinted with permission of the journal.

lists mere petty bourgeois ideologues.

The problem of the Russian *mir* has enormous significance for a proper understanding of dialectical materialism. Traditional interpreters of Marx[1] tend to view dialectical materialism as synonomous with a unilinear view of history. For them, dialectical materialism and economic determinism are the same. They interpret Marx as maintaining that history must move through necessary stages of societal evolution – feudalism to capitalism to communism. Europe was the first to pass through these stages; the rest of the globe must imitate this European development. History is a unilinear process which all societies must follow.

Newer interpretations of Marx,[2] revisionist interpretations, present Marx as a multilinearist. The revisionists maintain Marx believed each society was a unique structure, that each possessed unique conditions, and that each would advance in time in accordance with its own structure. Dialectical materialism, understood in these terms, emerges as a much more subtle, sensitive, and accurate method of social analysis, rather than as an indicator of social inevitability and macrocosmic determinism.[3] Such an understanding opens up the possibility of interpreting different societies as developing along various lines. All societies need not follow the three-stage sequence, feudalism, capitalism, communism; the rest of the globe need not imitate Europe.

The question of the *mir* will be used in this paper as a case study to ascertain what Marx meant by dialectical materialism. If it can be shown that Marx believed the *mir* must and should succumb to the forces of capitalism, this would lend support to the argument that Marx maintained a unilinear view of history. If the *mir* must and should succumb, then capitalism was a necessary antecedent to communism. Then the industrial proletariat, bred in the womb of capitalist society, was the only class that could build a communist society. If capitalism and the proletariat were necessary preconditions for the triumph of a communist society, then Marx indeed thought history a unilinear process.

Conversely, if it can be shown that Marx believed the *mir* could act as the transition to communism, this would lend support to the argument that Marx maintained a multilinear view of history. If communism could evolve out of the *mir*, then Russian development might clearly differ from that of Western Europe. It might be the peasants, rather than the proletariat, who would build a communist society. Consequently, since capitalism and the proletariat were not necessary preconditions for communism, there existed no predetermined, necessary stages of societal evolution.

It is the intention of this paper to gain new insight into Marx's approach to the problem of the *mir* by examining the notes Marx took on his reading in early Russian, Asian and German institutions.[4] These *exzerpte* do not contain direct, positive statements by Marx himself. Rather, the notes Marx took were almost uniformly quotes from the authors he was reading. Thus, while it is impossible to assert definitively on the basis of the *exzerpte* that Marx believed in a particular concept, it is nevertheless possible to see the kinds of information Marx was exposed to, the kinds of reading he selected, and, in terms of the quotes themselves, the kinds of data he found interesting. In short, the *exzerpte* do not tell us what Marx categorically believed. They do, however, acquaint us with the ideas which influenced him, the direction of his research, and the probable direction of his thinking.

The *exzerpte* document clearly that beginning in 1853, Marx grew increasingly interested in ancient Asian, Russian, and Germanic institutions. From 1843 until 1853, Marx read predominantly in political economy. His notebooks during this decade were filled with *exzerpte* from Smith, Ricardo, Malthus, the French Physiocrats, Sismondi, and List. There were also ample citations from books dealing with the history of trade, banking, agriculture, and industry. Clearly Marx was concentrating his major efforts during these ten years on the gathering of data for his attack upon English classical political economy and for his analysis of capitalism. The *Critique of Political Economy* was published in 1859.

In the notebooks of 1853, we find the first indication that Marx was reading in Asian history. In that year he read eight books on India, including such works as J. F. Royle's *Essay on the Productive Resources of India* and *An Inquiry into the Causes of the long continued stationary condition of India,* Thomas St Raffles' *The History of Java,* and Robert Patton's *The Principle of Asiatic Monarchies.* In the same year Marx was also reading heavily in Russian history. There were eleven titles for this year.

Marx's interest in primitive Asian and Slavic institutions did not bear fruit only in his journalism of this time for the *New York Daily Tribune.* From 1857–1858 Marx composed the *Grundrisse der Kritik der Politischen Okonomie.* One section of this work, the *Formen die der Kapitalistischen Produktion vorhergehen* dealt basically with ancient Oriental, Slavic, and German communal forms of life.[5] Clearly, much of the material Marx used in the *Grundrisse* was gathered from the reading on Asia and Russia which he began in 1853.

In 1868 Marx began his reading of G. L. von Maurer. In that year he read Maurer's *Einleitung zur Geschichte der Mark, Hof, Dorf und*

*Stadtverfassung.* His reading in Maurer deepened, and during 1876 he read Maurer's *Geschichte der Markenverfassung, Geschichte der Fronhofe,* and *Geschichte der Dorfverfassung in Deutschland.* Marx's interest and involvement with ancient Slavic institutions continued throughout 1876 and 1878. In the former year he finished M. Utiesenovic's *Die Hauskommunionen der Sudslaven,* and in the latter year Haxthausen's *Die landliche Verfassung Russlands.*

In 1881 and 1882 Marx took up again his study of ancient institutions. Marx studied, in 1881, L. H. Morgan's *Ancient Society,* J. W. B. Money's *Java, or how to manage a Colony,* and H. J. S. Maine's *Lectures on the Early History of Institutions.* One year later Marx was to finish J. Lubbock's *The Origin of Civilization and the Primitive Condition of Man,* and D. M. Wallace's *Russia.*[6]

This listing of the books Marx studied serves two purposes. It tells us what Marx read, as well as what he did not read. After 1851 Marx's interest in economics waned. There were no more *exzerpte* from Smith, Ricardo, Malthus, or the French Physiocrats. There was no intensive or prolonged study of banking, trade, industry, or population. In terms of the study of society, Marx was increasingly drawn to anthropology. He was studying the ancient condition of man. This indicated a major shift in the direction of his thought. He was moving away from economics, away from English industrial problems, away from the nineteenth-century Western European world of *Das Kapital.* Increasingly he was scrutinizing world-wide pre-capitalist economic formations.

In chapter twenty-four of Book I of *Das Kapital,* Marx described the evolution of the capitalist mode of production from its feudal, agrarian antecedent. Marx's reading in ancient Asian, Russian, and Germanic history clearly documents that Marx's interest during the last half of his life was focusing on the problem of the breakdown of primitive, communal forms of social existence. Marx's *exzerpte* on anthropology show that there existed in his mind an outline, a tentative structure for a comparative study of the destruction of communal life and its supercession by a different form of society. In 1878 Marx started to read J. B. Jukes' *Student Manual of Geology.* In essence, Marx was involved with sociological geology. He was studying how one layer of human history had been destroyed by a new layer of human history, that is, how societies with different structures based on communal property were replaced by societies with different structures based on private property. Marx was dealing with sociological deposits, sociological ages, accepting all the while the unique structure of each society and its unique path of development.

It is abundantly clear from the books Marx selected to read, and from the passages Marx copied from these books, that he believed communal forms of property had been and were being destroyed on a world-wide basis. From his reading in G. L. von Maurer, he learned that the tribal communalism of the ancient Germans broke down as a result of their conquest of Roman territories. The acquisition of new land gave an opportunity, eagerly exploited, for the nobles of the tribe to acquire private property outside of the traditional cooperative possessions of the tribe.[7] From his reading in M. Utiesenovic, he learned how the family communism of the South Slavs had been destroyed by the imposition of laws making it mandatory for property to be assigned to one male and his heirs.[8] The books of Sir J. Phear, George Campbell, J. F. Royle, and George Patton on India all indicated that the Indian village commune was being dissolved under the impact of British imperialism.[9] Furthermore, the research of Haxthausen and of D. M. Wallace on Russian village life indicated that the Russian *mir* was undergoing the same fate as the Indian commune. The emancipation act of 1861 did not afford freedom to the serfs, but dissolved their old village associations and placed them at the mercy of the capitalistic-minded landowners.[10]

In the 1870s, when the question was raised as to whether the Russian *mir* could serve as the point of transition to communism, Marx had before him a body of literature which depicted the overthrow of communal forms of life by capitalistic forms of life. According to historical precedent, the chances of communal *mir* expanding into communist society seemed slight. Thus in 1877 Marx wrote to the editor of the Russian journal *Otyecestvenniye Zapisky*:

> I have arrived at this conclusion: If Russia continues to pursue the path she has followed since 1861 she will lose the finest chance [of escaping capitalist development] ever offered by history to a nation, in order to undergo all the fatal vicissitudes of the capitalist regime. If Russia is tending to become a capitalist nation after the example of the Western European countries, and during the last years she has been taking a lot of trouble in this direction – she will not succeed without having just transformed a good part of her peasants into proletarians; and after that, once taken to the bosom of the capitalist regime she will experience its pitiless law like other profane peoples. That is all.[11]

Ever the realist, Marx understood that the *mir* was tending toward extinction. But the probability of destruction was not the same as the necessity of destruction. Although Marx was aware that the considerable powers of Russian Tzardom were moving for destruction, he never asserted that it was a necessary and inevitable historical law for the *mir* to be destroyed. In fact, Marx believed just the opposite. He believed that, left to itself, the *mir* could act as the transition point to communism. He believed that there were forces in the *mir* which, if allowed to develop, could transform Russia into a communist society. He did not think, in short, that it was an adamantine law that Russia follow the exact path of evolution of Western Europe.

In order to prove these assertions it will be necessary to show: (1) that Marx was aware of at least one occasion in the past when different societies (for example, Western and Oriental society) took different paths of development; (2) that social forces which were non-industrial and non-capitalistic could, in themselves, create a communist consciousness; (3) that the peasants rather than the proletariat could act as a revolutionary class to bring communism into existence.

**1.** In 1853 Marx read Robert Patton's *The Principle of Asiatic Monarchies*. To Patton it was clear that Europe and Asia had taken two different paths of social evolution. In the West the effect upon all the 'pastoral tribes who subdued the agricultural provinces of the Roman Empire was to strengthen the tendency among them to form at least great land proprietors.'[12] The communal basis of German tribal existence was destroyed by the conquest of new territories, giving rise to an independent nobility who could assert their authority against that of the crown. Later, the law of primogeniture was established among the European nobility, and thus the descent of private property in land was engrained in the essential social fabric of European civilization.

On the other hand, in Asia it was the sovereign who became the universal proprietor of the land. No independent nobility, no center of social or political power, developed outside of the sovereign to contest or limit the absolute power of the monarch. Patton maintained that it was the need for irrigation in arid Asia which shifted to the monarch the predominance of economic and political power. The building, maintenance, and supervision of indispensable irrigation projects became the province of the crown and its bureaucracy. Taxing powers, in order to finance these projects, fell concomitantly to the sovereign. Thus the need for a socio-political power to ensure the existence of water for agriculture served as the foundation for Oriental despotism. Although local villages organized their land on a communal basis, ultimate ownership resided in the monarchial proprietor.[13]

At the end of 1880 Marx read H. J. S. Maine's *Lectures on the Early History of Institutions*. The major thrust of Maine's book was to trace the different forms of landed proprietorship which evolved in Europe, Brittany, England, and Ireland. While dealing basically with Western Europe, Maine could not help but be aware that other races (Oriental) had pursued a path of development different from the Germanic. Marx copied the following quote from Maine's monograph: '. . . modern research conveys a stronger impression than ever of the separation between the Aryan race and races of other stocks.'[14] For Maine, the breakdown of tribal communalism stemmed from two factors: (a) the disentanglement of individual rights from the collective rights of the tribe; (b) the 'transmutation of the sovereignty of the tribal chief.'[15] It was evident to Maine that the feudal decentralization of Western Europe was a stark contrast to the hydraulic despotism of the Orient, which proved that different historical evolutions had led to a 'separation between the Aryan races and races of other stocks.'

Thus, when Marx was asked by Vera Zasoulich to comment on the course of Russian development, he was already acquainted with a scholarship which showed that East and West had taken different paths of development. On 8th March, 1881 he wrote to Vera Zasoulich:

> At the bottom of the capitalist system is, therefore, the radical separation of the producer from the means of production – The basis of this whole evolution is the expropriation of the peasants – It has been accomplished in a final form only in England – but all the other countries of Western Europe are going through the same movement.
> The 'historical necessity' of this movement is thus explicitly restricted to the countries of Western Europe.[16]

In short, Marx knew that East and West had evolved differently. Russia, therefore, could take a course of development different from that of the West. There was no macrocosmic determinist law which necessitated that Russia follow the example of the West. The path of evolution which brought capitalism to the Occident was 'explicitly restricted to the countries of Western Europe.'

**2.** For Marx the development of a communist consciousness was a necessary and irreplaceable step prior to the revolutionary establishment of a communist society. In the West, the proletariat must be aware that its interests would be better served in a communist society. The European proletariat must wish, must will, must act to achieve the victory of communism. Without this consciousness, this intention, communism would never prove triumphant.

Communist consciousness would be created in the Western proletariat, according to Marx, through their life experience in the industrial system. Factory life required cooperation; it illustrated clearly the dependence of one worker upon another. The production line was the prime example of the interrelatedness of industrial labor. Made conscious that cooperation was the basis of the industrial system, the

168

European worker would subsequently become conscious that society in general should be organized as a cooperative system.

Western capitalism inadvertently produced the seeds of its own destruction. By imposing the system of industrial interdependence upon the worker, Western capitalism would unknowingly instill in that same worker the awareness that the total society should be interdependent. Such was the process by which communism would come in the West; this was how communism would have to evolve from the unique conditions and structures in Europe. This did not mean that communism could realize itself historically only in this way. It did not mean that communist or cooperative consciousness could develop only in the factory. It was possible for such a consciousness to develop from a different basis.

In early 1881 Marx finished Lewis Henry Morgan's book *Ancient Society*. In this work Morgan attempted to describe how primitive life, based on the *gens,* was destroyed. The *gens* was a primitive form of society in which kinship relationships determined economic and political structures. That is, property was distributed along family lines, rather than to individuals. Political representation was determined by family. In the European cases which Morgan studied, Rome and Greece, the acquisition of a territorial base for the tribe spelled the doom of the *gens.* That is, territorial considerations and rights soon superseded kinship considerations and rights. The important point in this context, however, was that for many centuries during man's tribal non-territorial condition, kinship relations were the dominant relations in the society. In other words, it was kinship relationships which determined property and productive relationships. Purely economic forces played a secondary role during the tribal stage of human evolution. The rights of the family were the primary determinant of the use and appropriation of the means of production. With these rights came communal ownership of the means of production.[17]

In 1882 Marx read J. Lubbock's *The Origin of Civilization and the Primitive Condition of Man.* Lubbock's work also acquainted Marx with the fact that in primitive society, kinship relationships were the dominant social forces and conditioned the use and distribution of productive materials. Furthermore, in his reading of H. J. S. Maine, Marx exposed himself to a similar opinion and supporting documentation. Lastly, in this particular case the *exzerpte* do contain marginal comments by Marx himself. It is one of the rare cases in the *exzerpte* when Marx spoke in the first person. In the Maine notes, Marx wrote: '. . . from the moment when a tribal community settles down finally land begins to be the base of society in place of kinship.'[18] In the Lubbock notes, Marx wrote: '(Lubb) has taken some of the following evidence from his [James McLennan's][19] valuable works, adding, however, (!) several additional cases. (great, greatest Lubb!).'[20]

What Marx learned from his reading in anthropology, and what he agreed with, was that kinship relationships had been and therefore could be determining social forces. The ancient *gens* were matriarchies. Kinship groups were therefore rather extensive. Because descent was traced through the mother, and no sons or daughters were excluded from the kin, property was shared communally by the *gens*. Communalism was a necessary outgrowth of a society where kinship relations were dominant social forces. Since all members were equal in the *gens*, property would belong to the *gens* collectively.

Most importantly, however, the *gens* already possessed a communist consciousness like that of the proletariat of the nineteenth century. In *The German Ideology* Marx did distinguish the communist consciousness of the tribe from that of the European industrial worker.[21] But the essential quality was present: the consciousness of cooperation. This consciousness of cooperation did not arise from an industrial environment. Therefore, it was not absolutely necessary to create an industrial environment in order to create a collectivist consciousness. The communist consciousness of the tribe arose from the social force of kin awareness. Therefore, it was possible to create a communist consciousness in any society where there is collective ownership of the means of production.

The question of a communist consciousness is inseparable from the problem of whether the *mir* could act as a transition point to communism. Did Marx think it possible to evolve from an agrarian society to a highly industrialized society organized on the basis of socialist principles? A close examination of Marx's *exzerpte* suggests that he did indeed think so. The collectivist consciousness of the *mir* could act as the organizing principle and the philosophical context and fiber around which industrial organization would be structured. The *mir* could be a transitional stage because it was historically possible for society to develop from agrarian feudalism to socialist industrialism. The crucial element, the core factor, was a communist consciousness, an intellectual structuring of social life on a collectivist and communal basis.

The argument that the *mir* could expand directly into socialism offers compelling evidence of Marx's multilinear view of history. In short, there were at least two possible paths to socialism. First, there was the path of Western Europe, a three-stage progression from feudalism to capitalism to communism. Second, there was the possible path of agrarian Russia, a two-stage sequence bypassing capitalism and developing directly from feudal agrarianism to communism. Societies, depending upon their own internal structure, could evolve along either of these two paths (or perhaps some alternative paths). The factor that was crucial was the fruition of communist consciousness, rather than some universally necessary stage of economic development.

Marx addressed many of these issues in a letter he sent to Vera Zasoulich on 8th March, 1881. There were three drafts of this letter, and in the second one, which he did not mail, he wrote:

> In appropriating the positive results of the capitalist mode of production, (Russia) is capable of developing and transforming the archaic form of its village community, instead of destroying. (I observe, by the way, that the form of community property in Russia is the most modern form of the archaic type, which in turn has passed through a number of evolutionary changes.)
>
> The Russian village community belongs to the youngest type in this chain. Here the peasant cultivator already owns the house in which he lives and the garden belonging to it. Here we have the first dissolving element of the archaic formation unknown to older types. On the other hand all these are based on blood relationships between the members of the community while the type to which the Russian commune belongs, is already emancipated from these narrow bonds and is thus capable of greater evolution. The isolation of the village communities, the lack of links between their lines, this locally founded microcosm is not everywhere an immanent characteristic of the last of the primitive types. However, wherever it does occur, it permits the emergence of a central despotism above the communities. It seems to me that in Russia the original isolation caused by the vast extent of this territory is easily to be eliminated, once the fetters imposed by the government will have been burst.[22]

Since a communist consciousness already existed, the *mir* did not have to be destroyed. Russia did not have to become capitalized and proletarianized. However, two other conditions were necessary in order to realize the potential of the *mir*, in order to give full expression to its generative forces. First, the *mir* must appropriate the industrial system. Second, Tzarism must be overthrown.

The appropriation of the industrial system by the *mir* means that cooperation becomes the determining social force of technological society. Clearly, advanced industrial society will destroy outmoded technological and economic features of agrarian and *mir* existence. But the modern economy will be organized in accordance with *mir* collectivist mentality. On the level of social meaning and interrelationship, the communist consciousness of the *mir* will not only be the structural essence of the modernized society, but also the ground of human behavior and interpersonal exchange. The collectivist principle of the *mir* will become the primary social ethic of the society as a whole. The progressive and communal ethos of the *mir* will become the ground on which the materiality of advanced technology will be given meaning and social relevance.

The revolutionary overthrow of Tzarism would remove the political force which most hindered and retarded the generative power of the *mir*. Only when this hostile political barrier was removed could the *mir* reach its full potential. But there existed in the *mir* the vital factor: cooperative consciousness. All that was needed was to create the proper political environment so that the communist principles of the *mir* could readily extend their force to industrial society.

**3.** Not only did Marx recognize the possibility of peasants building a communist society through the evolution of the *mir*, he also believed that the peasantry could become a revolutionary communist force. In short, the peasantry could be proletarianized; their proletarianization would make them a revolutionary force.

The proletarianized peasantry we are discussing here is the non-*mir* peasantry. The bulk of the Russian peasants were those who did not live in communal surroundings, who were impoverished, who either did not own or rent any land, who worked as agricultural wage-laborers, or who owned or rented such small parcels of land that they were unable to satisfy their basic needs. The problem we are addressing in this section is thus different from the problem of the peasantry in the *mir*. The *mir* peasants possessed a collectivist consciousness because of their collectivist environment. The problem for the non-*mir* peasantry was how they were going to develop a revolutionary consciousness. We are not concerned here with the question of communal behaviour, but rather with the creation of a consciousness to fundamentally revolutionize society. The question that Marx had to face was whether it was possible for peasants living in a private-propertied environment to rise to the consciousness of revolutionizing society: not to provide the principles of the new, socialist society, but rather to overturn and topple an old society, to be the cadres of the revolutionary army.

In Western Europe, during the advent of capitalism, the peasantry had been almost completely destroyed. Chased from the land, the peasants had moved to the great industrial centers to become the exploited proletariat. For Marx, then, the proletariat was the revolutionary class in Western Europe. But this did not mean that only an industrial proletariat could be a communist revolutionary force. Other classes could fulfill this role. The crucial question was whether the social condition of a particular society produced in a class in that society a

172

revolutionary consciousness, that is, the intent to reconstruct society at all costs. In the Occident, capitalist society had given the proletariat a revolutionary consciousness. However, Marx also believed it possible for the peasantry to acquire a revolutionary consciousness.

Marx held this opinion as early as 1844. In one of his early manuscripts entitled *Rent of Land*, Marx wrote:

> Consequently, the agricultural workers are soon reduced to the minimum level of subsistence, and the farmer class establishes the power of industry and capital within landed property. Through competition with foreign countries the rent of land ceases, in the main, to constitute an independent source of income. A large section of the landowners is obliged to take the place of the tenant farmers who sink in this way into the proletariat.[23]

The theme of the proletarianization of the farmer was more fully developed in the third volume of *Das Capital*. However, before the peasant could be transformed into a wage-laborer, it was necessary for capitalist practices to dominate agriculture. According to Marx, this was exactly what had happened in the European countryside:

> We assume, then, that agriculture is dominated by the capitalist mode of production, just as manufacture is; in other words, that agriculture is carried on by capitalists who differ from other capitalists primarily in the manner in which their capital, and the wage-labor set in motion by this capital, are invested. So far as we are concerned, the farmer produces wheat, etc., in much the same way as the manufacturer produces yarn or machines . . . Just as the capitalist mode of production in general is based on the expropriation of the conditions of labor from the laborers, so does it in agriculture presuppose the expropriation of the rural labourers from the land and their subordination to a capitalist who carries on agriculture for the sake of profit.[24]

The capitalization of the countryside meant that the peasant would suffer from the same alienation and dehumanization as the industrial wage-laborer. Confronted by the same conditions, confronted by the same capitalist exploitation, peasant and proletarian would suffer the same degradation. Marx wrote:

> It is true that the peasant for example, expends much labor on his small plot of land. But it is labor isolated from objective social and material conditions of productivity, labor robbed and stripped of these conditions.[25]

Dehumanized, abandoned to the profit system, the peasant would suffer the same emiseration as the proletarian. The once independent peasant, unable to compete with the large capitalist landowning aristocracy, would gradually lose his land and his autonomy, and become a totally dependent wage-laborer.

Since the invasion of agriculture by the capitalist mode of production, transformation of independently producing peasants into wage-workers, is in fact the last conquest of this mode of production, these inequalities are greater here than in any other line of production.[26]

Since the peasants could be proletarianized, they could be a revolutionary force. They could develop a communist consciousness, that is, because they faced social conditions in which their labor was expropriated; they would become aware that only the common ownership of the means of production would prevent further exploitation of their productive praxis. Peasant and industrial laborer worked in different environments, but their social conditions were the same: alienating and exploitative. The communist consciousness of both the proletarianized peasant and the proletarianized industrial laborer stemmed from similarly oppressive social conditions.

In the case of the *mir*, as we have seen, consciousness was already communistic by virtue of the cooperative relations of production. Collectivist practices themselves could produce among the members of the *mir* the awareness that all means of production should be organized on a collectivist basis. In the case of the non-*mir* peasant, its proletarianization could create a revolutionary consciousness like that of the industrial worker; the agrarian worker could also come to believe that society must be fundamentally reconstructed.

Marx then was not primarily concerned with developing a 'historico-philosophical theory, of which the supreme virtue consists in its being suprahistorical, i.e. beyond the pale of history,'[27] but rather with depicting the variety of concrete historical processes in which communist consciousness can arise. Marx was not a unilinear determinist. Rather, he understood that revolutionary praxis was needed to bring communism into history. In his frame of reference, the Russian *mir* and non-*mir* peasant were entirely equal to this challenge. From his perspective, the *mir* and non-*mir* peasant were social forces with enough potency to develop the socialist society.

Marx's own certainty about the revolutionary potential of the *mir* and the peasantry becomes even more clear from a close reading of the second and third drafts of his 1881 letter to Vera Zasoulich. The fact that Marx wrote three drafts of the same letter indicates that he experienced some difficulty in specifying his ideas in so short a form. Nevertheless, the letters illustrate that Marx had at his disposal a wealth of information concerning the primitive forms of communal ownership in Asia, Russia, and among the German tribes. Marx apparently had worked out a theory regarding the historical succession of the various communal forms.[28] The impact of Marx's reading in anthropology and ancient history is quite apparent. At the end of his life he had moved away from an almost exclusive concentration on depicting the origin and genesis of capitalism in the West, toward a study of the historical evolution of agrarian collectivist societies, basically in non-Western areas. Trying to relate his extensive scholarship on primitive communism to the question of the *mir*, Marx wrote:

> I now come to the crux of the question. We cannot overlook the fact that the archaic type, to which the Russian commune belongs, conceals an internal dualism, which may under certain historic circumstances lead to its ruin. Property in land is communal, but each peasant cultivates and manages his plot on his own account, in a way recalling the small peasant of the West. Common ownership, divided petty cultivation: this combination which was useful in remoter periods, becomes dangerous in ours. On one hand mobile property, an element which plays an increasing part even in agriculture, gradually leads to differentiation of wealth among the members of the community, and therefore makes it possible for a conflict of interests to arise, particularly under the fiscal pressure of the state. On the other hand the economic superiority of communal ownership, as the base of an operative and combined labor, is lost . . .[29]
> But does this mean that the historic career of the agricultural community must inevitably lead to this result? Certainly not. The dualism within it permits of an alternative: either the property element in it will overcome the collective element, or the other way round. Everything depends on the historical environment in which it occurs.[30]

What Marx was saying was that the *mir* need not be destroyed. It could act as the transition to communism. The cooperative elements in it could serve as one of the origins for a general collectivization of society. On the other hand, the elements of private property which the *mir* also contained could serve as a decomposing force. If the course of development in Russia accentuated, selected, supported the private-propertied elements of the *mir*, it was doomed. If the *mir* was to survive, external forces must support its internal forces of collectivism. The potentiality for historically progressive communism already existed in the *mir*, but this was not sufficient in itself. Actual sociopolitical conditions must insure the future of the *mir*.

Dialectical materialism, then, is no dogma of historical inevitability. Marx never claimed to have discovered the macro-cosmic social laws which compelled all societies to move in a unilinear development. Dialectical materialism is rather an instrument for social analysis. It views all social formation as existing in a state of tension. In every socioeconomic structure there exists a conflict between retrogressive and progressive forces. The ascendancy of one or the other is determined in large part by external factors. The support of retrogressive or progressive elements, and therefore the revolutionary potential of a given socio-economic structure, is determined by the external conditions in which that structure finds itself.

It is fair to say that, in Marx's understanding, the *mir* was not an orphan of history. Rather, it had direct revolutionary potential. Communism could evolve in Russia, with the *mir* as inspiration, without the capitalization of its society. I shall leave it to the historian of Russian social development to determine the extent to which the *mir* realized that potential. I have cited the *mir* in this paper with a view toward demonstrating that Marx's approach to history was multilinear, not unilinear.

NOTES AND REFERENCES

1. Recent scholarship has begun to unravel the differences between Marx and Engels. Because the once assumed unanimity of view between the two men did not in fact exist, the paper deals solely with the work of Marx. On the relationship between Marx and Engels, see the following essays: Herman Bollnow, 'Engels Auffassung von Revolution und Entwicklung in Seinen Grundsatzen des Kommunismus (1847),' *Marxismusstudien* (Tübingen: J. C. B. Mohr, 1954), pp. 77–144; Ludwig Landgrede, 'Das Problem der Dialektik,' *Ibid.*, 1960, pp. 1–65; Erhard Lucas, 'Marx und Engels Auseinandersetzung Mit Darwin,' *Ibid.*, 1964, pp. 443–469; Thilo Ramm, 'Die Kunftige Gesellschaftsordnung Mach Theorie von Marx und Engels,' *Ibid.*, 1957, pp. 77–119; Erich Thier, 'Etappen der Marx Interpretation,' *Ibid.*, 1954, pp. 1–38. Also the following book makes penetrating comments about the whole problem: Iring Fetscher, *Karl Marx und der Marxismus* (München: R. Piper, 1967).

2. On the newer interpretations of Marx's view of dialectical materialism see the following works: Henri LeFebvre, *The Sociology of Marx*, trans. Norbert Guterman (New York: Pantheon Books, 1968); Alfred Schmidt, *Beitrage Zur Marxistischen Erkenntnistheorie* (Frankfurt: Suttekamp Verlag, 1969); Irving M. Zeitlin, *Marxism: A Reexamination* (Princeton: D. van Nostrand, 1967). For some revisionist classics, see George Lukács, *History and Class Consciousness*, trans. Rodney Livingstone (Cambridge, Mass.: M. I. T. Press, 1968); Antonio Gramsci, *Prison Notebooks*, trans. Quintin Hoare (New York: International Publishers, 1971).

3. On the question of Marx as a determinist, see my article 'Humanism without Eschatology,' *Journal of the History of Ideas* (January – March, 1972).

4. The author acknowledges the support of the American Philo-

sophical Society which allowed him to spend the summer of 1971 at the International Institute of Social History in Amsterdam. The International Institute possesses the entire corpus of Marx's notebooks. All the information contained in this essay regarding Marx's *exzerpte* was obtained from the archives at the Institute.

5. Karl Marx, *Pre-Capitalist Economic Formations*, trans. by Jack Cohen (New York: International Publishers, 1965).

6. *Exzerpte* of Karl Marx [vols. B65, B112, B162], International Institute of Social History, Archives, Amsterdam.

7. Marx, *exzerpte* on G. L. von Maurer, *Einleitung zur Geschichte der Mark, Hof, Dorf und Stadtverfassung* [vol. B133], pp. 4–95.

8. *Exzerpte* on M. Utiesenovic, *Die Hauskommunionen der Sudslaven* [vol. B137], pp. 18–45.

9. *Exzerpte* on Sir J. Phear, *The Aryan Village in India and Ceylon* [vol. B162], pp. 131–157; George Campbell, *Modern India* [vol. B65], pp. 12–24; J. F. Royle, *An Inquiry into the causes of the long continued stationary condition of India* [vol. B65], p. 9; Robert Patton, *The Principles of Asiatic Monarchies* [vol. B65], pp. 32–37.

10. *Exzerpte* on G. Haxthausen, *Die landliche Verfassung Russland* [vol. B138], pp. 16–39; D. M. Wallace, *Russia* [vol. B167], pp. 40–41.

11. Karl Marx and Friedrich Engels, *Selected Correspondence* (New York: International Publishers, 1964), pp. 353–354.

12. *Exzerpte* on Robert Patton, p. 32.

13. On the hydraulic basis of Oriental despotism, see *exzerpte* on Robert Patton. Also see Karl Wittfogel, *Oriental Despotism* (New Haven: Yale University Press, 1964).

14. *Exzerpte* on H. J. S. Maine, *Lectures on the Early History of Institutions* [vol. B162], p. 164.

15. *Ibid.*, p. 166.

16. Karl Marx and Friedrich Engels, *The Russian Menace to Europe*, ed. Paul W. Blackstock and Bert F. Hoselitz (Glencoe: Free Press, 1952), pp. 278–279.

17. *Exzerpte* on Lewis Morgan, *Ancient Society* [vol. B162], pp. 4–101.

18. *Exzerpte* on H. J. S. Maine, *Lectures on the Early History of Institutions*, p. 163.

19. Brackets are mine. Reference is to James McLennan, *Primitive Marriage* (London: Lawrence Press, 1865).

20. *Exzerpte* on J. Lubbock, *The Origin of Civilization and the Primitive Condition of Man* [vol. B168], p. 4.

21. Karl Marx, *The German Ideology* (London: Lawrence & Wishart, 1965), pp. 29–49.

22. Marx, *Pre-Capitalist Economic Formations*, pp. 142–143.

23. Marx, *Early Writings*, trans. T. B. Bottomore (New York: McGraw-Hill, 1963), pp. 142–143.

24. Marx, *Capital* (New York: International Publishers, 1967), pp. 614–615.

25. *Ibid.*, p. 677.

26. *Ibid.*, p. 650.

27. Marx, *The Russian Menace to Europe*, p. 218.

# SECTION III

# THE SOCIOLOGY OF CAPITALISM

# INTRODUCTION TO SECTION III

The centerpiece of Marx's sociology is, of course, his analysis of capitalism. The focus of his major theoretical works, the capitalist mode of production preoccupied Marx both as an object of scientific analysis and as the object of immediate political praxis. The intersection of these two interests has long been a source of confusion within Marxian scholarship.

Within this general problematic one poi..t, however, should be quite clear. For Marx, the unity of theory and practice did *not* mean the reduction of theory to the level of ideology or polemic, the intellectual justification of tactical political decisions. All too often, this has been the practice of Marxist political parties and repressive state apparatuses, when these have become entrenched in power. The concept that theory should be put at the service of the party is one wholly foreign to Marx's way of thinking.

What Marx did believe was that an informed understanding of the laws of motion of capitalist society should serve as a guide to the political practice of socialist movements and parties. And it was this belief which served as one of the mainsprings of Marx's life-long attempt to theoretically comprehend the growth and internal logic of capitalism as an historically unique and all-encompassing form of social relations.

Marx viewed the capitalist mode of production as historically unique, and his attitude toward it was in many ways quite ambivalent. Although he hated the exploitative nature of the capitalist-worker relationship and the tendency of the acquisitive market nexus to reduce all human to economic relationships, Marx was still capable of composing long paeans of praise to the majestic productive apparatus brought into being by capitalism. This ambivalence in Marx's attitude rose directly from his perception of the internal contradictions of capital itself. At once the most productive and exploitative of economic systems, capitalism as a mode of production was seen by Marx as a form of life which was constantly betraying its own promise. Capitalism, while producing unprecedented wealth in society ultimately fails as a form of productive and social relations because it cannot organize this production and its fruits for socially useful goals. Social production leads to private accumulation and the simultaneous creation of the polar opposites of wealth

181

and misery in its ruling and subordinate classes.

For Marx, this state of affairs was intolerable, and in his greatest work *Capital* he patiently presented the working out of these contradictory forces which determine the laws of motion of the capitalist mode of production. As capitalism develops into its mature form, it is exploded by its internal contradictions. The natural antagonism of labor and capital develops into open warfare and out of this, Marx hoped, would emerge the structural conditions which would make possible for the first time in human history the establishment of non-antagonistic forms of productive relations – a society which would no longer be divided into hostile camps, a classless society.

These twin themes of capitalist development and revolution lie at the center of Paul Sweezy's contribution to this volume. Sweezy, a noted economist and editor of the socialist journal *Monthly Review* for thirty years, is the dean of American Marxist scholarship. In this essay, he addresses the historical transformation of capitalism which took place in the transition from the period of capitalist manufacture, based on the introduction of a division of manual labor in the workshop, to the period of modern industry based on machinery. It is, Sweezy contends, only in this second stage of capitalism that Marx identified the development of a revolutionary working class. While earlier political economists such as Adam Smith and David Ricardo had dealt with only the earlier stage of capitalist manufacture in their written works, Marx, with his characteristic focus upon the role of technological change, felt that the 19th century industrial revolution, with its large-scale introduction of productive machinery into manufacturing, had produced a crucial change in the structure of capitalism. As the introduction of machinery made an anachronism of the old craft skills and enforced a new, more 'democratic' work regimen, at the same time it broke down old geographical and guild divisions and jealousies, creating a new consciousness of class among the working masses and making possible the emergence of a unified class-conscious working class movement and politics. In a few concluding comments, Sweezy addresses the theoretical problem posed by the failure of this working-class movement to achieve socialist revolution in the industrial heartland of Western Europe. This failure, Sweezy concludes, can be accounted for by further developments in the capitalist world unforeseen by Marx, primarily state intervention to ameliorate economic crises and the development of a 'new and international division of labor' displacing some of the worst effects of capitalist development onto the underdeveloped nations of the Third World. However, the creation of a new world-proletariat, Sweezy contends, while it postpones revolution in Europe, inevitably leads to the same result predicted by Marx, revolutionary overthrow of the capitalist system as a whole.

The second contribution, by Ian Gough, continues this examination of the interrelation of economic and political factors in Marx's work by re-examining the relevance of Marx's distinction between productive and non-productive labor for contemporary political practice. Generally, Gough concludes after a careful analysis of Marx's use of the two categories of labor, Marxists have taken an overly narrow interpretation of Marx's definition of productive labor, excluding a number of categories of productive workers (such as those producing luxury goods) which were explicitly included by Marx. These errors, according to Gough, have resulted from a confusion between the labor necessary to produce a final use value regardless of how or why that use value has been generated (Marx's definition) and ideas of the 'necessity' or social usefulness of various commodities produced by labor. In taking this stand distinguishing the intrinsic usefulness of the product of labor from the category of productive labor, Gough opts for a reading of Marx which emphasizes the scientific as opposed to moralistic nature of the analytical categories in Marx's economics.

Gough insists that the key role assigned to the proletariat by Marx was a consequence not of the misery this class suffers under capitalist relations of production, but rather was because of the place the class occupies in the productive process. In this respect, the distinction in Marx's economics between productive and unproductive labor remains of more than simply academic value.

In his brilliant piece on Marx and the middle class, Martin Nicolaus distinguishes in Marx's theory of surplus value the roots of a scientific analysis of the rise of a 'surplus' or middle class under conditions of advanced capitalism. Like Gough, Nicolaus is concerned with the productive/unproductive labor dichotomy and its implications for political action. Nicolaus, however, is interested primarily in exploding the myth of a Marxism which reduces everything to the fundamental contradiction of labor and capital.

Nicolaus attributes this 'Hegelian' reading of Marx to his early works, especially the 1848 *Communist Manifesto* in which, all too often, serious economic analysis is reduced to a dialectical catechism. However, in Marx's later works, beginning with the 1857–58 *Grundrisse* manuscript, Nicolaus finds a much more sophisticated class analysis based upon the theory of surplus value and the law of the tendential decline of the rate of profit. Nicolaus argues that, according to Marx, as the rate of profit falls, there is a necessary increase in both the rate and mass of surplus value as well as in the mass of profits. This increase generates a growing middle strata which performs two necessary services for capitalism: first, staffing the increasing number of non-productive service and maintenance (white-collar) positions which are required by a growing capital establishment and second, consuming an increasing number of commodities as the absolute surplus product continues to rise. Marx's theory of the new middle class, Nicolaus concludes, must be considered one of Marx's greatest, if least understood, scientific achievements.

In the final essay in this section, Ralph Miliband, senior editor of the annual collection *Socialist Register* and author of the noted *The State in Capitalist Society*, examines Marx's writings on the role of the state in capitalist society. While Miliband accedes to the classical Marxist view of the state as 'a committee for managing the common affairs of the whole bourgeoisie,' he advances a number of qualifications to this interpretation of Marx's thought on this subject. Particularly of interest are Miliband's analyses of Marx's writings on Bonapartism, the 'exceptional state' of capitalism in crisis, and 'Asiatic despotism.'

Miliband is especially concerned to defend Marx against the criticism of authoritarianism. He successfully demonstrates, largely through the use of quotations from Marx's own writings, a passionate attachment to democratic forms and methods in Marx's work. For Marx, socialism was the logical completion, not the negation, of 18th century liberal democracy. As the 18th and 19th century democratic revolutions in Europe had aimed at the destruction of feudal political privilege, so Marx saw the coming socialist revolution shattering the bonds of bourgeois economic privilege, completing the revolutionary promise of the French Enlightenment. Miliband concludes that, far from bearing any authoritarian imprint, Marx's writings on the state are marked by a thoroughly anti-authoritarian and anti-bureaucratic bias.

# KARL MARX AND THE
# INDUSTRIAL REVOLUTION*

PAUL M. SWEEZY

I have long been greatly impressed by the fact that Karl Marx, though using a conceptual framework derived from and in many ways very similar to classical economic theory, nevertheless reached conclusions radically different from those of the classical economists. Noting that Marx viewed the capitalist process as 'one which, in principle, involves ceaseless accumulation accompanied by changes in methods of production,' I wrote in 1942:

> It is at once apparent that this view of the capitalist process differs radically from that which underlies the classical theory of economic evolution. The latter is, in principle, unconcerned with changes in methods of production; economic development is viewed exclusively in terms of (gradual) quantitative changes in population, capital, wages, profits, and rent. Social relations remain unaffected; the end product is simply a state of affairs in which all these rates of change equal zero [the stationary state]. Since the Marxian view lays primary stress on changes in methods of production, it implies qualitative change in social organization and social relations as well as quantitative change in economic variables as such. The way is thus paved for regarding the 'end product' as a revolutionary reconstitution of society rather than a mere state of rest.[1]

Part of the explanation of this fundamental difference between Marx and the classics may well lie in the opposing personal and class interests that they represented. But I think it would be a mistake to leave the matter there. Classical political economy, especially in its Ricardian form, was not incompatible with a theory of class conflict: indeed, Ricardo himself pointed out and emphasized the conflict of interest between capitalists and landlords, and the so-called Ricardian socialists soon showed that the theory could equally well be used to underpin a theory of class struggle between capital and labor. Like them, Marx could have espoused the cause of the working class without making any

* Originally published in *Events, Ideology and Economic Theory*, (ed.) Robert V. Eagly, Detroit: Wayne State University Press, 1968. Reprinted with permission of the publisher.

important changes in classical economic theory. That he did not do so but instead transformed classical political economy into a radically new theory of economic development must be explained by something other than, or at any rate additional to, class interest. In what follows I shall try to show that Marx, in contrast to the classics, systematically took into account and incorporated into his theoretical system that inter-related series of events and processes which is generally known as the in-dustrial revolution. Marx's conceptualization of the industrial revolution is, I believe, the basis of his theory of economic development.

Let us begin by noting that Marx used the term 'industrial revolution' again and again,[2] not as a mere catch phrase to characterize a period of rapid change but as a descriptive designation of the process of transfor-mation between what Engels called 'two great and essentially different periods of economic history: the period of manufacture proper, based on the division of manual labor, and the period of modern industry based on machinery.'[3] These are not, in Marx's view, two different social systems but rather two phases of capitalism.

Manufacture differs from handicraft production in its organization of the labor process, not in its basic methods and instruments. In handi-craft production artisans produce saleable commodities and buy what they need (both consumption goods and means of production) from other similarly situated commodity producers. Division of labor within the workshop is severely limited by the fact that the master work-man has at most a few journeymen and apprentices working with him. The guilds, with their strict rules and standards, gave appropriate insti-tutional form to this mode of production and fought a long and bitter, though unsuccessful, battle to preserve its integrity.

The transition from handicraft production to capitalist manufacture was a part of the stormy process which Marx named 'primitive ac-cumulation.'[4] It had two sides to it: the separation of a sizeable body of working people from their means of production, and the emergence of a group of persons with liquid wealth which they wished to put to profitable use. The uprooting of peasants through such measures as en-closures and the expropriation of Church lands created the necessary landless proletariat, while trade and plunder, given enormous impetus by the geographical discoveries of the late 15th and early 16th cen-turies, spawned an eager and willing capitalist class. The result was the emergence and spread of capitalist manufacture, at first largely in areas outside the jurisdiction of the guilds.

The methods and instruments of production in the new factories were essentially those of the artisan workshop; but now, owing to the larger number of workers involved and the complete domination of the production process by the capitalist, it became possible to subdivide the work and specialize the workers. The result was a tremendous increase in productivity due largely to the increased division of labor within the factory, a process that was so eloquently and lovingly described in Book I of *The Wealth of Nations*.

In Marx's view, an economic system based upon manufacture is essentially conservative. 'History shows how the division of labor peculiar to manufacture, strictly so called, acquires the best adapted form at first by experience, as it were behind the backs of the actors, and then, like the guild handicrafts, strives to hold fast that form when once found, and here and there succeeds in keeping it for centuries.'[5] But it is not only in this technological sense that such an economy is conservative. It also creates a highly differentiated labor force, dominated, numerically and otherwise, by skilled workers who tend to be contentious and undisciplined but incapable of sustained revolutionary activity. The economy and society based on manufacture is thus inherently change-resistant: it expands under the impact of capital accumulation but does not generate forces capable of altering its structure or, still less, of transforming it into something else.

It was this system that provided the model for classical political economy, which found its fullest and best known expression in Adam Smith's *Wealth of Nations*. 'What characterizes . . . him [Smith] as the political economist par excellence of the period of manufacture,' Marx wrote, 'is the stress he lays on the division of labor.'[6] By comparison, Smith paid scant attention to machinery, so little, indeed, that Schumpeter felt justified in saying that with him 'division of labor is practically the only factor in economic progress.'[7] Nathan Rosenberg argues, persuasively I think, that Schumpeter's view needs qualification. Rosenberg holds that Smith recognized that the progress fostered by division of labor was limited to improvements within the existing technology and that major inventions are made not by workmen at all, or by capitalists either for that matter, but by 'philosophers' who are totally separated from the productive process.[8] Nevertheless, as applied to Smith's economic theory proper, the point made by Schumpeter seems entirely valid: Smith allows for no dynamic force other than the division of labor. And Rosenberg's argument simply underscores the basically conservative character of that force.

Classical political economy reached its intellectual and scientific apex in the work of David Ricardo, and it was of course Ricardo who had the greatest influence on Marx. If Ricardo had shared Smith's interest in productive processes, it seems quite possible that he would have developed a different conception of the dynamics of capitalism; for in the four decades that separated *The Wealth of Nations* from the *Principles*, industrial technology advanced by giant strides. But Ricardo's interest was largely focused on the distribution of income among the major classes of capitalist society. What he had to say about the dynamics of the system was largely incidental.[9] In fact it is in the work of Ricardo that we find in its purest form the view of economic development 'exclusively in terms of (gradual) quantitative changes in population, capital, wages, profits, and rent.'[10]

Marx did share Smith's interest in productive processes,[11] and the reality which confronted him was so different from that which had confronted Smith nearly a century earlier that he could hardly help coming to radically different conclusions. Marx was certainly the first economist to develop a rounded conception of the industrial revolution and to take full account of its consequences in building his theoretical model of the capitalist process.[12]

We have already noted that for Marx the industrial revolution marked the transition between two essentially different periods of capitalist development, the first being characterized by the dominance of manufacture and the second by the dominance of 'modern industry.' Although quite aware that 'epochs in the history of society are no more separated from each other by hard and fast lines of demarcation than are geological epochs,'[13] he nevertheless found it useful to tie the industrial revolution to a specific date.[14] By bringing out his spinning machine in 1735, John Wyatt 'began the industrial revolution of the 18th century.'[15] In the nature of the case, no comparable date for the end of the industrial revolution could be set, but we can infer that Marx considered that the decisive structural change in the system had been effected by the third decade of the 19th century. This inference follows from (1) his view that the business cycle is the unique and necessary attribute of the modern-industry phase of capitalist development, and (2) his dating of the first business cycle from the crisis of 1825.[16]

For Marx, the essence of the industrial revolution was the replacement of handwork by machinery, a process which takes place 'from the moment that the tool proper is taken from man and fitted into a mechanism' and regardless of 'whether the motive power is derived from man or from some other machine.'[17] Once started in an important part of the economy, this process of mechanization tends to spread in a series of chain reactions. As Marx put it:

> A radical change in the mode of production in one sphere of industry involves a similar change in other spheres. This happens at first in such branches of industry as are connected together by being separate phases of a process, and yet are isolated by the social division of labor

in such a way that each of them produces an independent commodity. Thus spinning by machinery made weaving by machinery a necessity, and both together made the mechanical and chemical revolution that took place in bleaching, printing, and dyeing imperative. So too, on the other hand, the revolution in cotton spinning called forth the invention of the gin for separating the seeds from the cotton fiber; it was only by means of this invention that the production of cotton became possible on the enormous scale at present required. But more especially, the revolution in the modes of production of industry and agriculture made necessary a revolution in the general conditions of the social process of production, i.e. in the means of communication and transport . . . Hence, apart from the radical changes introduced in the construction of sailing vessels, the means of communication and transport became gradually adapted to the modes of production of mechanical industry by the creation of a system of river steamers, railways, ocean steamers, and telegraphs. But the huge masses of iron that had now to be forged, to be welded, to be cut, to be bored, and to be shaped, demanded, on their part, cyclopean machines for the construction of which the methods of the manufacturing period were utterly inadequate.

Modern Industry had therefore itself to take in hand the machine, its characteristic instrument of production, and to construct machines by machines. It was not till it did this that it built up for itself a fitting technical foundation, and stood on its own feet. Machinery, simultaneously with the increasing use of it, in the first decades of this century, appropriated, by degrees, the fabrication of machines proper. But it was only during the decade preceding 1866 that the construction of railways and ocean steamers on a stupendous scale called into existence the cyclopean machines now employed in the construction of prime movers.[18]

From this passage one could perhaps conclude that it was Marx's view that he was writing the first volume of *Capital* during the final stage of the transition from manufacture to modern industry. If he had had to pick out the single most important step forward in this whole vast movement, it would undoubtedly have been the perfection of the steam engine. Here again it is worth while to quote his own words:

Not till the invention of Watt's second and so-called double-acting steam engine was a prime mover found, that begot its own force by the consumption of coal and water, that was mobile and a means of locomotion, that was urban and not, like the water-wheel, rural, that permitted production to be concentrated in towns instead of, like the water-wheels, being scattered up and down the country, that was of universal technical application, and, relatively speaking, little affected in its choice of residence by local circumstances. The greatness of Watt's genius showed itself in the specification of the patent that he took out in April, 1784. In that specification his steam engine is described, not as an invention for a specific purpose, but as an agent universally applicable in Mechanical Industry. In it he points out applications, many of which, as for instance the steam hammer, were not introduced until half a century later.[19]

I cannot refrain from pointing out in passing the very striking similarity between the steam engine in the industrial revolution and the technology of automation in the radical transformation of production processes through which we are living in the second half of the 20th century. 'What the feedback and the vacuum tube have made possible,' wrote the late Norbert Wiener, the father of cybernetics, 'is not the sporadic design of individual automatic mechanisms, but a general policy for the construction of automatic mechanisms of the most varied type.'[20] Here again we have a technological advance the importance of which stems not from its capacity to serve a specific purpose but from its universal applicability. And, as in the case of the steam engine, it seems certain that many of the applications will not be realized until many years later.[21]

To return to Marx's theory of the industrial revolution: Marx saw two respects in which an economy based on modern industry differs fundamentally from one based on manufacture. The first relates to the *modus operandi* of the production process itself; the second to the composition and nature of the working class. The net effect of these factors was to transform capitalism from a relatively conservative and change-resistant society into a super-dynamic society, headed, in Marx's view, for inevitable revolutionary overthrow.

With respect to the production process in modern industry, Marx held that technological progress ceases to depend on the ingenuity of the skilled laborer and/or the genius of the great inventor as it did in manufacture, and, instead, becomes the province of the rational sciences. A few quotations from the chapter on 'Machinery and Modern Industry' (*Capital*, I) will show how explicit Marx was on this point and what enormous importance he attached to it:

Intelligence in production . . . is lost by the detail laborers (and) is concentrated in the capital that employs them. . . . This separation . . . is completed in modern industry, which makes science a productive force distinct from labor and presses it into the service of capital.[22]

In Manufacture it is the workmen who, with their manual implements, must, either singly or in groups, carry on each particular detail process. If, on the one hand, the workman becomes adapted to the process, on the other, the process was previously made suitable to the workman. This subjective principle of the division of labor no longer exists in production by machinery. Here the process as a whole is examined objectively, in itself, that is to say, without regard to the question of its execution by human hands, it is analyzed into its

190

constituent phases; and the problem, how to execute each detail process and bind them all into a whole, is solved by the aid of machines, chemistry, etc.[23]

The implements of labor, in the form of machinery, necessitate the substitution of natural forces for human force, and the conscious application of science instead of rule of thumb. In . . . its machinery system, Modern Industry has a productive organism that is purely objective, in which the laborer becomes a mere appendage to an already existing material condition of production.[24]

When machinery is first introduced into an industry, new methods of reproducing it more cheaply follow blow upon blow, and so do improvements, that not only affect individual parts and details of the machine, but its entire build.[25]

The principle, carried out in the factory system, of analyzing the process of production into its constituent phases, and of solving the problems thus proposed by the application of mechanics, of chemistry, and of the whole range of the natural sciences, becomes the determining principle everywhere.[26]

Modern Industry rent the veil that concealed from men their own social process of production, and that turned the various, spontaneously divided branches of production into so many riddles, not only to outsiders but even to the initiated. The principle which it pursued of resolving each into its constituent movements without any regard to their possible execution by the hand of man, created the new modern science of technology. The varied, apparently unconnected, and petrified forms of the production processes now resolved themselves into so many conscious and systematic applications of natural science to the attainment of given useful effects. Technology also discovered the few main fundamental forms of motion which, despite the diversity of the instruments used, are necessarily taken by every productive action of the human body; just as the science of mechanics sees in the most complicated machinery nothing but the continual repetition of the simple mechanical powers.[27]

Immediately following the last passage, Marx stated in its most explicit and succinct form the general conclusion which he deduced from these arguments: '*Modern Industry never looks upon and treats the existing form of a process as final. The technical basis of that industry is therefore revolutionary, while all earlier modes of production were essentially conservative.*[28] *By means of machinery, chemical processes, and other methods, it is continually causing changes not only in the technical basis of production, but also in the functions of the laborer and in the labor-process.*'[29]

Marx's theory of the effects of machinery on the working class is certainly among his best-known doctrines and need not be reviewed in any

191

detail here. His central thesis, from which the rest followed quite logically, was that machinery does away with, or at any rate drastically reduces, the need for special skills and instead puts a premium on quickness and dexterity. It thereby opens the door to the mass employment of women and children and cheapens the labor power of adult males by obviating the need for long and expensive training programs. There follows a vast expansion of the labor supply which is augmented and supplemented by two further factors: (1) once solidly entrenched in the basic industries, machinery invades ever new branches of the economy, underselling the old handworkers and casting them onto the labor market; and (2) the progressive improvement of machinery in industries already conquered continuously eliminates existing jobs and reduces the employment-creating power of a given rate of capital accumulation. The effects of machinery are thus, on the one hand, to expand, homogenize, and reduce the costs of production of the labor force; and, on the other hand, to slow down the rate of increase of the demand for labor. This means a sea-change in the economic power relation between capital and labor, to the enormous advantage of the former. Wages are driven down to, and often below, the barest subsistence minimum; hours of work are increased beyond anything known before; the intensity of labor is stepped up to match the ever increasing speed of the machinery. Machinery thus completes the process of subjecting labor to the sway of capital that was begun in the period of primitive accumulation. It is the capitalistic employment of machinery, and not merely capitalism in general, which generates the modern proletariat as Marx conceived it.

But there are no medals without two sides. Economically, the power of the proletariat under modern industry is much reduced compared to that of its predecessor in the period of manufacture. But politically, its potential power is infinitely greater. Old geographical and craft divisions and jealousies are eliminated or minimized. The nature of work in the modern factory requires the organization and disciplining of the workers, thereby preparing them for organized and disciplined action in other fields. The extremes of exploitation to which they are subjected deprives them of any interest in the existing social order, forces them to live in conditions in which morality is meaningless and family life impossible, and ends by totally alienating them from their work, their products, their society, and even themselves. Unlike their predecessors in the period of manufacture, these workers form a proletariat which is both capable of, and has every interest in, revolutionary action to overthrow the existing social order. They are the ones of whom Marx and Engels had already said in the *Communist Manifesto:* 'The proletarians have nothing to lose but their chains. They have a world to win.' In *Capital* this bold generalization is supported by a painstaking analysis of the immanent characteristics and tendencies of capitalistic 'modern industry' as it emerged from the industrial revolution.

In this paper I have tried to explain the difference between the theory of capitalist development of the classics and that of Marx as being due, at least in part, to the fact that the former took as their model an economy based on manufacture, which is an essentially conservative and change-resistant economic order; while Marx, recognizing and making full allowance for the profound transformation effected by the industrial revolution, took as his model an economy based on modern machine industry, which is certainly highly dynamic and which Marx himself thought was headed for inevitable revolution. In conclusion, I should like to add a few remarks contrasting Marx's treatment of technological change with that of post-classical bourgeois economics and assessing the validity – or perhaps it would be better to say the fruitfulness – of his views on the implications of machinery for the functioning and future of the capitalist system.

While Marx put technological change at the very center of economic theory, it is hardly an exaggeration to say that the bourgeois successors of classical political economy – the marginalists of various countries and schools – banished it altogether. Consumption rather than production became the starting point of economic theorizing, and its adepts concerned themselves more and more with tendencies to equilibrium and less and less with the macrodynamics of the system as a whole. This of course did not happen all at once or completely: men like Marshall and Taussig, for example, were very much interested in methods of production or, to use a term which was current around the turn of the century, the state of the industrial arts. But their interest was akin to that of the historian, the intelligent observer, the educated man – it was not vitally related to their economic theory. And later on, as economists became increasingly specialized and decreasingly educated, interest in real production was progressively replaced by interest in imaginary 'production functions.'

There was one great exception among bourgeois economists, one outstanding figure who sought, under the influence of Marx and in opposition to the Marxists, to establish a rival theory of economic development centering on technological change. I refer of course to Joseph Schumpeter whose *Theory of Economic Development* was first published (in German) in 1912. A detailed comparison of the theories of

Schumpeter and Marx would certainly be a useful project but one which obviously cannot be undertaken within the scope of the present essay. I will content myself with observing that Schumpeter's treatment of technological change departed from Marx's on an issue that Marx considered to be of decisive importance, namely, the objective character of the process. For Marx, once machinery had taken firm hold it was bound to spread, to evolve into progressively more elaborate and productive forms, to harness all the natural sciences to its imperatives – and all this quite apart from the desires or intentions of individual capitalists or scientists.[30] For Schumpeter, on the other hand, technological change is essentially a by-product of the spontaneous innovating activity of individual entrepreneurs. There is no need for us, living in the second half of the 20th century, to pass judgement on this theory: history has already done so. The interconnection between science, technology, and production was still largely informal and unstructured a hundred years ago; since then, and especially during and after the Second World War, it has become ever closer, more institutionalized, more deliberately planned. Without denying that individual inventors and entrepreneurs still play a role in the process of technological change, we surely cannot compare their importance to that of the great government- and industry-financed laboratories where the bulk of research and development in today's advanced technologies takes place.

Schumpeter himself saw this coming as long ago as the 1920s, and in his book, *Capitalism, Socialism, and Democracy*, he included a section ('The Obsolescence of the Entrepreneurial Function') in which he virtually abandoned his old theory of innovation. 'Technological progress,' he wrote, 'is increasingly becoming the business of teams of trained specialists who turn out what is required and make it work in predictable ways.'[31]

Nothing in Schumpeter's original theory of economic development could have led us to expect this outcome. But, from the point of view of Marx's theory of the objectivization of the process of technological progress and the harnessing of science to its requirements, it is precisely the outcome which is most logical and natural. Indeed, what must strike one today as one re-reads Marx's chapter on 'Machinery and Modern Industry' in the light of recent history is its modernity, its direct relevance to what is happening under our very eyes. One is even tempted to assume that much of what Marx wrote on the subject a hundred years ago was more prophetic than literally true of mid-19th century Britain.

The same cannot be said about Marx's analysis of the effects of machinery on the working class. The trends which he stressed and projected into the future – flooding of the labor market by women and

194

children, homogenization of the labor force, abasement of living standards and conditions, etc. – reached their maximum intensity in the first half of the 19th century and had already been checked or reversed before the publication of the first volume of *Capital*. There were many factors at work here. One was state action, resulting partly from the political struggles of the working class itself and partly from the interest of the bourgeoisie in a healthier and better-trained labor force. Another was the growing strength of trade unions. And still another was the expansion of what is nowadays called the service sector of the economy, an expansion made possible by, and sustained from, the rising surplus product associated with the progressive mechanization of production.

Marx's failure was not that he did not recognize the existence of these counteracting forces. In the case of state action, he provided a detailed analysis of legislation regulating the length of the working day and of the factory acts; and the principles underlying this analysis could easily be extended to apply to other forms of social welfare legislation. And in various passages scattered throughout his writings he showed that he was well aware not only of the importance of trade unions as weapons in the working class struggle but also of the proliferation of what he, following the classics, called the 'unproductive' occupations. Marx's failure was rather in not understanding that all these counteracting forces taken together could actually come to prevail and thus turn a potentially revolutionary proletariat into an actual reformist force.

But we must also note another failure of Marx which cuts in a rather different direction. He saw very clearly the most striking international consequence of the industrial revolution:

So soon . . . as the general conditions requisite for production by the modern industrial system have been established, this mode of production acquires an elasticity, a capacity for sudden extension by leaps and bounds that finds no hindrance except in the supply of raw material and in the disposal of the produce. On the one hand, the immediate effect of machinery is to increase the supply of raw material in the same way, for example, as the cotton gin augmented the production of cotton. On the other hand, the cheapness of the articles produced by machinery, and the improved means of transport and communication furnish the weapons for conquering foreign markets. By ruining handicraft production in other countries, machinery forcibly converts them into fields for the supply of its raw material. In this way East India was compelled to produce cotton, wool, hemp, jute, and indigo for Great Britain . . . A new and international division of labor, a division suited to the requirements of the chief centers of modern industry springs up, and converts one part of the globe into a chiefly agricultural field of production for supplying the other part which remains a chiefly industrial field.[32]

What Marx did not foresee was that this 'new and international division of labor' might harden into a pattern of development and underdevelopment which would split mankind into haves and have-nots on a scale far wider and deeper than the bourgeois/proletarian split in the advanced capitalist countries themselves. If Marx had foreseen this momentous development, he could have easily conceded the existence of meliorative trends within the advanced countries without for a moment giving up the prediction of inevitable revolutionary overthrow for the system as a whole.

NOTES AND REFERENCES

1. Paul M. Sweezy, *The Theory of Capitalist Development* (New York, 1942), p. 94.
2. See especially the first section of Karl Marx's chapter on 'Machinery and Modern Industry,' *Capital*, ed. Kerr (Chicago, 1906), I, 405–522. (Chapter numberings differ in different editions: all references in this paper are to the Kerr edition.)
3. Editor's Preface to the First English Translation, *ibid.*, p. 29.
4. The German is *ursprüngliche Akkumulation* which literally means 'original accumulation,' and in this case the literal translation would have been better since what Marx wanted to convey was that this kind of accumulation preceded capitalist accumulation proper. 'Primitive accumulation,' however, is the generally accepted translation and to change it is to risk being misunderstood.
5. Marx, *Capital*, I, 399.
6. *Ibid.*, p. 383n.
7. Joseph A. Schumpeter, *History of Economic Analysis* (New York, 1961), p. 187.
8. Nathan Rosenberg, 'Adam Smith on the Division of Labour: Two Views or One?,' *Economica*, XXXII (May, 1965), 128.
9. David Ricardo's chapter 'On Machinery' was tacked onto the third edition of the *Principles* and was concerned entirely with the question of whether it was possible for machinery to displace labor. In the course of this analysis, he stated that 'with every augmentation of capital, a greater proportion of it is employed on machinery' and that the demand for labor 'will continue to increase with an increase in capital, but not in proportion to its increase; the ratio will, necessarily, be a diminishing ratio.' (*Principles of Political Economy and Taxation* (Everyman's ed., 1933) p. 387). These propositions could have formed the starting point of a fruitful line of analysis, but with Ricardo they remained hardly more than *obiter dicta*. It was left for Marx to explore their implications.
10. See above, p. 185.
11. In his biography of Marx, Mehring tells of an incident in which a manufacturer remarked that Marx too must have been a manufacturer

at some time. Marx's reply (in a letter to Engels) was: 'If people only knew how little I know about all this business!' Franz Mehring, *Karl Marx: The Story of His Life* (New York, 1935), p. 285.

12. I am tempted to say that the whole idea of the industrial revolution, which in my student days was commonly associated with the name of the elder Toynbee, really originated with Marx. But I confess that I do not know the relevant literature well enough to be sure.

13. Marx, *Capital*, I, 405.

14. Similarly the recognition that 'a critical history of technology would show how little any of the inventions of the 18th century are the work of a single individual' (*ibid.*, p. 406) did not prevent him from associating inventions with the names of individuals.

15. *Ibid.*

16. Speaking of the period 1820 to 1830 in the Preface to the second edition of volume I of *Capital*, Marx wrote that 'modern industry itself was only just emerging from the age of childhood, as is shown by the fact that with the crisis of 1825 it for the first time opens the periodic cycle of its modern life.' *Ibid.*, p. 18.

17. *Ibid.*, p. 408.

18. *Ibid.*, pp. 418–420.

19. *Ibid.*, pp. 411–412.

20. Norbert Wiener, *The Human Use of Human Beings: Cybernetics and Society* (Boston, 1950), p. 179.

21. Should the current technological transformation of the process of production, in which automation unquestionably plays a decisive role, be called a new industrial revolution? In purely technological terms it is doubtless as radical and thoroughgoing as the industrial revolution of the 18th and 19th centuries. And yet to a Marxist, at any rate, the appropriateness of the designation must seem at least doubtful. Capitalism has entered a new phase since Marx's day, the phase of monopoly capitalism. In technological terms, however, as Marx well understood, this transition was but the logical consequence of trends inherent in the very modern industry which he described and analyzed in *Capital* ('concentration' and 'centralization' of capital: see Marx, *op. cit.*, I, especially pp. 685–689). It has yet to be shown that the current technological transformation is introducing yet another phase of capitalist development. Unless this can be shown, it seems to me that the use of the term 'revolution' to describe what is now taking place can only lead to confusion.

22. *Ibid.*, pp. 396–397.

23. *Ibid.*, pp. 414–415.

24. *Ibid.*, p. 421.

25. *Ibid.*, p. 442.

26. *Ibid.*, p. 504.

27. *Ibid.*, p. 532.

28. In order to drive home the point still further and to extend the scope of its significance, Marx here adds a footnote quoting a famous passage from the *Communist Manifesto*:
'The bourgeoisie cannot exist without continually revolutionizing the instruments of production, and thereby the relations of production and

all the social relations. Conservation, in an unaltered form, of the old modes of production was on the contrary the first condition of existence for all earlier industrial classes. Constant revolution in production, uninterrupted disturbance of all social conditions, everlasting uncertainty and agitation, distinguish the bourgeois epoch from all earlier ones. All fixed fast-frozen relations, with their train of ancient and venerable prejudices and opinions, are swept away, all new formed ones become antiquated before they can ossify. All that is solid melts into air, all that is holy is profaned, and man is at last compelled to face with sober senses his real conditions of life, and his relations with his kind.'

If, in the *Manifesto*, this can be said to have had the character of a brilliant insight, the corresponding but less sweeping passage in *Capital* has the character of a reasoned deduction from an exhaustive study of the actual processes of production prevailing in England in the middle of the 19th century.

29. Marx, *Capital*, I, 532–533. Emphasis added.

30. The *objectivity* of technique and technological advance must not be confused with the *supremacy* of technique as preached for example by the Frenchman Jacques Ellul (*The Technological Society* (New York, 1964)). Technique does not operate and advance independently of the social framework but only independently of the will of individuals within the social framework. Ellul's book is a wonderful demonstration of what nonsense can result from failing to make this crucial distinction.

31. Joseph A. Schumpeter, *Capitalism, Socialism and Democracy* (New York, 1942), p. 132.

32. Marx, *Capital*, I, 492–493.

# MARX'S THEORY OF PRODUCTIVE
# AND UNPRODUCTIVE LABOUR*

IAN GOUGH

This essay will attempt, first and foremost, a definitive exposition of Marx's theory of productive and unproductive labour.[1] This theory is presented in the three volumes of *Capital* and in *Theories of Surplus Value* – Marx's projected historico-critical fourth volume.[2] This seems useful and necessary for several reasons. First, as one of the most suspect legacies of classical political economy, its importance in Marxist political economy is disputed.[3] As a result, it has not been accorded a central place in most expositions of Marx's political economy, and its relation to the fundamental concept of surplus value has not been sufficiently emphasized.[4] To anticipate, if the essential problem for Marx in his mature economic writings was the explanation of surplus value under capitalism, then, on any count, the distinction between productive labour which creates surplus value, and unproductive labour much of which is supported out of surplus value – this distinction is a critical one. Its analysis is the more urgent since several Marxist writers, notably Baran,[5] have recently reinterpreted the concept in the course of focusing on the disposal and absorption of the surplus under monopoly capitalism. Lastly, there has been a recent growth of awareness that the concepts of productive and unproductive labour may have political implications, by influencing our interpretation of the class structure of present-day monopoly capitalism.[6]

With these requirements in mind, this paper is divided into three parts (or rather two and a half, since the third is relatively brief and inadequate). First, there is an attempt to spell out precisely what Marx meant by the terms productive labour and unproductive labour, by summarizing and reproducing where necessary, his writings on the subject. In so doing, I shall follow Marx's own order of analysis by beginning with the basic concepts of *Capital* volume I, as developed and expanded in the first volume of *Theories of Surplus Value*, and by then

* Originally published in *New Left Review*, 76, November/December 1972. Reprinted with permission of the editors.

proceeding with their modification to take account of commercial labour in volumes II and III. In the second part, the concept of productive and unproductive labour is situated in its context, by relating it to the central propositions of Marx's political economy. The questions and ambiguities which this raises are then analysed, by comparing the role and status of the concept for Marx with Adam Smith and classical political economy on the one hand, and with more recent Marxist writers on the other. Lastly, there is a very brief consideration of the political implications of the theory of productive and unproductive labour.

## I  MARX'S CONCEPT

### 1. Labour productive of use value

> Only bourgeois narrow-mindedness, which regards the capitalist forms of production as absolute forms – hence as eternal, natural forms of production – can confuse the question of what is productive labour from the standpoint of capital with the question of what labour is productive in general, or what is productive labour in general; and consequently fancy itself very wise in giving the answer that all labour which produces anything at all, which has any kind of result, is by that very fact productive labour. [IV/1, 393]

For Marx, the concept of productive labour was an historically specific concept, and for this very reason it was necessary to distinguish at the outset productive labour under capitalism from 'productive labour in general.'[7] We begin, therefore, with his analysis of the latter, which Marx in volume I, Chapter 1 of *Capital* calls *useful* labour. This – the production of use values through the labour process – is a necessary condition of human existence:

> In the use value of each commodity there is contained useful labour, i.e.: productive activity of a definite kind and exercised with a definite aim . . . so far therefore as labour is a creator of use value, is useful labour, it is a necessary condition, independent of all forms of society, for the existence of the human race; it is an eternal nature – imposed necessity, without which there can be no material exchanges between man and Nature, and therefore no life. [I, 1, 42–43]

This necessary condition holds, therefore, for all commodity production and for all capitalist production:

> In order that his labour may reappear in a commodity, he must, therefore, before all things, expend it on something useful, on something capable of satisfying a want of some sort. Hence, what the capitalist sets the labourer to produce, is a particular use-value, a specified article. The fact that the production of use-values, or goods, is carried on under the control of a capitalist and on his behalf, does not alter the general character of that production. [I, 7, 177]

However, a few pages later in this chapter on the labour-process, Marx terms this general attitude of all human labour, *productive* labour:

> In the labour-process, therefore, man's activity, with the help of the instruments of labour, effects an alteration, designed from the start, in the material worked upon. The process disappears in the product; the latter is a use-value, Nature's material adapted by a change of form to the wants of man . . . If we examine the whole process from the point of view of its result, the product, it is plain that . . . the labour itself is productive labour. [I, 7, 181]

A footnote to the above continues:

> This method of determining, from the standpoint of the labour-process alone, what is productive labour, is by no means directly applicable to the case of the capitalist mode of production.

It seems clear that the labour viewed from the standpoint of the labour-process alone is *useful* labour, as Marx has used the term up to that point. To help distinguish this from productive labour under capitalism, we shall continue to denote all labour productive of use-values 'useful labour.'

This distinction also aids the interpretation of the following well-known passage in volume I:

> As the co-operative character of the labour-process becomes more and more marked, so, as a necessary consequence, does our notion of productive labour, and of its agent the productive labourer, become extended. In order to labour productively, it is no longer necessary for you to do manual work yourself; enough if you are an organ of the collective labourer, and perform one of its subordinate functions. The first definition of productive labourer . . . still remains correct for the collective labourer, considered as a whole. But it no longer holds good for each member taken individually. [I, 16, 508–509]

With spreading division of labour, it is increasingly rare for a single person to produce unaided a use-value. Hence he cannot be called a *useful* labourer as first defined. Nevertheless the collectivity of individuals does produce a use-value and does therefore labour usefully. The necessity for reinterpreting this passage in terms of useful labour will, I hope, emerge later on. Similarly, the important question of what constitutes a use-value is left to one side for the time being.

## 2. *Labour productive of surplus-value*

Productive labour specific to the capitalist mode of production is labour which produces surplus-value. This definition is presented in volume I of *Capital*:

> That labourer alone is productive, who produces surplus-value for the capitalist, and who thus works for the self-expansion of capital . . . Hence the notion of a productive labourer implies not merely a relation between work and useful effect, between labourer and product of labour, but also a specific, social relation of product, a relation that has sprung up historically and stamps the labourer as the direct means of creating surplus-value. [I, 16, 509]

Marx then says no more on the subject in volume I but refers us to 'Book IV, which treats of the history of the theory.' In Part I of *Theories of Surplus Value* a long chapter considers Adam Smith's views on productive and unproductive labour, and those of his followers. One must be careful in interpreting these passages, since Marx follows his usual policy here of simultaneously recounting and criticizing the views of other economists. But we are left in no doubt of his views on productive and unproductive labour, since he sets them out clearly in a separate addendum to Part I. It is this text that we shall use as our guideline and main source of information in this and the following three sections.

In a dozen and more places, Marx repeats this fundamental property of productive labour:

> *Only labour which is directly transformed into capital is productive.* [IV/1, 393]

> From the capitalist standpoint only that labour is productive which creates a surplus-value. [IV/1, 153]

> Productive labour, in its meaning for capitalist production, is wage-labour which, exchanged against the variable part of capital . . . reproduces not only this part of capital (or the value of its own labour-power), but in addition produces surplus-value for the capitalist. [IV/1, 152]

This must not be confused with the simple purchase of labour services with money, which, we shall see, is precisely what characterises *unproductive* labour.[8] Marx emphasizes that 'productive labour in the first sense' – what we have called 'useful' labour – is a necessary, but not sufficient condition for productive labour in this second, correct sense.

> Labour which is to produce *commodities* must be useful labour; it must produce a *use-value* . . . And consequently only labour which manifests itself in *commodities*, that is in use-values, is labour for which capital is exchanged. But it is not this concrete character of labour, its use-value as such . . . which forms its specific use-value for capital and consequently stamps it as *productive labour* in the system of capitalist production. [IV/1, 400]

If productive labour is labour exchanged with capital to produce surplus-value, unproductive labour is labour exchanged with revenue:

> This also establishes absolutely what unproductive labour is. It is labour which is not exchanged with capital, but directly with revenue, that is wages or profits (including of course the various categories of those who share as co-partners in the capitalist profit, such as interest and rent). [IV/1, 157]

Here Marx is clearly referring to the Ricardian gross revenue, or what we would call income. In other words wage-labourers can purchase unproductive labour no less than capitalists and those with whom they share surplus-value:

> The labourer himself can buy labour, that is commodities which are provided in the form of services . . . As buyer – that is a representative of money confronting commodity – the labourer is in absolutely the same category as the capitalist where the latter appears only as a buyer . . . [IV/1, 404]

The capitalist *qua* capitalist purchases *labour-power* with which to create surplus-value. The capitalist (or worker for that matter) *qua* consumer purchases *labour services* for the direct use-value they provide. The former labour is productive, the latter unproductive. Included in the latter are all state employees, whose services are purchased with revenue whether the original taxes are paid out of wages or out of the various categories of surplus-value.[9]

Marx stresses the importance of this distinction between productive and unproductive labour in the following passage:

> Productive labour is only a concise term for the whole relationship and the form and manner in which labour power figures in the capitalist production process. The distinction from *other* kinds of labour is however of the greatest importance, since this distinction expresses precisely the specific form of the labour on which the whole capitalist mode of production and capital itself is based . . . [IV/1, 396]

Productive labour is the *sine qua non* of capitalism, a category which expresses the 'form and manner in which labour power figures in the capitalist production process.'


## 3. Labour productive of material goods

The bulk of Chapter 4 of Part I of *Theories of Surplus Value* is concerned to demonstrate, first, that Adam Smith correctly defined productive labour in the way we have just considered, and second, that he confused this with another, incorrect distinction. This second definition of Adam

Smith's, and Marx's comments on it, are considered in this section. Smith also saw productive labour as that which 'fixes and realizes itself in some particular subject or vendible commodity, which lasts for some time at least after labour is past,' whilst services are unproductive labour because they 'generally perish in the very instant of their performance, and seldom leave any trace or value behind them.'[10] Thus this second distinction was based on the *material characteristics of the product*, rather than on the social relations embodied in the labour. This concept was the source of great confusion among economists following Smith, and Marx vehemently rejected it on every occasion, including the passage in *Capital*, volume I:

> If we may take an example from outside the sphere of production of material objects, a schoolmaster is a productive labourer, when, in addition to belabouring the heads of his scholars, he works like a horse to enrich the school proprietors. That the latter has laid out his capital in a teaching factory, instead of a sausage factory, does not alter the relation. [I, 16, 509]

More specifically:

> It follows from what has been said that the designation of labour as *productive labour* has absolutely nothing to do with the *determinate content* of that labour, its special utility, or the particular use-value in which it manifests itself. *The same* kind of labour may be *productive* or *unproductive*. [IV/1, 401]

> An actor for example, or even a clown, according to this definition, is a productive labourer if he works in the service of a capitalist (an entrepreneur) to whom he returns more labour than he receives from him in the form of wages; while a jobbing tailor who comes to the capitalist's house and patches his trousers for him, is an unproductive labourer. The former's labour is exchanged with capital, the latter's with revenue. [IV/1, 157]

There are several other passages just as explicit, but Marx does note that *in practice*, at the time Smith and he were writing there was a large overlap between the two concepts. As the capitalist mode of production spreads, it gradually conquers the field of material production, but impinges very little on non-material production. Thus labourers producing material goods were often productive labourers employed by capitalists, and labourers providing services were often paid for out of revenue, were unproductive labourers. But the conceptual distinction is in no way obscured by this fact:

> In considering the essential relations of capitalist production it can therefore be assumed that the entire world of commodities, all spheres of material production, are (formally or really) subordinated

to the capitalist mode of production (for this is happening more and more completely . . .) . . . It can then be said to be a characteristic of *productive labourers*, that is, labourers producing capital, that their labour realizes itself in *commodities*, in material wealth.[11] And so *productive labour*, along with its determining characteristic – which takes no account whatever of the *content of labour* and is entirely independent of that content – would be given a second, different and subsidiary definition. [IV/1, 409–410]

In the case of services proper,

here the capitalist mode of production is met with to only a small extent, and from the nature of the case can only be applied in a few spheres . . . All these manifestations of capitalist production in this sphere are so insignificant compared with the totality of production that they can be left entirely out of account. [IV/1, 410–411]

Though Marx has in mind here 'artists, orators, actors, teachers, physicians, priests, etc.,' many of whom are now employed by the State – thus are supported out of revenue and unproductive on this count, nevertheless the growth of services supplied by capitalist enterprises must qualify this observation today.

## 4. The labour of handicraftsmen and peasants

Marx's brief observations here are relevant to the labour of all self-employed persons in capitalist societies, though he considers only those producing a material commodity for sale – not a service. He criticizes contemporary analyses of the peasant which regarded him as simultaneously capitalist and wage-labour, setting himself to work with his own capital.

The means of production become capital only in so far as they have become separated from labourer and confront labour as an independent power. But in the case referred to the producer – the labourer – is the possessor, the owner, of his means of production. They are therefore not capital, any more than in relation to them he is a wage labourer. [IV/1, 408]

Independent handicraftsmen and peasants are not therefore productive labourers. But neither are they unproductive whose labour is exchanged directly for revenue:

They confront me as sellers of commodities, not as sellers of labour, and this relation therefore has nothing to do with the exchange of capital for labour, therefore also has nothing to do with the distinction between *productive* and *unproductive labour*, which depends entirely on whether the labour is exchanged for money as money or for money as capital. They therefore belong neither to the category of

205

*productive* or *unproductive* labourers, although they are producers of commodities. But their production does not fall under the capitalist mode of production. [IV/1, 407]

In other words labour outside the capitalist mode of production cannot be analysed in terms of Marx's distinction between productive and unproductive labour – there is a third category of labour which is neither. This is consistent with his aims of analysing productive and unproductive labour from the standpoint of capitalist production.

## 5. Collective labour

We consider further here Marx's observations on the 'collective labourer' and on 'fringe' groups in the productive process, such as transport workers. He remarks that the expanding division of labour under capitalist production, means that for many workers:

the direct relation which their labour bears to the object produced naturally varies greatly. For example the unskilled labourers in a factory . . . have nothing directly to do with the working up of raw material. The workman who functions as overseer of those directly engaged in working up the raw material is one step further away; the works engineer has yet another relation and in the main works only with his brain, and so on. [IV/1, 411]

Nevertheless, they are all productive labourers because (a) they *collectively* produce a use-value – they are all 'organs of the collective labourer,' and (b) they are all *individually* wage-labourers who have exchanged their labour for capital.

But *the totality of these labourers* . . . produce the result, which, considered as the *result* of the labour-process pure and simple, is expressed in a *commodity* or *material product*; and all together, as a workshop, they are the living production machine of these *products* – just as, taking the production process as a whole, they exchange their labour for capital . . . The relation of each one of these persons to capital (is) that of wage-labourer and in this pre-eminent sense (is) that of productive labourer. All these persons are not only *directly* engaged in the production of material wealth, but they exchange their labour *directly* for money as capital. [IV/1, 411–412][12]

Of course in contemporary analysis, the problem is to decide how direct is 'directly'. But Marx throughout interprets this broadly:

Included among these productive workers, of course, are those who contribute in one way or another to the production of the commodity, from the actual operative to the manager or engineer (as distinct from the capitalist). [IV/1, 156–157]

This would suggest the inclusion nowadays of large numbers of scientists, technologists, technicians and engineers, plus substantial sections of management and white collar workers – which groups precisely will emerge in the next section.

The transport industry is regarded by Marx as the 'fourth sphere of material production,' in addition to extractive industry, agriculture and manufacture [IV/1, 412]. Consequently,

> The relation of *productive labour* – that is, of the wage-labourer – to capital is here exactly the same as in the other spheres of material production. [IV/1, 412]

The reasoning behind this is quite consistent: it is that transport alters the use-value of the commodity – and the labour is therefore useful labour:

> Quantities of products are not increased by transportation. Nor, with a few exceptions, is the possible alteration of their natural qualities brought about by transportation an intentional useful effect; it is rather an unavoidable evil. But the use-value of things is materialized only in their consumption, and their consumption may necessitate a change of location of these things, hence may require an additional process of production, in the transport industry. [II, 6, 153]

> Its [the commodity's] spacial existence is altered, and along with this goes a change in its use-value, since the location of this use-value is changed. [IV/1, 412]

On this basis:

> Its exchange-value increases in the same measure as this change in the use-value requires labour ... although in this case the real labour has left no trace behind it in the use-value ... [IV/1, 412–413]

Marx's analysis of transport workers therefore both confirms the concept of productive labour that we have thus far arrived at (as the production of use-value and surplus-value), and helps us in interpreting the term 'use-value.'

## 6. Labour employed in the circulation process

On the last page of *Theories of Surplus Value*, Part 1, at the end of the important appendix that has so far guided us, Marx writes:

> Here we have been dealing only with *productive* capital, that is, capital employed in the *direct process of production*. We come later to capital in the *process of circulation*. And only after that, in con-

sidering the special form assumed by capital as *merchant's capital*, can the question be answered as to how far the labourers employed by it are productive or unproductive. [IV/1, 413]

We must therefore now turn to the relevant passages in *Capital*, volumes II and III, beginning with the treatment of 'pure' merchant's capital in volume III. This treats of commercial capital:

... stripped of all heterogeneous functions, such as storing, expressing, transporting, distributing, retailing, which may be connected with it, and confined to its true function of buying in order to sell. [III, 17, 282]

We leave entirely out of consideration all possible processes of production which may continue in the process of circulation, and from which the merchant's business can be altogether separated; as, in fact, the actual transport industry and expressage may be, and are, industrial branches entirely distinct from commercial. [III, 17, 288–289]

The remaining merchant's capital, devoted solely to buying and selling and their associated functions, is capital functioning in the sphere of circulation, *hence creates no surplus-value*.

The pure functions of capital in the sphere of circulation ... the acts of selling and buying – produce neither value or surplus-value. [III, 17, 281]

Merchant's capital is simply capital functioning in the sphere of circulation. The process of circulation is a phase of the total process of reproduction. But no value is produced in the process of circulation, and, therefore, no surplus-value. Only changes of form of the same mass of value take place. In fact, nothing occurs there outside the metamorphosis of commodities, and this has nothing to do as such either with the creation or change of values. [III, 16, 279]

This analysis is in no way altered if these functions become the special concern of a separate group of merchant capitalists who themselves employ wage-labourers:

If selling and buying commodities by industrial capitalists themselves are not operations which create value or surplus-value, they will certainly not create either of these when carried out by persons other than industrial capitalists. [III, 17, 281]

The important conclusion, therefore, is that commercial workers are unproductive labourers, despite the characteristics they have in common with workers in the process of production – above all the fact that they are similarly exploited through having to supply unpaid labour (discussed below in Part III). The previous definition of productive labour has been narrowed, from all labour exchanged with capital to all labour exchanged with *productive* capital; whereas the definition of unproductive labour has been expanded to include labour employed in the process of circulation.

But what precisely is the distinction between production and circulation or realization? This question is all the more important with the increasing penetration of the sales effort into the production process under monopoly capitalism.[13] The answer is provided elsewhere in volume III and in Marx's earlier analysis of the costs of circulation in *Capital* volume II. The critical distinction is between *those activities necessary to production in general, and those activities peculiar to commodity production*. That labour is unproductive which is historically specific to the commodity form, including capitalist production:

> If commercial capital and money-dealing capital do not differ from grain production any more than this differs from cattle-raising and manufacturing, it is plain as day that production and capitalist production are altogether identical . . . [III, 20, 324]

It is the 'apologetic endeavours of the vulgar economist' that treats:

> commercial capital and money-dealing capital as forms arising necessarily from the process of production as such, whereas they are due to the specific form of the capitalist mode of production, which above all presupposes the circulation of commodities, and hence of money, as its basis. [III, 20, 324]

This criterion is chiefly developed in Marx's analysis of the costs of storage in volume II, though at times the text is so unclear that the interpretation of certain passages will always be open to doubt. Nevertheless, the overall picture that emerges is of the necessity to distinguish among these costs, between those that arise because of the general nature of social production – the necessity to store and distribute goods – and those due solely to the commodity form:

> Whatever may be the social form of the products-supply, its preservation requires outlays for buildings, vessels etc. . . . also for means of production and labour, more or less of which must be expended, according to the nature of the product, in order to combat injurious influences . . . It may now be asked to what extent these costs enhance the value of commodities . . . Insofar as the formation of a supply entails a stagnation of circulation, the expense incurred thereby does not add to the value of the commodities . . . The costs are the same, but since they now arise *purely out of the form*, that is to say, out of the

209

necessity of transforming the commodities into money . . . they do not enter into the values of the commodities but constitute deductions, losses of value in the realization of the value. [II, 6, 147–151, my emphases]

Thus it is necessary to distinguish, within storage costs, between those arising purely out of the commodity-form, such as the involuntary pile-up of goods when circulation stagnates, and those necessary under any mode of production. Labour employed for the former reason does not add to value or surplus-value and is therefore unproductive. But when the 'commodity-supply is nothing but the commodity-form of the product-supply,' when, that is, storage and distribution must necessarily be undertaken as part of the general productive process, then the labour involved adds to value and is productive. As with transport, storage, etc., does not improve the intrinsic quality of the use-value (except for a few exceptional goods), but it does *alter* it by preventing it from deteriorating:

The use-value is neither raised nor increased here; on the contrary, it diminishes. But its diminution is restricted and it is preserved. [II, 6, 142]

On this basis, the labour employed is useful labour, hence, if employed by a capitalist, is also productive. The same analysis could be applied to workers in distribution. Those who are really part of the productive process working in the sphere of supply (such as workers who unload goods, move them to the counters, etc.) are productive labourers; those who operate the cash registers and are otherwise employed solely because the products assume a commodity form are, on Marx's criterion, unproductive labourers.

Marx uses the same approach to distinguish elsewhere between *supervisory* labour that is productive and unproductive, but here the criterion of unproductive labour is extended to include labour specific to all *class* societies based on exploitation:

The labour of supervision and management is naturally required wherever the direct process of production assumes the form of a combined social process, and not of the isolated labour of independent producers. However, it has a double nature. On the one hand, all labour in which many individuals co-operate necessarily requires a commanding will to co-ordinate and unify the process . . . This is a productive job, which must be performed in every combined mode of production. [III, 23, 383]

The remaining labour of management and supervision is unproductive:

One part of the labour of superintendence merely arises from the antagonistic contradiction between capital and labour, from the antagonistic character of capitalist production, and belongs to the incidental expenses of production in the same way as nine-tenths of the 'labour' occasioned by the circulation process. [IV/3, 505. cf. IV/2, 355–356]

These passages clearly reveal the historical dimension which Marx has incorporated into the analysis of productive and unproductive labour. Mandel's conclusion provides a useful summary of the concept we have now discerned:

In general, one can say that all labour which creates, modifies or conserves use-values or which is *technically indispensable* for realizing them is productive labour, that is, it increases their exchange-value. In this category belong not only the labour of industrial production properly so called, but also the labour of storing, handling and transport without which the use-values cannot be consumed.[14]

## 7. Labour productive of 'unnecessary' goods

At first sight, Marx appears to contradict his analyses reproduced in the previous section when he writes:

The use-value of the commodity in which the labour of a productive worker is embodied may be of the most futile kind. [IV/1, 158]

Or, the opposite side of the same coin:

Labour may be necessary without being productive.[15]

Thus at no time, Marx argues, does the criterion of productiveness depend on any notion of the 'necessity' or 'social usefulness' of the actual content of the labour. When elaborating these statements he distinguishes different historical periods and the labour necessary to each of them. Thus some functions would appear to be 'necessary' in any society based on class contradictions. Referring to 'the great mass of so-called 'higher-grade' workers – such as state officials, military people,' etc. Marx comments:

The necessity for the inherited social combination of these classes, which in part (are) totally unproductive, (arises) from its own organization. [IV/1, 174–175][16]

Circulation workers are essential for the smooth functioning of *commodity* production, for instance the buying and selling agent is indirectly productive:

211

He performs a necessary function, because the process of reproduction itself includes unproductive functions. He works as well as the next man, but intrinsically his labour creates neither value nor product. [II, 6, 134]

Merchant's capital . . . insofar as it contributes to shortening the time of circulation, may help indirectly to increase the surplus-value produced by the industrial capitalist. [III, 16, 280]

Other unproductive labour, devoted to meeting human needs, would expand with the development of communism, for instance the employment of teachers and doctors.[17] But nowhere is the necessity or intrinsic usefulness of the labour confused with productive labour. As Mandel puts it:

When they produce dum-dum bullets, opium or pornographic novels, workers create new value, since these commodities, finding as they do buyers on the market, possess a use-value which enables them to realise their exchange-value. But from the standpoint of the general interests of human society, these workers have done work which is absolutely useless, or even harmful.[18]

By contrast with Baran (see Part II below), Marx rigorously eschews a historical perspective to determine the usefulness of the end-product of the labour, and thus the productiveness of the labour itself.

But does this not contradict the analysis of the previous section where, as we have shown, the historical necessity of a particular form of labour precisely determines whether or not it is productive? In theory the answer is no. One must distinguish the labour necessary to produce a final use-value, whether consumer goods, capital goods, arms or social services, from the labour employed in producing 'necessary' use-values. Marx's approach (the former) is concerned solely with the labour technically required to produce a given useful effect (at a given level of productivity) without questioning how the demand for this particular use-value has arisen. For Marx in this context, a use-value is anything which is demanded. Thus a historical perspective is adopted to distinguish that labour common to production in general from that generated solely as a result of the commodity-form, but this is *not* extended to question the nature of the goods produced themselves. A further discussion of this is postponed to the next section since we have here reached the end of our projected exposition of Marx's writings on productive and unproductive labour.

To conclude, productive labour is labour exchanged with capital to produce surplus-value. As a necessary condition it must be useful labour, must produce or modify a use-value – increasingly in a collective fashion; that is, it must be employed in the process of production. Labour in the process of pure circulation does not produce use-values, therefore cannot add to value or surplus-value. It does not add to the production of use-values because it arises specifically with commodity production out of the problems of realizing the value of commodities. Alongside this group of unproductive labourers are all workers supported directly out of revenue, whether retainers or state employees. This group differs from circulation workers, however, in that they do produce use-values – all public teachers, doctors, etc., would be included in this category today. The following diagram makes clear the two groups of unproductive workers.

|  | Labour producing use-values | Labour not producing use-values |
|---|---|---|
| Labour producing surplus-value | Productive workers in industry, agriculture, distribution and services. | ———— |
| Labour not producing surplus-value | Unproductive workers: all State employees, domestic servants, etc. | 'Pure' circulation workers: salesmen, advertising workers, etc, and 'unnecessary' supervisory workers. |

## II  THE ROLE OF THE CONCEPT IN MARXIST POLITICAL ECONOMY

From an exposition of the nature and content of Marx's concept of productive and unproductive labour, we now turn to a consideration of its role within the systems of Marxist and classical political economy.

## 1. The Problem of Exploitation

For Marx, the central purpose of his mature economic writings was the explanation of exploitation under capitalism utilizing the concept of surplus-value.[19] Thus his concept of productive labour was developed to this end – it specified that labour which alone produced surplus-value under capitalism. Since, for Marx, the terms productive and unproductive labour are historical categories, 'the value or validity of the concepts is determined by the specific problems of the epoch.'[20] With the rise of industrial capital this became the creation, rather than the worldwide redistribution, of the surplus, and moreover its creation in value form. Inseparably linked as it was to the labour theory of value, surplus-value was premised on the production of use-values in the labour process. Hence followed Marx's elaboration of the concept in volumes II and III, and the distinction between the production and realization of value incorporated in his analysis of commercial workers. Joan Robinson wishes to disassociate Marx's analysis of the historical necessity of certain groups of workers, which she regards as 'important,' from his analysis of the production of value and surplus-value, which she regards as an 'unnecessary puzzle.'[21] But she can only suggest this because she rejects (or once rejected) the basis of the labour theory of value. It is this which forges the link between the quantities of social labour embodied in a commodity and its value, as well as between production of use-values – useful labour as the necessary basis to human society – and the production of surplus-value.[22] Marx's concept of productive and unproductive labour was shown above to be intimately linked to his basic theoretical categories: it cannot be thrown out without bringing these into question.

Nevertheless, it can be modified in various ways. There are three reasons why one may wish to consider alternative formulations of this or any concept in political economy. First, real conditions may have changed so much since the time Marx wrote that new problems have arisen, or phenomena which existed at that time may have changed qualitatively in importance, even though the mode of production remains capitalist. Three notable trends over the past century that have a bearing on the productive and unproductive labour debate are (a) the growth of state expenditures, some of which (such as health and education expenditure) are now important components of real wages, hence enter into the reproduction of variable capital; (b) the growth of commercial and distribution workers, including advertising and sales executives, financial advisers, etc.; and (c) the growth of products designed to meet consumer needs which may be regarded as 'unnecessary' or 'inessential,' having been either purposely created by capitalist enterprises and their sales organs, or shaped by more diffuse forces at work in capitalist society. Marx himself was well aware of the trends in capitalism, as he shows in the following prescient remarks:

What he [Ricardo] forgets to emphasize is the constantly growing number of the middle classes, those who stand between the workman

214

on the one hand and the capitalist and the landlord on the other. [IV/2, 573]

New ramifications of more or less unproductive branches of labour are continually being formed and in these revenue is directly expended. [IV/2, 560]

Second, and partly in response to a changing reality, the *object of analysis* of political economy may shift, so that theory is directed to answering different questions. From Marx's (successful) attempts to explain surplus-value under capitalism, attention among many Marxist economists today has focused on the *disposal* of this surplus under conditions of monopoly capital. This in turn leads to an analysis of *accumulation* and *growth* on the one hand, and to capitalist *waste* on the other.[23]

Third, these two factors – changes in the economic and social reality, and shifts in the goal of economic theory – may in turn reveal ambiguities in Marx's original formulations which previously remained hidden. The principal ambiguity in Marx's theory of productive and unproductive labour emerged at the end of our exposition in part I. It is the use of a historical perspective to distinguish the labour necessary to produce a given use-value, whilst rigorously denying the use of such a perspective to determine the 'necessity' of the final 'use-value' itself. The productiveness of labour depends on the former, but not the latter, according to Marx. The three trends noted above have each put fresh strain on this tenuous distinction.

The growth of state *productive* enterprises – the nationalized industries – presents few problems. Where labour is exchanged with capital to produce goods or services for sale, and where the enterprises 'usually aim to make enough surplus-value to cover the going rate of interest on government obligations,'[24] then the workers are productive just as in the private sector. As for remaining government activities, Marx is aware that these comprise both useful, historically necessary functions and functions arising from the class nature of capitalist society:

Supervision and all-round interference by the government involves both the performance of common activities arising from the nature of all communities, and the specific functions arising from the antithesis between the government and the mass of the people. [III, 23, 384]

But in this case the distinction has no implications for the productive *versus* unproductive labour debate since all labour employed by government (except in productive concerns) is exchanged with revenue, hence is unproductive.

This is not the case, however, if a second mode of distinguishing different government expenditures is adopted, i.e. that based on Marx's

215

concept of *luxury goods* developed in his analysis of reproduction in *Capital*, volume II. For Marx, luxuries are goods 'which enter into the consumption of only the capitalist class' (II, 20, 407), and which therefore do not re-enter the cycle of reproduction as elements of variable and constant capital, unlike necessities or means of production. Now this may be a fruitful way of categorizing modern state expenditures. Several writers have suggested that arms and military services in general are luxury goods on this definition – the products are not productively consumed, they 'cannot under any circumstances enter the production of other commodities.'[25] Yet, on the other hand, there has been the expansion of the social services which supply a rising share of the components of real wages – in the form of health, education, housing, etc. Thus the state now supplies directly part of the products which comprise the value of labour-power and which directly enter the cycle of reproduction as elements of variable capital. The question of whether this conflicts with Marx's concept of productive labour, and of the relevance of reproduction and accumulation to his concept, is analysed in more depth in section 2 below.

Second, the growth of distribution costs, of the commercial middle classes, etc., has placed added strain on Marx's distinction between the processes of production and circulation, and thus on the notion of productive and unproductive labour. Sweezy, Baran and others have attempted to incorporate not only the growth of salesmen, advertising workers, etc., but also increasing numbers of workers in distribution and production within Marx's original schema. Part of current distribution costs are 'unnecessary' under monopoly capitalism:

> These activities are, as we know, a part of the process of production proper. But now they become expanded far beyond the limits of what would be socially necessary under competitive conditions. Under monopoly only a part of distributive activities can be considered as productive of value; the rest are essentially similar to selling in the strict sense and share with the latter the attribute of using up value without producing any.[26]

Here the criterion of necessity is that which would exist under competitive conditions – an un-Marxist approach. Later, Baran and Sweezy extend the unproductive group still further to include those workers who are, in fact, concerned with realization, but are working within the process of production itself, such as those employed on product redesign, packaging, built-in obsolescence, etc. At the same time they alter the criterion of 'usefulness' or 'necessity' into a hypothetical appeal to the 'structure of output that could be produced under a more rational economic order.'[27] The comparison is no longer carried backwards with a previous era of competitive capitalism, but forwards with a future socialist (or communist?) era. This would appear a fruitful extension of Marx's historical analysis and critique of commercial workers, which throughout is premised on the notion of a *future* society without commodity production, or, in the case of supervisory staff, without class conflict. 'To the Marxist . . . the specific historical (i.e. transitory) character of capitalism is a major premise. It is by virtue of this fact that the Marxist is able, so to speak, to stand outside the system and criticize it as a whole.'[28]

But, in reinterpreting Marx's analysis to take account of a changing economic structure, Baran and Sweezy also accentuate yet further the ambiguity noted above. The dividing line between a critique of the labour necessary to produce a given use-value, and a critique of the necessity of the use-value itself becomes ever harder to draw. The second and third trends mentioned earlier draw together here. If the labour required to produce a new car model incorporating several sales gimmicks is unproductive, why not the labour to produce entirely 'useless' goods and services (American funeral parlours; poodle-trimming boutiques; even cars themselves if, in a more rational economic order, a less wasteful and costly system of transport is attainable)? If this is rejected, following Marx's explicit analysis, there still remains the problem of distinguishing 'final' from 'intermediate' goods and services. Is much present-day packaging a means to the consumption of the product, or part of the product itself; is expenditure on roads or commuting services part of final consumption expenditure, or a necessary expense to further social production?[29] Yet, there are grounds for supposing that Marx, if confronted with the volume and composition of production today, would have incorporated this new range of activities under the heading of unproductive labour. This view is based on his analysis of the determination of needs under capitalism. The problem has been confronted by Baran in *The Political Economy of Growth*. This, the second fundamental reinterpretation of Marx's concept of productive and unproductive labour, is considered in section 3.

## 2. The problem of accumulation

To understand how the problem of accumulation relates to the Marxist notion of productive labour, it is necessary first to go back to Adam Smith's development of the concept, which Marx devoted much of his labour in *Theories of Surplus Value*, Part I, to understanding and criti-

217

cizing. The twofold characteristic of productive labour in Smith's theory has already been noted. For Smith, productive labour was intimately linked with accumulation, as the title of Chapter 3, Book II, of the *Wealth of Nations* makes plain: 'Of the Accumulation of Capital, or of Productive and Unproductive Labour.' The chapter begins:

> There is one sort of labour which *adds to the value of* the subject upon which it is bestowed: there is another which has no such effect. The former, as it produces a value, may be called productive; the latter, unproductive labour.[30]

This can be explained in terms of the contemporary corn-model of the economy, where a single commodity – corn – serves both as means of production and consumption good. At the beginning of the agricultural year the farmer divides his stock of corn. One part he plants and advances to his agricultural workers, the other he himself consumes or uses to support servants, etc. The first part is constant plus variable capital C which yields a further crop of corn equivalent to $C + \Delta C$ next year. The latter part is revenue consumed by the farmer and his retainers. The capital supports productive workers – farm hands – who produce a value and surplus value next year. The corn consumed as revenue 'adds to the value of nothing.' Hence the smaller the expenditure out of revenue on servants or state officials or armies, the greater the employment of productive labour and the faster the rate of capital accumulation.

Allied to this – the core of the concept in Smith's theory – were two other distinguishing features between productive and unproductive labour, which followed both logically from the model of economy used, and historically from the time in which he was writing. First, as Marx noted and criticized, productive labourers produce storable commodities and unproductive labourers ephemeral services. As Myint says of Smith: 'the bias for accumulation involves a materialist bias, because only material commodities can store up labour.'[31] The corn model of the economy involves a physical commodity in recurring cycles, part of which is stored and consumed over the next cycle. Second, associated with this, was an implicit distinction between the production of necessities and luxuries. 'The classical economists were working on the basis of an economic system where the bulk of material commodities consisted of "necessities" or basic wage-goods, and where "luxuries" were mainly made ''p of the services of the menial and professional classes.'[32] In Smith's political economy, therefore, the notion of productive labour refers to labour that *adds to value* by means of producing *material* and

218

*necessary* commodities.

In a major reformulation of the Smithian concept of productive labour Gillman, Morris and Blake interpret these characteristics to mean *labour productive of constant or variable capital*, as opposed to labour which produces luxury goods which is therefore not productively consumed in the cycle of reproduction. 'The test of durability is to be sought not in the physical properties of commodities, but in their capacity to preserve value by transferring it to other products'[33] – many 'services' are therefore now important in the reproduction of variable and constant capital. Similarly, the test of necessity is not the social usefulness or otherwise of the product (this contrasts with Baran – see below) but 'the relationships to capital consumption and accumulation.'[34] This formulation takes note of Marx's criticism of the 'materiality criterion' in Smith, whilst retaining its essential core – the identification of labour which contributes to the accumulation of capital. Thus Marx's category of productive labourers is further narrowed – from all workers producing surplus-value, to (in his notation) all workers producing surplus-value in 'departments I and II', i.e. means of production and wage-goods. The distinction between wage-goods and luxuries here assumes great importance. If the value of labour-power is socially determined, then the real wage in a period of economic growth will also rise, and new commodities and services be incorporated into it. The distinction between necessities – so defined – and luxuries is difficult to draw in practice, but this is a problem inherent in the concept of 'the value of labour-power' itself. Besides, the major items of 'luxury' production today no doubt consist of arms and military services, as noted above.

Marx nowhere relates his three-department analysis of volume II to his analysis of productive and unproductive labour. When specifically confronting the problem, he is adamant that a worker who produces a use-value and surplus-value labours productively, whether he produces guns, or jewellery or millionaires' yachts. But, as Blake notes, the object of his analysis was quite different to Adam Smith's. For the purposes of explaining surplus-value under capitalism, the difference between workers producing means of production, wage-goods or luxury goods was of no importance; for the purposes of explaining reproduction and accumulation it is critical, as Marx himself is clearly aware in *Capital*, volume II. One must not confuse the criterion of productive and unproductive labour required 'for a political economy of growth with the criteria required by a theory of exploitation.'[35]

Nevertheless, it is highly probable that, at the time Marx was writing, he considered productive labour to consist almost entirely of labour which produced necessary wage-goods and means of production, whereas luxuries were chiefly services supplied by unproductive workers supported directly out of revenue. In this case, his explicit analyses cited earlier, would be less relevant – they would indicate that he was aware of the logical problem when forced to confront it, but did not consider it of any *practical* importance. Evidence for this view is to be found in several passages in *Theories of Surplus Value* where the growing productivity of the productive class is shown to provide the necessary *material base* for the growth of the unproductive classes.

> Productive labourers produce the material basis of the subsistence, and consequently, the existence, of the unproductive labourers. [IV/ 1, 186]

> A larger proportion of the surplus product, consisting of means of subsistence, is consumed by unproductive workers or idlers or exchanged for luxuries. [IV/3, 363]

Even so, if faced with the widening gulf which has developed today between these two categories of productive labour following the growth of arms and 'luxury' production, Marx would no doubt stand firm on his original definition – that productive labour *does* include output of luxuries. Given the theoretical task he set himself, it is the only logical interpretation of productive labour.

One further problem arises from the Gillman/Morris/Blake interpretation of the Marxist concept. Is the second criterion of productive labour (labour working in department I and II) an addition to or substitute for the first criterion (labour productive of surplus-value)? Gillman and Morris argue the former, Blake the latter.[36] The following diagram illustrates the alternatives more clearly.

| Labour employed in: | Department I and II | Department III |
| --- | --- | --- |
| *Labour producing surplus-value* | (1) Productive labour | (2) Marx—productive labour. Gillman/ Morris/Blake— unproductive labour |
| *Labour not producing surplus-value* | (3) Marx—unproductive labour. Gillman/Morris —unproductive labour. Blake—productive labour. | (4) Unproductive labour |

The major divergence is over workers creating surplus value but producing luxury goods (category 2). However, Blake suggests that, for a political economy of growth, a *sufficient* definition of productive labour is 'labour whose products can re-enter the cycle of production as elements of variable and constant capital . . . even when such employment does not directly produce surplus-value.'[37] Thus he would include as productive, labour in category 3, for instance health and education services provided by the state, and labour employed in scientific and research institutions (which contribute to the production of constant capital). This is a logical development of the neo-Smithian concept, but one which serves to divorce it clearly from the Marxist concept.

## 3. The Problem of Waste

The most explicit attempt to reinterpret Marx's concept in terms of necessity or social usefulness has been made by Baran. Unproductive labour

> consists of all labour resulting in the output of goods and services the demand for which is attributable to the specific conditions and relationships of the capitalist system, and which would be absent in a rationally ordered society.[38]

Here the historical viewpoint which Marx utilized to separate workers in the circulation process from production workers, is applied to categorize *all* workers, whether or not they produce a 'use-value'. It thus represents, on the one hand, a logical extension of Marx's mode of analysis to take account of the 'waste' and 'distortion' of output which occurs under monopoly capitalism. But on the other, it diverges radically from Marx, as does the neo-Smithian approach, by divorcing the concept of productive labour from the concept of surplus-value. Baran is explicit that not all remaining labour is productive of surplus-value – this is attributable only to labour producing 'essential consumption.' There is a second group of workers supported out of the surplus, but who are productive on Baran's definition:

> Scientists, physicians, artists, teachers and similarly occupied people live off the economic surplus but engage in labour the demand for which in a rationally ordered society, far from disappearing, would become multiplied and intensified to an unprecedented degree.[39]

Thus, just as with the Blake concept, there are two groups supported out of surplus-value (categories 3 and 4), but one is productive, the other unproductive. The actual categorization of workers is remarkably similar to Blake's: workers producing arms, luxury products, etc., are unproductive; scientists, doctors, teachers, etc., employed by the state are productive – but the theoretical derivation is quite distinct. The criterion here is not whether they re-enter the reproduction cycle as elements of constant or variable capital, but their necessity from the standpoint of 'a more rationally ordered society.'

Is there any theoretical antecedent in Marx for this mode of analysis? I think there is in his treatment of the determination of needs. Needs, according to Marx, are socially-determined, hence in our time are shaped by the capitalist mode of production. This theory is set out in its most abstract form in the *Introduction to the Critique:*

> Production thus produces consumption; first, by furnishing the latter with material; second, by determining the manner of consumption; third, by creating in consumers a want for its products as objects of consumption. It thus produces the object, the manner and the desire for consumption.[40]

It is concretely developed chiefly in the *Grundrisse*:

> The production of relative surplus-value, based on the growth of productive forces, requires the creation of new consumption; at the heart of circulation, the sphere of consumption must therefore grow in line with the sphere of production. Consequently: 1. existing consumption is quantitatively expanded, 2. increased needs are created in propagating needs to a wider sphere, 3. new needs are created, new use-values are discovered and produced.[41]

Much of this writing is in the context of the 'civilizing mission' of capitalism, and does not involve a critique, from the future standpoint of a communist society, of the needs thus created. An explicit condemnation of these is found only in his earlier writings, for instance:

> the extension of products and needs falls into contriving and ever-calculating subservience to inhuman, unnatural and imaginary appetites.[42]

There is still controversy on whether Marx later abandoned or incorporated this critical view in his mature writings. For some, such early observations constitute an aberration on Marx's part.[43] For Mandel, however, 'Marx keeps in view all the time the *two contradictory aspects* of the historical reality he has experienced'[44] – in this instance, the positive role of capitalism in creating the all-round development of man's needs and the negative role in distorting and trivializing these needs. If Mandel is correct, then there exists in the *Grundrisse* and his mature writings the basis for a Marxist critique of the needs fostered by capitalism.

The fact that Marx did not use this in his determination of unproductive labour can be explained in one of two ways. First, that he did not consider this relevant to the creation of surplus-value – his sole aim in utilizing the concept. Once again Baran's concept focuses attention on the *disposal* of this surplus and its wasteful or productive uses, as distinct from its *creation*. Indeed he quite explicitly dissociates the productiveness of labour from the production of surplus-value.[45] If this explanation is correct one is left with a choice of concepts, according to the goal of one's analysis. On the other hand, it is possible that the problem did not arise for Marx since he identified the production of trivial, luxury goods, etc., with unproductive labour hired directly by capitalists, landlords and the consuming classes. In this case the way is open for reinterpreting the Marxist concept along Baran's lines in the light of changing objective conditions. But at this point large questions are raised about the materialist basis of the labour theory of value, questions which are beyond the scope of this article.

## III  POLITICAL IMPLICATIONS

Two extreme views can be held regarding the political implications of the Marxist distinction between productive and unproductive labour. The first rigorously identifies productive workers with the working class, thus deduces the political class structure of capitalist society from these economic categories. The second denies any theoretical link or practical correlation between the two. Both viewpoints can lay claim to supporting evidence in Marx's writings on the subject.

To deny any simple identification of the proletariat with productive workers,[45] one has only to return to Marx's analysis of commercial workers in *Capital*. Here, he explicitly notes that commercial wage-labourers have in common with productive workers the fact that (a) their labour is exchanged with *capital*, albeit capital in the sphere of circulation, (b) that consequently they perform surplus labour, in the sense that they work part of the day for nothing, and (c) that their wages are determined in the same way as those of productive workers, reflecting the cost of production of their specific labour power:

> In one respect, such a commercial employee is a wage-worker like any other. In the first place, his labour-power is bought with the variable capital of the merchant, not with money expended as revenue, and consequently it is not bought for private service, but for the purpose of expanding the value of the capital advanced for it. In the second place, the value of his labour-power, and thus his wages, are determined as those of other wage-workers, i.e., by the cost of production and reproduction of his specific labour-power, not by the product of his labour. [III, 17, 292]

Whatever (the commercial worker's) pay, as a wage-labourer he works part of his time for nothing. He may receive daily the value of the product of eight working hours, yet functions ten. But the two hours of surplus-labour he performs do not produce any more than his eight hours of necessary labour, although by means of the latter a part of the social product is transferred to him. [II, 6, 135]

The unpaid labour of these clerks, while it does not create surplus-value, enables (the merchant capitalist) to appropriate surplus-value . . . It is therefore a source of profit to him. [III, 17, 294]

Finally, Marx specifically uses the term 'the commercial proletariat' on at least one occasion (III, 17, 301n.).

Yet elsewhere the germs of an alternative, contradictory political and class analysis can be found. In Part II of *Theories of Surplus Value*, Marx follows his remarks on the growth in the middle classes supported out of the increasing productivity of productive labour, by noting the *objective interest* of the former class in the exploitation of the latter:

For the worker it is equally consoling that because of the growth in the net product, more spheres are opened up for unproductive workers, who live on his product and whose interest in his exploitation coincides more or less with that of the directly exploiting classes. [IV/2, 571]

What he [Ricardo] forgets to emphasise is the constantly growing number of the middle classes, those who stand between the workman on the one hand and the capitalist and the landlord on the other. The middle classes maintain themselves to an ever-increasing extent directly out of revenue, they are a burden weighing heavily on the working base and increase the social security and power of the upper ten thousand. [IV/2, 573]

Here the political affiliations of the new middle class, are related in a striking way to its objective economic situation in the capitalist mode of production. This is developed by Sweezy: besides enjoying 'a standard of living which, from a subjective standpoint, ties them more or less closely to the ruling class of capitalists and landlords', there also exists 'an objective bond' linking the fortunes of the new middle class with those of the ruling class:

For both of these reasons the new middle class tends to provide social and political support for the capitalists rather than for the workers; its members constitute, so to speak, a mass army which readily accepts the leadership of capitalist generals.[47]

Sweezy has in mind here both 'necessary' and 'unnecessary' unproductive workers – both teachers, professionals, etc., and salesmen, advertising agents, publicists and many others in distribution. It is not clear whether he includes the mass of poorer-paid commercial wage workers, who certainly do not enjoy the standard of living thus described. If these are excluded, following Marx's approach above, then already any simple correlation between economic functions, class position and political consciousness has disappeared.

It seems clear that the political analysis, to be productive, must move beyond the confines of the opposing theories postulated above. Two questions arise at this stage. First, are productive workers the only potentially *revolutionary* group in capitalist society because of their objective situation in the process of production, even though other groups share their characteristics as wage-labourers? Second, are there not potential differences in political attitudes *within* the unproductive workers; between for instance, on the one hand, those whose functions are specific to capitalist society and, on the other, those groups the need for which might be expected to expand under a socialist mode of production? In answer to the first, it would seem evident that white-collar and commercial workers are increasingly displaying trade-union and political militancy on a par with associations of productive workers (e.g. ASTMS). This spread of political consciousness follows from the increasing proletarianization of the workforce, forecast by Marx long ago. To this extent, his distinction between productive and unproductive workers is not relevant for deriving their political attitudes.

Mandel has emphasized that the proletariat, as a *revolutionary subject*, requires more than a common situation as wage-labourers *vis-à-vis* capitalists. Marx and Engels in their later analyses 'assigned the proletariat the key role in the coming of socialism not so much because of the misery it suffers as because of *the place it occupies in the production process*.'[48] This general observation of Mandel's is fruitfully developed elsewhere, and it is no coincidence that, in so doing, he draws upon the theory of productive and unproductive labour:

> The massive reintroduction of intellectual labour into the process of production . . . has created the pre-requisite for a much broader layer of the scientific intelligentsia to regain the awareness of alienation which it had lost through its removal from the process of direct production of surplus value and its transformation into a direct or indirect consumer of surplus value . . . This is the material basis . . . for the possibility of involving increasing numbers of scientists and technicians into the revolutionary movement.[49]

Here employment in the process of production, hence involvement in the creation of surplus value, makes this group of workers potentially revolutionary. This follows, first, from the common experience of alienation, which Mandel attributes to workers only, and second, from the critical role of scientists and technologists in the process of production.

They:

> can only enhance the impact of the working class and revolutionary organization *because theory equips them with the knowledge that is indispensable for . . . the successful taking over of the means of production by the associated producers.*[50]

Their role is contrasted with that of unproductive workers – in the sphere of circulation, producers of ideology, trade union functionaries, etc. – whose influence on the developing class consciousness of the proletariat is 'permanently and unremittingly' negative. But the distinction is not rigorously maintained. At times Mandel seems to be following Baran's formulation of unproductive labour as when he includes teachers with scientists and technicians in the first group, and includes journalists and other wage-labourers producing ideology in the second, non-revolutionary category. The criterion then is between that labour, the demand for which is due to the specific conditions of capitalist production, and that which would expand in a socialist system. The former workers would have an 'objective interest' in ensuring the continuation of capitalism, the latter would not and would thus constitute a potential addition to the revolutionary movement.

Such a mode of reasoning appears fruitful but it has its dangers, above all the danger of economic reductionism and a failure to relate the economic situation of groups of workers with the other contradictions of capitalist society. All that can be said with certainty is that, because of both their experience of alienation *and* their objective situation in the productive process, the involvement of the mass of *productive* workers is essential to a successful socialist revolution.

NOTES AND REFERENCES

1. This essay originated in a Manchester study group which for two years systematically read and discussed the three volumes of Marx's *Capital*.

2. To avoid unnecessary footnotes, references to these volumes are placed immediately after any quotation. References to *Capital* give first the volume, second the chapter and third the page numbers in the Moscow editions of 1961 (vol. I), 1967 (vol. II) and 1966 (vol. III). Treating *Theories of Surplus Value* as the fourth projected volume of *Capital*, I refer to the three parts as IV/1, IV/2, and IV/3, followed by the page numbers in the Moscow editions of 1969 (part 1), 1968 (part 2) and 1972 (part 3).

3. Compare for instance Joan Robinson's view of the status of the concept with Baran's: J. Robinson, *An Essay on Marxian Economics*, 2nd ed., London 1966, pp. 20–21. P. Baran, *The Political Economy of*

*Growth* (London, 1957), ch. 2.

4. The best, though brief, expositions are found in P. Sweezy, *The Theory of Capitalist Development,* London, 1962 and E. Mandel, *Marxist Economic Theory,* 2 vols., London, 1968. See S. H. Coontz, *Productive Labour and Effective Demand* (London, 1965), for an extended discussion.

5. P. Baran, *The Political Economy of Growth.* See also J. Gillman, *The Falling Rate of Profit* (London, 1957); the stimulating debate between J. Morris and J. Blake in *Science and Society,* vol. 22, 1958 and vol. 24, 1960; and J. Gillman, *Prosperity in Crisis* (New York, 1965). These alternative interpretations are discussed in part II.

6. See M. Nicolaus, 'Proletariat and Middle Class in Marx', *Studies on the Left,* VII, 1, January–February 1967.

7. It is *precisely because* the historical specificity of concepts is central to Marx's political economy, that he utilizes abstractions referring to phenomena common to all societies, such as 'the labour process' and 'production in general.' cf. '*Production in general* is an abstraction, but it is a rational abstraction,' Introduction to A Contribution to a *Critique of Political Economy, Marx's Grundrisse* (London, 1971), p. 18.

8. The transformation or exchange of labour with *capital* consists of 'two essentially different though interdependent phases' (IV/1, 397). First, labour power is bought with money, and second, it is consumed, the labour power is set to work to produce surplus value: 'Labour is directly *materialized,* is transformed *directly* into capital, after it has been *formally* incorporated in capital through the first transaction . . . The statement that *productive labour* is labour which is *directly* exchanged with capital embraces all these phases.' (IV/1, 398–399.)

9. See IV/1, 84.

10. A. Smith, *The Wealth of Nations* (London, 1970), p. 430.

11. *Sic.* One reason why a reader can still leave Marx with the impression that productive labour is identified with labour producing material goods, is in his use of the term 'commodity' to mean a material good, rather than *any* use-value produced by human labour for exchange. However, in the following passage, Marx clarifies this usage and answers his critics: 'The materialization, etc., of labour is, however, not to be taken in such a Scottish sense as Adam Smith conceives it. When we speak of the commodity as a materialization of labour – in the sense of its exchange-value – this itself is only an imaginary, that is to say, a purely social mode of existence of the commodity which has nothing to do with its corporal reality; it is conceived as a definite quantity of social labour or of money. It may be that the concrete labour whose result it is leaves no trace in it' (IV/1, 171). We consider in Part II an alternative reason why Adam Smith maintained that productive labour necessarily produced material goods, which suggests that this was intentional and not necessarily due to any 'confusion' on his part.

12. See the interesting passage in K. Marx, *Resultate* (Frankfurt, 1969), p. 66, quoted in E. Mandel, *The Leninist Theory of Organization* (London, 1971), p. 23. Also J. Gillman, *The Falling Rate of Profit,* ch. 7.

13. Cf. P. Baran and P. Sweezy, *Monopoly Capital* (London, 1968), ch. 5.

14. E. Mandel, *Marxist Economic Theory*, pp. 191–192. I would substitute the term 'distributing' for 'realizing,' to make clear that it is the physical modification of the use-value that is critical.

15. K. Marx, *Grundrisse der Kritik der Politischen Okonomie* (*Robentwurf*) (Berlin, 1953), p. 432. Quoted in P. Baran, *The Political Economy of Growth*, p. 33. Though Marx treats of productive and unproductive labour in the *Grundrisse*, he does not add there to his fundamental analysis in *Theories of Surplus Value* and *Capital*.

16. See also IV/1, 288–289.

17. K. Marx, *Critique of the Gotha Programme*, in K. Marx and F. Engels, *Selected Works* (Moscow, 1949–50), vol. II.

18. E. Mandel, *Marxist Economic Theory*, p. 191.

19. Cf. J. Blake, 'Jacob Morris on Unproductive Employment: A Criticism,' in *Science and Society*, 24, 1960, p. 169.

20. S. H. Coontz, *Productive Labour and Effective Demand*, p. 67.

21. J. Robinson, *An Essay on Marxian Economics*, p. 20, n. 1.

22. Cf. R. Meek, *Studies in the Labour Theory of Value* (London, 1958), chs. 1–3.

23. These two strands are brought together in the work of P. Baran, *op. cit.*, P. Baran and P. Sweezy, *op. cit.*, J. Gillman, *op. cit.*, S. Coontz, *op. cit.*

24. P. Sweezy, *op. cit.*, p. 232.

25. M. Kidron, *Western Capitalism since the War* (London, 1970), p. 56. See also J. Morris, 'Unemployment and Unproductive Employment,' *Science and Society*, 22, 1958, pp. 194–195; J. Blake, 'Jacob Morris on Unproductive Employment: a Criticism,' *Science and Society*, 24, 1960, p. 171.

26. P. Sweezy, *op. cit.*, p. 282.

27. P. Baran and P. Sweezy, *op. cit.*, p. 141.

28. P. Sweezy, *op. cit.*, p. 22. The comparison could scarcely be *backwards* with a pre-capitalist mode of production, or, in the case of supervising staff, with primitive communism!

29. A similar dispute has centred on the items to be included in the national income of capitalist economies. See S. Kuznets, *National Income and its Composition*, 1919–1928, National Bureau of Economic Research, 1954, ch. 1. Marxist political economy brings with it the historical, critical standpoint – the question at issue is how far it should be used to distinguish productive from unproductive labour.

30. A. Smith, *op. cit.*, pp. 429–430.

31. H. Myint, *Theories of Welfare Economics* (London, 1948), p. 73.

32. *Ibid.*, pp. 73–74.

33. J. Blake, *op. cit.*, p. 171.

34. J. Morris, *op. cit.*, p. 195.

35. J. Blake, *op. cit.*, p. 172.

36. J. Gillman, *op. cit.*, p. 23; J. Morris, *op. cit.*, p. 194; J. Blake, *op. cit.*, pp. 172–173.

37. *Ibid.*, p. 173.

38. P. Baran, *op. cit.*, p. 32.

39. *Ibid.*, pp. 23, 33.

40. *Marx's 'Grundrisse,'* p. 26.

41. K. Marx, *Grundrisse*, p. 312. See also pp. 313–314. Part of this is translated in M. Nicolaus, 'The Unknown Marx,' *New Left Review*, 48, 1968, p. 56.

42. K. Marx, *Economic and Philosophic Manuscripts of 1844*, London 1970, pp. 147 *et seq.*

43. For example, P. Sedgwick, 'Natural Science and Human Theory,' in R. Miliband and J. Saville (eds.), *The Socialist Register* (1966), p. 189.

44. E. Mandel, *The Formation of the Economic Thought of Karl Marx* (London, 1971), p. 110, cf. pp. 34, 38.

45. Just as Joan Robinson wishes to, but for Baran this does not involve ditching the labour theory of value.

46. For instance 'To Marx, the proletariat meant *productive* workers only,' M. Nicolaus, 'Proletariat and Middle Class in Marx,' *op. cit.*, p. 49, n. 40.

47. P. Sweezy, *op. cit.*, p. 284. This is developed further in Sweezy's analysis of their role under imperialism and fascism, cf. chs. 17, 18.

48. E. Mandel, *The Formation of the Economic Thought of Karl Marx*, p. 23. (My emphasis.)

49. E. Mandel, *The Leninist Theory of Organization*, p. 15.

50. *Ibid.*, p. 14.

# PROLETARIAT AND MIDDLE CLASS IN MARX: HEGELIAN CHOREOGRAPHY AND THE CAPITALIST DIALECTIC*

MARTIN NICOLAUS

## I. HEGELIAN CHOREOGRAPHY

To bring more clarity into the delicate subject of Marx's Hegelianism, it is necessary to make a distinction among three aspects of the dialectic. There is, first, the *context* of the dialectical movement, which in Hegel is either the timeless realm of pure logic or a sphere which is called History but is only the ephemeral context in which an abstract Idea unfolds its purpose. Second, there is the *content* of the dialectical categories, which in Hegel is typically abstract, void of concrete reference. Finally, there is the dialectical *movement* itself, the inevitable process by which contradictions unfold, affirm, negate and gracefully vanish from the scene with a dazzling *Aufhebung* – annulment, preservation and supersession in one motion. With polemical intent I have called this *movement* of the categories in Hegel his 'choreography,' for, it seems to me, Marx remained under the spell of this dance long after he had succeeded in bringing the *context* and the *content* of the dialectic down to earth and under a plain light. It was Marx's captivation with this choreography, I shall argue, which led him to the prediction that capitalist society must inevitably become polarized into two directly antagonistic classes, and that, in this polarization, the industrial proletariat must play the role of successful negation.

That this prediction has proved to be mistaken, and that its fulfillment seems least probable precisely where it was most to be expected, namely in the *advanced* industrial nations, has been apparent for some time. In the second section of this paper, I argue that Marx himself developed the theoretical principles on which this prediction can be shown to be invalid, and that on occasion these principles led Marx himself to make predictions which explicitly contradict those of the *Communist Manifesto*. My thesis is that Marx's major contributions to the under-

* Originally published in *Studies on the Left*, 7:1, January/February 1967. Reprinted with permission of James Weinstein.

standing of capitalism – the labor theory of value, the theory of the surplus, the law of the tendential decline of the profit rate – constitute a body of theory from which the failure of capitalist society to polarize, the rise of a new middle class, and the declining militancy of the industrial proletariat – in other words, the essential features of advanced industrial society – can be accurately predicted and explained, and indeed that Marx himself did so. In discussing Marx's theory of classes I shall be concerned chiefly with his theory of classes arising out of industrial capitalism and not with his general theory. By the latter I understand the series of propositions centered on the ideas that class struggles are the moving force of history, that classes and their conflicts arise out of contradictions in the means and modes of production, etc. Nothing in this general theory, unfortunately, permits instant and spontaneous deductions to the specific conditions which prevail in a given society. In the *German Ideology* Marx was quite unambiguous about the necessity for empirical investigation. The general theory is that 'given individuals who are active in production in a given way, enter into certain social and political relationships.' However, 'The connection between production and the social and political structure must in every case be uncovered by empirical observation, without mystification or speculation.'[1] But Marx himself did not carry out a program of thorough empirical investigation of capitalist production until several years after the *Manifesto*, and it was the resulting weakness in his understanding of the capitalist social structure which permitted the Hegelian choreography to exercise so strong a hold over him.

Although biographical information about the genesis of an idea can provide no more than circumstantial evidence, that sort of evidence has its usefulness when it arouses skepticism; and when skepticism leads to a fresh examination of certain ritual formulations, then the introduction of biographical evidence may prove to be instrumental in bringing back to life an idea long after the period out of which it first arose. In the present case, the key item of circumstantial information which should arouse our skepticism and lead us to look at Marx afresh is the biographical fact that Marx proclaimed the historic liberating mission of the proletariat *before* he had more than the vaguest notions of the political economy of capitalism, before he had read the bourgeois economists of his day, and long before he had grappled with the economic problems to which his mature theory is the solution.

The proclamation that the proletariat would make the revolution came in the third of a series of philosophical papers in which the young Marx worked out a critical stance toward Hegel and his followers. In the first of these papers, the *Kritik des Hegelschen Staatsrechts* (written summer 1843, when Marx was twenty-five years old), he still held, with the Hegelians, that the French Revolution had created a political state in which the distinctions that existed in the private lives of its citizens, in 'civic society,' had no material relevance, or, in other words, that rich and poor were equal in the political sphere.[2] In the second paper *Zur Judenfrage* (autumn 1843), he amends this position drastically by stating that differences of civil standing might not be of importance in the political sphere, but that the political sphere itself was of little importance, and that civil distinctions nevertheless remained civil distinctions, which must not be ignored.[3] A short time later in the *Kritik der Hegelschen Rechtsphilosophie, Einleitung* (winter 1843–1844), the 'distinctions' of civil standing become 'contradictions within civil society,' a most important change; the relevance of the political sphere and of the philosophy that deals with it as if the state were the celestial realm here on earth is completely denied; philosophy itself is given a properly philosophical funeral with the proclamation that deeds, not words, will change society; and finally, the men who will wield the historical broom to sweep German thought and German politics clear of their interlocking cobwebs are ushered on stage:

> Where, then, is the *positive* possibility of German emancipation? *Answer:* In the formation of a class with *radical chains*, a class within civil society which is not a class of civil society, an estate which is the dissolution of all estates, a sphere which possesses a universal character because of its universal suffering . . . This dissolution of society as a special estate is the *proletariat*.[4]

Here the Hegelian context has been liquidated, and the Hegelian categories have received a historical content, but the choreography has, for all that, emerged more strongly. Marx has discovered no more about the proletariat than that it develops and grows larger as industry does,[5] and already he has it dancing the leading negative role in the dialectic of History. Only after this proclamation did Marx begin to read the political economists to find, as he wrote later, the anatomy of civil society.[6]

The record of the collision between Hegelian philosophy and the political economy of Adam Smith, Ricardo, and others, appears in Marx's *Economic-Philosophic Manuscripts of 1844*. None of his works reveals more clearly the difficulties Marx experienced, and probably those which anyone must experience, in attempting to grasp the dismally pragmatic confusion of data and theory that prevails in so unpoetic a discipline as economics with the intellectual equipment of a sphere so clear, uncluttered and even elegant as the Hegelian philosophy. The struggle is uncompromising and complex. On the one hand, Marx writes that '. . . my conclusions are the fruit of an entirely empirical analysis, based upon a careful critical study of political economy.'[7] And then: 'Political economy has merely formulated the laws of alienated labor.'[8] However: 'Hegel's standpoint is that of modern political economy. He conceives *labor* as the *essence*, the self-confirming essence of man.'[9] Nevertheless: Hegel is wrong 'because his conception is *formal* and *abstract*, [and therefore] the annulment of alienation becomes a confirmation of alienation.'[10] This is a battle of methods, of ways of seeing and explaining the world, a struggle between disparate epistemologies. Here the dialectic power of German idealism struggles like Hercules against the giant, Antaeus, the son of Earth; and, it must be said, the outcome is the same as in that mythical trial: philosophy lifts its antagonist off the ground, away from the source of his strength, and crushes him in midair. Thus Marx seizes upon the capitalist production process, its relations of property, together with its system of exchange and circulation, and lifts this entire edifice of empirical fact and empirical fancy into the Hegelian air, where he compresses the pragmatic giant into the single concept of 'alienated labor.' And Marx aims higher than Hercules; he not only crushes his antagonist, but he also believes that he can then reconstitute him on a higher level by unfolding the content of the fundamental core to which he has been reduced. Thus he writes, as only a philosophical idealist could write:

> As we have discovered the concept of *private property* by an *analysis* of the concept of *alienated labor*, so with the aid of these two factors we can evolve all the categories of political economy, and in every category, e.g. trade, competition, capital, money, we shall discover only a particular and developed expression of these fundamental elements.[11]

Here metaphysics has won over empiricism, not only in method but also in substance. Marx's theory of classes, as it was forged in this crucible, represents a two-fold defeat for economics. First, Marx sees both the division of society into classes and the division of labor as equivalent aspects of the touchstone concept 'alienated labor.'[12] Only from a perspective beyond economics can one afford to ignore the difference between them. A political economist, on the other hand, must grasp and explicate the fact that the division of labor is not the same thing as class division, or else his entire craft runs into confusion. As late as the *German Ideology* (1846) Marx still stands outside political economy in that respect, as is shown by his famous remark that communism will abolish the division of labor, so that man may be a hunter, a fisherman, or a critic as he pleases.[13] This is a brilliant philosophical vision, but a less poetic spirit would not have ventured it without first asking where the hunter is to get his rifle, the fisherman his rod and reel, and the critic his books – and the answer to those questions is again within the realm of the economist, not of the philosopher. There is a measure of irony in the fact that Marx puts the division of labor and the division of classes into proper economic perspective only when he notes that Proudhon has committed a similar philosophic confusion – for Marx himself, he later wrote, was responsible for 'infecting' Proudhon with Hegelianism.[14]

The second and more disastrous effect of the victory of philosophy over economics on Marx's theory of classes was his discovery that the antagonism of labor vs. capital could be made to 'fit' neatly into the dialectical pattern. The earlier proclamation of the proletariat as universal negation was strengthened and amplified here to the point where the development of capitalist industrialization appeared to Marx as a fateful unfolding of a contradiction whose path *must* conform to the choreography *because* it was dialectical. 'The relations of private property,' he writes – and here he still speaks of 'private property' instead of capitalism, of *'buergerliche Gesellschaft'* (civil society) instead of bourgeois society – 'are capital, labor, and their interconnections.' And then the pattern that is fundamental to his thought: 'The movements through which these elements have to go are: First – *unmediated and mediated unity of the two* . . . [then:] *opposition between the two* . . . *opposition* of each *to* itself . . . [and] *clash of reciprocal contradictions.*'[15] Although it became filled out with a great deal of historical material, this dialectical schema remained the basis of Marx's view of social classes and their conflict up to and including the *Manifesto*, and to a great extent for the rest of his life. The notion that 'capital' and 'labor' may not be the only determining components of a fully developed capitalist society, and the idea that 'the movements through which these elements have to go' may not be the movements through which any self-respecting dialectical contradiction must go, but that these movements may be determined by the specifically capitalist contradiction, which may be quite different – these notions do not occur until later in his work and will be discussed in the second part of this paper. Meanwhile, however, the movement of history seemed to confirm the dialectical prognosis, making a detailed analysis of the capitalist economic process unnecessary; for it was a fact, as Engels reported in his *Condition of the Working Class in England*, that the onrush of industrial capitalism was destroying the previous small middle classes of tradesmen, manufacturers and craftsmen, and that the social and economic distance between a small number of big capitalists and the swelling propertyless proletarians was growing wider and wider.[16] Was it so wrong to project the impact of primary capitalist accumulation into the future, as in this crucial passage from the *Manifesto*?

> Our epoch, the epoch of the bourgeoisie, possesses, however, the distinctive feature that it has simplified class contradictions. The whole society more and more splits into two great antagonistic camps, two great classes directly opposed to one another: Bourgeoisie and Proletariat.[17]

Only a small leap of faith was required to envision a society in which this initial polarization had continued to sharpen, finally reaching the outer limits of human endurance; that is, a society in which an absolutely wealthy capitalist class confronts an absolutely impoverished proletariat – and one does not need to be a Hegelian to predict that a revolution will occur under such circumstances. Yet it was a peculiarly Hegelian exaggeration, a Hegelian leap of faith, to assume that the contradiction between capital and labor would continue to develop and unfold in this manner until the two classes confronted each other with all the unmediated antagonism of a pure negation confronting an absolute affirmation. To assume without further analysis of the capitalist economic process that the dialectic of capitalism must conform to the dialectic of ideas was a most Hegelian error of procedure; and the error of procedure resulted in an error of substance. The advance of capitalist society has not meant increasingly sharp conflict between capital and labor. The most industrially advanced capitalist nations typically have the most quiescent, noninsurrectionary proletariats – witness the United States; and in every capitalist country there has arisen a broad, vocal and specifically new middle class to thwart Marxist theory and to stifle and crush Marxist action. Marx's captivation with the Hegelian choreography has cost his followers in advanced industrial society a heavy price. The prophets of class conflict have too often stood powerless to explain or to deal with the class structure of the society that their reading of Marx leads them to think should never have been.

## II. THE CAPITALIST DIALECTIC

### A. *The model of capitalist economics in the* Manifesto

Marx's contributions to political economy – the labor theory of value, the theory of the surplus, the law of the tendential fall of the profit rate – all date from about 1857–1858, the years during which Marx wrote the *Grundrisse*.[18] None of these discoveries is foreshadowed in the *Manifesto* (1848), and indeed this early work shows no clear evidence that

Marx had yet become aware of the *problems* to which his later contributions were the *solutions*.

Although Marx writes repeatedly in the *Manifesto* that capital employs labor in order to increase or augment itself (*vermehren*),[19] one looks in vain here for a theory of precisely how this process of capital accumulation takes place. The closest approach to an understanding of capitalist accumulation, and thereby to a theory of the surplus, comes when Marx mentions that communism wants to do away with the capitalist's appropriation of the net yield (*Reinertrag*) of production.[20] But this insight remains unconscious of itself, and the various references to capital accumulation are so rudimentary and cursory that no systematic theory of accumulation can be extracted from them or projected into them. The *Manifesto*'s economic theorizing in general suffers from a great amount of vagueness. Here, for instance, is one example of a powerful prediction based on a chain of diffuse economic reasoning:

> The essential condition for the existence, and for the sway of the bourgeois class, is the formation and augmentation of capital; the condition for capital is wage-labor. *Wage-labor rests exclusively on competition between the laborers.* The advance of industry, whose involuntary promoter is the bourgeoisie, replaces the isolation of the laborers, due to competition, by their involuntary combination, due to association. The development of Modern Industry therefore cuts from under its feet the very foundation on which the bourgeoisie produces and appropriates products. What the bourgeoisie therefore produces, above all, are its own gravediggers. Its fall and the victory of the proletariat are equally inevitable.[21]

I have italicized the phrase 'wage-labor rests exclusively on competition between the laborers' in order to emphasize what strikes me as the weakest link in this argument. The statement is at best a half-truth; it is not even a full truth if one says that the *level of wages* rests exclusively on competition. But even if the statement were correct, then the conclusion that workers' associations will bury the bourgeoisie does not follow; the only thing that follows is that wage labor will get more expensive, from the capitalist's standpoint. And that, of course, is precisely what has occurred wherever workers' associations (unions) have succeeded in defeating competition from non-unionized labor; the reduction of competition has by no means done away with wage labor or with capitalism. Only if the bourgeoisie were absolutely economically incapable of granting wage demands put forth by associated workers would there be any necessary revolutionary consequences in the elimination of competition between the laborers. Had Marx at this time worked out an economic theory to account for the fact that the bourgeoisie is *not* incapable of raising wages, this particular prediction would have had to be argued differently. What the excerpt above shows chiefly is that Marx's analysis of bourgeois production had at this point penetrated little further than the insight that the bourgeoisie turns all human values into market values, all human beings into commodities. Thus, here and elsewhere in the *Manifesto*, Marx sees the *market* as the center of gravity of bourgeois society; in this case he goes so far as to believe that a change in the market (the labor market, here) will produce a drastic change in the whole social structure. While this emphasis on the importance of the market cannot be discounted, Marx himself in his mature economic works came to see the market as a dependent variable, and he then identified *capital accumulation* and *production* as the real fulcrum around which all the other phenomena of bourgeois society gravitate.[22]

Insofar as the *Manifesto* contains any theory of capitalist accumulation and production at all, which is debatable, that theory centers on the concept of exploitation. 'Wage labor,' Marx writes, 'creates capital, i.e. that kind of property which exploits wage labor, and which cannot increase except upon condition of creating a new supply of wage labor for fresh exploitation.'[23] But here all clarity stops, for what exactly does exploitation mean? It should be noted that in *Capital*, after Marx had developed the theory of the surplus, he gives this term a very precise, quantifiable meaning; here, however, it is more a physical and moral term, denoting suffering, degradation, destruction, dehumanization, etc. The closest economic term for this usage of 'exploitation' would be destructive consumption; that is, capital is accumulated by using up, destroying the labor commodity in the act of production. The more the capitalist deprives the laborer of his commodity, labor, the richer the capitalist gets; the fatter the capitalist, the leaner the worker. Eventually the workers will become absolutely impoverished, and at the same time, the capitalists will have all the wealth of any kind in the nation. The capitalists will have everything but no one to sell it to, and the workers will have nothing but a world to win. Then, in the terms of the *Manifesto*, a classic overproduction crisis sets in ('too much civilization, too much means of subsistence, too much industry, too much commerce,')[24] or rather, there is a series of such crises, which culminates in the grand, final crisis which will bring the revolution. That approximately is the *Manifesto*'s model of capitalist accumulation, and this also appears to be the model many Marxists still cling to.

The affinities between this model and the Hegelian choreography should strike the eye. For if this is indeed how capitalism operates, then it follows that capitalism must throw all possible parts of the population into the industrial labor supply, which means that all intermediate classes must and will be destroyed (which is exactly what the *Manifesto* says), thus creating a society perfectly polarized between an absolutely rich capitalist class and an absolutely poor industrial proletariat, the two facing each other with the undiluted antagonism of a logical contradiction. And then indeed the *Aufhebung* is nigh.

But, to return a last time to this economic model, what if for one reason or another the total wealth of the nation were not a fixed constant; what if there were an increment, say $x$, which arose to augment the total without diminishing the wealth of either labor or capital proportionately? The existence of this extra increment, this surplus, removes the weight of the iron law of destructive consumption. Absolute wealth on one side would not necessarily mean absolute impoverishment on the other side; which means that capitalist accumulation would not necessarily mean absolute social polarization. And this would be especially true if it were discovered that this $x$ were not an arbitrary *deus ex machina* conjured into the system from outside, but a regular and essential feature of capitalist production itself.

## B. The discovery of surplus value

If I am correct in saying that the validity of the Hegelian social choreography depends on the validity of the simple, surplus-less model of destructive consumption outlined above, then the liquidation by Marx of the Hegelian choreography can be fixed in time and space with considerable precision. The spell of that dance is broken in principle in the *Grundrisse der Kritik der Politischen Oekonomie (Rohentwurf)* of 1857–1858, a voluminous work which has not been translated into English. After a lengthy critique of economic theory which treats capitalist production as if it were production in general, as if its special characteristics were not worth investigating, Marx brings up the central problem of the theory of capitalism and proceeds to solve it. How is it, he asks, that at the end of the production process the capitalist has a commodity which is worth more than the elements that went into it? He pays the price of machinery, raw materials and the price of labor, yet the product is worth more than all three together. What, in other words, is the source of the surplus value (*Mehrwert*) which the capitalist appropriates? The problem is insoluble, Marx writes, so long as 'labor' is considered a commodity like any other commodity (as it was, specifically, in the *Manifesto*).[25] If labor were such a commodity, then capitalist production would be: price of machinery + price of raw materials + price of labor = price of product. Where, then, is the capitalist's profit? If we evade the question by saying that the capitalist fixes an arbitrary profit percentage and simply adds it to the price of the product, as high as the market will bear, then it appears that the buyer of the commodity is the source of the capitalist's profit. Yet what the capitalist gains in this way, the buyer loses, and it is impossible to see how an aggregate surplus could arise out of such transactions. Marx rejected this mercantilist theory, according to which one nation could get richer only by cheating another in commerce. This theory is overcome, and the problem of surplus value is solved, when one realizes that the worker sells the capitalist not 'labor,' but labor *power* (*Arbeitskraft*). Although its price varies with supply and demand, this specific commodity has the exceptional quality of being able to produce more value than is necessary to reproduce it.[26] For example, all the commodities necessary to keep a worker alive and able to work, i.e. groceries, clothes, shelter, etc., have a value represented by the letter $n$. Working in a factory, the worker produces for the capitalist a quantity of commodities whose value is equal to the value of the commodities he needs to consume, in $n$ hours. This $n$ is what Marx calls necessary labor time, that is, the time necessary to produce enough value to allow the worker to live and work on. But once he is fed and clothed, the worker is able to continue to work more than $n$ hours, and that is exactly what the capitalist forces him to do. If at a given stage of social productivity it takes on the average six hours to produce enough for the worker to live, i.e. if $n$ is 6, then any hours worked in addition to 6 are what Marx calls surplus labor, and the product of this surplus labor is the surplus product, which, when sold, yields surplus value, a part of which the capitalist pockets as profit.

The specific nature of capitalist production, then, is the creation and appropriation of surplus value by the capitalist class. To increase surplus value, the capitalist must increase the amount of the workers' surplus labor. Marx distinguishes between two methods of increasing surplus labor. In the early stages of industrialization the first method was the prolongation of the working day over and above the necessary labor time, thus stretching the day to twelve, fourteen, sixteen and more hours, up to and beyond the limits of human endurance. This form of surplus accumulation Marx calls the production of 'absolute surplus.'[27] However, eventually the labor force becomes exhausted in this way; the worker dies too young, the laboring population diminishes through disease and wages must rise. Then, Marx writes, the capitalist class finds it in its own interests to limit the working day by law to a humanly endurable 'normal' length.[28] Once that stage has been reached, a point which according to Marx occurs when capitalism has taken over all branches of production and becomes altogether the

239

dominant form of production,[29] then the capitalist class turns to the creation of what Marx calls 'relative surplus,' that is, the extraction of more surplus labor within a fixed number of hours.[30] While the production of absolute surplus is possible with the instruments and machinery of earlier periods, the relative surplus can only be increased by revolutionizing the whole basis of production, which means principally the rapid introduction of modern machinery. Machinery raises the productivity of each worker, so that he produces the equivalent value necessary to sustain him in less time; that is, $n$, necessary labor time, is reduced relative to surplus labor time. In this way, the capitalist can appropriate greater and greater amounts of surplus without necessarily working the worker to death in the process, although he can also do both. For Marx, the production of relative surplus by the use of ever more efficient machinery resulting in ever greater productivity was one of capitalism's fundamental historical tendencies.

Here we must briefly discuss what Marx called the solution to the mystery which had plagued all of political economy since Adam Smith, namely, the 'law of the tendential decline of the profit rate.'[31] This law states quite simply that as the capitalist class as a whole invests more and more heavily in machinery, and proportionally less in wages, the *rate* of profit will tend to decline. The fact that Marx assumed competitive market conditions, and that these no longer are typical today, however, does not destroy the usefulness of this law as an explanatory concept. What Baran and Sweezy in *Monopoly Capital* have called the 'tendency of the surplus to rise' is not only not contradictory to Marx's law, but is in fact only another aspect of it.[32] Marx was quite specific, and repeatedly so, in stating that the tendential decline in the profit *rate* not only can but *must* lead to a corresponding rise in the *mass* of profits, and that a decline in the profit rate *must* tend to *increase* both the *rate* and the *mass* of the *surplus*.[33] (The surplus is computed only on the basis of necessary versus surplus labor time; but the profit is computed on the basis of investment in machinery also, which explains the seemingly contradictory movement of profit and surplus.) Thus in the course of capitalist development, Marx held, the capitalist class tends to realize a smaller profit rate on its investments, but the volume of profits, as well as the rate and volume of the surplus which it controls, tends to grow disproportionately faster. For example, an eighteenth-century manufacturer employing one thousand workers with hand tools might make a profit of fifty per cent, for a mass of profit measured in a few thousands of dollars; but a modern corporation with an equal number of workers, and a multi-million-dollar investment in machinery, may make only five per cent, but its profits may also be in the millions.

This tendency has important implications for the relationship between the capitalist class and the working class. One of them is that the process of advanced capitalist development enables the capitalist class to face workers' demands for higher wages with an unprecedented degree of flexibility. The small capitalist of an earlier period sometimes literally could not increase wages without eventually going out of business. For the huge corporation with its voluminous reserves, the refusal to grant wage increases is less a matter of life-and-death necessity and more a matter of policy. What happens then, Marx foresaw, is that the workers' submission to the capitalist class is clothed

> . . . in bearable, or, as Eden says, 'comfortable and liberal' forms. . . . From the workers' own swelling surplus product, a part of which is constantly being converted into additional capital, a greater portion flows back to them in cash, so that they can broaden the sphere of their consumption, equip themselves better with clothing and furniture, etc., and develop a small reserve of savings.[34]

Since a large capital can and does expand faster, although with a smaller profit rate, than smaller capital, wage increases of this sort at this stage of capitalist development may be safely granted, for they in no way hinder the accumulation of capital or its concentration in the hands of the class of big capitalists.[35] Elsewhere, Marx writes that what really matters under capitalism is not the absolute level of wages, but the incomes of the classes relative to one another.[36] Once capital has accumulated a certain volume of surplus, in other words, the absolute impoverishment of the workers becomes a negligible possibility because it is no longer the essential precondition of capitalist accumulation. Exploitation itself becomes a relative term; in *Capital* the rate of exploitation means the ratio of necessary labor to surplus labor in the working day. Thus the rate of exploitation may escalate almost *ad infinitum*, yet at the same time the working class may live more comfortably than ever. The rising surplus makes it possible for the capitalist class to exchange its tyranny for a benevolent despotism.

The saddest victims of capitalist accumulation in its advanced stage, as Marx charted it, are not the workers but the unemployed, the 'industrial reserve army.' As productivity rises, the demand for productive labor in a given industry or in all industries generally may drop temporarily, or in the long run, will tend to drop permanently. Thus is created a constant stream of under-employed, unemployed, prematurely used up, obsolete, or unemployable individuals.[37] When unskilled labor is the standard mode in the society, as Marx posited in *Capital*, then this reserve army serves to depress the wages of the employed; but, he might have added, at a certain stage in the development of productivity only skilled labor can be used (e.g. the replacement of ditch-digging gangs by earth-moving machinery), so that the unskilled unemployed lose even their competitive link with the working class, and as one generation of unemployed begets another, a permanent welfare class comes into being. At the same time, the greater volume of surplus makes it possible to support growing numbers of these people, however miserably. In the advanced stages of capitalist development, the 'exploitation' of the working class appears as prosperity beside the poverty of this never-working subproletariat.

The implications of Marx's theory of the surplus, in short, destroy the relationship between capital and labor which the *Manifesto* had foreseen. In the hands of an intelligent capitalist class bent on its own survival, the swelling surplus provides a cushion against the more acute forms of class conflict, and prevents absolute social polarization along the lines laid out by the Hegelian choreography. The specifically capitalist dialectic does not obey the laws of the great philosopher.

## C. The rise of the surplus class

The rise of the surplus not only alters the relationship between the capitalist class and the working class, but it also creates an entirely new class between them. While the term 'surplus class' to designate this stratum does not to my knowledge occur in Marx's writings, the idea and its implications were clearly seized and expressed by him.

The essential feature of capitalism, Marx says, is to appropriate surplus labor. That is to say, labor is productive for capitalism only insofar as it yields surplus labor; or, as Marx put it succinctly, 'labor is productive only insofar as it produces its own opposite.'[38] As labor becomes more and more productive, it produces more and more of its own opposite. This tendency yields what may be called the 'law of the surplus class' in its most general form: as less and less people are forced to produce more and more, more and more people are forced to produce less and less. As Marx put it:

> Given an advance of industrial productivity to the point where only one third of the population takes a direct part in material production, instead of two thirds as before, then one third furnish the means of life for the whole, whereas before two thirds were required to do so. Before, one third was net revenue (as distinct from the workers' income), now net revenue is two thirds. Disregarding the class contradiction, the whole nation would now need only one third of its time for direct production, whereas earlier it had needed two thirds. With equal distribution, everyone would now have two thirds of his time for unproductive labor and for leisure. But in capitalist

242

production, everything appears and is contradictory.[39]

The contradiction resides in the fact that the distribution of disposable time cannot be equal so long as the capitalist system operates by appropriating surplus labor, i.e. so long as it is the capitalist system of production; for if everyone worked only long enough to reproduce the means of life, there would be no surplus for the capitalists to appropriate. What does happen, under capitalism, to the mass of people who are released from direct, productive labor by the advance of productivity? The question is the same as the question of what happens to the mass of surplus value generated by advanced capitalist production.

Marx divided the surplus value into a number of categories, of which we need distinguish only the broadest, capital and revenue. Capital is that part of the surplus value which the capitalist reinvests in further production. Revenue includes everything the capitalist pays out to himself and others, such as dividends, interest payments, land rent, taxes, and most importantly, payment for services rendered to his enterprise by *other than productive workers*. A great number of people who produce no commodities for profitable sale are essential to the capitalist enterprise and consume a part of its revenue; e.g. book-keepers, clerks, secretaries, lawyers, designers, engineers, salesmen, etc. – in general, all the people who do not themselves control capital (as bankers do) and who fulfill a function in the vast system of financing, distributing, exchanging, improving and maintaining the commodities produced by the proletariat and appropriated by the capitalist class.[40] From the law of the rising surplus, it follows that except during times of exceptionally heavy capital investment, the mass of disposable revenue must also tend to rise; that is, there must be an increase in that part of the surplus which can be expended for the utilization of unproductive labor.

The surplus not only can, it *must* be expended for unproductive labor, for two reasons.

First, as productivity rises, the number of unproductive laborers required to service and maintain the growing capital establishment also rises. The number of the traditional unproductive workers increases, e.g. clerks, book-keepers. More significantly, entirely new branches of unproductive work are called into being, of which the banking system, the credit system, insurance empires and advertising are the most obvious examples, but the growth of the scientific and technological establishments, as well as an increase in public education generally, are also in this category. Marx himself pointed to the growth of this requirement for nonproductive services.[41]

The second reason why there must be an increase of nonproductive workers is that an increase in the surplus product requires an increase in the number of people who can afford to consume it. Surplus production requires surplus consumption. The capitalist system is based on the extraction from the laboring class of more commodities than that class is permitted to consume; the system would collapse if there were not also a class which consumed more than it produced. Some excerpts from Marx on this problem will be quoted below.

Together, these two corollaries of Marx's theory of the surplus make up what I have called the 'law of the surplus class,' that is, the law of the tendential rise of a new middle class.

That Marx formulated precisely such a law may come as something of a surprise to many Marxists. The reasons for this surprise, if my conjecture is correct in that regard, are not difficult to find. First, Marx's theory of the new middle class remained embryonic, though explicit; it was one of the many implications of his economic discoveries which he chose not to develop further, or was prevented by time from developing. The phenomenon which this theory describes, after all, had not emerged in its full dominance at the time he wrote. Secondly, the works in which Marx does develop this theory most clearly (the *Grundrisse* and the *Theorien Ueber den Mehrwert*) have not been translated into English (as far as I know), and the originals are not available in every library. Third, the theory of the middle class follows directly from the labor theory of value, the theory of the surplus and the law of the tendential fall in the profit rate, and there seems to be considerable tacit acquiescence on the left in the orthodoxly academic refusal to take these Marxist theses seriously.[42] Finally, there are still some Marxists, particularly in the New Left, who have not taken the trouble to read attentively anything that Marx wrote after the *Manifesto*, or, worse, anything after the *1844 Manuscripts*. There is an amusing tendency, at least in the academic circles known to me, to repeat an experiment Marx ventured when he was twenty-six, namely to try to squeeze the concept of alienated labor hard enough to make all the categories of sociology, politics and economics come dripping out of it, as if this philosopher's touchstone were a lemon. The drippings are flavorful but somewhat lacking in substance.

To make the data on Marx's theory of the middle class more widely available, I should like here to quote a number of excerpts at length, all of them from the untranslated works.

It was apparent to Marx from the beginning of his investigation of the surplus problem that the class of capitalists could not and did not consume all of the surplus which it extracted from the workers. Thus, in the *Grundrisse*, a few dozen pages after the surplus problem had been raised, we find the following footnote:

244

... the creation of surplus labor on one side corresponds to the creation of minus-labor, relative idleness (or *nonproductive* labor at best) on the other. That goes without saying as far as the capitalist class itself is concerned; but it also holds for the classes with whom it divides; thus, for the paupers, flunkeys, bootlickers and the whole train of retainers living off the surplus product; the part of the *servant* class which lives not from capital but from revenue. Essential difference between this *servant* class and the *working* class. . . . Thus Malthus is entirely logical when he calls not only for surplus labor and surplus capital but also for surplus idlers, consuming without producing, or the necessity for waste, luxury, ostentatious philanthropy, etc.[43]

Here Marx is thinking only of workers, rather, nonworkers who perform *personal* services for the capitalist, not those who fulfill a necessary unproductive function for the capital establishment. As the following excerpt from the *Theorien Ueber den Mehrwert* shows, he is not entirely clear that there is a difference.

Although the bourgeoisie is initially very frugal, with the growth in the productivity of its capital, i.e. its workers, it imitates the feudal system of retainers. According to the last (1861 or 1862) Factory Report, the total number of persons employed in the factories of the United Kingdom (managers included) was only 775,534 – while the number of female servants in England alone was one million. What a beautiful arrangement, where a factory girl sweats in the shop for 12 long hours so that the factory owner can use a part of her unpaid labor to take her sister as maid, her brother as groom, and her cousin as policeman or soldier into his personal service![44]

When one sees the individual capitalist as the embodiment of the capitalist class, however, as Marx does consistently, the inclusion of soldiers and policemen together with domestic servants in the single category of *servants* makes more sense. In a relatively well-known section of *Capital*, he measures out his scorn and ridicule impartially to all unproductive workers, including valets, politicians, churchmen, lawyers, soldiers, landowners, rentiers, paupers, vagabonds and criminals,[45] regardless of whether they perform their services for the individual capitalist or for the class as a whole.

His contempt for these people vents itself with particular fury (in the *Theorien*) on the dismal parson, Malthus, who advocated the creation of ever larger masses of these idlers to keep the capitalist economy going by consuming its surplus product. 'What a ridiculous idea,' Marx writes, 'that the surplus has to be consumed by servants and cannot be consumed by the productive workers themselves.'[46] Yet, he writes that Malthus is right about the necessity for unproductive consumers in a *capitalist* economy.[47] The fact that Malthus' 'remedies' for the evil of overproduction – 'heavy taxes, a mass of state and church sinecures, great armies, pensioners, tithes for the churchmen, a heavy national debt and periodic costly wars'[48] – have been in great part adopted by every advanced capitalist system would not have surprised Marx. He writes of Malthus that

> His greatest hope – which he himself indicates as more or less utopian – is that the middle class will grow in size and that the working proletariat will make up a constantly decreasing proportion of the total population (even if it grows in absolute numbers). That, in fact, is the course of bourgeois society. [*Das ist in der Tat der Gang der Bourgeoisgesellschaft.*][49]

Although Marx had nothing but spit and venom for any scheme designed deliberately to foster the growth of an unproductive class, he was repeatedly forced to recognize that the growth of productivity, i.e. the rise of the surplus, created precisely such a class. A few excerpts will make that clear:

> In order to produce 'productively' one has to produce in a manner that excludes the mass of the producers from a part of the market demand for the product; one must produce in contradiction to a class whose consumption stands in no relationship to its production – since precisely this excess of production over consumption makes up the profit of capital. On the other hand, one has to produce for classes which consume without producing.[50]
>
> On a low level of development of the social productivity of labor, where therefore surplus labor is relatively small, the class of those who live off the labor of others will in principle be small in relation to the number of workers. This class can grow to significant proportions to the degree that productivity, i.e. relative surplus value, develops.[51]
>
> The progressive transformation of a part of the workers into servants is a lovely prospect, just as it is a great consolation for them [the workers] that, as a consequence of the growth of the net product, more spheres open up for unproductive workers who live off surplus labor and whose interests more or less compete with the directly exploiting class in exploiting them.[52]

Marx's consistency in this matter can be tested negatively as well; if he agrees, as we have seen, with economists who predict a growth of the unproductive class in the course of capitalist development, then he should also disagree with economists who think that they can do away with this class without abolishing the capitalist system itself. The bourgeois economist Ramsay advocated the abolition of interest on capital, i.e. the dividends paid by industrialists to investors and coupon-clippers, and the abolition of land rent. Ramsay saw no useful function for either of these groups. Marx's acid comment on this proposal should be read with the phrase about the simplification of class contradictions (from the *Manifesto*) in mind:

> If this bourgeois ideal could really be put into practice, its consequence could only be that the entire surplus value would fall directly into the hands of the industrial capitalists, and all of society would be economically reduced to the simple contradiction between capital and wage labor, a simplification which certainly would hasten the dissolution of this form of production.[53]

Here again is the role of the surplus as a complicator of the simple class antagonisms reckoned with earlier. (A further, minor, example of the distance Marx's theory has carried him comes when he discusses economic crises in volume II, Part 2 of the *Theorien*; he writes that his analysis proceeds without dealing with 'the real constitution of society, which by no means consists only of the class of workers and the class of industrial capitalists.'[54])

The clearest statement of Marx's theory of the middle class known to me occurs in his critique of Ricardo's analysis of the effect of increased productivity on the labor force. Ricardo, like Marx, was a bitter enemy of all forms of unproductive labor, which were to him as to Marx so many '*faux frais de production*,' false production costs; and consequently Ricardo called for the extension of productive labor on a maximal scale. While Ricardo saw that only machinery permits the efficient utilization of vast quantities of industrial laborers, he was troubled by the fact that the growing productivity of machinery tended at the same time to make the worker superfluous. Marx comments:

> One tendency throws the workers onto the pavement and creates a superfluous population. The other tendency absorbs it again and expands wage slavery on an absolute scale, so that the worker's lot changes constantly but he can never escape it. That is why the worker correctly considers the development of the productive capacities of his labor as a hostile tendency, and why the capitalist treats him as an element to be constantly eliminated from production. These are the contradictions with which Ricardo struggles in this chapter. *What he forgets to emphasize is the constant increase of the middle classes, who stand in the middle between the workers on one side and the capitalists and landed proprietors on the other side, who are for the most part supported directly by revenue, who rest as a burden on the laboring foundation, and who increase the social security and the power of the upper ten thousand.*[55] [Italics mine – MN]

These excerpts represent, as far as I know, the most explicit statements of Marx's theory of the new middle class in the entire Marxian opus. It seems entirely possible to explain why Marx did not carry this theory further, and it may even be possible for someone to show somehow that this theory does not contradict Marx's prediction of class polarization and proletarian revolution (although I doubt it); but one thing cannot be done with Marx's theory of the middle class: it cannot be explained away. Even if Marx himself had never mentioned the terms 'unproductive class' or 'middle class,' someone else would have to draw these implications of his theory, for the rise of the middle class follows directly from the law of the tendency of the surplus to rise, which is part of the law of the tendency of the profit rate to fall, which arises directly out of the solution of the surplus value problem, which consists of the labor theory of value. Let me review this chain of ideas once more. The labor theory of value holds that the only agency which is capable of creating more value than it represents is labor; that is, only labor is capable of creating *surplus* value. The capitalist system of production consists of the appropriation by the capitalist class of ever greater quantities of this surplus value. In a developed capitalist system, the capitalist class will concentrate on increasing *relative* surplus value. That is, it will introduce machinery in order to decrease that portion of the working day which is necessary to reproduce the workers' labor power, and to increase that portion which is surplus labor. On the one hand, increased productivity requires increased investment in machinery, so that the *rate* of *profit* will tend to fall. On the other hand, the mass of profit will rise, and both the *rate* and the *volume* of *surplus* must rise. What happens to this swelling surplus? It *enables* the capitalist class to create a class of people who are not productive workers, but who perform services either for individual capitalists or, more important, for the capitalist class as a whole; and at the same time, the rise of productivity *requires* such a class of unproductive workers to fulfill the functions of distributing, marketing, researching, financing, managing, keeping track of and glorifying the swelling surplus product. This class of unproductive workers, service workers, or servants for short, is the middle class. In short, the middle class follows from the central principles which Marx spent the best decades of his life and his health in elaborating, and which he considered his historic contribution to the understanding of capitalism. If one denies, as it seems to me one must, the validity of Marx's class polarization and proletarian revolution predictions from the *Manifesto*, one does not deny that Marx was a champion of the proletarian cause; one cuts out of Marxism only its youthful optimism, the product of excessive captivation with the elegance of Hegelian idealism. But in order to cut out of Marx his theory of the middle class, one has to overthrow Marxism, scientific socialism, at its core – and fly in the face of contemporary reality. There *is* after all a middle class in advanced industrial society; and it must be considered one of Marx's great scientific achievements (and a great personal achievement, considering where his sentiments lay) to have not only predicted that such a new middle class would arise, but also to have laid down the fundamental economic and sociological principles which explain its rise and its role in the larger class structure. The outlines of what may become an adequate theory to account for the generation, growth, economic function and movement of the middle class have to my knowledge not been contributed by any other social scientist before Marx or after him. Here is a rare accomplishment and a rare challenge.

## NOTES AND REFERENCES

1. 'Die Deutsche Ideologie,' in Karl Marx, Friedrich Engels, *Werke* (Berlin: Dietz), vol. 3, p. 25.
2. Cf. *Werke*, vol. 1, esp. pp. 283–284.
3. Cf. *Werke*, vol. 1, esp. pp. 354–355, 368–369.
4. *Werke*, vol. 1, p. 390.
5. *Ibid.*
6. 'Zur Kritik der Politischen Oekonomie. Vorwort,' *Werke*, 13, p. 8.
7. For reasons unclear to me, the *Werke* edition does not contain the 1844 MSS. Because of its reliability and wide availability, I have quoted from the Bottomore translation, in Erich Fromm, *Marx's Concept of Man* (New York: Ungar, 1961). The present quotation is on p. 91.
8. *Ibid.*, p. 106.
9. *Ibid.*, p. 177.
10. *Ibid.*, p. 189.
11. *Ibid.*, p. 107.
12. 'The consideration of *division of labor* and *exchange* is of the greatest interest, since they are the *perceptible, alienated* expression of human *activity* and *capacities* as the activity and capacities *proper to a species*.' *Ibid.*, p. 161.
13. *Werke*, 3, p. 33. A page earlier, Marx writes that 'private property and division of labor are identical expressions' for the same thing, i.e. that the division of classes is only another aspect of the division of labor, and vice versa.
14. 'Ueber P. J. Proudhon,' in *Werke*, 16, p. 27. For Marx's clarification of the difference between division of labor and division of classes, see *Misère de la Philosophie* (1847), in *Werke*, 4, pp. 122, 144–156.
15. 'Economic-Philosophical Manuscripts of 1844,' in Fromm, *op. cit.*, pp. 117–118.
16. 'Lage der arbeitenden Klasse in England,' in *Werke*, 2, pp. 250–251.
17. 'Manifest der Kommunistischen Partei,' in *Werke*, 4, p. 463. I have relied in general on the English translation appearing in *The Communist Manifesto* (New York: Monthly Review Press, 1964) for my renderings of the original. However, some of the technical economic terms

in that translation are not quite accurately put; see notes 20 and 23 below.

18. Karl Marx, *Grundrisse der Kritik der Politischen Oekonomie* (*Rohentwurf*), Marx-Engels-Lenin Institut, Moscow (Berlin: Dietz, 1953). The actual *Grundrisse* of 1857–1858 occupy 760 pages in this huge volume. A complete translation, or at the very least a translation of selected excerpts, would be highly desirable.

19. *Werke*, 4, pp. 468, 473, 475.

20. *Ibid.*, p. 476. 'Reinertrag' is misleadingly rendered as 'surplus' in the English translation cited above, note 17.

21. *Ibid.*, p. 474.

22. For example, see Marx's polemic against the tendency to 'explain' capitalist economics with reference to the so-called laws of supply and demand, i.e. the laws of the market, in *Capital*, III, *Werke*, 25, p. 191 and elsewhere.

23. *Werke*, 4, p. 475. The English translation renders 'erzeugen' as 'getting' instead of 'creating' a new supply of wage labor; the point, however, is not vital.

24. *Ibid.*, p. 468.

25. 'Der Preis einer Ware, also auch der Arbeit, ist aber gleich ihren Produktionskosten.' *Ibid.*, p. 469. The editors of the *Werke* duly note that Marx would have said 'Arbeitskraft' instead of 'Arbeit' in his later writings, a crucial difference on which may be said to hinge the entire distinction between Marxist and non-Marxist economics – as well as the distinction, perhaps, between the 'young Marx' and the 'mature Marx.' See *Ibid.*, footnote 298, p. 649, and footnote 198, p. 636.

26. This definition is restated frequently, notably in 'Lohn, Preis und Profit,' *Werke*, 16, pp. 121–132, in *Capital*, and elsewhere.

27. *Kapital*, I, *Werke*, 23, p. 532.

28. *Ibid.*, p. 281.

29. *Ibid.*, p. 533.

30. *Ibid.*, p. 534.

31. *Kapital*, III, *Werke*, 25, p. 223.

32. Paul Baran and Paul Sweezy, *Monopoly Capital* (New York and London: Monthly Review Press, 1966). The authors of this monumental study consider the 'law of the rising surplus' a *substitution* for Marx's law of the tendential fall of the profit rate (see p. 72) without however discussing the fact that the law of the rising surplus is really no substitution at all, but merely another aspect of Marx's law.

33. This is already stated in *Grundrisse*, p. 649: 'Thus the profit rate stands in an inverse relationship to the growth of relative surplus value . . .' More explicitly in *Kapital*, III: 'As the process of production and accumulation progresses, the mass of surplus labor that can be and is appropriated, and thus the absolute mass of the profits appropriated by the capitalist class, *must* grow.' (*Werke*, 25, p. 229; also pages 228, 230, and elsewhere in the same chapter.

34. *Kapital*, I, *Werke*, 23, p. 646.

35. *Ibid.*, p. 647.

36. Karl Marx, *Theorien Ueber den Mehrwert*, Karl Kautsky, editor, (Stuttgart: Dietz, 1919), volume II, Part 1, p. 141. A new edition of this

important work is being issued by the editors of the *Werke* series; however, only Volume I of the new edition was available to me, and I have preferred to quote from the Kautsky edition, which seems to be more widely available in libraries. This work, consisting of three volumes in four books, figures in the *Werke* edition as 'Volume Four' of *Capital*; it was written in manuscript by Marx in 1861–1862, however, and thus predates the other volumes of *Capital*. I shall refer to it as '*Theorien*' in the notes below.

37. *Kapital*, I, *Werke*, 23, p. 673; also *Kapital*, III, *Werke*, 25, p. 232.

38. *Grundrisse*, p. 212.

39. *Theorien*, I, p. 189; see also p. 199.

40. These are of course the so-called white-collar proletarians, and the fact that this class also works for wages has aroused hopes that it also might in time be stimulated to develop along the classic lines of increasing proletarian militancy. Whatever the merit of this idea, however, it should be clear that to Marx, the proletariat meant *productive* workers only. If the proletariat is defined to include all those who work for wages, then many corporation executives and managers are proletarians too. Marx's early view of wage labor shows, by contrast, considerable lack of rigor; thus in the *Manifesto* he writes that the bourgeoisie has turned the judge, the parson, the poet, the scientist into its 'paid wage laborers' (*Werke*, 4, p. 465), which would put these worthy gentlemen into the proletariat, too, or so it would seem. Here again, as mentioned before, Marx sees the transformation of human values into market values as the overriding characteristic of the capitalist epoch, and has not yet become aware of the profounder characteristic, namely the creation and appropriation of surplus by the capitalist class. The shift from the market concept to the surplus concept marks, in my opinion, the central difference between 'young' and 'mature' Marxist thought. See note 25, above.

41. *Kapital*, III, *Werke*, 25, p. 310. The necessary connection between the rising requirement for such auxiliary services and the rise of the middle class is evident, but Marx does not state it at this point.

42. For example, even so sympathetic an economist as Joan Robinson dismisses the labor theory of value as an 'incantation' which is insubstantial for the rest of his work, which is a bit like saying that the concept of motion has no relevance for the understanding of Newton's laws. See Joan Robinson, *An Essay on Marxian Economics* (London: Macmillan, 1949), p. 22.

43. *Grundrisse*, pp. 304–305, fn.

44. *Theorien* I, p. 171. See also p. 189.

45. *Kapital*, I, *Werke*, 23, pp. 469–470. See also Engels summarizing Marx in 'Zur Wohnungsfrage,' *Werke*, 18, p. 214, where he speaks of the division of the surplus among unproductive workers, ranging from valets to the Pope, the Kaiser, the night watchman, etc. At one point Marx calls the various strata of civil servants, churchmen, etc., nothing but 'elegant paupers.' (*Theorien*, I, p. 189.)

46. *Theorien*, I, p. 184.

47. *Ibid.*; see also note 43 above.

48. *Theorien*, III, p. 49.

49. *Ibid.*, p. 61.
50. *Ibid.*, p. 139 fn.
51. *Theorien*, II, Part 1, p. 127.
52. *Theorien*, II, Part 2, p. 365.
53. *Theorien*, III, p. 423.
54. *Theorien*, II, Part 2, p. 264.
55. *Ibid.*, p. 368. A part of this excerpt appears in a not-quite-tight translation in T. B. Bottomore and Maximilien Rubel, editors, *Karl Marx, Selected Writings in Sociology and Social Philosophy* (McGraw-Hill paperback, 1964), p. 191.

# MARX AND THE STATE*

## RALPH MILIBAND

### 1

As in the case of so many other aspects of Marx's work, what he thought about the state has more often than not come to be seen through the prism of later interpretations and adaptations. These have long congealed into *the* Marxist theory of the state, or into *the* Marxist-Leninist theory of the state, but they cannot be taken to constitute an adequate expression of Marx's own views. This is not because these theories bear *no* relation to Marx's views but rather that they emphasize some aspects of his thought to the detriment of others, and thus distort by oversimplification an extremely complex and by no means unambiguous body of ideas; and also that they altogether ignore certain strands in Marx's thought which are of considerable interest and importance. This does not, in itself, make later views better or worse than Marx's own: to decide this, what needs to be compared is not text with text, but text with historical or contemporary reality itself. This can hardly be done within the compass of an essay. But Marx is so inescapably bound up with contemporary politics, his thought is so deeply buried inside the shell of official Marxism and his name is so often invoked in ignorance by enemies and partisans alike, that it is worth asking again what he, rather than Engels, or Lenin or any other of his followers, disciples or critics, actually said and appeared to think about the state. This is the purpose of the present essay.

Marx himself never attempted to set out a comprehensive and systematic theory of the state. In the late 1850s he wrote that he intended, as part of a vast scheme of projected work, of which *Capital* was only to be the first part, to subject the state to systematic study.[1] But of this scheme, only one part of *Capital* was in fact completed. His ideas on the state must therefore be taken from such historical *pièces de circonstance* as *The Class Struggles in France*, the *18th Brumaire of Louis Bonaparte* and *The Civil War in France*, and from his incidental remarks on the

* Originally published in *The Socialist Register*, 1965, (eds.) Ralph Miliband and John Saville. Reprinted with permission of the Merlin Press, London.

subject in his other works. On the other hand, the crucial importance of the state in his scheme of analysis is well shown by his constantly recurring references to it in almost all of his writings; and the state was also a central preoccupation of the 'young Marx': his early work from the late 1830s to 1844 was largely concerned with the nature of the state and its relation to society. His most sustained piece of work until the 1844 *Economic and Philosophical Manuscripts*, apart from his doctoral dissertation, was his *Critique of the Hegelian Philosophy of Right*, of which only the *Introduction*, actually written after the *Critique* itself, has so far appeared in English.[2] It is in fact largely through his critique of Hegel's view of the state that Marx completed his emancipation from the Hegelian system. This early work of Marx on the state is of great interest; for, while he soon moved beyond the views and positions he had set out there, some of the questions he had encountered in his examination of Hegel's philosophy recur again and again in his later writings.

2

Marx's earliest views on the state bear a clear Hegelian imprint. In the articles which he wrote for the *Rheinische Zeitung* from May 1842 to March 1843, he repeatedly spoke of the state as the guardian of the general interest of society and of law as the embodiment of freedom. Modern philosophy, he writes in July 1842, 'considers the state as the great organism in which must be realized juridical, moral and political freedom and where the individual citizen, in obeying the laws of the state only obeys the natural laws of his own reason, of human reason.'[3]

On the other hand, he also shows himself well aware that this exalted view of the state is in contradiction with the real state's actual behaviour: 'a state which is not the realization of rational freedom is a bad state,' he writes,[4] and in his article on the Rhineland Diet's repressive legislation against the pilfering of forest wood, he eloquently denounces the Diet's denial of the customary rights of the poor and condemns the assignation to the state of the rôle of servant of the rich against the poor. This, he holds, is a perversion of the state's true purpose and mission; private property may wish to degrade the state to its own level of concern, but any modern state, in so far as it remains true to its own meaning, must, confronted by such pretensions, cry out 'your ways are not my ways, and your ideas are not my ideas.'[5]

More and more, however, Marx found himself driven to emphasize the external pressures upon the state's actions. Writing in January 1843 on the plight of the wine growers of the Moselle, he remarks that 'in the examination of the institutions of the state, one is too easily tempted to overlook the concrete nature of circumstances ('*die sachliche Natur der Verhältnisse*') and to explain everything by the will of those empowered to act.'[6]

It is this same insistence on the need to consider the 'concrete nature of circumstances' which lies at the core of the *Critique of Hegel's Philosophy of Right*, which Marx wrote in the spring and summer of 1843, after the *Rheinische Zeitung* had been closed down. By then, his horizons had widened to the point where he spoke confidently of a 'break' in the existing society, to which 'the system of acquisition and commerce, of ownership and of exploitation of man is leading even more rapidly than the increase in population.'[7] Hegel's 'absurdity,' he also writes in the *Critique*, is that he views the affairs and the activities of the state in an abstract fashion; he forgets that the activities of the state are human functions: 'the affairs of the state etc., are nothing but the modes of existence and activity of the social qualities of men.'[8]

The burden of Marx's critique of Hegel's concept of the state is that Hegel, while rightly acknowledging the separation of civil society from the state, asserts their reconciliation in the state itself. In his system, the 'contradiction' between the state and society is resolved in the supposed representation in the state of society's true meaning and reality; the alienation of the individual from the state, the contradiction between man as a private member of society, concerned with his own private interests, and as a citizen of the state finds resolution in the state as the expression of society's ultimate reality.

But this, says Marx, is not a resolution but a mystification. The contradiction between the state and society is real enough. Indeed, the political alienation which it entails is the central fact of modern, bourgeois society, since man's political significance is detached from his real private condition, while it is in fact this condition which determines him as a social being, all other determinations appearing to him as external and inessential: 'real man is the private man of the present constitution of the state.'[9]

But the mediating elements which are supposed, in Hegel's system, to ensure the resolution of this contradiction—the sovereign, the bureaucracy, the middle classes, the legislature – are not in the least capable, says Marx, of doing so. Ultimately, Hegel's state, far from being above private interests and from representing the general interest, is in fact subordinate to private property. What, asks Marx, is the power of the state over private property? The state has only the illusion of being determinant, whereas it is in fact determined; it does, in time, subdue private and social wills, but only to give substance to the will of private property and to acknowledge its reality as the highest reality of the political state, as the highest moral reality.[10]

In the *Critique*, Marx's own resolution of political alienation and of the contradiction between the state and society is still envisaged in mainly political terms, i.e. in the framework of 'true democracy.' 'Democracy is the solution to the riddle of all constitutions'; in it, 'the constitution appears in its true reality, as the free product of man.' 'All other political systems are specific, definite, particular political forms. In democracy, the formal principle is also the material principle.' It constitutes, therefore, the real unity of the universal and the particular.[11] Marx also writes: 'In all states which differ from democracy, the state, the law, the constitution are sovereign without being properly dominant, that is to say without materially affecting the other non-political spheres. In democracy, the constitution, the law, the state itself are only the people's self-determination, a specific aspect of it, in so far as that aspect has a political constitution.'[12]

Democracy is here intended to mean more than a specific political form, but Marx does not yet define what else it entails. The struggle between monarchy and republic, he notes, is still a struggle within the framework of what he calls the 'abstract state,' i.e. the state alienated from society; the abstract political form of democracy is the republic. 'Property and all that makes up the content of law and the state is, with some modifications, the same in the United States as in Prussia; the republic in America is thus only a purely political form as is the monarchy in Prussia.'[13] In a real democracy, however, the constitution ceases to be purely political; indeed Marx quotes the opinion of 'some modern Frenchmen' to the effect that 'in a real democracy the political state disappears.'[14] But the concrete content of 'true democracy' remains here undefined.

The *Critique* already suggests the belief that political emancipation is not synonymous with human emancipation. The point, which is, of course, central to Marx's whole system, was made explicit in the two articles which he wrote for the *Franco-German Annals*, namely the *Jewish Question*, and the *Introduction* to a *Contribution to the Critique of Hegel's Philosophy of Right*.

In the first essay, Marx criticizes Bruno Bauer for confusing political and human emancipation, and notes that 'the limit of political emancipation is immediately apparent in the fact that the *state* may well free itself from some constraint, without man himself being *really* freed from it, and that the state may be a *free state*, without *man* being free.'[15] Even so, political emancipation is a great advance; it is not the last form of human emancipation, but it is the last form of human emancipation within the framework of the existing social order.[16] Human

256

emancipation, on the other hand, can only be realized by transcending bourgeois society, 'which has torn up all genuine bonds between men and replaced them by selfishness, selfish need, and dissolved the world of men into a world of atomized individuals, hostile towards each other.'[17] The more specific meaning of that emancipation is defined in the *Jewish Question*, in Marx's strictures against 'Judaism,' here deemed synonymous with trade, money and the commercial spirit which has come to affect all human relations. On this view, the political emancipation of the Jews, which Marx defends,[18] does not produce their social emancipation; this is only possible in a new society, in which practical need has been humanized and the commercial spirit abolished.[19]

In the *Introduction*, which he wrote in Paris at the end of 1843 and the beginning of 1844, Marx now spoke of 'the doctrine, that man is for man the supreme being' and of the 'categorical imperative' which required the overthrow of all conditions in which 'man is a degraded, enslaved, abandoned and contemptible being.'[20] But he also added another element to the system he was constructing, namely the proletariat as the agent of the dissolution of the existing social order;[21] as we shall see, this view of the proletariat is not only crucial for Marx's concept of revolution but also for his view of the state.

By this time, Marx had already made an assessment of the relative importance of the political realm from which he was never to depart and which also had some major consequence for his later thought. On the one hand, he does not wish to underestimate the importance of 'political emancipation,' i.e. of political reforms tending to make politics and the state more liberal and democratic. Thus, in *The Holy Family*, which he wrote in 1844 in collaboration with Engels, Marx describes the 'democratic representative state' as 'the perfect modern state,'[22] meaning the perfect modern *bourgeois* state, its perfection arising from the fact that 'the public system is *not* faced with any privileged exclusivity,'[23] i.e. economic and political life are free from feudal encumbrances and constraints.

But there is also, on the other hand, a clear view that political emancipation is not enough, and that society can only be made truly human by the abolition of private property. 'It is natural necessity, *essential human properties*, however alienated they may seem to be, and *interest* that holds the members of civil society together; *civil*, not *political* life is their *real* tie. It is therefore not the state that holds the *atoms* of civil society together . . . only *political superstition* today imagines that social life must be held together by the state, whereas in reality the state is held together by civil life.'[24] The modern democratic state 'is based on emancipated slavery, on bourgeois society . . . the society of industry, of universal competition, of private interest freely following its aims, of anarchy, of the self-alienated natural and spiritual individuality . . .',[25] the 'essence' of the modern state is that 'it is based on the unhampered development of bourgeois society, on the free movement of private interest.'[26]

A year later, in *The German Ideology*, Marx and Engels defined further the relation of the state to bourgeois society. 'By the mere fact that it is a *class* and no longer an *estate*,' they wrote, 'the bourgeoisie is forced to organize itself no longer locally but nationally, and to give a general form to its mean average interest'; this 'general form' is the state, defined as 'nothing more than the form of organization which the bourgeois necessarily adopt both for internal and external purposes, for the mutual guarantee of their property and interest.'[27] This same view is confirmed in the *Poverty of Philosophy* of 1847, where Marx again states that 'political conditions are only the official expression of civil society' and goes on: 'It is the sovereigns who in all ages have been subject to economic conditions, but it is never they who have dictated laws to them. Legislation, whether political or civil, never does more than proclaim, express in words, the will of economic relations.'[28]

This whole trend of thought on the subject of the state finds its most explicit expression in the famous formulation of the *Communist Manifesto*: 'The executive of the modern state is but a committee for managing the common affairs of the whole bourgeoisie;'[29] and political power is 'merely the organized power of one class for oppressing another.'[30] This is the classical Marxist view on the subject of the state, and it is the only one which is to be found in Marxism-Leninism. In regard to Marx himself, however, and this is also true to a certain extent of Engels as well, it only constitutes what might be called a primary view of the state. For, as has occasionally been noted in discussions of Marx and the state,[31] there is to be found another view of the state in his work, which it is inaccurate to hold up as of similar status with the first,[32] but which is none the less of great interest, not least because it serves to illuminate, and indeed provides an essential context for, certain major elements in Marx's system, notably the concept of the dictatorship of the proletariat. This secondary view is that of the state as independent from and superior to all social classes, as being the dominant force in society rather than the instrument of a dominant class.

3

It may be useful, for a start, to note some qualifications which Marx made even to his primary view of the state. For in relation to the two most advanced capitalist countries of the day, England and France, he often makes the point that, at one time or another, it is not the ruling class as a whole, but a fraction of it, which controls the state;[33] and that those who actually run the state may well belong to a class which is not the economically dominant class.[34] Marx does not suggest that this *fundamentally* affects the state's class character and its rôle of guardian and defender of the interests of property; but it obviously does introduce an element of flexibility in his view of the operation of the state's bias, not least because the competition between different factions of the ruling class may well make easier the passage of measures favourable to labour, such as the Ten Hours Bill.[35]

The extreme manifestation of the state's independent rôle is, however, to be found in authoritarian personal rule, Bonapartism. Marx's most extensive discussion of this phenomenon occurs in *The 18th Brumaire of Louis Bonaparte*, which was written between December 1851 and March 1852. In this historical study, Marx sought very hard to pin down the precise nature of the rule which Louis Bonaparte's *coup d'état* had established.

The *coup d'état*, he wrote, was 'the victory of Bonaparte over parliament, of the executive power over the legislative power'; in parliament, 'the nation made its general will the law, that is, made the law of the ruling class its general will;' in contrast, 'before the executive power it renounces all will of its own and submits to the superior command of an alien will, to authority;' 'France, therefore, seems to have escaped the despotism of a class only to fall back beneath the despotism of an individual and, what is more, beneath the authority of an individual without authority. The struggle seems to be settled in such a way that all classes, equally impotent and equally mute, fall on their knees before the rifle butt.'[36]

Marx then goes on to speak of 'this executive power with its enormous bureaucratic and military organization, with its ingenious state machinery, embracing wide strata, with a host of officials numbering half a million, besides an army of another half million, this appalling parasitic body which enmeshes the body of French society like a net and chokes all its pores.'[37] This bureaucratic power, which sprang up in the days of the absolute monarchy, had, he wrote, first been 'the means of preparing the class rule of the bourgeoisie,' while 'under the Restoration, under Louis Phillipe, under the parliamentary Republic, it was the instrument of the ruling class, however much it strove for power of its own.'[38] But the *coup d'état* had seemingly changed its rôle: 'only under the second Bonaparte does the state seem to have made itself completely independent;' 'as against civil society, the state machine has consolidated its position so thoroughly that the chief of the Society of 10 December [i.e. Louis Bonaparte] suffices for its head . . .'[39]

This appears to commit Marx to the view of the Bonapartist state as independent of any specific class and as superior to society. But he then goes on to say, in an often quoted phrase: 'And yet the state power is not suspended in mid-air. Bonaparte represents a class, and the most numerous class of French society at that, *the small-holding peasants*.'[40] However, their lack of cohesion makes these 'incapable of enforcing their class interests in their own name whether through a parliament or a convention;'[41] they therefore require a representative who 'must at the same time appear as their master, as an authority over them, as an unlimited governmental power that protects them against the other classes and sends them rain and sunshine from above. The political influence of the small-holding peasants, therefore, finds its final expression in the executive power subordinating society to itself.'[42]

'Represent' is here a confusing word. In the context, the only meaning that may be attached to it is that the small-holding peasants *hoped* to have their interests represented by Louis Bonaparte. But this does not turn Louis Bonaparte or the state into the mere instrument of their will; at the most, it may limit the executive's freedom of action somewhat. Marx also writes that 'as the executive authority which has made itself an independent power, Bonaparte feels it his mission to safeguard bourgeois order.' But the strength of this bourgeois order lies in the middle class. He looks on himself, therefore, as the representative of the middle class and issues decrees in this sense. Nevertheless, he is somebody solely due to the fact that he has broken the political power of this middle class and daily breaks it anew;' and again, 'as against the bourgeoisie, Bonaparte looks on himself, at the same time, as the representative of the peasants and of the people in general, who wants to make the lower classes of the people happy within the frame of bourgeois society. . . But, above all, Bonaparte looks on himself as the chief of the Society of 10 December, as the representative of the *lumpenproletariat* to which he himself, his *entourage*, his government and his army belong . . .'[43]

On this basis, Louis Napoleon may 'represent' this or that class (and Marx stresses the 'contradictory task' of the man and the 'contradictions of his government, the confused groping about which seeks now to win, now to humiliate first one class and then another and arrays all of them uniformly against him . . .'[44]); but his power of initiative remains very largely unimpaired by the specific wishes and demands of any one class or fraction of a class.

On the other hand, this does *not* mean that Bonapartism, for Marx, is in any sense neutral as between contending classes. It may *claim* to represent all classes and to be the embodiment of the whole of society. But it does in fact exist, and has been called into being, for the purpose of maintaining and strengthening the existing social order and the domination of capital over labour. Bonapartism and the Empire, Marx wrote much later in *The Civil War in France*, had succeeded the bourgeois Republic precisely because 'it was the only form of government possible at a time when the bourgeoisie had already lost, and the working class had not yet acquired, the faculty of ruling the nation.'[45] It was precisely under its sway that 'bourgeois society, freed from political cares, attained a development unexpected even by itself.'[46] Finally, Marx then characterizes what he calls 'imperialism,' by which he means Napoleon's imperial régime, as 'at the same time, the most prostitute and the ultimate form of the State power which nascent middle-class society had commenced to elaborate as a means of its own emancipation from feudalism, and which full-grown bourgeois society had finally transformed into a means for the enslavement of labour by capital.'[47]

In *The Origin of the Family, Private Property and the State*, written a year after Marx's death, Engels also notes: 'By way of exception, however, periods occur in which the warring classes balance each other so nearly that the state power, as ostensible mediator, acquires, for the moment, a certain degree of independence of both.'[48] But the independence of which he speaks would seem to go much further than anything Marx had in mind; thus Engels refers to the Second Empire, 'which played off the proletariat against the bourgeoisie and the bourgeoisie against the proletariat' and to Bismarck's German Empire, where 'capitalists and workers are balanced against each other and equally cheated for the benefit of the impoverished Prussian cabbage junkers.'[49]

For Marx, the Bonapartist state, however independent it may have been *politically* from any given class, remains, and cannot in a class society but remain, the protector of an economically and socially dominant class.


4


In the *Critique of Hegel's Philosophy of Right*, Marx had devoted a long and involved passage to the bureaucratic element in the state, and to its attempt 'to transform the purpose of the state into the purpose of the bureaucracy and the purpose of the bureaucracy into the purpose of

261

the state.'[50] But it was only in the early 'fifties that he began to look closely at a type of society where the state appeared to be genuinely 'above society,' namely societies based on the 'Asiatic mode of production,' whose place in Marx's thought has recently attracted much attention.[51] What had, in the *Critique*, been a passing reference to the 'despotic states of Asia, where the political realm is nothing but the arbitrary will of a particular individual, where the political realm, like the material, is enslaved,'[52] had, by 1859, become one of Marx's four main stages of history: 'In broad outlines,' he wrote in the famous Preface to *A Contribution to the Critique of Political Economy*, 'Asiatic, ancient, feudal and modern bourgeois modes of production can be designated as progressive epochs in the economic formation of society.'[53]

The countries Marx was mainly concerned with in this connection were India and China, and also Russia as a 'semi-Asiatic' or 'semi-Eastern' state. The Asiatic mode of production, for Marx and Engels, has one outstanding characteristic, namely the absence of private property in land: 'this,' Marx wrote to Engels in 1853, 'is the real key, even to the Oriental heaven. . .'[54] 'In the Asiatic form (or at least predominantly so),' he noted, 'there is no property, but individual possession; the community is properly speaking the real proprietor;'[55] in Asiatic production, he also remarked, it is the state which is the 'real landlord.'[56] In this system, he also wrote later, the direct producers are not 'confronted by a private landowner but rather, as in Asia, [are] under direct subordination to a state which stands over them as their landlord and simultaneously as sovereign;' 'the state,' he went on, 'is then the supreme lord. Sovereignty here consists in the ownership of land concentrated on a national scale. But, on the other hand, no private ownership of land exists, although there is both private and common possession and use of land.'[57]

A prime necessity of the Asiatic mode of production, imposed by climate and territorial conditions, was artificial irrigation by canals and waterworks; indeed, Marx wrote, this was 'the basis of Oriental agriculture.' In countries like Flanders and Italy the need of an economical and common use of water drove private enterprise into voluntary association; but it required 'in the Orient, where civilization was too low and the territorial extent too vast to call into life voluntary associations, the interference of the centralized power of Government. Hence an economical function devolved upon all Asiatic governments, the function of providing public works.'[58]

Finally, in the *Grundrisse*, Marx speaks of 'the despotic government which is poised above the lesser communities,'[59] and describes that government as the '*all-embracing unity* which stands above all these small common bodies . . . since the *unity* is the real owner, and the real pre-condition of common ownership, it is perfectly possible for it to appear as something separate and superior to the numerous real, particular communities . . . the despot here appears as the father of all the numerous lesser communities, thus realizing the common unity of all.'[60]

It is therefore evident that Marx does view the state, in the conditions of Asiatic despotism, as the dominant force in society, independent of and superior to all its members, and that those who control its administration are society's authentic rulers. Karl Wittfogel has noted that Marx did not pursue this theme after the 1850s and that 'in the writings of the later period he emphasized the technical side of large scale waterworks, where previously he had emphasized their political setting.'[61] The reason for this, Professor Wittfogel suggests, is that 'obviously the concept of Oriental despotism contained elements that paralysed his search for truth;'[62] hence his 'retrogressions' on the subject. But the explanation for Marx's lack of concern for the topic would seem much simpler and much less sinister; it is that he was, in the 'sixties and the early 'seventies, primarily concerned with Western capitalism. Furthermore, the notion of bureaucratic despotism can hardly have held any great terror for him since he had, in fact, worked through its nearest equivalent in capitalist society, namely Bonapartism, and had analysed it as an altogether different phenomenon from the despotism encountered in Asiatic society. Nor is it accurate to suggest, as does Mr Lichtheim, that 'Marx for some reason shirked the problem of the bureaucracy' in post-capitalist society.[63] On the contrary, this may be said to be a crucial element in Marx's thought in the late 1860s and in the early 1870s. His concern with the question, and with the state, finds expression in this period in his discussion of the nature of political power in post-capitalist societies, and particularly in his view of the dictatorship of the proletariat. This theme had last occupied Marx in 1851–1852; after almost twenty years it was again brought to the fore by the Paris Commune, by his struggles with anarchism in the First International and by the programmatic pronouncement of German Social Democracy. It is to this, one of the most important and the most misunderstood aspects of Marx's work on the state, that we must now turn.

5

It is first of all necessary to go back to the democratic and representative republic, which must be clearly distinguished from the dictatorship of the proletariat: for Marx, the two concepts have nothing in common. An element of confusion arises from the fact that Marx bitterly denounced the class character of the democratic republic, yet supported its coming into being. The contradiction is only apparent; Marx saw the democratic republic as the most advanced type of political régime in *bourgeois society*, and wished to see it prevail over more backward and 'feudal' political systems. But it remained for him a system of class rule, indeed the system in which the bourgeoisie rules most directly.

The limitations of the democratic republic, from Marx's point of view, are made particularly clear in the *Address of the Central Committee of the Communist League* which he and Engels wrote in March 1850. 'Far from desiring to revolutionize all society for the revolutionary proletarians,' they wrote, 'the democratic petty-bourgeois strive for a change in social conditions by means of which existing society will be made as tolerable and comfortable as possible for them.' They would therefore demand such measures as 'the diminution of state expenditure by a curtailment of the bureaucracy and shifting the chief taxes on to the big landowners and bourgeois . . . the abolition of the pressure of big capital on small, through public credit institutions and laws against usury . . . the establishment of bourgeois property relations in the countryside by the complete abolition of feudalism.' But in order to achieve their purpose they would need 'a democratic state structure, either constitutional or republican, that will give them and their allies, the peasants, a majority; also a democratic communal structure that will give them direct control over communal property and over a series of functions now performed by the bureaucrats.'[64] However, they added, 'as far as the workers are concerned, it remains certain that they are to remain wage workers as before; the democratic petty-bourgeois only desire better wages and a more secure existence for the workers . . . they hope to bribe the workers by more or less concealed alms and to break their revolutionary potency by making their position tolerable for the moment.'[65]

But, Marx and Engels go on, 'these demands can in no wise suffice for the party of the proletariat;' while the petty-bourgeois democrats would seek to bring the revolution to a conclusion as quickly as possible, 'it is our interest and our task to make the revolution permanent, until all more or less possessing classes have been forced out of their position of dominance, until the proletariat has conquered state power, and the association of proletarians, not only in one country but in all the dominant countries of the world, has advanced so far that competition among the proletarians of these countries has ceased and that at least the decisive productive forces are concentrated in the hands of the proletarians. For us the issue cannot be the alteration of private property but only its annihilation, not the smoothing over of class antagonisms but the abolition of classes, not the improvement of existing society but the foundation of a new one.'[66]

At the same time, while the demands and aims of the proletarian party went far beyond anything which even the most advanced and radical petty-bourgeois democrats would accept, the revolutionaries must give them qualified support and seek to push the democratic movement into even more radical directions.[67] It was, incidentally, precisely the same strategy which dictated Marx's later attitude to all movements of radical reform, and which led him, as in the *Inaugural Address* of the First International in 1864, to acclaim the Ten Hours Act or the advances of the cooperative movement as the victories of 'the political economy of labour over the political economy of property.'[68]

In 1850, Marx and Engels had also suggested that one essential task of the proletarian revolutionaries would be to oppose the decentralizing tendencies of the petty-bourgeois revolutionaries. On the contrary, 'the workers must not only strive for a single and indivisible German republic, but also within this republic for the most determined centralization of power in the hands of the state authority . . .'[69]

This is not only the most extreme 'statist' prescription in Marx's (and Engels') work – it is the only one of its kind, leaving aside Marx's first 'Hegelian' pronouncements on the subject. More important is the fact that the prescription is intended *not* for the proletarian but for the bourgeois democratic revolution.[70] In 1850, Marx and Engels believed, and said in the *Address*, that the German workers would not be able 'to attain power and achieve their own class interest without completely going through a lengthy revolutionary development.'[71] The proletarian revolution would see the coming into being of an altogether different form of rule than the democratic republic, namely the dictatorship of the proletariat.

In a famous letter to J. Wedemeyer in March 1852, Marx had revealed the cardinal importance he attached to this concept by saying that, while no credit was due to him for discovering the existence of classes in modern society or the struggles between them, 'what I did that was new was to prove (1) that the *existence of classes* is only bound up with *particular historical phases in the development of production,* (2) that the class struggle necessarily leads to the *dictatorship of the proletariat*, (3) that this dictatorship itself only constitutes the transition to *abolition of all classes* and to a *classless society*.'[72]

Unfortunately, Marx did not define in any specific way *what* the dictatorship of the proletariat actually entailed, and more particularly what was its relation to the state. It has been argued by Mr Hal Draper in an extremely well-documented article that it is a 'social description, a statement of the class character of the political power. It is not a statement about the forms of the government machinery.'[73] My own view, on the contrary, is that, for Marx, the dictatorship of the proletariat is *both* a statement of the class character of the political power *and* a description of the political power itself; and that it is in fact the nature of the political power which it describes which guarantees its class character.

In the *18th Brumaire*, Marx had made a point which constitutes a main theme of his thought, namely that all previous revolutions had 'perfected this [state] machine instead of smashing it. The parties that contended in turn for domination regarded the possession of this huge state edifice as the principal spoils of the victors.'[74] Nearly twenty years later, in *The Civil War in France*, he again stressed how every previous revolution had consolidated 'the centralized State power, with its ubiquitous organs of standing army, police, bureaucracy, clergy and judicature;' and he also stressed how the political character of the state had changed 'simultaneously with the economic changes of society. At the same pace at which the progress of modern history developed, widened, intensified the class antagonism between capital and labour, the State power assumed more and more the character of the national power of capital over labour, of a public force organized for social enslavement, of an engine of class despotism. After every revolution marking a progressive phase in the class struggle, the purely repressive character of the State power stands out in bolder and bolder relief.'[75]

As Mr Draper notes, Marx had made no reference to the dictatorship of the proletariat in all the intervening years. Nor indeed did he so describe the Paris Commune. But what he acclaims above all in the Commune is that, in contrast to previous social convulsions, it sought not the further consolidation of the state power but its destruction. What it wanted, he said, was to have 'restored to the social body all the forces hitherto absorbed by the State parasite feeding upon, and clogging the free movement of, society.'[76] Marx also lays stress on the Commune's popular, democratic and egalitarian character, and on the manner in which 'not only municipal administration but the whole initiative hitherto exercised by the State was laid into the hands of the Commune.'[77] Moreover, while the communal form of government was to apply even to the 'smallest country hamlet,' 'the unity of the nation was not to be broken, but, on the contrary, to be organized by the Communal Constitution, and to become a reality by the destruction of the State power which claimed to be the embodiment of that unity independent of, and superior to, the nation itself, from which it was but a parasitic excrescence.'[78]

In notes which he wrote for *The Civil War in France*, Marx makes even clearer than in the published text the significance which he attached to the Commune's dismantling of the state power. As contributing evidence of his approach to the whole question, the following passage from the Notes is extremely revealing: 'This [i.e. the Commune] was,' he wrote, 'a Revolution not against this or that, legitimate, constitutional, republican or Imperialist form of State power. It was a Revolution against the *State* itself, of this supernaturalist abortion of society, a resumption by the people for the people of its own social life. It was not a revolution to transfer it from one fraction of the ruling class to the other but a Revolution to break down this horrid machinery of Classdomination [*sic*] itself . . . the Second Empire was the final form (?) [*sic*] of this State usurpation. The Commune was its definite negation, and, therefore, the initiation of the social Revolution of the nineteenth century.'[79] It is in the light of such views that Marx's verdict on the Commune takes on its full meaning: this 'essentially working-class government,' he wrote, was 'the political form at last discovered under which to work out the economic emancipation of labour.'[80]

It is of course true that, while Engels, long after Marx's death, did describe the Paris Commune as the dictatorship of the proletariat,[81] Marx himself did not do so. The reason for this would seem fairly obvious, namely that, for Marx, the dictatorship of the proletariat would be the outcome of a socialist revolution on a national scale; the Commune, as he wrote in 1881, was 'merely the rising of a city under exceptional conditions,' while 'the majority of the Commune was in no wise socialist, nor could it be.'[82] Even so, it may justifiably be thought that the Commune, in its de-institutionalization of political power, did embody, for Marx, the essential elements of his concept of the dictatorship of the proletariat.

Precisely the opposite view has very generally come to be taken for granted; the following statement in Mr Lichtheim's *Marxism* is a typical example of a wide consensus: 'His (Marx's) hostility to the state was held in check by a decidedly authoritarian doctrine of political rule during the transition period: prior to being consigned to the dustbin of history, the state was to assume dictatorial powers. In different terms, authority would inaugurate freedom – a typically Hegelian paradox which did not worry Marx though it alarmed Proudhon and Bakunin. . . .'[83]

The trouble with the view that Marx had a 'decidedly authoritarian doctrine' is that it is unsupported by any convincing evidence from

Marx himself; and that there is so much evidence which directly runs counter to it.

Marx was undoubtedly the chief opponent of the anarchists in the International. But it is worth remembering that his central quarrel with them concerned above all the manner in which the struggle for a socialist revolution ought to be prosecuted, with Marx insisting on the need for political involvement within the existing political framework, against the anarchists' all or nothing rejection of mere politics; and the quarrel also concerned the question of the type of organization required by the international workers' movement, with Marx insisting on a *degree* of control by the General Council of the International over its affiliated organizations.

As for the role of the state in the period of transition, there is the well-known passage in the 'private circular' against the anarchists issued by the General Council in 1872, *Les Prétendues Scissions dans l'Internationale*, and most probably written by Marx: 'What all socialists understand by anarchism is this: as soon as the goal of the proletarian movement, the abolition of class, shall have been reached, the power of the state, whose function it is to keep the great majority of the producers beneath the yoke of a small minority of exploiters, will disappear, and governmental functions will be transformed into simple administrative functions. The Alliance [i.e. Bakunin's Alliance of Socialist Democracy] turns the thing upside down. It declares anarchism in the ranks of the workers to be an infallible means for disrupting the powerful concentration of social and political forms in the hands of the exploiters. Under this pretext, it asks the International, when the old world is endeavouring to crush our organization, to replace organization by anarchism. The international police could ask for nothing better . . .'[84]

This can hardly be construed as an authoritarian text; nor certainly is Marx's plaintive remark in January 1873 quoted by Lenin in *State and Revolution* that 'if the political struggle of the working class assumes violent forms, if the workers set up this revolutionary dictatorship in place of the dictatorship of the bourgeoisie, they commit the terrible crime of violating principles, for in order to satisfy their wretched, vulgar, everyday needs, in order to crush the resistance of the bourgeoisie, instead of laying down their arms and abolishing the state, they give the state a revolutionary and transitory form . . .'[85]

Nor is there much evidence of Marx's 'decidedly authoritarian doctrine' in his marginal notes of 1875 on the Gotha Programme of the German Social-Democratic Party. In these notes, Marx bitterly attacked the programme's references to 'the free state' ('free state – what is this?') and this is well in line with his belief that the 'free state' is a contradiction in terms; and he then asked: 'What transformation will the state undergo in communist society? In other words, what social functions will remain in existence there that are analogous to present functions of the state?' Marx, however, did not answer the question but merely said that it could only be answered 'scientifically' and that 'one does not get a flea-hop nearer to the problem by a thousandfold combination of the word people with the word state.'[86] He then goes on: 'Between capitalist and communist society lies the period of the revolutionary transformation of the one into the other. There corresponds to this also a political transition period in which the state can be nothing but *the revolutionary dictatorship of the proletariat.*'[87]

This does not advance matters much, but neither does it suggest the slightest 'authoritarian' impulse. In the *Critique of the Gotha Programme*, Marx as always before, made a sharp distinction between the democratic republic and the dictatorship of the proletariat, and Engels was clearly mistaken when he wrote in 1891 that the democratic republic was 'even the specific form of the dictatorship of the proletariat.'[88] On the contrary, Marx's critical attitude towards the democratic republic in the *Critique of the Gotha Programme* shows that he continued to think of the dictatorship of the proletariat as an altogether different and immeasurably freer form of political power. 'Freedom,' he wrote in the *Critique of the Gotha Programme*, 'consists in converting the state from an organ superimposed upon society into one completely subordinated to it. . . .'[89] This would seem a good description of Marx's view of the state in the period of the dictatorship of the proletariat. No doubt, he would have endorsed Engels' view, expressed a few weeks after Marx's death, that 'the proletarian class will first have to possess itself of the organized political force of the state and with this aid stamp out the resistance of the capitalist class and reorganize society.'[90] But it is of some significance that, with the possible exception of his remark of January 1873, referred to earlier, Marx himself always chose to emphasize the liberating rather than the repressive aspects of post-capitalist political power; and it is also of some interest that, in the notes he made for *The Civil War in France*, and which were not of course intended for publication, he should have warned the working class that the 'work of regeneration' would be 'again and again relented [*sic*] and impeded by the resistance of vested interests and class egotisms,' but that he should have failed to make any reference to the State as an agent of repression. What he did say was that 'great strides may be [made] at once through the communal form of political organization' and that 'the time has come to begin that movement for themselves and mankind.'[91]

The fact is that, far from bearing any authoritarian imprint, the whole of Marx's work on the state is pervaded by a powerful anti-authoritarian and anti-bureaucratic bias, not only in relation to a distant communist society but also to the period of transition which is to precede it. True, the state is necessary in this period. But the only thing which, for Marx, makes it tolerable is popular participation and popular rule. If Marx is to be faulted, it is not for any authoritarian bias, but for greatly understating the difficulties of the libertarian position. However, in the light of the experience of socialist movements since Marx wrote, this may perhaps be judged a rather less serious fault than its bureaucratic obverse.

NOTES AND REFERENCES

1. K. Marx to F. Lassalle, 22 February 1858, and K. Marx to F. Engels, 2 April 1858 (*Selected Correspondence*, Moscow, n.d.), pp. 125, 126.
2. For the *Critique*, see *Marx/Engels Gesamtausgabe* (MEGA) (Moscow, 1927), I, 1/1, pp. 403–553; for the *Introduction*, first published in the *Franco-German Annals* of 1844, *ibid.*, I, 1/1, pp. 607–621, and T. B. Bottomore, ed., *K. Marx, Early Writings* (London, 1963).
3. MEGA, *ibid.*, p. 249.
4. *Ibid.*, p. 248.
5. *Ibid.*, p. 283.
6. *Ibid.*, p. 360. Note also his contemptuous reference in an article of May 1842 on the freedom of the Press to 'the inconsistent, nebulous and timorous reasoning of German liberals, who claim to honour freedom by setting it up in an imaginary firmament, rather than on the solid ground of reality' (*ibid.*, p. 220; A. Cornu, *Karl Marx et Friedrich Engels. Leur Vie et leur Oeuvre* (Paris, 1958), II, p. 17).
7. K. Marx to A. Ruge, May 1843, MEGA, p. 565; see also K. Marx to A. Ruge, March 1843, *Sel. Cor., op. cit.*, p. 25.
8. MEGA, *ibid.*, p. 424.
9. *Ibid.*, pp. 498–499. See also J. Hyppolite, *Etudes sur Marx et Hegel* (Paris, 1955), pp. 123 ff., and M. Rubel, *K. Marx. Essai de Biographie Intellectuelle* (Paris, 1957), pp. 58 *et seq.*
10. MEGA, *ibid.*, p. 519.
11. *Ibid.*, pp. 434–435.
12. *Ibid.*, p. 435.
13. *Ibid.*, p. 436.
14. *Ibid.*, p. 435.
15. *Ibid.*, p. 582. (Italics in original.)
16. *Ibid.*, p. 585.
17. *Ibid.*, p. 605.
18. See S. Avineri, 'Marx and Jewish Emancipation,' in *Journal of the History of Ideas*, vol. XXV (July–September 1964), pp. 445–450.
19. MEGA, *op. cit.*, p. 606.

20. *Ibid.*, p. 615.

21. *Ibid.*, pp. 619 *et seq.*

22. K. Marx and F. Engels, *The Holy Family* (Moscow, 1956), p. 154.

23. *Ibid.*, p. 157. (Italics in original.)

24. *Ibid.*, p. 163. (Italics in original.)

25. *Ibid.*, p. 164.

26. *Ibid.*, p. 166.

27. K. Marx and F. Engels, *The German Ideology* (New York, 1939), p. 59. (Italics in original.)

28. K. Marx, *The Poverty of Philosophy* (London, 1936), p. 70.

29. K. Marx and F. Engels, *Selected Works*, hereafter noted as *S. W.* (Moscow, 1950), I, p. 35.

30. *Ibid.*, p. 51.

31. See, e.g. J. Plamenatz, *German Marxism and Russian Communism* (London, 1954), pp. 144 *et seq.*; J. Sanderson, 'Marx and Engels on the State' in the *Western Political Quarterly*, vol. XVI, No. 4 (December 1963), pp. 946–955.

32. As is suggested by the two authors cited above.

33. See, e.g. *The Class Struggles in France, passim, The 18th Brumaire of Louis Bonaparte, passim.*

34. See, e.g. 'The Elections in Britain,' in K. Marx and F. Engels, *On Britain* (Moscow, 1953), pp. 353 *et seq.* 'The Whigs are the *aristocratic representatives* of the bourgeoisie, of the industrial and commercial middle class. Under the condition that the bourgeoisie should abandon to them, to an oligarchy of aristocratic families, the monopoly of government and the exclusive possession of office, they make to the middle class, and assist it in conquering, all those concessions, which in the course of social and political developments have shown themselves to have become *unavoidable* and *undelayable.*' (*ibid.*, p. 353. Italics in original.)

35. *Ibid.*, p. 368.

36. *S. W..*, I, p. 300.

37. *Ibid.*, p. 301.

38. *Ibid.*, p. 302.

39. *Ibid.*, p. 302.

40. *Ibid.*, p. 302. (Italics in original.)

41. Marx also notes that the identity of interest of the smallholding peasants 'begets no community, no national bond and no political organization among them,' so that 'they do not form a class' (*ibid.*, p. 302). For an interesting discussion of Marx's concept of class, see S. Ossowski, *Class Structure in the Class Consciousness* (London, 1963), ch. V.

42. *S. W.*, I, p. 303.

43. *Ibid.*, pp. 308–309.

44. *Ibid.*, p. 309.

45. K. Marx, *The Civil War in France, S. W.*, I, p. 470.

46. *Ibid.*, p. 470.

47. *Ibid.*, p. 470.

48. F. Engels, *The Origin of the Family, Private Property and the State, S. W.* II, p. 290.

271

49. *Ibid.*, pp. 290–291. For further comments on the subject from Engels, see also his letter to C. Schmidt, 27 October 1890, in *S.W.*, II, pp. 446–447.

50. MEGA, *op. cit.*, I, 1/1, p. 456.

51. See, e.g., K. Wittfogel, *Oriental Despotism* (Yale, 1957), ch. IX; G. Lichtheim, 'Marx and the "Asiatic Mode of Production,"' in *St Antony's Papers*, No. 14, Far Eastern Affairs (London, 1963). Also K. Marx, *Pre-Capitalist Economic Formations*, with an introduction by E. J. Hobsbawn (London, 1964). This is a translation of a section of Marx's *Grundrisse Der Kritik der Politischen Okonomie (Rohentwurf)* (Berlin, 1953).

52. MEGA, I, 1/1, p. 438.

53. *S.W.*, I, p. 329.

54. K. Marx to F. Engels, 2 June 1853, *Sel. Cor.*, p. 99.

55. K. Marx, *Pre-Capitalist Formations, op. cit.*, p. 79.

56. *New York Daily Tribune*, 5 August 1853, in Lichtheim, *op. cit.*, p. 94.

57. K. Marx, *Capital* (Moscow, 1962), III, pp. 771–772.

58. K. Marx and F. Engels, *The First Indian War of Independence* (1857–1859) (Moscow, n.d.), p. 16. In *Capital* (Moscow, 1959), I, p. 514, ft. 2, Marx also notes that 'one of the material bases of the power of the State over the small disconnected producing organisms in India, was the regulation of the water supply;' also, 'the necessity for predicting the rise and fall of the Nile created Egyptian astronomy, and with it the dominion of the priests, as directors of agriculture' (*ibid.*, p. 514, fn. 1); for some further elaborations on the same theme, see also F. Engels, *Anti-Dühring* (Moscow, 1962), p. 248.

59. K. Marx, *Pre-Capitalist Economic Formations, op. cit.*, p. 71.

60. *Ibid.*, p. 69. (Italics in original.)

61. K. Wittfogel, *Oriental Despotism, op. cit.*, p. 381.

62. *Ibid.*, p. 387.

63. Lichtheim, *op. cit.*, p. 110.

64. K. Marx and F. Engels, *Address of the Central Committee to the Communist League, S.W.*, I, p. 101.

65. *Ibid.*, p. 101.

66. *Ibid.*, p. 102.

67. *Ibid.*, p. 101.

68. *Ibid.*, pp. 307–309.

69. *Ibid.*, p. 106.

70. It is, in this connection, of some interest that Engels should have thought it necessary to add a Note to the 1885 edition of the Address, explaining that this passage was based on a 'misunderstanding' of French revolutionary experience and that 'local and provincial self-government' were not in contradiction with 'national centralization.' (*Ibid.*, p. 107.)

71. *Ibid.*, p. 108.

72. K. Marx to J. Wedemeyer, 5 March 1852, *Sel. Cor.*, p. 86. (Italics in original.)

73. H. Draper, 'Marx and the Dictatorship of the Proletariat,' in *New Politics*, vol. I, No. 4, p. 102. (Italics in original.)

74. *S.W.*, I, p. 301.
75. *Ibid.*, pp. 468–469.
76. *Ibid.*, p. 473.
77. *Ibid.*, p. 471.
78. *Ibid.*, p. 472.
79. *Marx-Engels Archives* (Moscow, 1934), vol. III (VIII), p. 324. (Italics in original.) I am grateful to Mr M. Johnstone for drawing my attention to these Notes. Note also, e.g., the following: 'Only the Proletarians, fired by a new social task to accomplish by them for all society, to do away with all classes and class rule, were the men to break the instrument of that class rule – the State, the centralized and organized governmental power usurping to be the master instead of the servant of society. . . . It had sprung into life against them. By them it was broken, not as a peculiar form of governmental (centralized) power, but as its most powerful, elaborated into seeming independence from society expression and, therefore, also its most prostitute reality, covered by infamy from top to bottom, having centred in absolute corruption at home and absolute powerlessness abroad' (*ibid.*, p. 326). The peculiar English syntax of such passages is obviously due to the fact that they are only notes, not intended for publication.
80. *S.W.*, I, p. 473.
81. 'Of late,' Engels wrote in an Introduction to the 1891 edition of *The Civil War in France*, 'the Social-Democratic philistine has once more been filled with wholesome terror at the words: Dictatorship of the Proletariat. Well and good, gentlemen, do you want to know what this dictatorship looks like? Look at the Paris Commune. That was the Dictatorship of the Proletariat.' (*S.W.*, I, p. 440.)
82. K. Marx to F. Domela-Nienwenhuis, 22 February 1881, in *Sel. Cor.*, p. 410.
83. G. Lichtheim, *Marxism* (London, 1961), p. 374.
84. G. M. Stekloff, *History of the First International* (London, 1928), pp. 179–180, and J. Freymond, ed., *La Première Internationale* (Geneva, 1962), II, p. 295.
85. V. I. Lenin, *State and Revolution* (London, 1933), p. 54.
86. K. Marx, *Critique of the Gotha Programme, S.W.*, II, p. 30.
87. *Ibid.*, p. 30. (Italics in original.)
88. Quoted in Lenin, *The State and Revolution*, p. 54. Lenin's own comment is also misleading: 'Engels,' he writes, 'repeats here in a particularly striking manner the fundamental idea which runs like a red thread through all of Marx's works, namely, that the democratic republic is the nearest approach to the dictatorship of the proletariat' (*ibid.*, p. 54). Engels' phrase does not bear this interpretation; and whatever may be said for the view that the democratic republic *is* the nearest approach to the dictatorship of the proletariat, it is not so in Marx.
89. *S.W.*, II, p. 29.
90. F. Engels to P. Van Patten, 18 April 1883, *Sel. Cor.*, *op. cit.*, p. 437.
91. *Marx-Engels Archives, op. cit.*, p. 334.

# SECTION IV

# MARX AND CONTEMPORARY SOCIOLOGY

# INTRODUCTION TO SECTION IV

The question of the relevance of Marx's work to contemporary social science remains a bitterly contested one. On the one hand, proponents of functionalist or order paradigms within the social sciences are prone to insist that Marxism is an outmoded theory describing a stage of capitalist development which has long been superseded. At best, according to adherents of this view, Marxism still offers some insight into the structure of 19th century European society, or it may be said to 'sensitize' us to the existence of conflict in social organizations. At worst, Marx's writings are declared to be a millenarian dogma masquerading as science, totalitarian in essence (if one thinks this picture to be a gross exaggeration, see Popper, 1950).

On the other hand, in both Europe and North America, an increasing number of scholars working in the social sciences out of an explicit Marxian perspective have challenged this politically conservative view of Marx's work as a caricature. In Europe, Marxian scholars working both within and without the framework of traditional Marxist parties (Communist and Socialist) have made enormous strides in systematically developing Marxist theory in many different areas of the human, or social, sciences. In the U.S.A., a number of Marxist scholars have emerged from the political collapse of the New Left and have begun to do theoretical work which is increasingly up to the standards of the most advanced work in Europe, especially in the analysis of the capitalist state.

The development of a coherent Marxist social science and the emergence of a long-drawn-out struggle for academic recognition and standing during the 1960s and 1970s has made the reassessment of Marx's work and its contribution to contemporary research problems a particularly important task. All three of the authors included in this final section attempt to carry out such an evaluation in which what is outmoded in Marx is criticized while what is valuable is conserved. Needless to say, the three scholars included here come to different conclusions concerning specific points of analysis, yet there is a striking sense of general agreement on fundamental issues of interpretation and evaluation.

The first essay in this final section is by Tom Bottomore, British sociologist and well-known author of such books as *Classes in Modern Society* and *Sociology as Social Criticism*. In his brief essay on Marx and contemporary sociology included here, Bottomore emphasizes the tentative and heuristic nature of Marx's completed theoretical formulations, seeing the value of Marx's work for contemporary sociological research to be mainly as a source for theoretical and methodological departures. In Bottomore's opinion, the most interesting research in recent years in several areas of sociological inquiry has been done on problems directly inspired by Marx's writings. Yet very little theoretically significant work has been done by what Bottomore calls 'orthodox Marxists.' Clearly, for Bottomore, the contemporary value of Marx's work lies more in the nature of the questions which it poses than in the answers which it offers to those questions. Yet, he concludes, the re-evaluation of Marx's work is a process with which we will never be done.

The other essay in this section is by George Lichtheim, one of the most brilliant essayists and political commentators of the twentieth century. Author of *Marxism: An Historical and Critical Study*, an excellent introduction to Marxism and nineteenth century European socialism, and numerous important essays and theoretical studies, Lichtheim wrote from within the Marxian tradition with great erudition and empathy while yet retaining a certain critical distance from that tradition and what he viewed as its historical tragedy.

In this article, Lichtheim attempts a brief survey of the historical development of European Marxism after Marx, stressing the relationships between Marxism and Hegel, and Marxism and Comtean Positivism. What Lichtheim finds to have occurred in the late nineteenth and early twentieth centuries is a severe decomposition of Marxian theory, arising from the failure of revolutionary transformation in Western Europe and the systematic reintroduction of Hegelian metaphysics into Marxist theory in the writings of Engels, Plekhanov, and Lenin. The very conception of 'Marxism' as a unified system of thought is, Lichtheim argues, part of the process of revision undertaken by Engels following Marx's death and finally carried to completion by Lenin in 'official' Soviet Marxism. Lichtheim rightly enough labels this development an 'intellectual disaster.' Even worse, in his view, is the fact that the only historically meaningful alternative to this reading of Marx has been the incorporation of themes from Comtean positivism into Marxist theory, transforming Marx's understanding of the evolution of bourgeois society in Western Europe into a fatalistic social evolutionism, complete with a 'law' of inexorable stages.

It is clear from the above that Lichtheim preferred Marxism in its original form to the fantastic development of its progeny. Although the premise is left unstated in this essay, like the other authors included in this volume, Lichtheim looked for a return to the original source in Marx's own writings to precipitate a revival in Western Marxism.

# KARL MARX: SOCIOLOGIST OR MARXIST?*

## T. B. BOTTOMORE

The question posed in the title of this paper is not intended to exhaust all the aspects from which Marx's work may be regarded; nor is it meant to prejudge the issue as to whether a thinker – and Marx in particular – may be *both* a sociologist *and* a Marxist. But there are advantages in putting just this question. First, the consideration of Marx's thought as one of the early systems of sociology, that is, as an attempt to formulate new concepts for depicting the structure of whole societies and for explaining massive social changes, brings into prominence the most distinctive and, I would say, the most interesting of his ideas. This has become clearer with the growth of sociological studies in the past few decades and with the accompanying reassessment of the history of modern social thought. It is evident that the marked revival of interest in Marxism as a theoretical scheme (which is in contrast with its declining intellectual appeal as a political creed) owes much to the recent work of sociologists; but even at an earlier time, at the end of the 19th century and in the first decade of the 20th century, the most fruitful discussions of Marx's thought seem to me to have been those which arose from sociological or philosophical concerns – in the writings of Max Weber, Croce, Sorel and Pareto, for example – rather than those which originated in strictly economic or political criticisms.[1]

One important reason for the present revival of interest is the fact that Marx's theory stands in direct opposition on every major point to the functionalist theory which has dominated sociology and anthropology for the past twenty or thirty years, but which has been found increasingly unsatisfactory. Where functionalism emphasizes social harmony, Marxism emphasizes social conflict; where functionalism directs attention to the stability and persistence of social forms, Marxism is radically historical in its outlook and emphasizes the changing structure of society; where functionalism concentrates upon the regulation of social life by general values and norms, Marxism stresses the divergence of in-

* Originally published in *Science and Society*, 30:1, Winter 1966. Reprinted with permission of the editors.

terests and values within each society and the role of force in maintaining, over a longer or shorter period of time, a given social order. The contrast between 'equilibrium' and 'conflict' models of society, which was stated forcefully by Dahrendorf in 1958,[2] has now become a commonplace; and Marx's theories are regularly invoked in opposition to those of Durkheim, Pareto and Malinowski, the principal architects of the functionalist theory.

This is not to claim that Marxism stands alone as a theory which gives due weight to social conflict, and to the historical and mutable nature of human societies; nor that mere delineation of the 'equilibrium' and 'conflict' models, as alternative constructions which may be useful in different contexts, appears to most sociologists as the final step which can be taken. Other scholars after Marx, and notably Simmel and Max Weber, contributed new elements to a theory of social conflict and of social change, and they brought corrections, amplifications or refutations of some of Marx's own propositions. It is true, nonetheless, that their work can only be fully understood when it is seen as *following* that of Marx.

The possibility of alternative models of society raises difficult problems which have been with sociologists since the beginning of their discipline. In a sense, modern sociologists are grappling anew with the old question of the reconciliation between 'order' and 'progress' which was one of the main themes of Comte's sociology. This intellectual affinity stems in part from the similarity in social conditions. Like Comte, we live in the aftermath of great revolutions, and in the midst of new revolutionary outbreaks and violent transformations of society. In consequence, the most important tasks of sociology now appear to be the comprehension of what is happening in the creation of new states, the accelerating growth of science and technology, the spread of industrialism throughout the world, and the revolutions in class structure, in the family, and in political systems. Unlike Comte, however, we are more concerned with finding a satisfactory theory than with expounding a new social philosophy; and we are more aware of the need to provide an explanation of social change, whereas Comte, who was confronted by the numerous theories of progress of his age, was more anxious to discover principles of 'order' and stability.

In Marx's theory, the main emphasis is put upon the conflicts within society and the structural changes which result from these conflicts; and there is an underlying scheme of the progressive development of mankind. At the same time, the theory does include some partial accounts of social solidarity and of the persistence of social forms. Marx deals at length, for instance, with the conditions in which class solidarity is generated and maintained; and at the level of a total society he explains the persistence of a particular structure by the relations between classes, the position of a ruling class, and the influence of 'ruling ideas.' Further, Marx predicts the advent of a type of society in which social conflict will be eliminated while social solidarity and harmony will be complete. In other words, we may see in Marx's theory a juxtaposition of 'conflict' and 'equilibrium' models of society in two different ways: first, that conflict predominates in the social relations within the total society, while solidarity and consensus prevail in many of the subgroups (especially social classes) in society; and secondly, that total societies may be arranged in a historical order such that in one historical period, the only one we have experienced up to now, conflict is predominant, and in another, located in the future, solidarity, peaceful co-operation and consensus will prevail.

Nevertheless, this theory does not provide an adequate reconciliation of the two models, quite apart from the errors which it may contain in the actual description and explanation of societal conflict or class solidarity. It does not, for example, allow for the possibility that conflict itself may engender or maintain social solidarity (a possibility which Simmel explored more systematically). Moreover, it eliminates conflict entirely in the hypothetical classless society of the future, and it seems also to postulate an original condition of human society, before the extension of the division of labor and the accumulation of private wealth, which was free from conflict. This view depends upon a historical conception which is at odds with the idea of a positive science which seems generally to inspire Marx's mature work. We may attribute greater or lesser importance to the Hegelianism or the positivism of Marx's theory, but it is impossible to reconcile them. Isaiah Berlin, for instance, has argued that: 'The framework of [Marx's] theory is undeviatingly Hegelian. It recognizes that the history of humanity is a single, non-repetitive process, which obeys discoverable laws. These laws are different from the laws of physics or of chemistry, which being unhistorical, record unvarying conjunctions and successions of interconnected phenomena, whenever or wherever these may repeat themselves; they are similar rather to those of geology or botany, which embody the principles in accordance with which a process of continuous change takes place.'[3] On the other hand, it may be claimed that many of Marx's propositions have the form at least of statements of universal laws. Thus, the famous phrase: 'The history of all hitherto existing society is the history of class struggles' may be interpreted, not as a historical principle, but as a universal law of conflict in human society. Similarly, the assertion that the form of social institutions and of ideas is determined by the economic structure of society has to be regarded either as the expression of a universal law, or as a rule of method. Even where Marx says he is formulating a law of change – for example, 'the law of motion of modern capitalist society' – this may be seen as a special law applicable to a particular type of society (capitalist or industrial), and in principle derivable from some more general law which refers to change in *all* societies. Thus, laws of social change do not have to be historical laws or principles; they may be universal, and applicable to all instances whenever or wherever they occur.

In Marx's own theory these two conceptions – the historical interpretation of a unique sequence of events, and the framing of universal laws covering repeatable events – co-exist, and later Marxists have in the main opted for one or the other view: the positivist or scientific school being represented to some extent by Engels, and most fully by Max Adler; the Hegelianizing school by Lukács, Korsch, Marcuse, and a number of recent opponents of positivism, particularly in France. My own contention is that the general inclination of Marx's work, when it is traced from his earlier to his later writings, is clearly away from the philosophy of history and towards a scientific theory of society, in the precise sense of a body of general laws and detailed empirical statements. I recognize, of course, that it is not along this path that the main development of Marxism has occurred. Indeed, it is striking that the major contributions of Marxist research have been in the historical field, though even here they have been confined to a narrow range of problems, and that empirical investigations in the sociological domain have been rare.

A recent essay by Hobsbawm[4] restates the point about the influence of Marxism upon economic and social history with great clarity. Introducing the first English translation of Marx's only extended analysis of pre-capitalist societies,[5] Hobsbawm argues that Marx formulates here a theory of historical *progress* rather than a scheme of social evolution, and that it is in these terms (i.e., from the standpoint of a historian) that his distinctions between different types of society should be considered. What Marxist historians have actually done Hobsbawm examines later, and he concludes that the recent contributions are in some ways unsatisfactory inasmuch as they have neglected certain types of society – notably the 'Asiatic society' – and have greatly expanded the notion of 'feudal society' to fill up the gaps. The preoccupation of Marxist historians with just those questions which Marx himself examined most fully – the rise of the *bourgeoisie* within feudal society, the transition from feudalism to capitalism, and the early stages of capitalist society – does, indeed, seem excessive; and aside from the neglect of other types of social structure, it has also meant that the Marxist contribution to modern social history has been less substantial than might have been expected. In the main, it is not the Marxists who have studied closely the development of modern social classes and elites, of ideologies, or of political parties, or who have attempted to analyse revolutionary movements. This domain, which is closest to sociology, has unquestionably been much influenced, if not actually created, by Marx's ideas, but most of the important studies have been made by scholars who were not Marxists – from Sombart, Max Weber and Michels to Geiger and Karl Mannheim, from Veblen to C. Wright Mills.

In the main line of sociological inquiry no Marxist scholar has emerged to equal the achievement of Max Weber in using Marx's very general propositions about the relation between ideologies and social structure as the starting point for a vast and fruitful investigation of the role of particular religious ideas and beliefs in social change and of their connections with various social classes. Those Marxists who, like Max Adler, wanted to present Marx's theory as a system of scientific sociology have generally confined themselves to methodological discussions,[6] while those of the Hegelian school have either wandered into the happily imprecise and imaginative field of literary criticism (Lukács) or have, like the positivists, turned to methodological reflections (Sartre).

The contrast between the accomplishments of the more orthodox schools of Marxism and of those scholars who were simply stimulated by Marx's ideas to embark upon fresh research of their own, reflects no discredit upon Marx himself. Marx was always passionately interested in factual social inquiries – from the investigations of Quételet and Buret to the reports of the English factory inspectors and his own projected 'enquête ouvrière' – and he undertook in *Capital* an empirical study of vast scope which is still unsurpassed in the literature of the social sciences. His whole work, which combines the construction of theoretical models of society with the elaboration of methods of inquiry, and with the imaginative use of these models and methods in the analysis of a type of social system and its transformations, is by any reckoning one of the great contributions to the formation of modern sociology; and when we consider how, outside the confines of the various Marxist orthodoxies, it has provoked new sociological investigations, new reflections upon problems of theory and method, and repeated reassessments (such as we are engaged upon today), then it may justifiably be regarded as the greatest single contribution – *the* decisive intellectual advance which established our subject in a recognizable form. If Marx sometimes contradicted himself, made mistakes, moved

285

ambiguously from a Hegelian idiom to the language of modern natural science, and back again, left some of his concepts in a logically untidy form, sometimes used essentialist definitions though he was in the main a nominalist, exaggerated social conflict in his theoretical model, this seems to me excusable in a pioneer thinker whose ideas had the power to create a new branch of knowledge which, in its own development, would produce the means of correcting and refining these early formulations.

The inexcusable would be that Marx had deliberately sacrificed positive science to metaphysics, that he had sought only that evidence which supported a vision of the world and of history created by a poetic and philosophic imagination and never afterwards questioned; in short, that he was pre-eminently a Marxist, the expounder of a creed. Marx, of course, *said* that he was not a Marxist, and there is little reason to doubt that he was extremely critical of the exposition of his ideas by self-styled disciples during his lifetime. Was it that he considered these expositions inadequate, or did he object to the presentation of his ideas as a political creed? Did he see his theory chiefly as an engine of discovery, and as one which required a great deal more hard intellectual work before it would be really adequate for its purpose? We must, in any case, make a distinction between the 'Marxism' of Marx and that of the Marxists. For Marx, his own system of thought could not possibly be something established or given, a simple framework for the expression of a social or political aim. It was his own creation, worked out laboriously over a long period of time, incessantly revised and admittedly incomplete. The record of his intellectual labors, which has been set out admirably by Maximilien Rubel,[7] shows the manner in which Marx arrived at his principal ideas – the anatomy of 'civil society,' the class system, ideologies, and revolutionary change – and the plans which he formed in his youth to investigate in detail these various aspects of modern society, but which he was never able to realize. On many occasions he declared that he had now, at last, completed his work on the economic system and would be able to turn to the problems of class, political regimes, ideologies, but he continued to write new drafts of his economic analysis, published a preliminary account of his discoveries in 1859, the initial volume of *Capital* in 1867, and then in the last fifteen years of his life was unable even to finish the remaining parts of his economic analysis, let alone embark upon new studies in the other spheres of society which he had repeatedly distinguished as vitally important for the full development of his theoretical system. The relative sterility of Marx's later years may be explained in various ways – by his discouragement in the face of scholarly indifference to his work, by his disillusionment with the labor movement after the demise of the International, by his failure to solve major problems in the economic analysis of capitalism, by illness and domestic anxieties – but it can certainly not be explained as a consequence of his self-satisfied contemplation of the completed edifice of Marxist theory, which needed henceforth only to be expounded. Marx was only too keenly aware of the incompleteness of his work, and he returned intermittently to a reconsideration of some of his fundamental conceptions; for example, the classification of pre-capitalist societies, and especially the nature of the Asiatic type of society.

In this sense, then, of considering himself the possessor of a complete and finished theory of society, Marx was not a Marxist. In another sense, which is still more important in relation to the political history of the twentieth century, Marx was also not a Marxist: he did not regard himself as the originator of a political creed which must be adopted as the unique doctrine of the working-class movement. From his earliest to his latest writings Marx takes a consistent view: in a letter to Ruge of September 1843 he writes '. . . I am not at all in favor of raising our own dogmatic banner. Quite the contrary . . . We do not confront the world in doctrinaire fashion with a new principle, saying: Here is the truth, bow down before it! We develop new principles for the world out of its own existing principles. . . We may sum up the outlook of our Journal[8] in a single phrase: the self-knowledge (critical philosophy) of the age about its struggles and aims. This is a task for the world and for ourselves.' And in 1880, Marx prefaces his 'enquête ouvrière' with an appeal to the French workers to reply to the questionnaire, since only they can describe 'with full knowledge the evils which they endure,' and 'only they, not any providential saviors, can energetically administer the remedies for the social ills from which they suffer.'

I do not claim that Marx never deviated from this view, or that he was never tempted to impose his own conception of the aims and the appropriate tactics of the working-class movement. But the recent publication of the records of the First International[9] has shown how little authoritarian Marx was in his political activities, and this is confirmed entirely by his attitude to the Paris Commune and its failure. In his relations with other socialists Marx sometimes gives an impression of dogmatism, but I believe that it was rather the irritation of a great and creative thinker in his encounters with men who were not only much less able, but who lacked Marx's dedication to scientific inquiry. Proudhon, for instance, was a purely speculative thinker, Bakunin a passionate and woolly-minded revolutionary. Neither of them ever conceived or carried out a rigorous social investigation, and, hence, they were treated by Marx with a contempt which is perhaps distasteful to us, but which is not without justification.

There runs unmistakably through all Marx's work (even in his youthful writings when he is still struggling out of the toils of the Hegelian philosophy) a profound commitment to the investigation of *social facts*; a commitment which again finds expression in his preface to the 'enquête ouvrière,' where he appeals to those who, '. . . desiring social reform, must also desire *exact* and *positive* knowledge of the conditions in which the working class, the class to which the future belongs, lives and works.' The 'Marxism' in Marx's own thought, and in that of his followers, has frequently been seen as the subordination of theoretical ideas and social investigations to a preconceived social ideal and a rigorously determined means of attaining it. I have already suggested that this view is mistaken with respect to Marx himself, inasmuch as it was his declared intention to make clear to his age *its own* strivings, and more particularly to display to the working class its real situation in capitalist society, the implications of its revolt against that situation, and the probable outcome of the working-class movement.

It will be profitable, however, to consider more closely the relations between theoretical judgments, judgments of fact, and judgments of value in Marx's work. The first point to note is that in Marx's life socialism and social science were closely interwoven. He became, at an early age, and probably through the influence of Saint-Simonian doctrines, a sympathizer with the working-class movement; and this commitment to socialism certainly preceded the full elaboration of his sociological theories. Nevertheless, from the beginning he was equally impressed by the new 'science of society' pre-figured in Saint-Simon's writings (and subsequently in Lorenz von Stein's book on the social movement in France); and his later reading of the historians of the French Revolution and of the political economists was sufficient to persuade him both that there was growing up a new field and a new method in the study of man's social life, and that the development of capitalism and the rise of the labor movement formed the essential subject matter of this study. From that time, about the middle of the 1840s, Marx's participation in the socialist movement and his efforts to advance the theoretical science of society proceeded together, and fructified each other. This, after all, is not surprising, nor uncommon. The greatest social scientists have been passionately concerned about some social problem, and usually extremely partisan (I think of Max Weber, Durkheim, and Pareto) and this may account for the significance and the intellectual excitement of their work. The question is whether this partisanship manifests itself too strongly, not simply in the selection of subjects for inquiry, but in the formation of concepts and models, which become ideal-types of too ideal a kind, and in the conduct and presentation of their investigations, which become too selective, too well insulated against the possible discovery of counter-instances.

In Marx's case (but also in some of the others, and notably in Durkheim's) there is also a more profound problem. Does the theory, or the broader scheme of thought, contain within itself a theory of knowledge which eliminates the distinction between fact and value? There are several features of Marx's thought which need to be considered here. The idea of the social determination of thought appears to destroy the autonomy of moral judgments; but in the same manner it destroys the autonomy of all judgments (including those judgments which constitute Marx's own theory, so that there is no longer any point in asking whether it is true or false). But this is not a problem in Marx's theory alone: it is a problem for any deterministic theory, and in a broad sense of any scientific theory, in psychology or sociology. It may, indeed, be argued, on the other side, that one of the virtues of Marx's social theory is that it makes a much greater allowance for the creative work of human reason in the fashioning of social institutions.[10]

A more specific problem appears in Marx's theory of ideologies, which, while it excludes science from the realm of socially determined ideas, makes moral notions wholly ideological in the sense of reflecting the interests of social classes. This makes moral ideas relative, yet Marx also expresses what appear to be absolute moral judgments. If this is, indeed, the case there is a contradiction in his thought. The controversy over this question has recently come to be expressed in somewhat different terms as a result of the interest in Marx's early writings. Is there, for Marx, a permanent, unchanging essence of man, which is alienated in certain forms of society, but which in others can find its full expression, and which can thus be treated as a moral ideal in some version of a morality of self-realization? Or is the essence of man a purely historical phenomenon, so that no universal ideal or criterion of morality can be formulated at all? I shall not attempt to resolve this problem here. Marx did not attempt to do so, and to say the least his thought is obscure on this subject, while the later Marxist contributions, such as Kautsky's *Ethics and the Materialist Conception of History*, fall far below the level of a genuine philosophical discussion. I will only say that I consider possible and plausible an interpretation of Marx's ethical conceptions as being both rationalist and historical; that is, as recognizing some basic and permanent human needs which ought to be satisfied, and which can be expressed in some coherent moral ideal, and yet seeing these needs as assuming different forms in different historical states of society.

A view of this kind would allow us to resolve another problem in the theory of ideology, namely, that although it appears as thoroughly relativistic it does nonetheless permit, in conjunction with other parts of Marx's theory, an unbounded dogmatism. This occurs in the following way: all moral ideas are class ideas and thus relative, but the working class is the rising class in modern society (as shown by the sociological part of the theory) and so its moral ideas are superior and should prevail. Criticisms of the social and political aims of the working class, and even of the means employed to attain them, can only arise from other class positions and are to be condemned out of hand as inferior because *dépassé*. Not only is it possible, in this way, to adopt an absolutist moral stance, on the basis of a relativistic moral theory, but the theory of ideology can be used to dismiss any arguments of one's opponents, whether these are moral or theoretical arguments.

It is hardly necessary to observe that Marxists have in fact used the theory in this manner literally *ad nauseam*. It may be more necessary to say that Marx himself did not argue in this fashion. First, there is the element in Marx's thought mentioned earlier, which is concerned with a permanent human essence or morality. Secondly, careful scrutiny of Marx's work shows that he never dismissed any serious theoretical view merely on the ground that it expressed a non-proletarian ideology. From his criticism of Bauer in *The Jewish Question*, through *The Poverty of Philosophy*, up to the critical examination of modern political economy in *Capital* and *Theories of Surplus Value*, Marx undertakes primarily to show by theoretical argument and empirical tests that the views he is opposing are *false*, and only later, if at all, does he refer to their ideological sources. There is a good example in one of the lesser known sections of *The German Ideology*, where Marx criticizes utilitarianism on the ground that its reduction of all human relationships to a single relation of utility results in a false conception both of human nature and of social life. Only in conjunction with this theoretical examination of the doctrine does he propose a sociological account of it as an ideology which faithfully reflects the kind of social relations that modern capitalism actually tends to produce. In this instance, I think both the theoretical and the sociological analyses are extraordinarily fruitful, and the latter could be pursued much further, as it was, for example, by Simmel in his *Philosophy of Money,* where the influence of Marx's ideas is extremely strong.

However, I do not wish to single out Marx's own scientific rectitude as the only restraint upon his ideological enthusiasms, even though it does form a striking contrast with the attitude of some of his followers. There is also the fact that in Marx's lifetime his theoretical analysis and his allegiance to the labor movement were congruent and, in a sense, mutually supporting. The labor movement developed spontaneously, and Marx could easily justify his claim to be analysing and explaining a real process of social change. The gulf between classes was widening, class consciousness was growing, the relations between classes did form the core of the social problem, and the new doctrines of working-class organizations did foreshadow the classless society which Marx predicted. Thus, Marx's theory could find empirical confirmation, and its empirical testing provided at the same time a degree of rational and factual support for Marx's moral convictions. How closely these two aspects were associated is shown especially well in the projected 'enquête ouvrière' of 1880, which is first of all in the tradition of a long series of empirical surveys of working-class conditions, but which, secondly, goes beyond these in attempting to establish the principle of an investigation of working-class conditions by the working class itself, and which does so in order to combine in a single effort of research both a factual inquiry and a heightening of class consciousness.

Here Marx's two aims are in perfect concord. We may ask whether the combination is legitimate, and I would answer with a qualified affirmative. If sociology is to have any application to actual social life, then one of its most important applications should be the wide diffusion of knowledge about the nature of social relationships in a given society in order to increase men's conscious self-regulation of their social life. And in societies where whole classes of men are excluded from any significant part in the regulation of public affairs, it is proper to concentrate upon awakening and fostering in those particular classes a consciousness of their place in society, of their material and intellectual poverty, their lack of rights, their exclusion from power. But as the knowledge of society increases, as the position of classes changes, so must sociological thought follow these movements, revise its initial propositions, and conceive new empirical tests. It is here that Marx and the Marxists diverge. To take only one example: I do not think that there has been a single important contribution to the study of modern social classes from the side of orthodox Marxism. Yet, Marx's influence has been immense, and two recent works – one theoretical, S. Ossowski's *Class Structure in the Social Consciousness*, the other historical, E. P. Thompson's *The Making of the English Working Class* – show how fruitful that influence may be, so long as one is not an orthodox Marxist.

In this paper I have been concerned with a reassessment of Marx's sociology in relation to his 'Marxism.' I have not said anything, except by implication, about the validity or usefulness of his theories at the present day. Does Marx's thought belong simply to the history of sociology, or does some part of it survive today as a significant element in the general body of accepted sociological theory? I believe that the latter is true – that Marx's 'conflict' model, and especially the theory of classes, his account of ideologies, his theory of revolution, must find a place in sociological theory – but also that both are important. For sociology is not quite like a natural science where theory advances in linear fashion and the history of the subject is simply its history, inessential to the comprehension of theoretical principles; it is also somewhat like philosophy, in which perennial problems are examined from different standpoints, and where knowledge of these diverse approaches and their successive appearances constitutes the theoretical grasp of the subject. In this sense I do not think that we shall ever be quite finished with the re-evaluation of Karl Marx.

NOTES AND REFERENCES

1. I have examined some of these early contributions more fully in an article on Marxist sociology which is to appear in the *International Encyclopedia of the Social Sciences* (New York, 1966 onwards).

2. Ralf Dahrendorf, 'Out of Utopia: Toward a Reorientation of Sociological Analysis,' *American Journal of Sociology*, vol. LXIV, No. 2 (1958).

3. Isaiah Berlin, *Karl Marx*, 3rd edition (London, 1963), p. 124.

4. E. J. Hobsbawm, 'Introduction' to Karl Marx, *Pre-capitalist Economic Formations* (New York, 1965).

5. In the manuscript dating from 1857–1858, which was an early draft of *Capital* and which was first published in Moscow (1939–1941) under the title *Grundrisse der Kritik der politischen Ökonomie (Rohentwurf)*.

6. Karl Renner's study of law in *The Institutions of Private Law and Their Social Functions* (London, 1949) is a notable exception.

7. Maximilien Rubel, *Karl Marx: Essai de biographie intellectuelle* (Paris, 1957).

8. The proposed *Deutsch-Französische Jahrbücher* of which one double issue was published in 1844.

9. *Documents of the First International*, vol. I: *1864–1866*, vol. II: *1866–1868* (Moscow, 1964).

10. Marcuse, in *Reason and Revolution* (New York, 1941), presents the case for Marx's 'critical philosophy' and against Comte's sociological positivism in these terms; and more recently Sartre, in his *Question de Méthode* (Paris, 1960), has argued in a similar fashion.

nified just this: the conviction that the 'proletarian revolution' was a *historical necessity*. If then we are obliged to note that the universal aims of the Marxist school and the actual tendencies of the empirical workers' movement have become discontinuous, we shall have to characterize Marxism and the 'ideology' of that movement during a relatively brief historical phase which now appears to be closed. The phase itself was linked to the climax of the 'bourgeois revolution' in those European countries where the labor movement stood in the forefront of the political struggle for democracy, at the same time that it groped for a socialist theory of the coming post-bourgeois order. Historically Marxism fulfilled itself when it brought about the upheaval of 1917–1918 in Central and Eastern Europe. Its subsequent evolution into the ideology of the world Communist movement, for all the latter's evident political significance, has added little to its theoretical content. Moreover as far as Soviet Marxism and its various derivations are concerned, the original 'union of theory and practice' has now fallen apart.

This approach to the subject is not arbitrary but follows from the logic of the original Marxian conception of the *practical* function of *theory*. It was not part of Marx's intention to found yet another political movement or another 'school of thought.' Rather his prime purpose as a socialist was to articulate the practical requirements of the labor movement in its struggle for emancipation. His theoretical work was intended as a 'guide to action.' If it has ceased to serve as such, one may only conclude that the actual course of events had diverged from the theoretical model which Marx had extrapolated from the political struggles of the nineteenth century. In fact it is today generally agreed among Western socialists that the model is inappropriate to the post-bourgeois industrial society in which we live, while its relevance to the belated revolutions in backward pre-industrial societies is purchased at the cost of growing divergence between the utopian aims and the actual practices of the Communist movement. From a different viewpoint the situation may be summed up by saying that while the bourgeois revolution is over in the West, the proletarian revolution has turned out to be an impossibility: at any rate in the form in which Marx conceived it in the last century, for the notion of such a revolution giving rise to a classless society has now acquired a distinctly utopian ring. Conversely the association of socialism with some form of technocracy – understood as the key role of a new social stratum in part drawn from the industrial working class which continues to occupy a subordinate function – has turned out to be much closer than the Marxist school had expected. In short, the 'union of theory and practice' has dissolved because the working class has not in fact performed the historic role assigned to it in

Marx's theory and because the gradual socialization of the economic sphere in advanced industrial society has become parallel with the emergence of a new type of social stratification. On both counts, the 'revisionist' interpretation of Marxism – originally a response to the cleavage between the doctrine and the actual practice of a reformist labor movement – has resulted in the evolution of a distinctively 'post-Marxian' form of socialist theorizing while the full doctrinal content of the original systematization is only retained, in a debased and caricatured form, in the so-called 'world view' of Marxism-Leninism: itself the ideology of a totalitarian state-party which has long cut its connections with the democratic labor movement. While the Leninist variant continues to have operational value for the Communist movement – notably in societies where that movement has taken over the traditional functions of the bourgeois revolution – the classical Marxian position has been undercut by the development of Western society. In this sense, Marxism (like liberalism) has become 'historical.' Marx's current academic status as a major thinker in the familiar succession from Hegel (or indeed from Descartes-Hobbes-Spinoza) is simply another manifestation of this state of affairs.[1]

## 2

While the interrelation of theory and practice is crucial for the evaluation of Marx – far more so than for Comte who never specified an historical agent for the transition to the 'positive stage' – it does not by itself supply a criterion for judging the permanent value of Marx's theorizing in the domains of philosophy, history, sociology or economics. In principle there is no reason why his theoretical discoveries should not survive the termination of the attempt to construct a 'world view' which would at the same time serve as the instrument of a revolutionary movement. This consideration is reinforced by the further thought that the systematization was after all undertaken by others – principally by Engels, Kautsky, Plekhanov and Lenin – and that Marx cannot be held responsible for their departures from his original purpose, which was primarily critical. While this is true, the history of Marxism as an intellectual and political phenomenon is itself a topic of major importance, irrespective of Marx's personal intentions. Moreover it is arguable that both the 'orthodox' codification undertaken by Engels and the various subsequent 'revisions' have their source in Marx's own ambiguities as a thinker.

As far as Engels is concerned, the prime difficulty arises paradoxically from his life-long association with Marx. This, combined with his editorial and exegetical labors after Marx's death, conferred a privileged status upon his own writings even where his private interests diverged from those of Marx, e.g. in his increasing absorption in problems peculiar to the natural sciences. While Engels was scrupulous in emphasizing his secondary role in the evolution of their common viewpoint,[2] he allowed it to be understood that the 'materialist' metaphysics developed in such writings as the *Anti-Dühring* was in some sense the philosophical counterpart of Marx's own investigations into history and economics. Indeed his very modesty was a factor in causing his quasi-philosophical writings to be accepted as the joint legacy of Marx and himself. The long-run consequences were all the more serious in that Engels, unlike Marx, lacked proper training in philosophy and had no secure hold upon any part of the philosophical tradition, except for the Hegelian system, of which he virtually remained a life-long prisoner. The 'dialectical' materialism, or monism, advanced in the *Anti-Dühring* and in the essays on natural philosophy published in 1925 under the title *Dialectics of Nature*, has only the remotest connection with Marx's own viewpoint, though it is a biographical fact of some importance that Marx raised no objection to Engels' exposition of the theme in the *Anti-Dühring*. The reasons for this seeming indifference must remain a matter for conjecture. What cannot be doubted is that it was Engels who was responsible for the subsequent interpretation of 'Marxism' as a unified system of thought destined to take the place of Hegelianism and indeed of classical German philosophy in general. That it did so only for German Social-Democracy, and only for one generation, is likewise an historical factum. The subsequent emergence of Soviet Marxism was mediated by Plekhanov and Lenin and differs in some respects from Engels' version (e.g. in the injection of even larger doses of Hegelianism) notably in the introduction by Lenin of a species of voluntarism which had more in common with Bergson and Nietzsche than with Engels' own rather deterministic manner of treating historical topics. In this sense Leninism has to be regarded as a 'revision' of the orthodox Marxism of Engels, Plekhanov and Kautsky.

The whole development has obvious political, as well as intellectual, significance. I have dealt with it at some length elsewhere and must here confine myself to the observation that Soviet Marxism is to be understood as a monistic system *sui generis*, rooted in Engels' interpretation of Marx but likewise linked to the pre-Marxian traditions of the Russian revolutionary intelligentsia. Unlike 'orthodox' Marxism, which in Central Europe functioned for at least one generation as the 'integrative ideology' of a genuine workers' movement, Soviet Marxism was a pure intelligentsia creation, wholly divorced from the concerns of

296

the working class. Its unconscious role has been to equip the Soviet intelligentsia (notably the technical intelligentsia) with a cohesive world view adequate to its task in promoting the industrialization and modernization of a backward country. Of the subsequent dissemination and vulgarization of this ideology in China and elsewhere, it is unnecessary to speak.[3]

In the light of what was said above about the transformation of Marxism from a revolutionary critique of bourgeois society into the systematic ideology of a non-revolutionary, or post-revolutionary, labor movement in Western Europe and elsewhere, this contrasting, though parallel, development in the Soviet orbit presents itself as additional confirmation of our thesis. The latter assigns to Marxism a particular historical status not dissimilar from that of liberalism: another universal creed which has evolved from the philosophical assumptions and hypotheses of the eighteenth-century Enlightenment. The universalist content is, however, differently distributed. Liberalism was from the start markedly reluctant to disclose its social origins and sympathies whereas Marxism came into being as the self-proclaimed doctrine of a revolutionary class movement. The humanist approach was retained in both cases, but whereas liberal philosophy in principle denies any logical relation between the social origin of a doctrine and its ethico-political content, Marxism approached the problem by designating the proletariat as the 'universal' class and itself as the theoretical expression of the latter's struggle for emancipation: conceived as synonymous with mankind's effort to raise itself to a higher level. Hence although for contemporary liberalism the unsolved problem resides in the unacknowledged social content of its supposedly universal doctrine, the difficulty for Marxism arises from the failure of the proletariat to fulfill the role assigned to it in the original 'critical theory' of 1843–1848 as formulated in Marx's early writings and in the *Communist Manifesto*. Since liberalism cannot shake off the death-grip of 'classical,' i.e. bourgeois, economics – for which the market economy remains the center of reference – Marxism (at any rate in its Communist form) is confronted with the awkward dissonance between its universal aims and the actual record of the class upon whose political maturity the promised deliverance from exploitation and alienation depends. There is the further difference that the Marxian 'wager' on the proletariat represents an 'existential' option (at any rate for intellectuals stemming from another class), whereas liberalism – at least in principle – claims to be in tune with the commonsense outlook of educated 'public opinion.' This divergence leads back to a consideration of the philosophical issues inherent in the original codification of 'orthodox Marxism.'

297

Marx's early theoretical standpoint, as set out in the *Holy Family* (1845) and the *German Ideology* (1845–1846), was a development of French eighteenth-century materialism, minus its Cartesian physics and the related epistemological problem in which he took no interest. The basic orientation of this materialism was practical, and its application to social life led in the direction of socialism, once it was admitted that between man and his environment there was an interaction which left room for a conscious effort to remodel his existence. As Marx put it in the *Holy Family*, 'If man is shaped by his surroundings, his surroundings must be made human. If man is social by nature he will develop his true nature only in society . . .'[4] Materialism or naturalism (the terms are employed interchangeably by Marx) is the foundation of communism. This conclusion follows *necessarily*, once it is grasped that the material conditions of human existence can and must be altered if man is to reach his full stature. Materialism is revolutionary because when applied to society it discloses what the idealist hypostatization of 'spirit' obscures: that man's history is a constant struggle with his material environment, a struggle in which man's 'nature' is formed and reformed. The historicity of human nature, which is a necessary consequence of this anthropological naturalism, raises the question as to what criterion we possess for judging the activities of men in their effort to subdue the nonhuman environment: an effort mediated by social intercourse with other men, since it is only in and through society that men become conscious of themselves.[5]

The answer Marx gives is open to criticism on the grounds of circularity, since it amounts to saying that man's 'nature' is constituted by his *Praxis*, i.e., his capacity for constituting a man-made world around him. However this may be, it is plain that for Marx the only 'nature' that enters into consideration is man's own plus his surroundings which he transforms by his 'practical activity.' The external world, as it exists in and for itself, is irrelevant to a materialism that approaches history with a view toward establishing what men have made of themselves. It is doubly irrelevant because, on the Marxian assumption, the world is never simply 'given' to consciousness, any more than man himself is the passive receptacle of sense impressions. An external environment, true knowledge of which is possible, is a fantasy in abstraction from man's active role in molding the object of perception. The only world we know is the one we have constituted – that which appears in our experience. The 'subjective' nature of this experience is checked by its social character which in turn is rooted in the permanent constituents of man as a 'species being' (*Gattungswesen*) who 'comes to himself' in society. There is in the strict sense, no epistemological problem for Marx. The dialectics of perception and natural environment cannot, in his view, be compressed into a formula, for 'reason' is itself historical and its interaction with nature is just what appears in history. Man has before him a 'historical nature,' and his own 'natural history' culminates in his conscious attempt to reshape the world of which he forms a part.

The notion that this anthropological naturalism is anchored in a general theory of the universe finds no support in Marx's own writings. There is no logical link between Marx's conception and the 'dialectical materialism' of Engels and Plekhanov, any more than there is a necessary connection between Marx's pragmatic view of conscious mental activity as an aspect of *Praxis* and the epistemological realism of Lenin. Indeed in the latter case there is positive incongruity. Perception as a mirror-image of an external reality which acts upon the mind through physical stimuli has no place in Marx's theory of consciousness. The copy theory of perception set out in *Materialism and Empiriocriticism* (apart from being inadequate and self-contradictory in the way Lenin presents it) is incompatible with the Marxian standpoint. Its formulation arose from the accidental problem of working out a new theoretical basis for the natural sciences – a problem in which Marx had taken no interest. It also involved a divergence from Engels' approach, since materialism for Engels was not the same as epistemological realism. In Engels' quasi-Hegelian discussion of this theme, 'matter' conserved some of the attributes of a primary substance which was somehow involved in the constitution of the universe. The difference between idealism and materialism was seen by Engels to lie in the former's claim to the ontological pre-eminence of mind or spirit whereas natural science was supposed by him to have established the materiality of the world in an absolute or ultimate sense. The resulting medley of metaphysical materialism and Hegelian dialectics (first described as 'dialectical materialism' by Plekhanov) was conserved by Lenin, but his own theory of cognition – which was what mattered to him – was not strictly speaking dependent on it. Matter as an absolute substance, or constitutive element of the universe, is not required for a doctrine which merely postulates that the mind is able to arrive at universally true conclusions about the external world given to the senses. Lenin's standpoint in fact is compatible with any approach which retains the ontological priority of the external world (however constituted) over the reflecting mind. Belief in the existence of an objective reality is not peculiar to materialists. It is, moreover, only very tenuously connected with the doctrine of nature's ontological primacy over spirit which Lenin had inherited from Engels and which was important to him as a defense against 'fideism.'

The whole confusion becomes comprehensible only when it is borne in mind that the transformation of Marx's own naturalism into a metaphysical materialism was a practical necessity for Engels and his followers without being a logical one. It was required to turn 'Marxism' into a coherent *Weltanschauung*, first for the German labor movement and later for the Soviet intelligentsia. As such it has continued to function, notwithstanding its philosophical inadequacies, but it has also suffered the fate of other systematizations undertaken for non-scientific reasons. At the same time it has paradoxically served to weaken the appeal of Marx's own historical materialism, since the latter was supposedly derived from a metaphysical doctrine of the universe – or an indefensible theory of cognitive perception – with which in reality it had no connection whatever.

4

To grasp the full extent of this intellectual disaster it is necessary to see what Marx intended when he applied his realistic mode of thought to the understanding of history. The doctrine sketched out in his early writings (notably in the first section of the *German Ideology*) and subsequently given a succinct formulation in the well-known Preface to the 1859 *Critique of Political Economy* was 'materialist' in that it broke with the traditional 'idealist' procedure wherein ordinary material history was treated as the unfolding of principles laid up in the speculative heavens. The primary datum for Marx was the 'real life-process' in which men are engaged, the 'production and reproduction of material existence,' as he put it on some occasions. In this context, the so-called higher cultural activities appeared as the 'ideological reflex' of the primary process whereby men organize their relationship to nature and to each other. Whatever may be said in criticism of this approach, it is quite independent of any metaphysical assumptions about the ontological priority of an absolute substance called 'matter,' though for evident psychological reasons it was easy to slide from 'historical' to 'philosophical' materialism. Even so, the grounding of the former in the latter does not necessarily entail the further step of suggesting that human history is set in motion and kept going by a 'dialectical' process of contradiction within the 'material basis.' Such a conclusion follows neither from the materialist principle nor from the quasi-Hegelian picture

Marx drew in the 1859 Preface where he referred briefly to the succession of stages from 'Asiatic society,' via Antiquity and the Middle Ages, to the modern (European) epoch. Marx's own historical research (notably in the *Grundrisse* of 1857–1858) stressed the radical discontinuity of these 'historical formations.' It is by no means the case that the emergence of European feudalism from the wreck of ancient society was treated by him as a matter of logical necessity. Even in relation to the rise of capitalism he was careful to specify the unique historical preconditions which made possible the 'unfolding' of the new mode of production. The notion of a dialectical 'law' linking primitive communism via slavery, feudalism and capitalism with the mature communism of the future was once more the contribution of Engels who in this as in other matters bore witness to the unshakable hold of Hegel's philosophy upon his own cast of mind.

The reverse side of this medal is the ambiguous relationship of Marx and Engels to Comte and of Marxism to Positivism. The point has occasionally been made[6] that in dealing with the rise of the 'historical school' in nineteenth-century Europe, one has to go back to the intermingling of Hegelian and Comtean strands in the 1830s – mediated in some cases by writers who had actually studied under both Comte and Hegel.[7] It is also arguable that Marx may have been more deeply influenced by Comte than he was himself aware since some of Saint-Simon's later writings are now known to have been in part drafted by his then secretary. However this may be, it is undeniable that the general effect of Engels' popularization of Marx ran parallel to the more direct influence of Positivism properly so called. With only a slight exaggeration it may be said that 'Marxism' (as interpreted by Engels) eventually came to do for Central and Eastern Europe what Positivism had done for the West. It acquainted the public with a manner of viewing the world which was 'materialist' and 'scientific,' in the precise sense which these terms possessed for writers who believed in extending to history and society the methods of natural sciences. While Marx had taken some tentative steps in this direction, it was Engels who committed German Socialism wholeheartedly to the new viewpoint.

At first sight it is not apparent why a Hegelian training in philosophy should predispose anyone in favour of the Comtean approach, which in some respects stands at the opposite pole. Moreover Marx owed more to the French materialists than did Engels; consequently there appears to be a certain paradox in the notion that the fusion of Hegelian and Comtean modes of thought was mediated by Engels. It must, however, be borne in mind that the *Philosophie Positive* had two aspects. In so far as it stressed the purely empirical character of science and dispensed

301

with metaphysical explanations, it belonged to the tradition of the Enlightenment in its specifically French 'materialist' form (which was the only one Marx took seriously). Where it aimed at a universal history of mankind, its influence ran parallel to that of Hegelianism. Now the peculiarity of Marx's 'historical materialism' is that it combines universalism and empiricism. For Marx (e.g. in the Preface to the 1859 work) the historical process has an internal logic, but investigation into the actual sequence of socioeconomic formations is a matter for empirical research. The link between the two levels of generality is to be found in the interaction between technology ('forces of production') and society ('relations of production'). This interaction, however, is not uniform, i.e. not of such a kind that the historical outcome can be predicted in each case with reference to a general law abstracted from the principle of interaction. Unlike Hegel, Marx does not treat history as the unfolding of a metaphysical substance and unlike Comte, he does not claim to be in possession of an operational key which will unlock every door. Even the statement that 'mankind always sets for itself only such tasks as it can solve'[8] is simply an extrapolation from the empirically observable circumstance that in every sphere of life (including that of art) problems and solutions have a way of emerging jointly. A formulation of this kind is at once too general and too flexible to be termed a 'law.' It is a working hypothesis to be confirmed or refuted by historical experience. Similarly the statement that socialism grows 'necessarily' out of capitalism is simply a way of saying that economic conflict poses an institutional problem to which socialism supplies the only rational answer. Whether one accepts or rejects this, Marx is not here laying down a 'law,' let alone a universal law. On his general assumptions about history, the failure to solve this particular problem (or any other) remained an open possibility. In such a case there would doubtless be regress, perhaps even a catastrophe. The 'relentless onward march of civilization' is a Comtean, not a Marxian, postulate. If the second generation of his followers understood Marx to have expounded a kind of universal optimism, they thoroughly misunderstood the meaning and temper of his message.[9]

In relation to bourgeois society the Marxian approach may be summarized by saying that this formation contains within itself the germs of a higher form of social organization. Whether these latent possibilities are utilized, depends upon historical circumstances which have to be investigated in their concreteness. One cannot deduce from a general law of social evolution the alleged necessity for one type of society to give birth to a more developed one – otherwise it would be incomprehensible why classical Antiquity regressed and made room for a primitive type of feudalism instead of evolving to a higher level. In fact Marx held that the collapse had been brought about by the institution of slavery, which was both the basis of that particular civilization and the organic limit of its further development.[10] In principle the same might happen again. If Marx makes the assumption that the industrial working class is the potential bearer of a higher form of social organization, he is saying no more than that no other class appears capable of transcending the *status quo*. What might be called the existential commitment of Marxism to the labor movement follows from this assumption. Like every commitment it carries with it the implied possibility of failure. Were it otherwise, there would be no sense in speaking of 'tasks' confronting the movement: it would be enough to lay down a 'law' of evolution in the Comtean or Spencerian manner. Belief in an evolutionary 'law' determining the procession of historical stages was not only the mark of 'orthodox' Marxism as formulated by Kautsky and Plekhanov under the influence of Spencer and other evolutionists but was also the mark of Engels whose synthesis of Hegelian and Comtean modes of thought made possible this fateful misunderstanding.

5

In justice to all concerned it has to be borne in mind that Marxism and Positivism did have in common their descent from the Saint-Simonian school. It was in the latter that the notion of history as a developmental process subject to 'invariable laws' was first adumbrated in confused fashion, later to be given a more adequate formulation by Comte and Marx. The justification for treating these two very disproportionately gifted thinkers under the same heading arises from the evident circumstance that their contemporaries were affected by them in roughly similar ways. In general it might be said that Marx did for the Germans – notably for German sociology and the 'historical school' (Schmoller, Weber, Sombart, Troeltsch and so on) – what Comte had earlier done for Durkheim and his school in France. And this assimilation of Comtean and Marxian modes of thought into the canon of academic sociology was evidently rendered possible by their commitment to the idea of history as the special mode of societal evolution. In saying this, one is simply stating the obvious, although on occasion this does no harm. It was Saint-Simon who had first declared that the proper business of social science is the discovery of laws of development governing the course of human history. To say that Marx, no less than Comte, remained true to this perspective is simply to say that he remained faithful to his intellectual origins (which in this case antedated the

303

Hegelianism of his student days since we know that he had come across Saint-Simonism while still a schoolboy). That human history forms a whole – in Hegelian terms a 'concrete totality' – was a certainty he never surrendered. There is the same attachment to the original vision in his oft-repeated statement that knowledge of the 'laws' underlying historical development will enable society to lessen the 'birthpangs' inseparable from the growth of a new social formation. Insight into the regularities of history is, by a seeming paradox, seen as a means of controlling the future course of development.

In all these respects Comte and Marx appeared to be saying the same thing, and it was this similarity which led so many Positivists to describe themselves as Marxists: notably in France, where indeed this identification became a factor in the evolution of the Socialist movement. Yet the differences are as important as the similarities. Comte's sociology dispensed with the notion of class conflict which for Marx was the central motor of historical progress. The Comtean view of society not only posited the latter as the basic reality – over against the state on the one hand, and the individual on the other – but also elevated it to a plane where the 'science of society' was seen to consist in the elucidation of an harmonious interdependence of all the parts. From the Marxian viewpoint this is sheer fantasy, a willful disregard of the reality of conflict whereby alone social progress takes place. In the subsequent evolution of the two systems this difference in approach translated itself *inter alia* into the conflicting doctrines of Russian Populism (heavily impregnated by Comte) and its Marxist rival. There is a sense in which the defeat of *Narodnichestvo* represented the victory of the Marxian over the Comtean school. The Russian Marxists were aware of this situation, and down to Lenin's polemics in the 1890s the need to differentiate themselves from the Positivist belief in the organic unity of society played an important role in the development of their thinking.[11]

The last-mentioned consideration, however, also serves to define the historical context within which the Marxian doctrine could expect to play a role in the formation of a revolutionary movement. When in the 1880s some former Populists turned from *Narodnichestvo* to Marxism, they did so because they found in Marx a convincing statement of the thesis that the economic process would 'slowly but unavoidably undermine the old regime,' so that the Russian proletariat, 'in an historical development proceeding just as inexorably as the development of capitalism itself,' would thereby be enabled to 'deal the deathblow to Russian absolutism.'[12] In other words, what they found was *a theory of the bourgeois revolution*. The latter being a 'necessary' process – in the sense that the political 'superstructure' was bound, sooner or later, to be transformed by the autonomous evolution of the socioeconomic realm – it was possible to interpret Marx's doctrine in a determinist sense. In *Das Kapital* Marx had done so himself, to the extent that he had treated the 'unfolding' of the new mode of production – once it had come into being – as a process independent of the conscious desires and illusions of its individual 'agents.' Hence the link between the 'materialist conception of history' and the notion of 'ideology' as 'false consciousness.' What his contemporaries (and the first generation of his followers) failed to see was that the entire construction was strictly appropriate only to the evolution of bourgeois society, which in Western Europe was coming to an end, while in Russia the 'bourgeois revolution' was about to be carried through by a movement hostile to the traditional aims of the middle class. Marxism as a theory of the bourgeois revolution was destined to celebrate its triumph on Russian soil at the very moment when it began to falter in the post-bourgeois environment of Western industrial society. This discontinuity was later to be mirrored in the cleavage between the determinist character of 'orthodox Marxism' and the voluntarist strain which came to the fore in the theory and practice of the Communist movement. The latter, faced with the evident exhaustion of the revolutionary impulse which had accompanied the great economic gearshift of the nineteenth century, was increasingly obliged to seek fresh sources of popular spontaneity in areas of the world not yet subjected to industrialism (whether capitalist or socialist). At the theoretical level, the uncomprehended necessity to find a substitute for the revolutionary proletariat of early capitalism – an aspect of the bourgeois revolution, for it is only the latter that rouses the working class to political consciousness – found its expression in the doctrine of the vanguard: an elite which substitutes itself for the class it is supposed to represent. This development signifies the dissolution of the Marxian 'union of theory and practice': a union originally built upon the faith that the working class *as such* can and will emancipate itself, and the whole of mankind, from political and economic bondage.

NOTES AND REFERENCES

1. Cf. *inter alia* the treatment of the subject in *Karl Marx – Selected Writings in Sociology and Social Philosophy*, ed. by T. B. Bottomore and M. Rubel (London, 1956), and the recent spate of editions of Marx's early writings. Historically, the interpretation of Marxism as the theory of a revolutionary movement which has now come to an end, goes back to the writings of Karl Korsch; cf. in particular his *Karl Marx* (London-New York, 1963).

# SELECTED BIBLIOGRAPHY OF SECONDARY SOURCES ON MARXISM AND SOCIOLOGY

NOTE: A date in parentheses succeeding a work gives the date of its original publication, or, in the case of unpublished or belatedly published works, the date of the original manuscript.

Aaronovitch, Sam
    1964  'Sociology, Class and Power.' *Marxism Today.* 8 (June): 170–178.

Althusser, Louis
    1970  *For Marx.* New York: Vintage Books.
    1971  *Lenin and Philosophy.* New York: Monthly Review Press.
    1972  *Politics and History.* London: NLB.

Althusser, Louis and Etienne Balibar
    1970  *Reading 'Capital'.* New York: Pantheon Books.

Arthur, C. J. (ed. and intro.)
    1970  Marx and Engels: *The German Ideology.* New York: International Publishers.

Avineri, Schlomo
    1971  *The Social and Political Thought of Karl Marx.* Cambridge: Cambridge University Press.
    (ed. and intro.)
    1968  *Karl Marx: On Colonialism and Modernization.* New York: Doubleday and Company.
    (ed. and intro.)
    1972  *Marx's Socialism.* New York: Lieber-Atherton.

Berger, Peter (ed.)
    1969  *Marxism and Sociology: Views from Eastern Europe.* New York: Appleton-Century-Crofts.

Berlin, Isaiah
    1963  *Karl Marx: His Life and Environment.* London: Oxford University Press.

Bernstein, Samuel
    1948  'Saint Simon's Philosophy of History.' Pp. 82–96 in Samuel Bernstein (ed.), *A Centenary of Marxism.* New York: Science and Society.

Blackburn, Robin (ed.)
 1973  *Ideology in Social Science: Readings in Critical Social Theory.*
        New York: Vintage Books.
Bloch, Ernest
 1971  *On Karl Marx.* New York: Herder & Herder.
Bloom, Solomon F.
 1968  *A Liberal in Two Worlds: The Essays of Solomon F. Bloom.*
        Washington: Public Affairs Press.
Blum, Alan F.
 1973  'Reading Marx.' *Sociological Inquiry.* 43: 23–34.
Blumenberg, Werner
 1972  *Karl Marx.* London: NLB.
Bober, M. M.
 1962  *Karl Marx's Interpretation of History.* New York: W.W.
        Norton & Company (1927).
Bottomore, Tom B. (ed. and intro.)
 1964  Karl Marx: *Early Writing.* New York: McGraw-Hill Book
        Company.
 1973  *Karl Marx.* Englewood Cliffs, N.J.: Prentice-Hall.
 1975  *Marxist Sociology.* New York: Holmes & Meier Publishers.
        (ed.)
 1975  *Crisis and Contention in Sociology.* London: Sage Publi-
        cations, Ltd.
Bottomore, Tom B. and Maximilien Rubel (eds. and intro.)
 1964  Karl Marx: *Selected Writing in Sociology and Social Philo-
        sophy.* New York: McGraw-Hill Book Company (1956).
Boudin, Louis
 1907  *The Theoretical System of Karl Marx.* Chicago: Charles H.
        Kerr.
Brown, Bruce
 1966  'The French Revolution and the Rise of Social Theory.' *Sci-
        ence and Society.* 30 (Fall): 385–432.
Bukharin, Nikolai I.
 1969  *Historical Materialism: A System of Sociology.* Ann Arbor:
        University of Michigan Press (1921).
Carver, Terrell
 1976  *Karl Marx: Texts on Method.* New York: Harper & Row.
 1976  'Marx – and Hegel's "Logic".' *Political Studies.* 24 (March):
        57–68.
Ceppa, Leonardo
 1976  'Korsch's Marxism.' *Telos.* 26 (Winter): 94–119.

Cohen, Gerald A.
  1968  'Bourgeois and Proletarians.' *Journal of the History of Ideas.*
        29: 211–230.

Cole, G. D. H.
  1964  *The Meaning of Marxism.* Ann Arbor: University of Michigan
        Press (1948).

Cole, Robert
  1966  'Structural-Functional Theory, the Dialectic and Social
        Change.' *Sociological Quarterly.* 7 (Winter): 39–58.

Colletti, Lucio
  1973  *Marxism and Hegel.* London: NLB.
  1972  *From Rousseau to Lenin: Studies in Ideology and Society.*
        London: NLB.

Cornforth, Maurice
  1953  *Dialectical Materialism:* vol. I – *Historical and the Dialectical
        Method.* New York: International Publishers.
  1954  *Dialectical Materialism:* vol. II – *Historical Materialism.* New
        York: International Publishers.
  1955  *Dialectical Materialism:* vol. III – *The Theory of Knowledge.*
        New York: International Publishers.
  1962  'Progress as a Scientific Category.' *Marxism Today.* 6:
        205–210.
  1965  'Some Questions About Laws of Dialectics.' *Marxism Today.*
        9: 330–337.

Cornu, Auguste
  1957  *The Origins of Marxian Thought.* Springfield: Charles C.
        Thomas, Publishers.

Coser, Lewis A.
  1970  'Karl Marx and Contemporary Sociology.' pp. 137–151 in
        Lewis Coser, *Continuities in the Study of Social Conflict.* New
        York: Free Press.

Dahrendorf, Ralf
  1958  'Out of Utopia: Toward a Reorientation of Sociological
        Analysis.' *American Journal of Sociology.* 64 (September):
        115–127.
  1959  *Class and Class Conflict in Industrial Society.* Stanford: Stan-
        ford University Press.

Daniels, Robert V.
  1960  'Fate and Will in the Marxian Philosophy of History.' *Journal
        of the History of Ideas.* 21: 538–552.

della Volpe, Galvano
1974    *Rousseau et Marx et autres essais de critique materialiste.*
        Paris: Maspero.
Deutscher, Isaac
1971    *Ironies of History.* Berkeley: Ramparts Press.
Dobb, Maurice
1947    *Studies in the Development of Capitalism.* New York: International Publishers.
1951    'Historical Materialism and the Role of the Economic Factor.' *History.* 36: 1–11.
1966    'Marx on Pre-Capitalist Economic Formations.' *Science and Society.* 30 (Summer): 319–325.
1968    'Classical Political Economy and Marx.' Pp. 49–67 in David Horowitz, ed. *Marx and Modern Economics.* New York: Monthly Review Press.
Doering, J. A. (ed.)
1962    *Marx vs. Russia.* New York: Frederick Ungar.
Dos Santos, Theotonio
1970    'The Concept of Social Classes.' *Science and Society.* 34, 2 (Summer): 166–193.
Draper, Hal
1970    'Marx and the Dictatorship of the Proletariat.' Pp. 285–304 in Michael Curtis (ed.), *Marxism.* New York: Atherton Press.
(ed. and intro.)
1971    Karl Marx and Frederick Engels. *Writings on the Paris Commune.* New York: Monthly Review Press.
Duggett, Michael
1975    'Marx on Peasants.' *Journal of Peasant Studies.* 2 (January): 159–182.
Dupré, Louis
1966    *The Philosophical Foundations of Marxism.* New York: Harcourt, Brace & World.
Durkheim, Émile
1958    *Socialism and Saint Simon.* Yellow Springs, Ohio: Antioch Press (1928).
Eaton, John
1963    *Political Economy.* New York: International Publishers.
Engels, Frederick
1940    *The Dialectics of Nature.* New York: International Publishers (1883).
1968    'Ludwig Feuerbauch and the End of the Classical German Philosophy.' Pp. 594–632 in Marx and Engels: *Selected*

*Works*. New York: International Publishers (1886).

1970 *Anti-Dühring: Herr Eugen Dühring's Revolution in Science.* New York: International Publishers (1878).

Fernbach, David
1969 'Avineri's View of Marx.' *New Left Review*. 56 (July-August): 62–68.

Fetscher, Iring
1967 'The Young and the Old Marx.' Pp. 19–39 in Nicholas Lobkowicz (ed.) *Marx and the Western World*. Notre Dame: University Press.
1971 *Marx and Marxism*. New York: Herder & Herder.

Feuer, Lewis S. (ed.)
1959 Marx and Engels: *Basic Writings on Politics and Philosophy.* Garden City: Anchor Books.

Feuerbach, Ludwig A.
1957 *The Essence of Christianity*. New York: Harper Torchbooks (1841).

Fine, Ben
1975 Marx's *Capital*. London: Macmillan Press.

Fischer, Ernest and Franz Marek
1970 *The Essential Marx*. New York: Herder & Herder.

Fleischer, Helmut
1973 *Marxism and History*. New York: Harper Torchbooks.

Frank, André Gunder
1969 'Functionalism and Dialectics.' Pp. 95–107 in André Gunder Frank, *Latin American: Underdevelopment or Revolution*. New York: Monthly Review Press.

Fraser, John
1977 'Louis Althusser on Science, Marxism and Politics.' *Science and Society*. 40 (Winter): 438–464.

Freedman, Robert (ed.)
1968 *Marxist Social Thought*. New York: Harcourt, Brace & World Inc.

Fromm, Erich
1961 *Marx's Concept of Man*. New York: Frederick Unger Publishing Company.

Garaudy, Roger
1967 *Karl Marx: The Evolution of His Thought*. New York: International Publishers.

Geras, Norman
1971 'Essence and Appearance: Aspects of Fetishism in Marx's *Capital*.' *New Left Review*. 65 (January-February): 69–85.

1972    'Louis Althusser – An Assessment.' *New Left Review*. 71
        (January–February): 57–86.

Gerratana, Valentino
1973    'Marx and Darwin.' *New Left Review*. 82 (November–
        December): 60–82.

Gerstein, Ira
1976    'Production, Circulation and Value.' *Economy and Society*. 5
        (August): 242–291.

Geymonat, Ludovico
1973    'Neopositivist Methodology and Dialectical Materialism.'
        *Science and Society*. 37 (Summer): 178–194.

Giddens, Anthony
1971    *Capitalism and Modern Social Theory*. Cambridge: Cam-
        bridge University Press.

Glezerman, G. and G. Kursanov
1969    *Historical Materialism:* Basic Problems. Moscow: Progress
        Publishers.

Glucksmann, André
1973    'The Althusserian Theater.' *New Left Review*. 72
        (March–April): 68–92.

Glucksmann, Miriam
1969    'Lucien Goldmann: Humanist or Marxist?' *New Left Review*.
        56 (July–August): 49–62.

Godelier, Maurice
1970    'System, Structure and Contradiction in *Das Capital*.' Pp.
        340–358 in Michael Lane (ed.) *Introduction to Scructuralism*.
        New York: Basic Books.
1972a   Rationality and Irrationality in Economics. New York:
        *Monthly Review Press*.
1972b   'The Thought of Marx and Engels in Today and Tomorrow's
        Research.' *International Journal of Sociology*. 2 (Summer–
        Fall): 133–177.

Goldmann, Lucien
1969    *The Human Sciences and Philosophy*. London: Jonathan
        Cape.

Gouldner, Alvin, W.
1970    *The Coming Crisis of Western Sociology*. New York: Basic
        Books.
1974    'Marxism and Social Theory.' *Theory and Society*. 1: 17–35.

Gramsci, Antonio
1957    *The Modern Prince and Other Writings*. New York: Inter-
        national Publishers.

1975    *Prison Notebooks*. New York: International Publishers.
Gurvich, Georges
1963    *La Vocation Actuelle de la sociologie* – Vol. II: *Antecedents et perspectives*. Paris: Presses Universitaires de France.
Habermas, Jurgen
1975    'Towards a Reconstruction of Historical Materialism.' *Theory and Society*. 2 (Fall): 287–300.
Harrison, Royden
1959    'E. S. Beesly and Karl Marx.' *International Review of Social History*. 4: 22–58; 208–238.
Hegel, George W. F.
1967    *The Phenomenology of Mind*. New York: Harper Torchbooks (1807).
Hempel, Carl G.
1965    *Aspects of Scientific Explanation*. New York: Free Press.
Henderson, Lawrence J.
1935    *Pareto's General Sociology: A Physiologist's Interpretation*. Cambridge: Harvard University Press.
Hepner, Benoit P.
        'History and the Future: The Vision of August Cieszkowski.' *Review of Politics*. 15: 328–349.
Hill, Christopher
1948    'The English Civil War Interpreted by Marx and Engels.' *Science and Society*. 12 (Winter): 130–156.
Hindess, Barry and Paul Q. Hirst
1975    *Pre-Capitalist Modes of Production*. London: Routledge & Kegan Paul.
Hirst, Paul Q.
1972    'Marx and Engels on Law, Crime, and Morality.' *Economy and Society*. 1 (February): 28–56.
Hobsbawn, Eric J.
1969    'Karl Marx's Contribution to Historiography.' Pp. 197–211 in International Social Science Council (ed.) *Marx and Contemporary Scientific Thought*. The Hague: Mouton.
        (ed. and Intro.)
1964    *Karl Marx: Pre-capitalist Economic Formations*. New York: International Publishers.
Hodges, Donald Clark
1959    'The Role of Classes in Historical Materialism.' *Science and Society*. 23: 16–26.
1961    'The "Intermediate classes" in Marxist Theory.' *Social Research*. 28 (Spring): 23–26.

1962 'The Dual Character of Marxian Social Science.' *Philosophy of Science*. 29 (October): 333–349.

1964 'The Unity of Marx's Thought.' *Science and Society*. 28 (Summer): 316–323.

1965 'Engels' Contribution to Marxism.' Pp. 297–310 in Ralph Miliband and John Saville (eds.) *The Socialist Register: 1965*. New York: Monthly Review Press.

1967 'The Method of *Capital*.' *Science and Society*. 31 (Fall): 505–514.

1973 'The Young Marx: A Reappraisal.' Pp. 19–35 in Schlomo Avineri (ed.) *Marx's Socialism*. New York: Lieber-Atherton.

Hodgson, Geoff
1974 'Marxian Epistemology and the Transformation Problem.' *Economy and Society*. 3 (November): 375–392.

Hoffman, David
1972 'Bukharin's Theory of Equilibrium.' *Telos*. 14 (Winter): 126–136.

Hook, Sidney
1933 *Towards the Understanding of Karl Marx*. New York: Humanities Press.

1940 *Reason, Social Myths and Democracy*. New York: Humanities Press.

1962 *From Hegel to Marx*. Ann Arbor: University of Michigan Press (1936).

Horton, John
1966 'Order and Conflict Theories of Social Problems as Competing Ideologies.' *American Journal of Sociology*. 71 (May): 701–713.

Howard, Dick
1972 *The Development of the Marxian Dialectic*. Chicago: University of Chicago Press.

Hunt, R. N. Carew
1950 *The Theory and Practice of Communism*. Baltimore: Pelican Books.

Hyppolite, Jean
1969 *Studies on Marx and Hegel*. New York: Harper Torchbooks.

Israel, Joachim
1971 *Alienation: From Marx to Modern Sociology*. Boston: Allyn and Bacon, Inc.

Jones, Gareth Stedman
1973 'Engels and the End of Classical German Philosophy.' *New Left Review*. 79: 17–36 (May–June).

Jordan, Z. A.
1967 *The Evolution of Dialectical Materialism.* New York: St Martin's Press.
(ed. and intro.)
1971 Karl Marx: *Economy, Class, and Social Revolution.* London: Michael Joseph.

Kalab, Milos
1969 'The Specificity of the Marxist Conception of Sociology.' Pp. 58–76 in Peter Berger (ed.) *Marxism and Sociology: Views from Eastern Europe.* New York: Appleton-Century-Crofts.

Kamenka, Eugene
1970a *The Philosophy of Ludwig Feuerbach.* London: Routledge & Kegan Paul.
1970b 'The Primitive Ethic of Karl Marx.' Pp. 118–127 in Michael Curtis (ed.) *Marxism.* New York: Atherton Press.

Kemp, Tom
1966 'Capitalism and Industrialization.' *Science and Society.* 30 (Summer): 288–309.

Kiernan, V. G.
1967 'Marx and India.' Pp. 159–189 in Ralph Miliband and John Saville (eds.) *The Socialist Register, 1967.* London: The Merlin Press.

Kojeve, Alexander
1969 *Introduction to the Reading of Hegel.* New York: Basic Books.

Kolakowski, Leszek
1968 *The Alienation of Reason: A History of Positivist Thought.* New York: Doubleday and Company.

Konstantinov, F. and V. Kelle
n.d. *Historical Materialism – The Marxist Sociology.* Moscow: Novosti Press Agency Publishing House.

Korsch, Karl
1938 *Karl Marx.* New York: Russell & Russell.
1970 *Marxism and Philosophy.* New York: Monthly Review Press (1923).
1972 *Three Essays on Marxism.* New York: Monthly Review Press.

Kosik, Karel
1967 'The Individual and History.' Pp. 177–191 in Nicholas Lobkowicz (ed.) *Marx and the Western World.* Notre Dame: University Press.

Krieger, Leonard
1953 'Marx and Engels as Historians.' *Journal of the History of Ideas.* 14: 381–403.

Labriola, Antonio
1966 *Essays on the Materialistic Conception of History.* New York: Monthly Review Press (1897).

Laffey, John
1965 'Auguste Comte: Prophet of Reconciliation and Reaction.' *Science and Society.* 29 (Winter): 44–65.

Lane, James
1976 'Marx's Conception of Truth and the Transition to the Sociological Dimension of Meaning.' *Sociological Analysis and Theory.* 6 (June): 109–166.

Lecourt, Dominique
1975 *Marxism and Epistemology.* London: NLB.

Lefebvre, Henri
1968a *Dialectical Materialism.* London: Jonathan Cape (1940).
1968b *The Sociology of Marx.* New York: Vintage Books.

Lenin, Vladimir I.
1967 *Materialism and Empirio-Criticism.* New York: International Publishers.
1971 *Selected Works.* New York: International Publishers.

Lepenies, Wolf
1974 'Lévi-Strauss and the Structuralist Reading of Marx.' *International Journal of Sociology* 4 (Spring): 15–81.

Levine, Donald
1976 *Marx Contra Engels.* New York: Halsted Press.

Levy, Hyman
1959 'Marx as Scientist.' *Centennial Review.* 3 (Fall): 407–422.

Lichtheim, George
1961 *Marxism: A Historical and Critical Study.* New York: Frederick A. Praeger.
1967a 'On the Interpretation of Marx's Thought.' Pp. 3–17 in Nicholas Lobkowicz (ed.) *Marx and the Western World.* Notre Dame: University Press.
1967b 'Oriental Despotism.' Pp. 62–93 in George Lichtheim, *The Concept of Ideology and Other Essays.* New York: Vintage Books.
1967c 'The Concept of Ideology.' Pp. 3–46 in George Lichtheim, *The Concept of Ideology and Other Essays.* New York: Vintage Books.
1969 *The Origins of Socialism.* New York: Praeger Publishers.
1970 *A Short History of Socialism.* New York: Praeger Publishers.
1971 *From Marx to Hegel.* New York: Herder & Herder.

Lichtman, Richard
  1975  'Marx's Theory of Ideology.' *Socialist Revolution.* 5 (April): 45–76.

Lifshitz, Mikhail
  1976  *The Philosophy of Art of Karl Marx.* London: Pluto Press (1933).

Lobkowicz, Nicholas
  1967  *Theory and Practice: The History of a Marxist Concept.* Notre Dame: University Press.
  (ed.)
  1967  *Marx and the Western World.* Notre Dame: University Press.
  1971  'Historical Laws.' *Studies in Soviet Thought.* 11 (December): 235–249.

Lockwood, David
  1964  'Social Integration and System Integration.' George K. Zollschan and Walter Hirsch (eds.) *Explorations in Social Change.* Boston: Houghton Mifflin.

Lopreato, Joseph
  1973  'Notes on the Work of Vilfredo Pareto.' *Social Science Quarterly.* 54 (December): 451–468.

Lopreato, Joseph and Letitia Alston
  1970  'Ideal Types and the Idealization Strategy.' *American Sociological Review.* 35 (February): 88–96.

Lopreato, Joseph and Lawrence Hazelrigg
  1972  *Class, Conflict, and Mobility.* San Francisco: Chandler Press.
Lubasz, Heinz
  1976  'Marx's Initial Problematic: The Problem of Poverty.' *Political Studies.* 24 (March): 24–42.

Ludz, Peter C.
  1975  'Marxism and Systems Theory.' *Social Research.* 42 (Winter): 661–674.

Lukács, George
  1966  'Technology and Social Relations.' *New Left Review.* 39: 27–34 (1925).
  1971  *History and Class Consciousness.* Cambridge: MIT Press (1923).
  1973  *The Young Hegel.* Cambridge, Mass.: MIT Press.
Luporini, Cesare
  1975  'Reality and Historicity: Economy and Dialectics in Marxism.' *Economy and Society.* 4 (May, August): 206–231; 283–308.

317

McGuire, David
    1973   *Marx's Paris Writings: An Analysis.* New York: Harper & Row.

Mandel, Ernest
    1971   *The Formation of the Economic Thought of Karl Marx.* New York: Monthly Review Press.

Mandic, Oleg
    1969   'The Marxist School of Sociology: What is Sociology?' Pp. 37–57 in Peter Berger (ed.) *Marxism and Sociology: Views from Eastern Europe.* New York: Appleton-Century-Crofts.

Manuel, Frank E.
    1963   *The New World of Henri St. Simon.* Notre Dame: University Press.
    1965   *The Prophets of Paris.* New York: Harper Torchbooks.

Manuel, Frank E. and Fritzie P. Manuel (eds.)
    1971   *French Utopias.* New York: Schocken Books.

Marcuse, Herbert
    1960   *Reason and Revolution: Hegel and the Rise of Social Theory.* Boston: Beacon Press (1944).
    1968   'Industrialization and Capitalism in the Work of Max Weber.' Pp. 201–226 in Herbert Marcuse, *Negation.* Boston: Beacon Press.

Markovic, Mihailo
    1969   'Marx and Critical Scientific Thought.' Pp. 155–167 in International Social Science Council. (ed.) *Marx and Contemporary Scientific Thought* The Hague: Mouton.

Martin, Neil A.
    1968   'Marxism, Nationalism, and Russia.' *Journal of the History of Ideas.* 29: 231–252.

Marx, Karl
    1963a  *The Poverty of Philosophy.* New York: International Publishers (1847).
    1963b  *Theories of Surplus Value: Vol. I.* Moscow: Progress Publishers (1862).
    1964   *The Economic and Philosophical Manuscripts of 1844.* New York: International Publishers (1844).
    1967a  *Capital: vol. I – A Critical Analysis of Capitalist Production.* New York: International Publishers (1867).
    1967b  *Capital: vol. III – The Process of Capitalist Production as a Whole.* New York: International Publishers (1862).
    1968a  *Theories of Surplus Value: vol. II.* Moscow: Progress Publishers.

1968b 'Wage Labour and Capital.' pp. 64–94 in Marx and Engels: *Selected Works*. New York: International Publishers (1847).

1968c 'Critique of the Gotha Program.' pp. 313–335 in Marx and Engels: *Selected Works*. New York: International Publishers.

1968d 'Wages, Price and Profit.' pp. 186–229 in Marx and Engels: *Selected Works*. New York: International Publishers.

1970a *Critique of Political Economy*. New York: International Publishers.

1970b *Critique of Hegel's 'Philosophy of Right.'* Cambridge: Cambridge University Press (1843).

1971 *The Grundrisse:* Selections. New York: Harper & Row (1858).

1973a *Grundrisse: Introduction to the Critique of Political Economy*. London: Pelican Books (1858).

1973b *Surveys from Exile* (*Political Writings:* vol. II). London: Pelican Books.

Marx, Karl and Frederick Engels

1955 *Selected Correspondence*. Moscow: Progress Publishers.

1970 *The German Ideology*. New York: International Publishers (1846).

1972 *On Colonialism: Articles from the 'New York Tribune' and Other Writings*. New York: International Publishers.

Márkus, György

1974 'Human Essence and History.' *International Journal of Sociology*. 4 (Spring): 82–125.

Mayer, Carl

1975 'Max Weber's Interpretation of Karl Marx.' *Social Research*. 42 (Winter): 701–719.

Mayo, H. B.

1970 'Marxism as a Philosophy of History.' pp. 197–206 in Michael Curtis (ed.) *Marxism*. New York: Atherton Books.

McGovern, Arthur F.

1970 'The Young Marx on the State.' *Science and Society*. 34 (Winter): 430–466.

McLellan, David

1969 *The Young Hegelians and Karl Marx*. New York: Praeger Publishers.

1970 *Marx Before Marxism*. New York: Harper Torchbooks.

1973 *Karl Marx: His Life and Thought*. New York: Harper & Row. (ed. and intro.)

1971 Karl Marx: *The Grundrisse*. New York: Harper & Row.

Meek, Ronald L.

1967 'The Scottish Contribution to Marxist Sociology.' pp. 34–50 in Ronald L. Meek, *Economics and Ideology and Other Essays*. London: Chapman & Hall.

Mehring, Franz
1962 *Karl Marx: The Story of His Life*. Ann Arbor: University of Michigan Press (1918).

Mengelberg, Kaethe
1961 'Lorenz von Stein and His Contribution to Historical Sociology.' *Journal of the History of Ideas*. 22: 267–274.

Merton, Robert K.
1968 *Social Theories and Social Structure*. New York: The Free Press.

Mészáros, István
1970 *Marx's Theory of Alienation*. New York: Harper & Row.

Mewes, Horst
1976 'On the Concept of Politics in the Early Work of Karl Marx.' *Social Research*. 43 (Summer): 276–294.

Meyer, Alfred G.
1959 'Marxism and Contemporary Social Science.' *Centennial Review*. 3 (Fall): 423–436.
1963 *Marxism: The Unity of Theory and Practice*. Ann Arbor: University of Michigan Press.
1976 'The Aufhebung of Marxism.' *Social Research*. 43 (Summer): 199–219.

Michels, Robert
1962 *Political Parties*. New York: The Free Press (1911).

Miliband, Ralph
1965 'Marx and the State.' pp. 278–296 in Ralph Miliband and John Saville (eds.) *The Socialist Register: 1965*. New York: Monthly Review Press.

Mills, C. Wright
1963 *The Marxists*. New York: Delta Books.

Mins, Henry F.
1948 'Marx's Doctoral Dissertation.' *Science and Society*. 12: 157–169.

Montano, Mario
1972 'The "Scientific Dialectics" of Galvano della Volpe.' pp. 342–364 in Dick Howard and Karl E. Klare (eds.) *The Unknown Dimension: European Marxism since Lenin*. New York: Basic Books.

Mosca, Gaetano
1939 *The Ruling Class*. New York: McGraw-Hill (1895).

Nagel, Ernest
1961 *The Structure of Science.* New York: Harcourt, Brace & World.

Needleman, Martin, and Carolyn Needleman
1961 'Marx and the Problem of Causation.' *Science and Society.* 33: 322–339.

Neurath, Otto
1959 'Sociology and Physicalism.' pp. 282–317 in A. J. Ayer (ed.) *Logical Positivism.* New York: The Free Press.

Nicolaus, Martin
1968 'The Unknown Marx.' *New Left Review.* 48 (March–April): 41–60.

1971 'The Crisis of Late Capitalism.' pp. 2–21 in George Fischer (ed.) *The Revival of American Socialism: Selected Papers of the Socialist Scholars Conference.* New York: Oxford University Press.

(ed. and intro.)
1973 *Grundrisse.* London: Penguin Books.

Nikolaevskii, Boris I. and Otto Menchen-Helfen
1936 *Karl Marx: Man and Fighter.* Philadelphia: J. B. Lippincott Co.

Ollman, Bertell
1968 'Marx's use of "Class".' *American Journal of Sociology.* 73 (March): 573–580.

1971 *Alienation: Marx's Conception of Man in Capitalist Society.* Cambridge: Cambridge University Press.

1973 'Marxism and Political Science: Prolegomenon to a Debate on Marx's Method.' *Politics and Society.* 3 (Summer): 491–510.

O'Malley, Joseph J.
1966 'History and Man's "Nature" in Marx.' *Review of Politics.* 28: 508–527.

1976 'Marx's "Economics" and Hegel's "Philosophy of Right": An Essay on Marx's Hegelianism.' *Political Studies.* 24 (March): 43–56.

O'Neil, John
1972 *Sociology as a Skin Trade.* New York: Harper & Row.

Ossowski, Stanislaw
1963 *Class Structure in the Social Consciousness.* London: Routledge & Kegan Paul.

Pachter, Henry M.
1974 'The Idea of Progress in Marxism.' *Social Research.* 41 (Spring): 136–161.

Padover, Saul K. (ed. and intro.)

1971 *Karl Marx on Revolution*. New York: McGraw-Hill.

1973 *Karl Marx on the First International*. New York: McGraw-Hill.

Pareto, Vilfredo

1925 *Les Systèmes Socialistes*. Paris: M. Giard and E. Brière (1901–1902).

1935 *The Mind and Society: A Treatise on General Sociology*. New York: Dover Publications (1916, 1923).

1971 *Manual of Political Economy*. New York: Augustus M. Kelley (1906, 1909).

Petrovic, Gajo

1967 *Marx in the Mid-Twentieth Century*. Garden City: Doubleday & Co.

Pelling, Geoffrey

1972 'The Law of Value in Ricardo and Marx.' *Economy and Society*. 1 (August): 281–307.

Plekhanov, George V.

1940 *The Materialist Conception of History*. London: Lawrence & Wishart Ltd. (1897).

1969 *Fundamental Problems of Marxism*. New York: International Publishers (1908).

1973 *Development of the Monist View of History*. New York: International Publishers (1895).

Popper, Karl R.

1950 *The Open Society and Its Enemies*. Princeton: Princeton University Press.

1957 *The Poverty of Historicism*. New York: Harper Torchbooks.

Poulantzas, Nicos

1969 'The Problem of the Capitalist State.' *New Left Review*. 58 (November–December): 67–68.

1973 *Political Power and Social Classes*. London: NLB.

Proudhon, Pierre-Joseph

1969 *Selected Writings*. Garden City: Anchor Books.

Ranciere, Jaques

1976 'The Concept of "Critique" and the "Critique of Political Economy" (from the 1844 Manuscripts to Capital).' *Economy and Society* 5 (August): 352–376.

Renner, Karl

1949 *The Institution of Private Law and Their Social Function*. New York: Harper & Row (1904).

Riazanov, David
   1973   *Karl Marx and Frederich Engels.* New York: Monthly Review
          Press (1927).
Rodinson, Maxime
   1966   'What Happened in History.' *New Left Review.* 35: 97–99.
Rooatti, Pier Aldo
   1973   'The Critique of Fetishism in Marx's *Grundrisse.*' *Telos.* 17
          (Fall): 56–69.
Ropers, Richard
   1973   'Mead, Marx and Social Psychology.' *Catalyst.* 7 (Winter):
          42–61.
Rosdolsky, Roman
   1977   *The Making of Marx's 'Capital.'* London: Pluto Press.
Rosenberg, Arthur
   1965   *Democracy and Socialism.* Boston: Beacon Press (1938).
Rowthorn, Bob
   1974   'Neo-classicism, Neo-Ricardianism, and Marxism.' *New Left
          Review.* 86 (July–August): 63–87.
Rubel, Maximilien and Margaret Manale
   1976   *Marx without Myth.* New York: Harper Torchbooks.
Ruhle, Otto
   1929   *Karl Marx: His Life and Work.* New York: Viking Press.
Ryan, Alan
   1967   'A New Look at Professor Tucker's Marx.' *Political Studies*
          15: 202–210.
Saint-Simon, Claude Henri
   1964   *Social Organization, the Science of Man and Other Writings.*
          New York: Harper & Row.
Sallach, David
   1973   'Critical Theory and Critical Sociology: The Second Syn-
          thesis.' *Sociological Inquiry.* 43: 131–140.
Sanderson, John
   1969   *An Interpretation of the Political Ideas of Marx and Engels.*
          London: Longmans.
Sarah, A. K.
   1963   'The Marxian Theory of Social Change.' *Inquiry.* 1 (Spring):
          70–127.
Sartre, Jean-Paul
   1963   *Search for a Method.* New York: Vintage Books.
Sayer, Derek
   1975   'Method and Dogma in Historical Materialism.' *Sociological
          Review.* 23 (November): 779–810.

Schmidt, Alfred
1971   *The Concept of Nature in Marx*. London: NLB.
Schneider, Louis
1971   'Dialectic in Sociology.' *American Sociological Review*. 31 (August): 667–678.
Schroyer, Trent
1973   *The Critique of Domination*. New York: George Brazilier.
Schuller, Peter M.
1975   'Karl Marx's Atheism.' *Science and Society*. 39 (Fall): 331–345.
Schumpeter, Joseph A.
1954   *History of Economic Analysis*. New York: Oxford University Press.
1962   *Capitalism, Socialism and Democracy*. New York: Harper and Row (1942).
Schwartzman, David W.
1975   'Althusser, Dialectical Materialism, and the Philosophy of Science.' *Science and Society*. 39 (Fall): 318–330.
Sedgwick, Peter
1966   'Natural Science and Human Theory.' pp. 163–192 in Ralph Miliband and John Saville (eds.) *The Socialist Register, 1966*. New York: Monthly Review Press.
Seé, Henri Eugene
1929   *The Economic Interpretation of History*. New York: Adelphi Company.
Seligman, Edwin
1902   *The Economic Interpretation of History*. New York: Columbia University Press.
Selsam, Howard, David Goldway and Harry Martel (eds.)
1970   *Dynamics of Social Change: A Reader in Marxist Social Science*. New York: International Publishers.
Séve, Lucien
1972   'The Structural Method and the Dialectical Method.' *International Journal of Sociology* 2 (Summer–Fall): 195–240.
Shaw, Martin
1974   'The Theory of the State and Politics: A Central Paradox of Marxism.' *Economy and Society*. 3 (November): 429–450.
1975   *Marxism and Social Science*. London: Pluto Press.
Sherman, Howard
1976   'Dialectics as a Method.' *The Insurgent Socialist*. 6 (Summer): 57–64.

Simon, Joan
 1962 'Stages in Social Development.' *Marxism Today.* 6: 183–188.
Simon, Walter M.
 1956 'History and Utopia: Saint-Simon and the Idea of Progress.'
 *Journal of the History of Ideas.* 17: 311–331.
Simorenko, Alex (ed.)
 1966 *Soviet Sociology.* Chicago: Quadrangle Books.
Smelser, Neil J. (ed. and intro.)
 1973 *Karl Marx: On Society and Social Change.* Chicago: University of Chicago Press.
Sohn-Rethel, Alfred
 1965 'Historical Materialist Theory of Knowledge.' *Marxism
 Today.* 9: 114–122.
Stinchcombe, Arthur L.
 1968 *Constructing Social Theories.* New York: Harcourt, Brace &
 World.
Struik, Dirk J.
 1948 'Marx and Mathematics.' *Science and Society.* 12: 181–196.
 (ed. and intro.)
 1964 Karl Marx: *The Economic and Philosophical Manuscripts.*
 New York: International Publishers
Sweezy, Paul M.
 1942 *The Theory of Capitalist Development.* New York: Monthly
 Review Press.
 1972 *Modern Capitalism and Other Essays.* New York: Monthly
 Review Press.
Swingewood, Alan
 1975 *Marx and Modern Social Theory.* London: Macmillan Press.
Syzmanski, Al
 1973 'Marxism and Science.' *The Insurgent Sociologist.* 3 (Spring):
 25–38.
Talmon, J. L.
 1960 *Political Messianism: The Romantic Phase.* London: Secker
 and Warbung.
Terray, Emmanuel
 1972 *Marxism and 'Primitive' Societies.* New York: Monthly Review Press.
Therborn, Göran
 1973 'The Working Class and the Birth of Marxism.' *New Left Review.* 79 (May–June): 3–16.
 1976 *Science, Class, and Society: On the Formation of Sociology and
 Historical Materialism.* London: NLB.

Thomas, Paul
    1976  'Marx and Science.' *Political Studies*. 24 (March): 1–23.

Tristam, Robert
    1975  'Ontology and Theory: A Comment on Marx's Analysis of Some of the Problems.' *Sociological Review*. 23 (November): 759–777.

Tucker, Charles W.
    1969  'Marx and Sociology: Some Theoretical Implications.' *Pacific Sociological Review*. 12 (Fall): 87–93.

Tucker, Richard C.
    1961  *Philosophy and Myth in Karl Marx*. Cambridge: Cambridge University Press.

    1969  *The Marxian Revolutionary Idea*. New York: W. W. Norton and Company.

Turner, Bryan S.
    1974  'The Concept of Social Stationariness: Utilitarianism and Marxism.' *Science and Society*. 38 (Spring): 3–18.

Turner, Jonathan H.
    1975  'Marx and Simmel Revisited: Reassessing the Foundations of Conflict Theory.' *Social Forces*. 53 (June): 618–627.

Urbanek, Edward
    1969  'Roles, Masks and Characters: A Contribution to Marx's Idea of the Social Role.' Pp. 168–201 in Peter Berger (ed.) *Marxism and Sociology: Views from Eastern Europe*. New York: Appleton-Century-Crofts.

van den Berghe, Pierre L.
    1963  'Dialectic and Functionalism: Toward a Theoretical Synthesis.' *American Sociological Review*. 28 (October): 695–705.

Veltmeyer, Henry
    1975  'Towards an Assessment of the Structuralist Interrogation of Marx.' *Science and Society*. 38 (Winter): 4.

Venable, Vernon
    1966  *Human Nature: The Marxian View*. Cleveland: World Publishing Company (1946).

von Stein, Lorenz
    1964  *The History of the Social Movement in France*. Totowa, New Jersey: Bedminster Press.

Walton, Paul and Andrew Gamble
    1972  *From Alienation to Surplus Value*. London: Sheed & Ward.

Weber, Max
    1949  *The Methodology of the Social Sciences*. New York: The Free Press (1903–1917).

1964 *The Theory of Social and Economic Organization.* New York: The Free Press.

Weingart, P.
1969 'Beyond Persons? A Critique of Ralf Dahrendorf's Conflict Theory.' *Social Forces.* 48 (March): 151–165.

Weiss, Hilde
1973 'Karl Marx's Enquête Ouvrière.' Pp. 172–184 in Tom Bottomore (ed.) *Karl Marx.* Englewood Cliffs, N.J.: Prentice-Hall.

Wesolowski, Wlodzimierz
1967 'Marx's Theory of Class Domination: An Attempt at Systemization.' Pp. 53–97 in Nicholas Lobkowicz (ed.) *Marx and the Western World.* Notre Dame: University Press.

Wetter, Gustav A.
1969 'The Ambivalence of the Marxist Concept of Ideology.' *Studies in Soviet Thought.* 9: 177–183.
1973 *Dialectical Materialism.* Westport, Conn.: Greenwood Publishers.

Williams, Robin Moore, Jr
1966 'Some Further Comments on Chronic Controversies.' *American Journal of Sociology.* 71 (May): 717–721.

Wilson, Edmund
1940 *To the Finland Station.* New York: Doubleday & Company.

Winfield, Richard
1976 'The Logic of Marx's *Capital*'. *Telos.* 27 (Spring): 111–139.

Zeitlin, Irving
1967 *Marxism: A Re-Examination.* New York: Van Nostrand Reinhold Company.
1968 *Ideology and the Development of Sociological Theory.* Englewood Cliffs, N.J.: Prentice-Hall.

Zivkovic, Ljubomir
1969 'The Structure of Marxist Sociology.' Pp. 98–127 in Peter Berger (ed.) *Marxism and Sociology: Views from Eastern Europe.* New York: Appleton-Century-Crofts.